Hierarchies in World Politics

Globalising processes are gathering increased attention for complicating the nature of political boundaries, authority and sovereignty. Recent examples of global financial and political turmoil have also created a sense of unease about the durability of the modern international order and the ability of our existing theoretical frameworks to explain system dynamics. In light of the inadequacies of traditional International Relations (IR) theories in explaining the contemporary global context, a growing range of scholars have been seeking to make sense of world politics through an analytical focus on hierarchies instead. Until now, the explanatory potential of such research agendas and their implications for the discipline went unrecognised, partly due to the fragmented nature of the IR field. To address this gap, this ground-breaking book brings leading IR scholars together in a conversation on hierarchy and thus moves the discipline in a direction better equipped to deal with the challenges of the twenty-first century.

Ayşe Zarakol is a University Lecturer in International Relations at the University of Cambridge and a Fellow at Emmanuel College. She is the author of *After Defeat: How the East Learned to Live with the West* (Cambridge, 2011).

T0371467

Cambridge Studies in International Relations 144

Hierarchies in World Politics

Cambridge Studies in International Relations is a joint initiative of Cambridge
University Press and the British International Studies Association (BISA).
The series aims to publish the best new scholarship in international studies,
irrespective of subject matter, methodological approach or theoretical
perspective. The series seeks to bring the latest theoretical work in International
Relations to bear on the most important problems and issues in global politics.

143 Lisbeth Zimmerman
     Global Norms with a Local Face

142 Alexandre Debs and Nuno P. Monteiro
     Nuclear Politics

141 Mathias Albert
     A Theory of World Politics

140 Emma Hutchison
     Affective Communities in World Politics
     Collective Emotions after Trauma

139 Patricia Owens
     Economy of Force
     Counterinsurgency and the Historical Rise of the Social

138 Ronald R. Krebs
     Narrative and the Making of US National Security

137 Andrew Phillips and J. C. Sharman
     International Order in Diversity
     War, Trade and Rule in the Indian Ocean

Series list continues after index

Hierarchies in World Politics

Edited by

Ayşe Zarakol

University of Cambridge

CAMBRIDGE
UNIVERSITY PRESS

CAMBRIDGE
UNIVERSITY PRESS

University Printing House, Cambridge CB2 8BS, United Kingdom

One Liberty Plaza, 20th Floor, New York, NY 10006, USA

477 Williamstown Road, Port Melbourne, VIC 3207, Australia

314-321, 3rd Floor, Plot 3, Splendor Forum, Jasola District Centre, New Delhi - 110025, India

79 Anson Road, #06-04/06, Singapore 079906

Cambridge University Press is part of the University of Cambridge.

It furthers the University's mission by disseminating knowledge in the pursuit of education, learning and research at the highest international levels of excellence.

www.cambridge.org
Information on this title: www.cambridge.org/9781108416634
DOI: 10.1017/9781108241588

© Cambridge University Press 2017

First published 2017

A catalogue record for this publication is available from the British Library

ISBN   978-1-108-41663-4   Hardback
ISBN   978-1-108-40402-0   Paperback

Contents

List of Contributors   *page* vii
Editor's Preface and Acknowledgements   xi

Theorising Hierarchies: An Introduction   1
AYŞE ZARAKOL

**Part I Forms of Hierarchy: Origins, Nature and
         Intersections**   15

1 Laws and Norms in the Making of International
   Hierarchies   17
   DAVID A. LAKE

2 Making Empires: Hierarchy, Conquest and
   Customization   43
   ANDREW PHILLIPS

3 Hierarchy and Paternalism   66
   MICHAEL BARNETT

4 Revealing International Hierarchy through
   Gender Lenses   95
   LAURA SJOBERG

5 Against Authority: The Heavy Weight of
   International Hierarchy   113
   VINCENT POULIOT

Part II How Actors Experience Hierarchies   135

6 Hierarchy in an Age of Equality: Micro-States and
   Dependencies   137
   J. C. SHARMAN

7   Command and Control? Hierarchy and the International
    Politics of Foreign Military Bases   154
    ALEX COOLEY

8   Leading Authority as Hierarchy among INGOs   175
    SARAH S. STROUP AND WENDY H. WONG

9   Are We 'Lazy Greeks' or 'Nazi Germans'? Negotiating
    International Hierarchies in the Euro Crisis   198
    REBECCA ADLER-NISSEN

10 'Delinquent Gangs' in the International System
    Hierarchy   219
    SHOGO SUZUKI

Part III Conclusion   241

11 Beyond Hierarchy   243
    JACK DONNELLY

12 Why Hierarchy?   266
    AYŞE ZARAKOL

    Bibliography   275
    Index   311

Contributors

REBECCA ADLER-NISSEN is a Professor of International Relations at the University of Copenhagen. Her research focuses on International Relations (IR) theory (especially international political sociology, stigma, status, norms and the practice turn), diplomacy, sovereignty and European integration, as well as fieldwork, participant observation and anthropological methods in IR. She has been a visiting research fellow at the Centre for International Security Studies (University of Sydney), Centre for International Peace and Security Studies (McGill University/Université de Montréal) and the European University Institute in Florence. In 2015, she received the Nils Klim Prize. Her most recent book is *Opting Out of the European Union: Diplomacy, Sovereignty and European Integration* (Cambridge University Press, 2014).

MICHAEL BARNETT is University Professor of International Affairs and Political Science at George Washington University's Elliott School of International Affairs. Currently, he is an associate editor of International Organization. He has published extensively on IR theory, global governance, humanitarian action and the Middle East. Dr Barnett is the author of many books, including a history of humanitarianism, *The Empire of Humanity: A History of Humanitarianism*, and, most recently, *The Stars and the Stripes: A History of the Foreign Policies of American Jews*.

ALEX COOLEY is a Professor of Political Science at Barnard College and the current director of Columbia University's Harriman Institute. His research examines how external actors – including international organizations, multinational companies, non-governmental organizations (NGOs) and foreign military bases – have influenced the development and sovereignty of the former Soviet states, with a focus on Central Asia and the Caucasus. His research has been supported by the Open Society Foundations, Carnegie Corporation, the Smith Richardson Foundation and the German Marshall Fund of the United States, among others. Dr Cooley is the author of many books, including *Great Games, Local Rules: The New Great Power Contest for Central Asia.*

JACK DONNELLY is the Andrew Mellon Professor and John Evans Professor at the Josef Korbel School of International Studies, University of Denver. His principal research interests are in IR theory, especially structural theories of international politics and the comparative analysis of historical international systems and the theory and practice of human rights. Dr Donnelly is the author of more than 100 refereed articles and book chapters and several books, the best known of which is *Universal Human Rights in Theory and Practice.*

DAVID A. LAKE is the Jerri-Ann and Gary E. Jacobs Professor of Social Sciences and Distinguished Professor of Political Science at the University of California, San Diego. He currently serves as president of the American Political Science Association (2016–17). Dr Lake has published widely in IR theory and international political economy. In addition to nearly 100 scholarly articles and chapters and several books, he is most recently the author of *The Statebuilder's Dilemma: On the Limits of External Intervention.* He is co-author of a comprehensive textbook entitled *World Politics: Interests, Interactions, and Institutions.* Dr Lake has served as the co-editor of the journal *International Organization* (1997–2001), founding chair of the International Political Economy Society (2005–12) and president of the International Studies Association (2010–11).

ANDREW PHILLIPS is an associate professor of International Relations and Strategy at the University of Queensland. During 2013–15, he was an Australian Research Council DECRA fellow. His research interests centre on the question of international orders – both how they have historically developed from the sixteenth century onwards and how today's global order is adapting to challenges ranging from the rise of non-Western Great Powers (especially China and India) through to unconventional security threats including religiously motivated terrorism and state failure. His most recent book is *International Order in Diversity: War, Trade and Rule in the Indian Ocean* (Cambridge University Press, 2015), co-authored with Jason C. Sharman.

VINCENT POULIOT is an associate professor and William Dawson Scholar at McGill University, where he is also the director of the Centre for International Peace and Security Studies (CIPSS). His research interests are political sociology of international organisations, global governance of international security and multilateral diplomacy. Dr Pouliot is the author of several books and many research articles, including most recently *International Pecking Orders: The Politics and Practice of Multilateral Diplomacy* (Cambridge University Press, 2016).

J. C. SHARMAN is the Sir Patrick Sheehy Professor of International Relations at the University of Cambridge. In 2012, Dr Sharman was awarded an Australian Research Council Future Fellowship, and since 2014, he has been a member of the ARC College of Experts. Dr Sharman's research is currently focused on corruption, money laundering and tax havens, as well as the international relations of the early modern Indian Ocean. He is the author of many books, including most recently *International Order in Diversity: War, Trade and Rule in the Indian Ocean* (Cambridge University Press, 2015), co-authored with Andrew Phillips.

LAURA SJOBERG is an associate professor of Political Science at the University of Florida. Her research interests are in the area of gender-based and feminist approaches to the study of IR generally and international security specifically. Her research has addressed gender and just-war theory, women's violence in global politics and feminist interpretations of the theory and practice of security policy. Dr Sjoberg is currently the editor of *International Studies Review*. She is also the author of many books, including most recently *Beyond Mothers Monsters Whores* (with Caron Gentry) and *Women as Wartime Rapists*.

SARAH S. STROUP is an associate professor of Political Science at Middlebury College. Her research focuses on the politics of humanitarianism, international political economy and non-state actors in world politics. Her first book, *Borders among Activists*, explored how the national roots of international NGOs shape their strategies and structures, using case studies of humanitarian and human rights INGOs in the United States, Britain and France. Her co-authored book with Wendy H. Wong, *The Authority Trap*, is forthcoming.

SHOGO SUZUKI is a senior lecturer in International Relations at the University of Manchester. His research focuses on IR theory with reference to East Asia, Sino-Japanese relations, Chinese foreign policy, Japanese foreign policy and Sino-Japanese reconciliation. Suzuki has held visiting appointments at the University of Cambridge, University of Copenhagen, Peking University and Tokyo University, among others. In addition to many research articles, he is the author of

Civilisation and Empire: China and Japan's Encounter with the European International Society.

WENDY H. WONG is the director of the Trudeau Centre for Peace Conflict and Justice and an associate professor of Political Science at the University of Toronto. Her main research interests lie at the crossroads of IR and comparative politics. She is interested in the politics of organisation, why human beings choose to act collectively, their choices to go about doing it and the effects of those choices. Other research interests include human rights, humanitarianism, international law, social movements, indigenous politics, the rights of ethnic minorities and the role of networks. Her co-authored book with Sarah S. Stroup, *The Authority Trap*, is forthcoming.

AYŞE ZARAKOL is University Lecturer in International Relations at the University of Cambridge and a Fellow at Emmanuel College. Her research is at the intersection of historical sociology and IR, focusing on East-West relations in the international system, problems of modernity and sovereignty, stigma and social hierarchies, rising and declining powers and Turkish politics in a comparative perspective. In addition to many articles, she is also the author of *After Defeat: How the East Learned to Live with the West* (Cambridge University Press, 2011), which deals with international stigmatisation and the integration of defeated non-Western powers (Turkey after World War I, Japan after World War II and Russia after the Cold War) into the international system. Zarakol has held fellowships with Council on Foreign Relations, the Norwegian Nobel Institute and the Centre for the Research in Arts, Social Sciences and Humanities at Cambridge.

Editor's Preface and Acknowledgements

This book is the product of many conversations among IR scholars who have not (entirely) given up the dream of overcoming the fragmentation of the discipline. It is our hope that thinking about hierarchies in world politics opens up underexplored avenues of research and thus helps bring the discipline into the twenty-first century. Reorienting the IR conversation to the concept of hierarchy also links previously disconnected clusters of scholarship around common questions, as opposed to various '-isms'. What first had started out as an ISA working group around this idea led to two more workshops. I would like to thank the International Studies Association (ISA), the Institute on Global Conflict and Cooperation, the Jacobs Chair of Social Sciences at the University of California San Diego (UCSD), the Cambridge Humanities Grant Scheme and the Department of Politics and International Studies at the University of Cambridge for funding and hosting these meetings.

There were also individuals without whose generous intellectual and logistical support the project would never have survived: Michael Barnett, David Lake and Jack Donnelly. Michael Barnett is in many ways the godfather of this collaboration: it was on his suggestion that the first working group on hierarchies was organised. He continued to play a key role with his guidance. David Lake almost singlehandedly made the project possible by first agreeing to attend the first ISA working group and then funding the first workshop in UCSD. His willingness to seriously engage with *all* kinds of IR scholarship and his generous mentorship of young scholars make him truly a role model for our discipline. Jack Donnelly is the contributor every collaboration of this sort needs: he kept all of us alert with his interlocutions and thus took some of the editing burden off my shoulders. Every chapter in the book is better as a result of his feedback. I am also grateful to the other contributors in the book for their dedication to the project over the years: Rebecca Adler-Nissen, Alex Cooley, Andrew Phillips, Vincent Pouliot, Laura Sjoberg, J. C. Sharman, Sarah Stroup, Shogo Suzuki and Wendy Wong. It truly was a privilege to work with such a group of scholars at the top of their game, who not only contributed some of the best examples of their research to this book but also helped improve the other contributions through substantive engagement with each other's approaches.

Many others have been involved in previous stages even though their work is not represented in this book: Anna Agathangelou, Tarak Barkawi, Charlotte Epstein, Evelyn Goh, Jonathan Havercroft, Kristen Hopewell, Naeem Inayatullah, Mark Laffey, Jenny Lobasz, Xavier Mathieu, David McCourt, Dan Nexon, Ben O'Loughlin, Alex Prichard, Bahar Rumelili, Mark Salter, Ann Towns, Karyn Wang and Yuan-Kang Wang. The project has benefitted greatly from their contributions to the conversation. The same applies especially to Janice Bially Mattern. But for her involvement, the hierarchies project would not have even started.

Theorising Hierarchies
An Introduction

*Ayşe Zarakol**

Globalising processes are gathering increased attention for complicating the nature of political boundaries, authority and sovereignty. Recent global financial and political turmoils have also created a sense of unease about the durability of modern international order and the ability of our existing theoretical frameworks to explain system dynamics. In light of the insufficiencies of traditional International Relations (IR) theories[1] in explaining the contemporary global context, a growing number of scholars have been seeking to make sense of world politics through an analytical focus on hierarchies instead.[2] Until now, the explanatory potential of such research agendas and the implications for the discipline went unrecognised due to the fragmented nature of the IR field.

Hierarchies, understood broadly as any system through which actors are organised into vertical relations of super- and subordination, have long been of interest to social scientists, including in IR.[3] In recent years, however, IR scholarship concerned with hierarchies has expanded considerably. Building upon economic, sociological, legal, philosophical and

---

* Some sections of this chapter borrow from Bially Mattern and Zarakol (2016). This introduction and the conclusion have also benefitted from the comments of Michael Barnett, Jack Donnelly, David Lake, Daniel Nexon, Ann Towns, George Lawson, Patricia Owens, Kamran Matin, Ole Jacob Sending, Maria Birnbaum, Halvard Leira and Einar Wigen, as well as the questions of many others to whom versions of this chapter were presented at the European International Studies Association (EISA, Sicily 2015), the University of Sussex and the Norwegian Institute of International Affairs (NUPI).

[1] Some have described (and others have lamented) this as evidence of the 'end of theory' in IR. See the special issue of *EJIR*, especially Mearsheimer and Walt (2013).

[2] Hierarchies themselves are not new phenomena in world politics, but recent developments in the system have drawn the attention of *more* scholars to hierarchy.

[3] See e.g. Lake 2007, 2009a, 2009b, 2010; Nexon and Wright 2007; Donnelly 2006; Cooley 2003, 2005; Keene 2002; Hobson and Sharman 2005; Hobson 2012; Wendt and Friedheim 1995; Simpson 2004; Anghie 2005; Kaufman, Little and Wohlforth 2007; Bowden 2009; Lebow 2008; Zarakol 2011; Buzan and Lawson 2015. There are also approaches that never conceded the anarchy assumption to begin with: for example, world systems theory (e.g. Frank 1978; Wallerstein 1974, 1984; Arrighi 1994), uneven and combined development (e.g. Rosenberg 2013; Anievas and Nişancıoğlu 2015) and post-colonial (see e.g. Grovugui 2006; Darby and Paolini 1994; Chowdhry and Nair 2004; Barkawi and Laffey 2006).

1

historical insights about the intertwined logics of formal equality and vertical stratification, researchers across the spectrum of theoretical and methodological commitments have undertaken inquiry into the effects of ranked differentiation among actors on the political dynamics of issues such as global governance, economic relations and security. This scholarship is diverse, but it also converges on two insights: first, that hierarchies are a ubiquitous feature of international (i.e. inter-state) politics and, second, that they generate social, moral and behavioural dynamics that are different from those created by other arrangements. In short, hierarchies matter in distinctive ways for world politics.

We owe the close association of IR and anarchy to neorealism. In *Theory of International Politics*, Waltz posited that '[i]n defining structures, the first question to answer is: What is the principle by which the parts are arranged?'[4] and that 'domestic systems are centralized and hierarchic', whereas 'international systems are decentralized and anarchic.'[5] From these postulates he derived a number of other components, e.g. that 'the units of an anarchic system are functionally undifferentiated'[6]; that 'in anarchic realms, like units coact'[7]; that 'so long as anarchy endures, states remain like units'[8]; and that 'like units work to maintain a measure of independence and may even strive for autarchy.'[9] Though Waltz was not, by any means, the first[10] scholar to make the argument that international relations was characterised primarily by its anarchic nature, he did make the statement more definitively than most and had a strong influence in this regard on the generations of scholarship that followed him[11]: 'Before 1979 three-fifths of the books use "anarchy" or "anarchic" three or fewer times. After 1978 four-fifths use these terms 10 or more times ... A sharp transition occurs around the publication of Waltz's *Theory of International Politics*.'[12] According to Donnelly, the subsequent success of the anarchy concept in IR can be explained in reference to three factors: its association with structural realism, which offered the promise of an elegant systemic theory of international politics; its appeal to rationalist approaches as a starting assumption; and its presentation 'as an analytically neutral demarcation criterion'.[13] Again in Donnelly's words: 'By the mid-1990s, anarchy had become "naturalized" across much of the discipline; treated as a taken-for-granted foundational assumption. Neorealism and neoliberalism, the leading research programmes of the era, even incorporated anarchy into the IR orthodoxy that no contrary evidence or argument can be permitted to challenge.' To this day,

[4] Waltz 1979, 82.   [5] *Ibid.*, 88.   [6] *Ibid.*, 97.   [7] *Ibid.*, 104.   [8] *Ibid.*, 93.
[9] *Ibid.*, 104.
[10] See Donnelly (2015a) for an overview of pre-Waltz usages of the concept in IR.
[11] Schmidt 1997, 40.   [12] Donnelly 2015a, 394–5.   [13] Donnelly 2015a, 402.

'anarchy' has been rarely questioned *explicitly* within the mainstream of IR as both *the* defining assumption of the discipline and *the* defining feature of international relations.

Many IR scholars have nevertheless been studying hierarchies because hierarchies feature heavily among *both* the problems of world politics that scholarship is interested in addressing *and* the possible solutions to those problems. Yet, scholars working on different types and aspects of hierarchies have not engaged each other, having trained their sights instead on dismantling or bypassing the anarchy assumption. Put another way, always having to confront the concept of anarchy as a starting point has impeded the productivity of hierarchy research in IR. Different strands of hierarchy scholarship should be challenging each other on conceptualisations of hierarchies (and their mechanisms) rather than continuously having to 'reinvent the-criticisms-of-the anarchy-assumption wheel' in different ways. This book aims to change this status quo and open up a productive space for hierarchy-oriented research through the mutual engagement of diverse approaches.[14] The concept of hierarchy thus promises to unite fragmented insights about world politics into an alternative explanatory framework.

A comprehensive survey of the existing IR literature[15] reveals some insights about how hierarchies have been understood in the discipline. First, the structures of differentiation at the core of hierarchical systems are deeply implicated with power. Hierarchical systems are thus intrinsically political. Second, in world politics, hierarchies stratify, rank and organise the relations not only among states but also among other kinds of actors as well and often even a mix of different actors within a single structure of differentiation. Third, there are many different kinds of hierarchical relations in world politics. However, since different hierarchies can and often do intersect each other, these logics can be nested. Taken together, these features suggest that a focus on hierarchies can both facilitate the kinds of systemic perspectives on world politics that made anarchy-centred theories so useful and, unlike anarchy-centred theories, account for on-going globalising processes as a part of the system.

IR research on hierarchy thus far could be summarised as having gravitated towards two major research questions: (1) 'What is the nature of hierarchy?' (with the accompanying questions, 'What is hierarchy

---

[14] The book itself is product of a series of conversations: (1) an ISA working group (2013 San Francisco Convention), (2) a 2014 workshop hosted by UCSD and (3) a 2015 workshop hosted by the University of Cambridge. There were also roundtables and panels at the ISA, EISA and CEEISA.

[15] See Bially Mattern and Zarakol 2016. Literature review sections below also draw from that article.

made of?'; 'How is hierarchy made?'; 'Where does hierarchy come from?'; etc.) and (2) 'How do actors exist in hierarchies?' (with the accompanying questions, 'How do actors use/navigate/reproduce/resist/escape existing hierarchies?'; 'How do existing hierarchies function?'; and 'How are existing hierarchies sustained or dismantled?'). Hierarchy research therefore can move forward by developing conversations around the two primary questions it has already focused upon: origin and nature of hierarchies, on the one hand, and actor behaviour in existing hierarchies, on the other.

It is not particularly difficult to demonstrate that the concept of hierarchy captures dynamics that exist in most, if not all, social systems. However, recognition of this fact alone does not get us very far empirically. Hierarchy research, if it is to open new paths for IR thinking, needs to first better specify where hierarch*ies* come from, how different hierarch*ies* interact and how actors navigate hierarch*ies* given the particular origin and interactive effects of existing hierarch*ies*. This introduction thus first reviews the existing research on these questions and contextualises the chapters in this book against that background. I suggest that one major existing cleavage in the literature has been around more agentic/institutional accounts of the origins of hierarchies versus more structural understandings. The former sees hierarchies as solutions to problems of order, whereas the latter sees hierarchies more as a constraining environment (or worse). The second part of this introduction reviews the literature on agency in hierarchies and contextualises the chapters in this book accordingly.

Origins and Nature of Hierarchies

One dominant strain of IR research understands hierarchies – and a given actor's position within a hierarchy – as arising in the first place from bargained solutions to problems of order. In this understanding, hierarchies are founded on exchanges in which actors trade degrees of freedom for a desired social or political arrangement. Hierarchies institutionalise interests in that order, and this distinctively affects actors' incentives and disincentives to create compliant and non-compliant outcomes.[16] This line of research generally operates with a *narrow* conception of hierarchy, understood as legitimate authority.

Within IR, the best example of this account is in David Lake's contract theory of hierarchies as expounded in *Hierarchy in International Relations*. Noting the general inattention of IR to the persistence of power asymmetries established through colonialism and alliances, Lake argues that such arrangements are best understood as authoritative institutions. They

[16] Pumain 2006, 7.

function, he argues, as (explicit or tacit) bargains in which subordinates give up rights to freedom in exchange for the provision of a social order that is valued by the subordinate. International hierarchies, in other words, are theorised as functional, intentional solutions to collective problems of global governance.[17] As 'bargains between ruler and ruled premised on the former's provision of a social order of value sufficient to offset the loss of freedom',[18] hierarchies uniquely structure incentives in ways that explain behaviour of super- and subordinate actors alike.[19]

In *Liberal Leviathan*, Ikenberry invokes a similar contract-functionalist logic to explain both America's long-standing position as hegemon in the liberal international order and the current crisis of American hegemony. As Ikenberry explains it, American hegemony is 'a hierarchical system that was built on both American power dominance and liberal principles of governance'[20] and that was 'made acceptable to other states . . . because it provided security and other "system services"'.[21] With US authority no longer securely established, the liberal international order needs 'a new bargain' through which to stabilise incentives and behaviours in world politics.[22]

In *Special Responsibilities: Global Problems and American Power*, Bukovansky et al. also treat hierarchies as functional bargains, though ones undertaken by international society as a whole rather than by individual states. Their account arises in the course of seeking to explain why international society has historically dealt 'with major global problems' through the allocation of differentiated responsibilities – or hierarchies – among sovereign states. Their argument is that hierarchies 'come to the fore and assume particular political importance' in instances where neither the formal principle of sovereign equality nor political power struggle provides an adequate basis on which to address challenges of co-existence and cooperation.[23] In such instances, international society has allocated special responsibilities 'to enhance the efficient working of international order'.[24] International society has, in other words, promulgated hierarchies because they give incentives to super- and subordinates to support and conform to the order it values.

The trade-off explanation has also been deployed to account for the creation of regional orders. Kang has argued that the hierarchy that ordered East Asian international relations from 1368 to 1841 rested on an implicit bargain in which Chinese authority was legitimated because China crafted the kind of Confucian-inspired social order that was

---

[17] Lake 2009a, 32.   [18] Lake 2007, 54.   [19] See Lake 2009a, Chapters 4 and 5.
[20] Ikenberry 2012, 6.   [21] *Ibid.*, 5.   [22] *Ibid.*, Chapters 7 and 8.
[23] Bukovansky et al. 2012, 6–7.   [24] *Ibid.*, 5.

generally valued by, and so conformed with, its subordinates.[25] Keene similarly turns to bargained hierarchy resting on a prior stock of shared culture in accounting for the European Union's normative power. Normative power, suggests Keene, arises from a sort of authorised leadership in an international social club in which others are followers – that is, from a social hierarchy. Such a hierarchy, in turn, arises from a social bargain. The European Union just 'construct[s] a distinctive identity and lifestyle'[26] that draws in a unique and exclusive way on the core social principles of international society and ... establish[es] the EU as a model society to whose normative authority others implicitly consent to defer'. Normative power, in this way, is explained at least partly as a trade-off.

There are significant differences between each of the hierarchy-oriented analyses represented in these examples. Most notable are differences in the basis of hierarchy-constituting agreements. Kang and Keene see the bargains upon which hierarchies are founded as authorised by the social appropriateness of the subordination, whereas Lake and Ikenberry focus positive consequences of subordination. Bukovansky et al. highlight both positive consequences *and* social appropriateness. Despite their differences, however, these accounts converge on at least three crucial points. First, hierarchies are understood *narrowly* as legitimate orders of authority in which super-ordinate and subordinate alike have some material, functional and/or social *interest*. Second, actors are understood (more and less) as *purposeful agents* in international life.[27] Finally, and most importantly, the *bargains encoded* in hierarchies are assumed to *structure subsequent action*, whether through social or interest-based incentives.

To put it another way, this vein of research is interested primarily in how and why hierarchies are *deliberately* erected by specific actors as solutions to problems of anarchy, i.e. in the origins of hierarchies. This is why the bulk of this research has focused on the incentives super-ordinate states face to exercise self-restraint in spite of their right to govern through power as they see fit. Ikenberry and Lake each characterise these incentives in terms of the contingency of the dominant states' authority on the buy-in of the super-ordinate, whereas Bukovansky et al. characterise them in terms of the norms of right action and the expectation of political accountability faced by super-ordinate power.[28] It is in this incentive for self-restraint that the value of this hierarchy heuristic becomes clear. Basically, this logic explains an aspect of uni-polarity that could not be apprehended through balance-of-power theory.[29] Some

[25] Kang 2010a.   [26] Keene 2013, 950.
[27] There are disagreements about how much agency and intention actors exert in this process, as well as who has it.
[28] Bukovansky et al. 2012, 16.   [29] Ikenberry 2012, 9; see also Finnemore 2009.

attention has also been paid to the distinctive effects of (bargained) hierarchy on subordinates, as well as the conditions under which non-compliance, resistance or under-compliance might emerge. With respect to subordinates, the matrix of incentives appears to encourage the delegation of responsibility for security – among other things – to superordinates.[30] With respect to noncompliant behaviour, research has focused on the incentives for contestation arising from the rather visible inequalities that hierarchies entail.[31] There is also a common concern with the internal dynamism of hierarchies. Bargained hierarchy rests on 'relational authority' such that superordinates' legitimacy depends upon how well those actors deliver upon the expectations of the role. But given that all actors in hierarchies face position-specific matrices of incentives, sustaining 'an equilibrium among interests' is an on-going process.[32] The implication is that whereas anarchy is under-stood as a given condition, or as deep structure, hierarchies, by contrast, are seen to be constantly subject to renegotiation as bargained orders. By contrast, this strand of research has mostly overlooked (until this book) the possibility of deep hierarchical structures influencing the creation and renegotiation of hierarchies as institutions of bargain.

In fact, in direct contrast to the agentic-contractual accounts outlined earlier, the other dominant strain of IR research on hierarchy conceives hierarchies *broadly* as deep structures of organised inequality that are neither designed nor particularly open to renegotiation. Such accounts suggest that hierarchy does not just shape the behaviours of actors in world politics but rather produces *both* the actors (or at least their worldview) and the space of world politics in which they act. Approached (depending upon the school of thought) as deeply ingrained social practices, inter-subjective structures or a superstructure rooted in material inequality, hierarchies are seen as deep patterns of inequality that are manifested through actors' habitus, role perceptions, bodily activity or discursive regimes.[33] In such accounts, hierarchies shape actors within their structure of differentiation as particular kinds of agents with particular capacities for action that belong, or do not, in some space of world politics. Hierarchies create the actors of world politics and/or their repertoires for action. They also produce the bound-aries that define who and what belongs where in world politics.

Within IR, understandings of hierarchy as deep structure are found most commonly in post-structuralist, post-colonial, feminist and critical scholarship, both of the more ideational variety and critical work within the historical materialist vein. To give just a few examples, Weldes et al.

---

[30] Lake 2009b.   [31] Bukovansky et al. 2012, 16.   [32] Lake 2009b, 16.
[33] E.g. Schatzki et al. 2001, Butler 1997.

argue that borders − physical, territorial, conceptual or collectively imagined − must be seen as sites of power, inequality and the practice of hierarchy.[34] This claim rests on the idea that discursive practices − like all practices − are founded not on universal truths but on historically contingent knowledge structures that signify objects, subjects and other phenomena by positioning them in relation to each other.[35] Discourses thus are forms of power, 'regimes of truth' that dominate and violate by arbitrarily defining 'the (im)possible, the (im)probable, the natural, the normal, what counts as a social problem' and so *who* is (im)possible, (im) probable, natural, normal and problematic.[36] They bring social beings into being, as particular identities, with particular capacities that mark them as superior or inferior. The discursive practices of bordering thus inscribe spaces of inside (superior) and outside (inferior) by 'making' the superior and inferior actors that populate them. For instance, in *Writing Security*, Campbell argues that discourses that drive US foreign policy have produced 'the boundaries of the identity in whose name it operates'. But at the same time it also produced the many dangers against which the US requires protection.[37] More recently, Barder has argued that international hierarchies, whether in the guise of imperialism or hegemony, have 'historically resulted in the experimentation and innovation of various norms and practices that (re)shape the domestic space of various imperial or hegemonic powers'.[38] In Barder's account, even *domestic* political outcomes in both the core and the periphery are produced by international hierarchies. Post-colonial approaches, such as that of Shilliam, also build their explanations around structures of inequality in the international system, for instance, that of race.[39] It is not just ideational approaches, however, that see hierarchy as a structural force in international political life. Such an understanding of hierarchy is also evident in the core, semi-periphery and periphery accounts of World Systems approaches.[40] Similarly, any theory that accepts formal anarchy among states as a defining feature of international politics implicitly presupposes the productive effects of hierarchies. After all, it is only through the distinctive hierarchical relation of states to their territorially bounded societies that they emerge as sovereign actors and that the formally anarchic space of international politics comes into being.[41]

---

[34] Weldes et al. 1999.   [35] Milliken 1999.
[36] Hayward as cited in Barnett and Duvall 2005, 21.
[37] Campbell 1988, 5. See also Weber 1999.   [38] Barder 2015, 2.
[39] See e.g. Shilliam 2010, 2015; Anievas, Manchanda and Shilliam 2014; see also the recent forum in *International Theory*: Epstein 2014; Jabri 2014; Shilliam 2014; Gallagher 2014; Zarakol 2014.
[40] Wallerstein 1984; Arrighi 1994.   [41] Ashley 1988.

To sum up thus far, the *narrow* understanding of hierarchy in IR as a designed institution assumes that hierarchies, once erected, will function more or less as planned. Actors' initial choices are significant in explaining the design of such hierarchies. The *broad* understanding of hierarchy as structure assumes that understanding the content of inequality and/or the shape of the structure will reveal more or less everything about how actors exist in hierarchies, and one does not need to pay much attention to the actors. The *narrow* approach, because it was operating with an implicit structure as anarchy assumption, has not considered very well how an institutional hierarchy, once erected, may interact with broad hierarchies, i.e. structures of inequality. It has also not considered the impact of broad hierarchies in shaping actors and their choices. The *broad* approach, however, has not considered the possibility that the solution to the problems created by broad hierarchies may be hierarchies of the *narrow* type.

It is apparent from the preceding discussion that approaches that posit that hierarchies can be erected as solutions to problems of order need to take more seriously the insights of research that understands the nature of hierarchy more broadly (and vice versa). How are contractual hierarchies of legitimate authority created in a world of broader hierarchies of organised inequality? How do 'consensually' erected hierarchies underwritten by international law intersect, for instance, with racial inequalities in the international system? Part I of this book brings together contributors with very different understandings of hierarchy, ranging from very agentic/institutional to very structural. The contributors display varying degrees of optimism as to whether hierarchies as institutions can be created independently of broader structural hierarchies, but they all genuinely engage with alternative understandings of hierarchy.

Part I starts with Lake, who is at one end of the spectrum in terms of his conception of hierarchy as legitimate authority. In Chapter 1, writing on international law and norms, with a particular focus on the principle of non-intervention, he maintains his emphasis on agency and deliberate action in explaining the origins of hierarchies. At the same time, he also fruitfully engages with a broader conception of hierarchy by recognising that the normative structure of racial inequality has to some extent undermined agent efforts in solidifying the principle of non-intervention in international law. The chapters that follow are ordered by their level of emphasis on the narrow (agentic/institutional) versus broad (structural) types of hierarchy as being more determinative. In Chapter 2, in his comparative study of the Chinese and British Empires, Phillips makes more room for the influence of social and cultural hierarchies but nevertheless maintains an emphasis on the agency of elites in creating empires as legitimate forms of authority. In Chapter 3, Barnett looks at paternalism, a narrow(er) type of hierarchy, but one that cannot be explained as a consensual trade-off and therefore one that points very clearly towards the influence of broader hierarchies on agent behaviour. In Chapter 4, Sjoberg examines both how narrow hierarchies are gendered and also at gender hierarchy as broadly defined. In Chapter 5, Pouliot takes the agentic explanations for the origin and existence of narrow hierarchies head on, arguing that no such legitimate authority exists independent of broader social hierarchies. In Part I, then, the main debate is about the origins and forms of hierarchy and how different hierarchies intersect.

How Actors Experience Hierarchies

The second major vein of research on hierarchies in IR has focused on actor behaviour within existing hierarchical environments. In other words, this growing body of IR research is much less focused on the nature of hierarchy and much more focused on how existing hierarchies shape *actors* or actor *behaviour*. As such, research in this cluster is able to operate both with a narrow institutional view of hierarchy *and* a broad structural view depending on the particular research question. This line of research generally asserts that the content of what actors want and what is important to them depends in part on where they are *positioned* in a hierarchical order. Such a view can be found in research in a variety of substantive areas: security,[42] foreign policy,[43] diplomacy,[44] international law[45] and even research on IR scholarship itself.[46] The shared analytical focus is on the socialising effects of hierarchies on the actors positioned within them; hierarchies appear as extant features of the world political environment in which actors simply find themselves and which teach actors to play certain roles, including having certain interests and expectations.

Scholarship on the distribution of power and its impact on state behaviour offers one important example of this type of research. Because of its theoretical origins in balance-of-power studies, this scholarship is not explicitly connected to the notion of 'hierarchy'. However, by underlining systemic, vertical differentiation-of-power capabilities, this approach implicitly invokes the broad conception of hierarchy (as organised inequality). Its focus, however, is on actors' position-contingent interests and expectations. In characterising the international system as a cycle of hegemony, challenge, war and restabilisation, power transition theory as discussed in Organski and Kugler's *The War Ledger*, for instance,

---

[42] See e.g. Ayoob 2003; Wendt and Friedheim 1995; Wendt and Barnett 1993.
[43] See e.g. Adler-Nissen and Gad 2013, Morozov 2013, Kösebalaban 2008.
[44] See e.g. Adler-Nissen 2014, Zarakol 2014.
[45] See e.g. Keene 2007, Subotic and Zarakol 2013.   [46] See e.g. Levine 2012.

presupposes that actors are always already positioned within a durable structure of vertical differentiation and that different positions stimulate different kinds of interests – status quo, revisionist and regional – for dominant, great and middle powers, respectively.

A similar understanding has also been used to explain other actor behaviour that the balance-of-power theory does not account for. For instance, in their essay in Paul et al.'s *Status in World Politics*, Larson and Schevchenko argue that materially stratified hierarchies are just part of the story, as most such hierarchies are also overlaid with a social hierarchy. In the latter, actors are positioned according to the level of status conferred on them by the social recognition of others. Social status matters for actor behaviour, but precisely *how* it matters depends on positionality. Those with superior material positions tend to become socially competitive when those with inferior material positions have a higher status rank. Writing in a similar vein, Volgy et al. in the same volume reverse the story: social hierarchies matter much more for the behaviour of those who are positioned *lower down* on a material hierarchy – like those who fall just short of great power standing. In such cases, improved social status is less costly to achieve and more attainable than great power standing. Still others have argued that to fully understand the impact of social hierarchies on world politics, their behaviour-generating effects ought to be treated on their own rather than fused analytically to material hierarchy.

There are some significant differences in works focused on agents in hierarchical environments. Some study behaviour in the context of material stratification, whereas others focus on social standing. While most emphasise the importance of structure, disagreements also exist over the degree of agency actors enjoy within hierarchical systems. Despite their differences, however, these accounts converge on a number of points: that hierarchies are relatively durable; that an actor's position within an existing hierarchy is not (just) a choice or the result of a bargain; that an actor's identity, role, interests and/or expectations are constituted by, or an effect of, his or her position in the existing system; and that it is through these socialising dynamics that existing hierarchies create effects in world politics.

Vibrant research has emerged around this common ground and could be pushed even further through a clearer articulation of the nature of hierarchies under investigation. For instance, a core area of inquiry regards which actors' behaviours are most affected by hierarchy: those at the top, the bottom or somewhere in between. Within this vein, research on social hierarchies (both in connection with and sometimes independent of material hierarchies) has developed particularly quickly, focusing especially upon the *intensity* of socialisation. Building on the idea that the impact of a hierarchy depends on socialisation at the bottom, many have turned their attention to lower-ranking actors. In *Women and States*, Towns sees the desire to move up ranks as part of being socialised to lower rankings, and as a result, she is more optimistic about the possibility of upward mobility. This explains why policy diffusion can come from below. For Adler-Nissen in *Opting Out of the European Union*, low-ranking agents are socialised enough to be negatively affected by their stigmatisation but not so socialised as to lack the agency to strive for change. By considering the conditions under which stigma would be managed by opting out, Adler-Nissen underlines how hierarchies may produce resistance as well as compliance.[47] Others see the impact on behaviour as going deeper, with actors as having less ability to resist socialisation to their position. Though drawing upon different social theories, Zarakol in *After Defeat* and Suzuki in *Civilization and Empire* converge on their view of the desire to move up rank as part of being socialised to the stigmatised lower rankings but also indicate that being socialised to try to move up leads to behaviours that actually reproduce stigmatisation. They are therefore less optimistic about the possibility of upward mobility. Hobson and Sharman observe that status hierarchies can also socialise the powerful: 'In the 18th and especially 19th centuries through to 1945/60 prevailing norms of great power status were grounded in racist norms which prescribed that a state is a great power when it can govern over large areas of land in the "inferior non-European world" … The British (and others) engaged in imperialism not simply because they could. Rather they engaged in it because they believed they should.'[48] The British superior racial standing and superior power standing not only legitimated but also required their superior political standing. In sum, actor behaviour within existing international hierarchies is a growing focus of empirically oriented research in IR. What is lacking from this body of work is a more direct engagement with the concept of hierarchy itself, as well as an explicit articulation of what form(s) of hierarchy actors under study find themselves in.

Part II of this book pushes this research agenda forward by demanding that studies that are concerned with actor behaviour in existing hierarchies become more deliberate in articulating how they define and understand hierarchy. As in Part I, the contributors range along a spectrum from those who see actors as being more concerned with narrow institutionalised hierarchies (even while acknowledging that broad hierarchies may exist) to those who argue that actors are oriented primarily

[47] See also Adler-Nissen 2014.   [48] Hobson and Sharman 2005, 87.

toward broader social and economic structural hierarchies (even within formal institutional orders). The chapters are therefore ordered by their degree of commitment to narrow versus broad understanding of hierarchy that defines the environment in which actors under investigation are operating. Part II starts with Sharman, who focuses on micro-states in Chapter 6 and finds them to be spared from most of the supposed constraints of narrow hierarchy. It continues with Cooley in Chapter 7, who finds that actor behaviour in narrow hierarchies defined within military alliances and basing networks is at times complicated by the social signals such arrangements send about status in ways not anticipated by the formal design of the authority relationship. In Chapter 8, Stroup and Wong examine how international non-governmental organisations (INGOs) navigate the social hierarchy among themselves, finding that a broad hierarchy underwrites the formal institutionalisation of hierarchical arrangements in this realm. In Chapter 9, Adler-Nissen looks at Greek and German responses to the social hierarchies made manifest by the Euro Crisis, which do not necessarily parallel the formal hierarchy of European Union. Finally, in Chapter 10, Suzuki analyses Chinese responses to East-West relations, understood as a broad hierarchy with a long history much more powerful than any narrow manifestation of the same that has existed over time. His account mirrors Sharman in that he also makes a case for agency of subordinate actors but differs sharply from Sharman in that he finds strong evidence of international hierarchy broadly understood as a structure of organised inequality.

Conclusion

Hierarchies in World Politics thus furthers two major research areas on hierarchy in IR through the productive engagement of its contributors with each other's conceptualisations. Part I contributors, who in previous work had focused on different visions of hierarchy, ranging from narrow to broad, reflect upon whether (and to what extent) narrow hierarchies as legitimate authority can be erected independently of broad hierarchies as organised inequality. Institutional/agentic accounts of hierarchy thus have to take into account the possibility of hierarchical structures in the international system, and structural accounts have to acknowledge that hierarchies can take institutional forms. Part II contributors, who in previous work had focused on actors' understanding and their responses to existing hierarchies, consider how those accounts can be enriched by articulating more clearly the type of hierarchy (or a particular intersection of hierarchies) that is being responded to by the actor. Each chapter develops its account not only theoretically but also through an empirical focus on a particular issue area relevant to contemporary world politics. The empirical richness of this book is yet another demonstration of the great promise of hierarchy research in IR.

Then, in a coda chapter (Chapter 11), Donnelly provides the reader with an alternative way of thinking of hierarchy that is not fully captured by the frameworks adopted in this book. Donnelly argues that 'neither hierarchy nor anarchy is a structural ordering principle' and that the phenomena discussed in this book would be better captured by the concepts of 'authority and (in)equality, and rule in international relations'. He suggests that we can get further analytical leverage on our deployment of the concept of hierarchy by thinking about the ways stratification and centralization intersect. He also observes that the modern commitment to equality has made it difficult to understand hierarchies. In the conclusion (Chapter 12), I answer Donnelly's challenge and make a positive case for organising IR research around the concept of hierarchy. Research programmes are not created out in a vacuum, and they have particular histories. The power of hierarchy as a concept lies not only in its heuristic but also its ability to connect diverse scholarship in a discipline that was most recently organised around the concept of anarchy. This book is thus not meant (just) as an intervention about the proper analytical lens for research but also as one with hopefully far-reaching implications about the future of IR as a coherent discipline that can make original contributions to our understanding of world politics.

Part I

Forms of Hierarchy

Origins, Nature and Intersections

1 Laws and Norms in the Making of International Hierarchies

David A. Lake

Hierarchies both produce rules and are reproduced through rules. Whether conceived as structures of organized inequality or authority, hierarchies require rules that order relations between actors of the same or different status and define the rights and duties of rulers and ruled. Yet these same hierarchies are themselves constituted by rules. How is stratification determined? Who adjusts the rankings when technological or environmental changes intrude? What are the rightful powers of a ruler? Which commands are legitimate – and which not? Even anarchic systems have rules,[1] however much they may be violated in practice.[2] Hierarchic systems, however, depend on rules and, indeed, could not exist without them.

As described by Zarakol in the Introduction to this book, hierarchies come in two primary forms.[3] Some hierarchies are sets of laws, intentionally enacted and enforced by authorities to shape human behavior and even motives. Authority and law are always the product of agency, made by someone for some purpose. It is this intentional quality of law that underlies Zarakol's notion of authority as narrow or agentic hierarchy, even if the subsequent effects of laws are not always those anticipated by their creators. Other hierarchies are composed of norms – widely held principles of acceptable behavior – that rank actors according to some often implicit but broadly understood rule. Although in their early stages principled ideas may be actively promoted by norms entrepreneurs,[4] once accepted and internalized, norms are disembodied.[5] Even after the fact, it is commonly difficult to identify who or what "authored" the norm and why a particular principled idea rather than another attained a normative status. Some norms are so deeply woven into the fabric of social life, in fact, that they seem "natural" and are taken for granted, though even these naturalized conventions, such as the norm of racial inequality, likely

---

[1] Reus-Smit 1999.   [2] Krasner 1999.
[3] These forms are sometimes associated with different logics of social action; see March and Olson 1998.
[4] Finnemore and Sikkink 1998.   [5] Bicchieri 2006.

had active entrepreneurs at some moment far distant in time. It is precisely this deep, widely shared ranking of actors that creates the organized inequality behind the broad, structural, or institutional conception of hierarchy discussed in this book.

In this chapter emphasizing the interaction of hierarchies as mutually constituted laws and norms, I explore how functional bargains in law – narrow hierarchies – combine with intersubjectively defined inequalities – broad hierarchies – to constrain social life. Although different authors place different weights on the relative importance of these two forms of hierarchy in political life, laws and norms are symbiotic or mutually constitutive. Law is created and enforced by authorities, which are themselves actors with legitimate power. Law legitimates power by solving collective-action problems and improving human welfare, but it is simultaneously conditioned and constrained by norms. Not only do social norms provide a language through which large numbers of individuals can communicate about what is or is not a legitimate use of power and therefore law, but they also create standards against which the use of power is judged, assessed, and possibly opposed by those to whom it would be applied. Without social norms structuring and facilitating how society relates to uses or abuses of power, legitimacy could not exist. Social norms, in turn, are nowadays increasingly codified into law, especially before they are internalized or have acquired a taken-for-granted quality. Indeed, though it has received little attention, a primary task of norms entrepreneurs as described in available case studies is precisely to translate their principled ideas into law.[6] The first section of this chapter therefore proposes a framework for understanding the interaction of these hierarchies. The second section then uses this framework to examine the evolution of the principle of nonintervention.

The Interaction of Law and Norms in Hierarchies

Law, and the corresponding authority on which it rests, and social norms are deeply intertwined with one another. Although often treated independently, we should strive toward an integrated approach.

Law as Socially Constituted Hierarchy

Law is the rule or set of rules enacted by an authority. Not all rules are laws, only those duly propagated by some recognized authority.

---

[6] Keck and Sikkink 1998.

Authority, in turn, is rightful rule or legitimate power.[7] When political authority is exercised, the ruler, A, commands a set of subordinates, B, to alter their actions, where command implies that A has the *right* to issue such orders. This right, in turn, implies a correlative obligation or *duty* by B to comply, if possible, with A's order. In short, B "surrenders judgment" and accepts the force of A's command. B's obligation implies a further correlative right by A to *enforce* its commands in the event of B's noncompliance. In an authority relationship, individuals choose whether to comply with a ruler's commands but are bound by the right of the ruler to discipline or punish their noncompliance. Many drivers exceed the speed limit, for instance, but if caught, they accept the right of the state to issue fines or other punishments for breaking the law.

Authority and, specifically, the right to punish noncompliance ultimately rest on the collective acceptance or legitimacy of the ruler's right to rule. As Thomas Hobbes himself recognized, "the power of the mighty (the Leviathan) hath no foundation but in the opinion and belief of the people."[8] Richard Flathman develops this point more fully, arguing that "sustained coercion is impossible without substantial agreement among the members of the association about those very propositions whose rejection commonly brings coercion into play."[9] If recognized as legitimate, the ruler acquires the ability to punish individuals because of the broad backing of others.[10] Because a sufficient portion of the ruled accepts the ruler and her edicts as rightful, the ruler can employ force against individual free riders and even dissidents. Knowing that a sufficient number of others support the ruler, in turn, potential free riders and dissidents are deterred from violating the rules, and overt force is rendered unnecessary or, at least, unusual.

Authority is a hierarchy created and sustained through practice by a ruler and the ruled. This has several noteworthy implications. First, authority is not a claim made by the ruler but a right granted by the ruled. A does not possess authority unless B acknowledges a duty to comply with A's will.[11] Obedience springs not from A's assertions. Rather, A's ability to expect compliance derives from B's conferral of the *right* to rule.

Second, authority is always a product and site of political struggle as both ruler and ruled contest at the margins the rights and duties in their relationship. What it means to be authoritative and what rights both the

[7] This section draws heavily on Lake (2009a, Chapter 2), which develops the approach to authority in greater detail.
[8] As quoted in Williams 2006, 265.   [9] Flathman 1980, 29.
[10] Bernard 1962, 162; Lasswell and Kaplan 1950, 133.
[11] Bernard 1962, 163–5; Simon 1976, 146.

ruler and ruled may legitimately possess are continually negotiated and renegotiated, as suggested by the ongoing struggle over reproductive rights even within a well-established legal system such as that of the United States. Acts of noncompliance by subordinates designed to test the ruler's tolerance and acts of discipline by the ruler to demarcate those limits are an inherent part of this struggle. Authority is a dynamic and constantly evolving relationship of domination and subordination.

Finally, the key problem in any hierarchy is limiting abuses of authority by the ruler.[12] Granting authority to the ruler to issue and enforce commands also gives her the ability to use coercion in her own self-interest. A may decide to coerce B to ensure her hold on office or to extract economic benefits for herself or her principal supporters or simply for her own, megalomaniacal purposes. Thus, to grant authority to A, B must be relatively confident that the authority conferred will be used appropriately. To receive this grant, therefore, A must commit to limits on her authority that are acceptable and credible to B. Within states, the creation of relatively more democratic institutions that diffuse power and ensure that popular preferences are represented in the policy process is one common method of creating credibility.[13] Between states, democracy within the dominant power and multilateralism abroad have been similarly used to enhance credibility.[14] Nonetheless, limiting potential abuses by the ruler is a necessary and typically prior step in any grant of authority. It is this implied self-restraint by the ruler that most clearly separates authority from coercion and legitimate order from pure "power" politics in international relations.

What distinguishes authority from other cognate concepts such as coercion and law from other rules is its legitimacy, or the recognition by the governed of the rightfulness of the rules enacted by the ruler. What makes any particular authority legitimate, of course, is highly contested, often because the foundations of legitimacy are themselves tightly tied to debates over the boundaries of authority. At a minimum, an authority and its rules – the law – must create a social order that improves the welfare of a sufficient portion of the community relative to the next-best conceivable option that individuals expect other members to support the ruler and comply with her rules – in other words, to legitimate her powers. Rules improve social welfare by facilitating cooperation. At the same time, rules nearly always bias outcomes in favor of the politically powerful and influential within society. Authority is almost never "fair" or equitable,

---

[12] Simon 1976, 134.   [13] North and Weingast 1989.
[14] On democracy, see Martin 2000; Lipson 2003. On multilateralism, see Ruggie 1993; Thompson 2009.

especially in the eyes of those whom it disadvantages. But even so, it must, on average, leave enough members of the community better off than the next-best alternative or the ruler will lose her legitimacy.

Because law is always consciously written and enacted by someone for some purpose, it is natural, I think, to conceive of law as the product of instrumental self-interest and intentional political strategies, contingent on the distribution of political power in society and existing political institutions. Even when motivated by principled ideas, attention to strategy and choice tends to favor a "rationalist" approach to politics. Indeed, one can read Keck and Sikkink (1998), one of the most highly cited works on the transformation of social norms, as a purely instrumental account of the pursuit of *principled* values and nascent social norms.

Yet even the minimum condition of improved social welfare is itself highly structured by social norms. What constitutes an adequate social order? In centuries past, social order implied only the absence of banditry, pestilence, and war. Today, societies commonly expect their governments to produce high levels of economic growth, full employment, and low inflation. How many and what members of a community must benefit from that social order to constitute a "sufficient" proportion? What is the next-best social order that members of the community can envision as a realistic alternative? The answers to all these questions rely on shared understandings of what is "good," right, and indeed appropriate. What makes any possible authority legitimate for any community at any moment in time is highly contingent on the norms of that society.

Norms as Socially Constituted Hierarchy

Social norms are shared understandings of appropriate behavior for a given actor in a given context. Like law, norms are rules governing behavior that are accepted by a community. Unlike laws, though, norms are disembodied or decentralized. Although there may be entrepreneurs who promote them, there is no ruler who articulates a norm or enforces it. Rather, norms emerge from within society and are enforced in a decentralized fashion by members of the community through social sanctions ranging from mild rebuke to permanent ostracism or exile. The strength of norms, in turn, can be seen in recurring behavior consistent with the norm and, when breeched, in the justifications and excuses offered to explain the deviation. The strength of the norm against torture, for instance, was seen clearly in the attempt by US President George W. Bush to redefine waterboarding and other practices previously understood as torture as "enhanced interrogation techniques"; recognizing that he could not violate a deeply held norm, he attempted to redefine the meaning of torture itself. Once accepted as norms, though, the rules and corresponding behaviors are naturalized, and it is difficult for those holding the norms to imagine how anyone could have thought differently. Slavery is perhaps the clearest example of this "mind shift": the previously common practice of holding other human beings in permanent bondage is today nearly unimaginable (though sometimes still practiced, especially in the sex trade).

By defining appropriate behavior, social norms create hierarchies of "good" actors who substantially comply with expectations or can persuasively explain and justify lapses and "bad" actors who inexplicably violate or even deny the existence of the community standard.[15] Norms are inherently judgmental. In specifying a standard to which actors should aspire and to which they will be held to account, norms equally identify "negative" behavior and, when consistently violated, actors who are inferior, deficient, or unworthy and who should be socially shunned in greater or lesser degree. Hierarchical orderings of states subtly reflect these judgments. In the nineteenth century, sovereign states were limited to Europe and North America, whereas all others were ranked as neutralized states, protected independent states, vassal states, protected dependent states, and autonomous colonies – with formal colonies further beyond the pale.[16] Little separated some of these categories other than the race of the majority population.[17] Today, "developed" states have social and institutional attributes that have led them to "succeed" and serve as models for others, whereas "developing" states are presently deficient in some way, though they have the capacity to transform themselves.[18] We have the P5, the G-7, the G-20, the Organisation for Economic Co-operation and Development (OECD), and the Group of 77 (now with 134 members). And democratic states defined by broadbased political participation and the protection of certain political and civil rights are commonly seen as superior to authoritarian states that restrict political participation and freedom.[19] Social identity theory posits that individuals inherently desire acceptance or respect by others, motivating them to conform to social norms, and it appears that this may apply to collectivities as well, creating a desire for "status."[20] If so, then it is precisely through the act of judging others that norms exert at least some of their effect.

---

[15] See also Towns 2012; Zarakol 2014; see also Chapters 9 and 10.
[16] Willoughby and Fenwick 1974.   [17] Reid 1932.
[18] On status rankings of states, stigmatization, and counterhegemonic strategies, see Zarakol 2011.
[19] Fukuyama 1992.   [20] Paul, Larson, and Wohlforth 2014.

It is difficult and often impossible to identify the origins of social norms. Principled ideas always have advocates – norms entrepreneurs – who seek to promote those ideas and their corresponding behavior. But there are lots of principled ideas floating around at any time – a sort of primordial normative soup, if you will – and some take hold and gain adherents, and some do not.[21] Although the Protestant dissenters in England were likely critical of the abolition of the slave trade,[22] the Abolitionist movement as a whole had many parents. Eleanor Roosevelt is justly credited with a key role in promoting universal human rights, but the idea of human rights evolved over centuries and through the efforts of many political thinkers and was likely not internalized until the 1970s in reaction to the abuses of the Argentine junta.[23] Isolating the precise "cause" of a norm or when an idea gains sufficient social support to be considered a standard of appropriate behavior remains hard precisely because of the shared nature of understanding that makes one idea and not another a norm. Although entrepreneurs may have been instrumental in creating the norm, their identities and histories become buried in time, the more so the more deeply internalized is the principle. Intentionality and strategy fade, and action (even enforcement) is taken because this is what "we" do.

Yet norms are nearly always ambiguous, at least at the margins. What exactly is the standard to which actors are held to account? What is an excusable breach or adequate justification? Ambiguity is inherent in any norm, which must be kept simple to be widely shared and understood but which then lacks nuance in specific situations or changing environments. Equally, though, ambiguity results from struggles over the content of specific norms. To the extent that norms matter, it should not be a surprise that they are continuously contested. Are economic, social, and cultural rights equal to political and civil rights? Do "Western" political and civil rights trump "Asian values"? As political statements, norms will always be open to interpretation, reflecting the lowest common denominator on which the community can agree.

Perhaps because of this inherent ambiguity there has been a steady movement in the modern world to legalize norms by rendering them into statute, treaty, or convention – to make them legible. Legalization not only renders norms more precise but also harnesses the adjudicatory powers of the state to their interpretation and enforcement.[24] The small communities of deep social capital, strict social norms, and "trust" idealized by Robert Putnam (2000) have given way in the United States and

---

[21] Lake and Wong 2009.   [22] Kaufman and Pape 1999.
[23] See e.g. Hunt 2007; Ishay 2008.
[24] On legalization in international relations, see Goldstein et al. 2001.

elsewhere to more mobile national communities regulated by legal contracts and public statutes. At the international level, "decent" behavior by diplomats ensured by "gentlemanly norms" that became encrusted as customary international law have become increasingly codified into treaties as international society has been enlarged and become more diverse, with the Law of the Sea being but one prominent example.

Recognizing the power of law, activists increasingly seek to use law to instill norms in the face of social resistance. The Civil Rights Act of 1964 could not have been passed without the civil rights movement in the United States, but the legislation also predated the change in norms – especially for many southern conservatives. Likewise, although there was considerable trepidation in the LGBT community about taking the "legal route" to marriage equality, the Supreme Court found in the Constitution the right to same-sex marriage before this principle was widely shared by all Americans, again especially in more conservative regions of the country. Internationally, the United Nations first began to address apartheid in South Africa in the early 1960s, long before the divestment movement reflecting a change in social norms began.[25] Although this trend is not sufficiently appreciated in the transnational advocacy networks (TANs) literature in my view, it is noteworthy that a significant fraction of the activities of norms entrepreneurs appears to be aimed at codifying principled ideas into law rather than simply changing the views of diverse publics. At the very least, writing norms into law ties the legitimacy of law to the principles advocated by norms entrepreneurs. Law transforms as well as reflects social norms.

Interactions

Figure 1.1 illustrates a framework for capturing the interactions of law, norms, and principles already identified in the existing literature and touched on earlier. Principles are rules for behavior not yet enacted into law or norms, and they form the primordial soup out of which law and norms emerge. The vertical arrangement in the figure is not intended to imply any ranking of constructs because it is the interactions that are of interest here. Political actions closer to the "top" of the figure are more intentional and strategic – or narrow in the language of this book – and actions closer to the "bottom" are more reflexive – or broad. The sides differ in what they take for granted or as exogenous. The left-hand side, moving "up" the figure, takes social norms as fixed and constraints on the choice of principles and law. The right-hand side, moving "down," takes law as given and examines how it influences the diffusion and choice of

[25] See Klotz 1995.

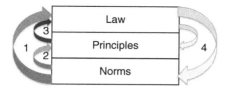

Figure 1.1 Interactions of law, norms, and principles.

principles and norms by society. The left-hand side is more fully articulated. It is harder to differentiate the effects of law on principles and norms, reflected in the single arrow labeled "4." Although for initial expository purposes the sides take different constructs as given, in actuality, law, principles, and norms are always simultaneously in play as they are renegotiated and shaped by political struggle.

Norms, legitimate authority, and, in turn, law (1). Legitimacy exists only when conferred by the ruled on the ruler. The central problem in constituting any authority relationship is empowering the ruler to create and enforce law while simultaneously limiting that power. To enforce limits on authority, in turn, requires coordinated action by the governed, which, while possible, is never a unique equilibrium.[26] Social norms serve two essential functions in determining the legitimacy of the ruler's actions and thus whether those actions are regarded as authoritative and lawful or coercive.

First, independent of any moral effect, norms provide a language for communicating among a large number of individuals about whether the ruler and her acts are rightful and legitimate. To act collectively, members of a community must agree that the ruler has transgressed the boundary of her appropriate powers. Precisely because social norms are widely shared, they provide a foundation for identifying and judging whether the ruler has crossed a "red line" that requires a response from society.[27]

Second, transgressions of social norms offend individuals and spur them to action despite collective-action problems that might otherwise thwart an effective societal response. Indirect reciprocity has been shown to be an evolutionarily stable equilibrium solution to the free-rider problem.[28] There is also considerable experimental evidence, spanning many cultures, that individuals are willing to bear at least some cost in sanctioning rule breakers without immediate benefit to themselves, especially when violations offend socially contingent

[26] Weingast 1997.   [27] Bicchieri 2006.
[28] Axelrod 1986; Panchanathan and Boyd 2004.

conceptions of fairness.[29] By extension, an authority's violation of a social norm on which its legitimacy rests is more likely to generate first- and second-order retaliation in which individuals both sanction the ruler and sanction others who fail to also sanction the ruler. Tying violations of legitimate powers by an aggrandizing ruler to a moral standard is likely to make collective action against that ruler more robust than rationalist theory alone expects.

Norms condition principles (2). At any moment in time, there are many principles that might guide behavior. The Universal Declaration of Human Rights (UDHR), for instance, contains thirty articles and enumerates even more rights. Only a handful of the principles contained therein have moved beyond aspiration to become norms to which states are held to account.[30] As Keck and Sikkink (1998) show, transnational advocacy network (TANs) are more likely to succeed in advancing principles when they can be framed in terms of existing social norms. Women's rights, for instance, failed to gain traction because of diverse views in different societies until they were connected to the more universally held norm of avoiding physical harm. The existing structure of norms thus favors some principles and limits others. This relationship, of course, is not deterministic. As framing effects show, norms entrepreneurs have some leeway in how principles are represented and to which norms they are attached. Overall, however, principles that are consistent with social norms will be more readily translated into new norms and laws.

Principles are strategically translated into law (3). The translation of principles into norms is a complex process. How, when, and why a norms cascade occurs remains uncertain.[31] Changing behavior by changing what people want to do (or feel they should do) is likely more efficient than changing incentives through law and its enforcement provisions. Nonetheless, in a way that is presently underappreciated, getting principles codified into law appears to be an important objective of norms entrepreneurs and an important step in stimulating a norms cascade. Codifying principles into law requires some degree of public support and consistency with established social norms, at least in democratic or semidemocratic societies. To be translated into law and regarded as legitimate, any principle must be framed in terms that receive sufficient political support to get onto the political agenda. Translating principle into law, however, both creates a standard against which practice is assessed and raises the expected costs of defection from that standard. In short, by changing incentives, law changes behavior, which is typically

---

[29] Henrich et al. 2006.   [30] Wong 2012.   [31] Finnemore and Sikkink 1998.

what activists seek to achieve rather than the transformation of a principle into a norm itself.

Law promotes principles and norms (4). In addition to altering behavior, however, there are also at least five indirect effects of law on principles and norms. First, by creating incentives that encourage ("make legal") and discourage ("outlaw") certain behaviors, law naturalizes or normalizes actions. By generating compliance, some behaviors become more common and others less so, creating over time collective expectations that individuals will act in some ways and not others. Second, if enacted legitimately – that is, by existing and accepted procedures – individuals are more likely to accept that a sufficient proportion of their society believes that the rule is consistent with other norms and that they should accept this principle and modify their behavior accordingly. If enacted "lawfully," one cannot call into question a particular law without calling into question all laws adopted in the same way. Opponents therefore must argue that a law was adopted "unconstitutionally." In both these first two indirect effects, the penumbra or status of law helps legitimate the principle and move it toward acceptance as a norm, but even here, as the abortion example suggests, the effect is neither universal nor automatic.

Third, once enacted, law imposes a specific form of reasoning on principles and norms surrounding the issue. Law must be consistent with established constitutional or more basic law. A legislature can write any norm or principle into law it chooses, but a constitutional court of review can render it null and void if it violates other laws. Having established a constitutionally protected right, no subsequent law, however rightly passed or popular, can then abridge that right.[32] This is a form of logic and practice that law imposes on social norms, no matter how widely held. Similarly, in a nearly unique form of legal reasoning, disputes over the law and its meaning are governed by standing, precedent, and *stare decisis*. Once decided, therefore, law places the burden on challengers to demonstrate that the law was wrongly decided, inappropriately applied in different circumstances, or trumped by subsequent law and developments. Law insists that principles and norms be bent to its will. Fourth, and related, principles and norms almost always contain ambiguities, as noted earlier, especially in application to novel circumstances. Ambiguity is exacerbated when multiple principles and norms may apply and point to different behaviors or justifications. Law either resolves these ambiguities itself in statute or provides a means of resolving them through the courts. Thus, through legalization, principles and

---

[32] See, e.g., the trajectory of Proposition 8 in California.

norms gain precision and create focal points around which social expectations converge.

Finally, through the force of these other indirect effects, law privileges some principles and norms over others. Law reshapes the playing field on which the struggle over principles and norms takes place. We see this process clearly at work in the continuing struggles for racial equality in the United States. The Civil Rights Act is justly celebrated. From the very first, however, the civil rights movement was bound up with changing the law first and social norms second. The law would not have changed, of course, without pressure from the civil rights movement, reaching national prominence in the Montgomery bus boycott in 1955–6, the freedom riders of 1961, and then the Selma to Montgomery marches of 1965. Yet protesters won their first success in the courts in *Brown v. Board of Education* in 1954 and with the advocacy of President Lyndon Johnson in the Voting Rights Act passed in 1965. The most important legal moves either preceded or coincided with the momentous protests, which themselves preceded large-scale change in social attitudes toward race. Court decisions and legislation did not by themselves overturn social norms of racial inequality and prejudice, and the struggle for equality continues. It is also hard to know exactly how social norms might have evolved in the absence of legislation in the United States, but now, decades after the Civil Rights Act, explicit appeals to norms of racial inequality are regarded as offensive and "beyond the pale." Law certainly contributed to this important change in social norms. A similar process unfolded in the movement for marriage equality. The law moved first or at least in tandem with public attitudes but certainly before any significant shift in social norms and in the face of still considerable social resistance. Having shifted, however, norms of equality have triumphed over social norms embodied in what opponents of this change still refer to as "traditional family values."

Social norms and principles condition law, and law moves social norms and principles. As social norms evolve in response to law, they change the foundations of law in real ways. The civil rights movement promoted social norms of human equality over norms of racial inequality. However imperfectly held, these social norms of human equality then laid the foundation for the movement to instill marriage equality as law and, perhaps, a new social norm. LGBT rights were built on the foundation of civil rights for racial minorities in the United States. Conservatives warned of the "slippery slope," most notably Supreme Court Justice Antonin Scalia, who famously mocked the Court majority in its decision in *United States v. Windsor*, arguing that it would lead inevitably to overturning state laws denying same-sex couples marital status. But such is the way of all social change. Norms condition principles, norms and principles condition law, law conditions norms and principles ad infinitum.

The International Principle and Law of Nonintervention

Nonintervention is a principle of international society and, since 1945, an increasingly elaborated international law. Widely referred to as a norm, states nonetheless routinely intervene in each other's internal affairs, not least in wars of regime change. Although violators seldom deny the existence of an international law against intervention – in this sense, it is a well-established doctrine – they demonstrate its weakness or tenuous normative status through practice and by appeals to other "higher" or more fundamental norms such as self-defense, the protection of lives and property, and increasingly the defense of minority rights. Nonintervention is a law that may be on the path to becoming a norm, but it has not yet achieved that status and is still actively contested by advocates of other principles, including the responsibility to protect (R2P).

This section provides a brief genealogy of the idea of nonintervention in world politics through the framework developed in the preceding section. The short version of the story is that the principle of nonintervention developed over centuries of political struggle. Although fully articulated by the eighteenth century, it was thwarted by incomplete norms of human equality that, in turn, conflicted with stronger norms of racial inequality. A decisive opening arose at the end of the nineteenth century as the United States sought to replace European dominance and colonial control in Latin American states, which, even if sovereign, were not recognized as full and equal members of international society. Emphasizing the Spanish ancestry and culture of their elites rather than the indigenous or former slave status of the majority of their populations, the Latin American states were best placed of all subordinate states to claim an equal sovereign status and the right to internal autonomy. Central to the struggle was the attempt by Latin Americans to write the principle of nonintervention into international law, an effort opposed by the United States until 1933. The principle was subsequently incorporated into the United Nations Charter and then – with the support of recently decolonized countries – elaborated by subsequent General Assembly resolutions over the succeeding decades. This legal foundation, along with declining support for the norm of racial inequality, then provided the platform on which postcolonial states, still vulnerable to external intervention, sought to propagate the norm of nonintervention – the struggle for which continues today.

30   *David A. Lake*

The Principle of Nonintervention

The principle of nonintervention in the internal affairs of states, often called *Westphalian sovereignty*, is one of several core principles of the more general concept of sovereignty.[33] Sovereignty itself is and will always remain a contested and contingent construct that evolves through political struggle.[34] It has no fixed meaning, even today.[35] Rather, the concept of sovereignty has emerged organically in response to specific challenges facing states and their rulers, filtered through the ideas of political philosophers in each era, and rendered into practice and, sometimes, international law.

Nonintervention is a corollary to the more basic principle of sovereignty that ultimate or final authority is vested in the sovereign, whether this be a monarch or the people as a corporate body. Where ultimate authority is vested was the central issue in the struggle over sovereignty in the centuries before and after Westphalia supposedly settled the issue. The history of sovereignty is usually encapsulated in a series of historical "signposts" wherein important steps were taken in the process of consolidating authority in the state, often through war with the principle advanced through the peace settlement that followed.[36] The process was actually far more gradual and less linear than in the orthodox version.

The investiture controversy of the eleventh and twelfth centuries began when Catholic officials revoked the right of the Holy Roman Emperor, then the child Henry IV, to appoint the pope, creating the College of Cardinals.[37] In 1075, now grown, Henry withdrew his support from Pope Gregory VII, declaring him a "false monk," and began once again appointing his own bishops. Pope Gregory VII then excommunicated Henry, deposing him as German king and settling off an internal struggle in the empire for control. One year later, Henry capitulated, only to later invade Italy to depose Gregory.[38] Successive popes continued to stimulate rebellions and wars within the Holy Roman Empire, leading to a dramatic decline in political centralization. This first stage of the controversy was eventually ended in the Concordat of Worms, signed in September 1122, through which some rights of investiture were returned

---

[33] On Westphalian sovereignty, see Krasner 1999, 20–5. For a slightly different formulation of the principles of sovereignty, see Lake 2009s, 45–51. On sovereignty as the basic constitutional structure of international relations, see Reus-Smit 1999; Philpott 2001. On the development of the principle of nonintervention, see Glanville 2014.

[34] Howland and White 2009, 1–2; Havercroft 2012; Onuf 1998, Chapter 5.

[35] On the socially constructed nature of sovereignty, see Biersteker and Weber 1996.

[36] See Hinsley 1986.   [37] On the period in general, see Bisson 2009.

[38] Gregory was removed only after his Norman allies, who defeated the Germans, sacked Rome and touched off a popular uprising against the pope.

to the pope. A similar controversy played out in England during this same period. The investiture controversy and subsequent concordat hardly settled the issue, however, and monarchs and popes continued to struggle over the division of authority in Christendom, with the pope continuing to claim the power to depose rulers.[39]

The next major signpost was the Peace of Augsburg in 1555. Following the Reformation, the Holy Roman Empire once again fell into near chaos, with the Catholic emperor, Charles V, now facing off against Lutheran monarchs resisting his authority, resulting in the Schmalkaldic War (1546–7). Although Charles won on the battlefield, instability continued, and Protestantism became entrenched. A compromise was eventually reached in the Peace of Augsburg, a legal treaty seeking to create a norm, which included the famous principle of *cuius regio, eius religio* (whose realm, his religion), granting princes within the empire the right to choose the official religion within the domains they controlled. This right, however, was limited to Lutherans, excluding the rapidly growing Calvinist sect and sowing the seeds of future instability. The Peace of Augsburg created a period of relative quiet in the religious wars, only to be broken by the start of the Thirty Year's War in 1618, once again pitching the Catholic emperor against Protestant princes struggling for greater autonomy.

The Thirty Year's War started as a local dispute over the appointment of a new king in Bohemia but soon became a "world war" involving all the German principalities, France, Spain, and Sweden, all pursuing interests of their own that sometimes conflicted with their religious affiliations. The war ended in 1648 with the Treaties of Münster and Osnabrück, forming the Peace of Westphalia. Described by Leo Gross (1948) as the "majestic portal" through which the age of sovereignty supposedly arrived, revisionists have conclusively shown that Westphalia was, if anything, merely one further step in the evolution of the principle we now call sovereignty.[40] Westphalia was a general legal settlement that sought to address the range of political and religious issues that had been scouring Europe for centuries. Affirming the principle of *cuius regio, eius religio* from Augsburg, Westphalia went further in claiming *rex est imperator in regno suo* (each king is an emperor in his own realm), effectively ending the Holy Roman Empire's claim to be a trans-European polity and, more important, asserting that ultimate authority in any territory was vested in the monarch.[41] Although none of the princes at Westphalia envisioned anything like the modern concept of sovereignty, by 1648, the seeds of the norm had been planted by the treaties that ended the war.

---

[39] Havercroft 2012, 124.   [40] Krasner 1999; Osiander 2001.   [41] Havercroft 2012, 120.

The legal consolidation of ultimate authority in the state at Westphalia implied the principle of nonintervention, but this was not made explicit for nearly another century. This has led revisionists to move the date at which the principle of sovereignty emerged to the late eighteenth century, but even here there was no radical breakpoint, only the slow, incremental elaboration of philosophical principles in the context of continuing political struggle. The first explicit statement of the principle of nonintervention was by Christian von Wolff, writing in 1748 that "[t]o interfere in the government of another, in whatever way indeed that may be done is opposed to the natural liberty of nations, by virtue of which one is altogether independent of the will of other nations in its action."[42] In this way, early legal reasoning was deployed to structure a subsequent understanding of a principle of behavior. Writing a decade later and seeking to popularize Wolff's more philosophical view, Emmerich de Vattel agreed that no state had a right to intervene in the internal affairs of any other. Since nations were "free and independent of each other, in the same manner as men are naturally free and independent," he wrote, "each nation should be left in the peaceable enjoyment of that liberty which she inherits from nature."[43] Now explicit, the principle still had to be translated into behavior, which has perhaps been even more problematic than the centuries-long process that led to this formulation.

The Role of Social Norms

The principle of nonintervention was conditioned by at least two underlying social norms, one supporting it and driving forward its translation into practice and law and one undermining it and severely limiting its application. The first, supportive norm was the liberal idea of fundamental human equality, which was, in turn, premised on the belief that all individuals possess certain natural rights simply by their existence as humans. Modern human rights law shares this same foundation. The theory of natural rights also laid the groundwork for Hugo Grotius' development of international law.[44] Key here was the extension of natural rights of individuals to collections of individuals in states interacting in the state of nature. Indeed, for some theorists, notably Thomas Hobbes, if corporate bodies were necessary to preserve the natural rights of individuals – most important, the right to self-preservation – then natural rights

---

[42] As quoted in Krasner 1999, 21.
[43] Emmerich de Vattel, *The Law of Nations, Preliminaries*, §15. Available at www.constitu tion.org/vattel/vattel_pre.htm (accessed April 20, 2014).
[44] Brown, Nardin, and Rengger 2002, 312–16.

applied even more to collectivities when they interacted with one another in the state of nature.[45]

It followed that if all individuals and states possessed certain natural rights, then all individuals and, in turn, states have equal status or are "formally" equal. As Vattel also wrote, "A dwarf is as much a man as a giant; a small republic is no less a sovereign state than the most powerful kingdom."[46] And it followed further, as earlier, that if all states are formally equal, no state has a *right* to intervene in the affairs of another. As the liberal norm of human equality spread in the seventeenth and eighteenth centuries, it laid the foundation on which the principle of nonintervention could rest and became a possible frame for those seeking to covert a principle into a more widely shared social norm.

Paralleling liberalism, however, was the countervailing norm of racial inequality. Race and especially racial hierarchies are seldom discussed in international relations.[47] There is a silence in the discipline, sometimes justified by apologists by the "obvious" nature of race and racism in world politics and by others as irrelevant when politics stops at the water's edge.[48] Nonetheless, the effects of racial hierarchies are seldom theorized. Alongside the norm of human equality has been the enduring status hierarchy of racial inequality. The contradiction has been reconciled de facto by limiting in practice the equality of individuals and, in turn, states to white Europeans while imposing a "color line" on the rest of the world.[49]

The norm of racial inequality was used to justify both massive systematic interventions against peoples of color through imperialism and other, more short-term interventions intended to protect white travelers, missionaries, diplomats, and investors.[50] The inherent racism in the Age of Discovery is exemplified in Pope Nicholas V's papal bull of 1455 declaring West Africa *terra nullis*, extended by Pope Alexander VI to all new lands in 1493. In this way, Europeans intentionally blinded themselves to

---

[45] *Ibid.*, 316–17.

[46] Emmerich de Vattel, *The Law of Nations, Preliminaries*, §18. Available at www.constitution.org/vattel/vattel_pre.htm (accessed April 20, 2014). On Vattel, see Goebel 1923; Dickenson 1972; Hinsley 1986.

[47] On the exclusion of race from international relations, see Chin 2009; Henderson 2013; Jones 2008; and especially Vitalis 2000, 2015.

[48] Vitalis 2000, 2015.

[49] This is a prominent theme in critical studies in international relations. See Hobson (2012) and the accompanying symposium on "Revisioning Eurocentrism" at The Disorder of Things, available at http://thedisorderofthings.com/2012/09/17/re-visioning-eurocentrism-a-symposium/ (accessed September 14, 2015).

[50] See Jones 2008; Vitalis 2000; Strang 1996. Although he does not emphasize racism, the two-tiered system of international relations is central to Keene (2002). Crawford (2002, 134) cites beliefs in the superiority of European society and on expanding Christianity.

indigenous political formations and justified to themselves, at least, a civilizing mission that imposed European culture, religion, and governance structures on "inferior" or "backwards" peoples.[51] It is impossible to disentangle formal and informal European imperialism, as well as various ad hoc interventions in non-European polities, from deeply held norms of racial inequality.

Thus, throughout modern history, the norm of human equality that supported the principle of nonintervention, limited in practice to European and later North American states, and the norm of racial inequality that permitted and – through the notion of the "white man's burden" – encouraged intervention have competed one against the other. As a result of the contradiction, the principle of nonintervention has never gained universal support, especially from the states most likely to be doing the intervening. As the norm of racial inequality came to be increasingly challenged after World War II, both in the United States, as discussed earlier, and in the decolonization movement, the norm of human equality appears to have become dominant, ushering in a period of greater support (if not respect) for the principle of nonintervention.[52] Even today, however, the norm of racial inequality continues to influence the debate over humanitarian intervention and the right to protect (R2P), to which I return later.

The Struggle for and Effects of Legalization

The political struggle over the principle of nonintervention, especially in non-European states that remained most vulnerable, eventually turned to international law. The first serious attempts to codify the principle into international law originated in Latin America in the Calvo and Drago doctrines, articulated in 1868 and 1902, respectively. The first doctrine – posed by Carlos Calvo, an Argentine jurist – holds that jurisdiction in international investment disputes lies with the country in which the investment is located. Articulated by then Argentine Foreign Minister Luis Maria Drago, the second doctrine declared that no foreign power could use force against a Latin American country to collect debt. Both doctrines have subsequently become recognized claims under customary international law, as well as embodied in several national constitutions and treaties. Nonetheless, the principle of nonintervention remained a topic of constant agitation in hemispheric relations. At the Sixth

[51] Crawford 2002, 144–52.
[52] On the comparatively recent dominance of the principle of nonintervention, see Glanville 2014.

International Conference of American States, convened in Havana in 1928, the Commission of Jurists recommended the adoption of the principle, "No state has a right to interfere in the internal affairs of another."[53] The proposal was rejected by the United States on the grounds that it had a right to intervene to protect the lives of its nationals should internal order break down. Under the new "good neighbor policy," however, the United States finally relented in 1933 at the seventh conference and agreed to the Convention on Rights and Duties of States, which included the language that "no state has the right to intervene in the internal or external affairs of another." Elaborating further, the Charter of the Organization of American States, signed in 1948, declared that "No State or group of States has the right to intervene, directly or indirectly, for any reason whatever, in the internal or external affairs of any other State. The foregoing principle prohibits not only armed force but also any other form of interference or attempted threat against the personality of the State or against its political, economic, and cultural elements." The principle was universalized in the Article 2(7) of the United Nations Charter, which declares that "nothing contained in the present Charter shall authorize the United Nations to intervene in matters which are essentially within the domestic jurisdiction of any state or shall require the Members to submit such matters to settlement under the present Charter." Although stated in very general terms, there is now a very large corpus of General Assembly resolutions, meeting records, reports, letters, and official documents clarifying the meaning of the principle and its specific applications.[54] The principle is now highly legalized: obligatory for all members of the United Nations and relatively precise.[55] Throughout the struggle, it was the fervent ambition of political entrepreneurs to create a norm of nonintervention through law. Entrepreneurs marshaled other norms to justify the principle, but it was the codification of the idea into law that ultimately and eventually gave it standing. As with the civil rights and marriage equality cases in the United States discussed earlier, the move to legalize the principle of nonintervention succeeded long before the establishment of a norm, which remains a work in progress.

It is no coincidence, one might say, that the push to legalize the principle of nonintervention first arose in Latin America. Although

---

[53] Krasner 1999, 31.

[54] Onuf 1998, 151. The most important documents are General Assembly Resolutions 2131 (XX), December 21, 1965; 2625 (XXV), October 24, 1970, and 36/103, December 9, 1981. For other documents, see www.un.org/en/sc/repertoire/princi ples.shtml.

[55] On legalization, see Abbott et al. 2000.

recognized as sovereign states after gaining independence from Spain, Latin American countries nonetheless held a second-class status in international relations, not least because the majority populations of most states in the region were of indigenous or slave descent. Highly stratified societies themselves, dominated by elite land owners of Spanish origin, Latin American states were not fully accepted into international society and were "excluded from the family of nations because it [was] believed they [had] not reached that stage of political development at which it [was] possible for them adequately to fulfill the obligations which international law imposes upon the adult international person."[56] Most notably, European states consistently asserted the right to collect private debts of Latin American states by force, if necessary. It was in this context that Calvo and Drago, both members of the Spanish elite, first put forth their doctrines as a plea for recognition of the real sovereignty of their states. No other states at the time had this unusual combination of sovereignty but "second class" status, nor significant minority elites that were acceptable in European society. Latin Americans had both the need and the access to international tribunals necessary to push the principle of nonintervention onto the international political agenda.

The focus then shifted to the United States, which began working after 1898 to replace European dominance in the region by taking over the debts owed to European investors and, sometimes, as in the Dominican Republic in 1904, fiscal control of the state. In justifying this new, more imperialist role for the United States, President Theodore Roosevelt asserted his famous corollary to the Monroe Doctrine, which claimed that "[c]hronic wrong-doing, or an impotence which results in a general loosening of the ties of civilized society, may in America, as elsewhere, ultimately require intervention by some civilized nation, and in the Western Hemisphere the adherence of the United States to the Monroe Doctrine may force the United States, however reluctantly, in flagrant cases of such wrongdoing or impotence, to the exercise of an international police power."[57] This bold claim of a right of intervention was then followed up by thirty-five US military deployments (shows of force to landing of troops) in Latin America between 1894 and 1921, which served to establish de facto American rule over the hemisphere.[58] The "good neighbor policy," instituted under TR's cousin, Franklin Delano Roosevelt, was less a change in policy than an indication of its prior success. Despite acceding to the principle of nonintervention as part of

---

[56] Willoughby and Fenwick 1974, 6. See also Philpott 2001, 33–4.
[57] See Lake 2009b, 4–7.   [58] Loveman 2010, 200–5.

this shift in nominal policy, the United States has continued to intervene in Latin America with some regularity ever since.

After World War II and decolonization, the primary advocates of the principle of nonintervention became the newly independent states, often fearful of their continued dependence on their former colonial masters and the residual rights that many imperial states continued to assert. This concern was reinforced by bipolarity, wherein two superpowers were so much more powerful than any other states that they could intervene within their exclusive spheres of influence with impunity and were checked only by their competition with each other outside those spheres, more often than not resulting in each supporting an opposing side in an otherwise internal struggle. Nonintervention became the hallmark of the Group of 77's demands and a continuing theme of the "nonaligned" movement, and it was this group that shifted the locus of legalization activity to the United Nations General Assembly, where their majority could enact resolutions opposed by the Great Powers.

Despite the absence of compliance, legalization of the principle of nonintervention was important in clarifying its scope and meaning. Intervention is, by common language, a broad concept, potentially encompassing many effects by one state on another, including trade in goods and services or transborder flows of pollution, for instance. In writing down the principle and limiting it to acts that affect a state's "territorial integrity and political independence," law now instructs governments to ignore whole classes of acts that might otherwise be regarded as infringements on their domestic or interdependence sovereignty. The only "interventions" that count *under the law* are forcible actions that are hostile in intent and substantial in scale (Onuf 1998, 150).[59] By limiting the principle in this way, states regulate how the principle is applied and when states can claim that another has violated their sovereignty. In so doing, the law on intervention conditions subsequent principles and norms regarding appropriate and inappropriate actions in world politics.

The Current Debate

The direct effects of legalizing the principle of nonintervention are, as always, hard to identify.[60] The Great Powers, at least, continue to intervene apparently at will, usually not challenging the law but justifying their

---

[59] On changing purposes of intervention, see Finnemore 2003. For a more philosophical treatment, which highlights the difficulty of distinguishing possibly acceptable interventions, see Lu 2006.

[60] On the compliance problem in international relations, see Downs, Rocke, and Barsoom 1996.

interventions along some other, more fundamental normative dimension, including the right of self-defense, as the United States did in Iraq, or the protection of lives and property, as Russia did in Ukraine. What we do not know is the number or types of interventions that would have happened were it not for the law. I suspect that the law's effect is significant, but given the number of violations, only at the margin.

The indirect effects of legalization are likely more profound. The prohibition on interventions permits juridically sovereign states to persist even though they lack effective domestic control over their territories (domestic sovereignty).[61] Forming a political cartel around the rule that they will not wage wars against one another,[62] "weak" but juridically sovereign states are following a different path from the European states that were forged in the crucible of battle.[63] At the same time, shared state weakness and transnational ethnic kin allow internal conflicts to diffuse rapidly and widely.[64] International law may or may not reduce the number of actual interventions – that remains a topic for future research – but it appears to have had a considerable indirect effect on the types and patterns of conflict in the modern world.

The law on nonintervention also strongly colors the debate about what to do with fragile states in the world today.[65] For better or worse, sovereignty has served as a decentralized governance structure for controlling interstate violence. As the concept of sovereignty developed, states came to be charged with responsibility for violence originating within their borders. Even when carried out by freebooters, mercenaries, pirates, and other private actors, states nonetheless became responsible for attacks on others carried out from within their territories.[66] Private, transnational violence was considered as an act of war. Today's fragile states, lacking effective domestic sovereignty, are unable to control their peripheries and have become, in some cases, safe havens for violent nonstate actors. Unable to count on fragile states to fulfill their responsibilities for policing their territories, other states wrestle with how to defend themselves against transnational terrorists and insurgents of all forms. Do other states intervene massively to change the regime in hopes of creating a new, more effective state? Do they apply their own law extraterritorially and target and hunt down "extremists" across national borders? Does it matter if assassinations are carried out by Special Forces teams on the ground or piloted aircraft and remotely controlled drones flying at 25,000 feet? The same problem arises in humanitarian

[61] Jackson 1990.   [62] Jackson and Rosberg 1982.   [63] Tilly 1990.
[64] Cederman, Gleditsch, and Buhaug 2013, Chapter 6.   [65] Ramos 2013.
[66] Thomson 1994.

interventions when governments cannot (fragile states that lack capacity) or will not (states that abuse their own) protect their citizens from violence. When are other states allowed or even encouraged to step in and protect vulnerable populations? And in both military and humanitarian interventions, who decides when and whether an intervention is permissible or legitimate? In ways reminiscent of the struggle between monarchs and the pope in early modern Europe over where ultimate authority was vested, can states themselves legitimately decide to intervene, or is this authority vested in some international body – and if so, which one?[67]

That the principle of nonintervention is now international law conditions the debates around and possible answers to all these questions.[68] Since military interventions are prohibited, they cannot be officially approved except when justified by some other, arguably more basic principle. The key issue in the debate surrounding R2P, for instance, is not whether states have a right to intervene to protect human lives and end suffering – this is well established now under international humanitarian law. Rather, the question is whether this right trumps the legal prohibition on intervention and, if so, under what circumstances? Without having previously codified the principle of nonintervention into international law, the current debates would be very different and more likely to find in favor of a broader range of humanitarian actions. Similarly, the legalization of nonintervention affects who can approve or legitimate a humanitarian intervention. If the law is grounded in the United Nations Charter and elaborated in an extensive body of United Nations General Assembly resolutions and other documents, is the United Nations then the only body that can decide when the law can be breached or subordinated to some higher principle? Or can NATO appeal to R2P to bomb Libya? Although it did not do so, could Russia have appealed unilaterally to R2P to justify intervening in Ukraine to protect ethnic Russians? Again, without a clearly established law against intervention, debates about who can decide to intervene where and for what reason would be far more open than they currently are. Whether we like it or not, the law on nonintervention is shaping the emergence of other principles and social norms, especially those regulating humanitarian protections that might be desirable and possibly defensible on other grounds.

Yet, although the spread of the norm of human equality has supported the principle and law of nonintervention, the norm of human inequality

---

[67] On the strictures of sovereignty on this question and the possibility of deciding rightfulness in a more decentralized manner, see Havercroft 2011.
[68] Glanville 2014.

and its effects on international relations have not faded entirely. The current debate on intervention – and especially humanitarian intervention – remains deeply affected by an implicit racial hierarchy. The norm has been sufficiently challenged that it is no longer possible to justify intervention on racial grounds, but it nonetheless remains salient. Norms do change. Today's racism is not the scientific Darwinism of a century ago that justified permanent imperial rule. Driven underground, racism has simply adopted a disguise or is left implicit – though it is still recognizable and sometimes recognized.

The emerging consensus on R2P appears to be that intervention is justified only when a state has "failed," the modern equivalent to the earlier doctrine of *terra nullis*. The only failed states in the world today, of course, are comprised mostly of people of color, deemed unable to govern themselves or abide by the laws of "civilized" international society. Humanitarian missions, in turn, are dominated by military forces from white-majority countries who want to teach the people of failed states, in the words of the well-known racist President Woodrow Wilson, "to elect good men." The International Criminal Court has come under similar criticism for indicting only African leaders. Although the terms have shifted, it is not much of a stretch to conclude that the push for humanitarian exceptions to the law of nonintervention is simply an updated version of the white man's burden. Over the centuries, repeated cycles through the framework identified in Figure 1.1 have changed the norms, principles, and laws at issue. The norm of human equality and the principle of nonintervention have been strengthened over time. Nonetheless, the norm of racial inequality that limited the rise of nonintervention and justified imperialism in its many forms continues to influence when, where, and why states may intervene in the affairs of others.

Conclusion

Hierarchies interact. Social norms matter because individuals believe them and, equally, believe that others believe them, that others believe they believe them, and so on.[69] Even the most instrumental egoists cannot navigate the political world without taking norms into account. At the same time, because norms matter, actors champion their preferred principles and, importantly, seek to codify them into law. This not only attaches the weight of law as a whole to any principle so favored, but it also creates a focal point around which sometimes ambiguous social

---

[69] See Morrow 2014.

expectations converge. In short, in a complex, mobile society in which individuals are seldom likely to "know" one another well prior to any interaction, law helps "institutionalize" norms.

Norms and law were intimately bound up in the propagation of the principle of nonintervention. The articulation of the principle, its connection to sovereignty, and its recognition by states was a slow, incremental, and organic process that unfolded over centuries. Critical to its emergence as a real constraint on behavior, however, was the legalization of the principle beginning in the early twentieth century. Once codified into international law, the principle took on a status and importance that it otherwise would have lacked and conditioned subsequent deliberations over other principles and norms, especially the current question of humanitarian interventions. The principle of nonintervention as law now stands as a baseline against which deviations in general (e.g., R2P) or in particular (e.g., the Iraq War) must be justified.

Although applied to the case of nonintervention, the framework outlined herein appears to be more general. As implied by the examples in the first section of this chapter, it captures the coevolution of norms and law in the cases of racial and marriage equality in the United States. It also seems to fit – at least to a first approximation – the spread of human rights norms *and* law in the latter half of the twentieth century. It may also apply to issues of transnational corporate responsibility and environmental regulation, where norms and laws are still in greater flux. The case of nonintervention, however, also highlights that social norms do not always point in the same "progressive" direction, whatever that might be. People appear to be able to hold inconsistent norms simultaneously, believing, for instance, that all humans are equal but that all races are not. This is often depicted as a puzzle about the "founding fathers" of the United States, especially Thomas Jefferson – one of the most enlightened thinkers of his day – who could pen that "all men are created equal" and yet hold some of those men (and women and children) as slaves. Codifying the principle of nonintervention into law may have been more central in this case than others because of these competing norms.

Yet the "victory" of nonintervention is incomplete. Although institutionalized racism is waning, or at least the norm of racial hierarchy is sufficiently under attack that it can no longer be used in public to justify inequality in principle, racism in international relations persists, albeit in different form. One cannot justify intervention today simply because a people are inherently "inferior" or deficient. Nonetheless, the "developed" states or the "advanced" industrialized democracies have innovated a series of euphemisms to capture some of the same hierarchical rankings of states. Today, one can support intervention because a state has "failed," or a leader abuses his citizens, or a government permits terrorists to operate from its territory or might share weapons of mass destruction with others. Such claims are more likely to be credible and to resonate with popular opinion if the majority population of the country at issue is of color. Such terms are a code to refer to the deficiencies of societies that require tutelage, at the least, and enlightened governance by a more civilized state, at the most. As the international community debates legitimate exceptions to the now-legalized principle of nonintervention, we should all be attentive to the social norms at play.

2 Making Empires
Hierarchy, Conquest and Customization

Andrew Phillips

> *Divide et Impera* was the Old Roman motto, and it should be ours.[1]

> [The] art of ruling native races is a thing of infinite variety not amenable to standardization.[2]

This chapter examines the nature and origins of (institutionalized) hierarchies, with particular reference to two of history's most powerful empires: Qing China and British India. International Relations (IR) scholars' preoccupation with understanding the perils of anarchy has obscured important relations of hierarchy in contemporary world politics. As problematic as the neglect of hierarchy is for making sense of the world today, it is even more confining when applied to global politics before 1945. For the vast majority of modernity, imperial hierarchy coexisted with sovereign anarchy as one of international politics' primary organizing principles. This was especially so in East and South Asia, two of the world's wealthiest and most populous regions before the nineteenth-century 'global transformation' that propelled the West to global dominance.[3] For us to comprehend how world politics played out for most people and for most of modern history, it is essential that we gain a better knowledge of how imperial hierarchies emerge. It is this task that I engage herein.

Consistent with recent IR scholarship, I understand empires as authoritarian systems of alien rule grounded in 'regimes of unequal entitlements'.[4] I furthermore endorse Nexon's characterization of empires as composite arrangements, characterized by extensive reliance on indirect rule and by patterns of government in which the centre is bound to subordinate communities through asymmetric customized compacts, which Nexon dubs 'heterogeneous contracting'.[5] Most critically, I accept that empires are generally sustained through 'divide and rule' strategies, in which rulers hold power by deliberately cultivating cultural divisions between subject communities.[6]

---

[1] Omissi 1991, 9. [2] Newbury 2003, 72. [3] Buzan and Lawson 2015.
[4] Reus-Smit 2013, 12. [5] Nexon 2007, 72. [6] Motyl 2013; Nexon and Wright 2007.

The rulers of Qing China and British India both conformed to this ideal type of empire. Both curated cultural diversity among their subject populations in furtherance of 'divide and rule' strategies. They did so mainly through official religious patronage and selective ethnic military mobilization, which I categorize as instances of customization. I develop the concept of customization from Amitav Acharya's idea of localization.[7] Acharya invoked localization to characterize non-Western actors' selective appropriation and adaptation of originally foreign Western ideas and normative resources to enhance their own power.[8] By contrast, customization describes a reverse process, through which outsiders win power over locals by selectively appropriating and adapting indigenous ideas and normative resources to imperial ends.

Practices of customization help empire-builders define, differentiate and segregate subject populations into discrete imperial constituencies. Once institutionalized, this differentiation then inhibits collaboration between these constituencies while enabling ruling elites to vertically incorporate local intermediaries from these constituencies into heterogeneous contracts favouring the imperial centre. Following the distinction between narrow and broad forms of hierarchy from this book's introduction, I recognize empires as constituting a narrow form of hierarchy.[9] Though empires are typically immensely exploitative, they rest on extensive collaboration between rulers and local intermediaries. To this extent only, they can be cast as 'legitimate orders of authority in which superordinate and subordinate alike have some material, functional and/or social interest'.[10] At the same time, however, imperial hierarchies are also built upon broad hierarchies, conceived as 'productive structures of organized inequality'.[11] Narrow hierarchies of formal imperial rule are typically embedded within and dependent upon broader productive hierarchies of religion, race and caste that fragment subject populations and confer differential capacities for agency upon them. What is distinctive about empires is rulers' self-consciousness in recognizing this embeddedness and their calculation in deliberately fostering these broad hierarchies through customization to sustain their rule. As parvenu conquerors, both the Manchus and the British were culturally distinct from local populations and also hugely outnumbered. Patronage of indigenous religious establishments provided both with a means of forging an 'identity bridge'[12] with local collaborators while entrenching religious difference as a basis for 'divide and rule'.[13] Likewise, selective ethnic military mobilization enabled Manchus and Britons to co-opt indigenous military

[7] Acharya 2004.   [8] *Ibid.*   [9] See Introduction.   [10] *Ibid.*   [11] *Ibid.*
[12] Goddard 2009, 270.   [13] Crossley 1999; Metcalf 1997.

capacities while providing a further wedge to differentiate and divide local populations.[14]

Post-colonial scholars have written extensively on how Western imperialists constructed their empires through a colonial 'rule of difference',[15] based on contrived identities of race, caste and sect manufactured through Western discursive practices.[16] I draw sparingly but appreciatively from this scholarship later. My case selection, however, encompasses cases of Asian (Manchu) as well as Western (British) imperialism. I pair these cases to contest the idea that the 'rule of difference' was idiosyncratic to the West. Far from being the product of purely Western pathologies, the curatorship of cultural difference through customization reflected governance challenges common to early modern empires. Despite their major differences, both the rulers of the 'Manchu Raj'[17] and British India faced remarkably similar challenges. They moreover responded to them in ways that powerfully illuminate the dependence of narrow hierarchies of rule on the broad hierarchies of difference constituted through practices of customization.

This chapter proceeds in four sections. The first section defines imperial hierarchies, canvasses their distinct characteristics, and rehearses the limits of existing theories of imperial hierarchy. The second section presents my alternative argument for imperial hierarchies' emergence. The third section empirically illustrates the argument through case studies of customization practices of religious patronage and ethnic military mobilization in Manchu China and British India. The final section teases out the implications of my findings for both the study of empires in IR and 'hierarchy studies' as introduced in this book.

Empires in World Politics: Definitions and Existing Explanations

Empires are systems of imperative control grounded in 'regimes of unequal entitlement'.[18] In empires, a narrow view of hierarchy of formalized command and obedience links a dominant core to a penumbra of dependent peripheral polities.[19] Empires are therefore distinct from most of the international hierarchies this book considers. Whereas the latter exist in a world defined by de jure norms of sovereign equality and nonintervention, empires are hierarchies in both the de jure and the de facto senses.[20]

---

[14] Elliott 2001; Streets 2004.   [15] See e.g. Chatterjee 1993.   [16] Dirks 2001.
[17] Darwin 2008, 132.   [18] Reus-Smit 2013, 12.
[19] Hobson and Sharman 2005, 69–70.   [20] *Ibid.*

In addition to constituting narrow hierarchies of imperative control, empires have historically been characterized by high levels of cultural diversity. Heterogeneity, as much as hierarchy, has traditionally been one of empires' defining features. Managing cultural diversity thus has always been a key challenge of imperial rule. Empires for most of world history also disposed of only limited amounts of 'infrastructural power'[21] and so lacked the capacity to directly rule their far-flung territories. Consequently, imperial elites have generally relied extensively on indirect rule through local intermediaries.[22] The combined challenges of managing diversity while relying on local intermediaries historically led to distinctly imperial modes of governance. These arrangements involved forging customized compacts between the imperial centre and its dependencies.[23] Such arrangements tied local intermediaries to the centre through asymmetric bargains involving specific material incentives but also tailored legitimation strategies aimed at cultivating intermediaries' allegiance to the imperial core.

Empires face distinct governance challenges owing to their grounding in foreign rule over diverse populations, their dependence on local intermediaries and their susceptibility to legitimation crises flowing from these characteristics. Two dangers to imperial rule – anti-colonial revolution and secession – warrant particular attention. First, empires face the danger of being toppled through a mobilization of anti-imperial sentiment that cuts across and unites dependent peoples in opposition to the imperial core. The sixteenth-century Reformation and mid-twentieth-century decolonization stand as important examples of empires' vulnerability to overthrow by subaltern 'revolutions in sovereignty'.[24] Alternatively, empires are also vulnerable to the piecemeal secession of their segments should local intermediaries choose to defect from the empire. These combined dangers of anti-imperial revolution and piecemeal secession impose corresponding imperatives on imperial elites: to prevent subversive collaboration between the empire's segments while keeping local intermediaries loyally bound to the core.

For all their immensity and historical significance, then, empires constitute a highly fragile form of (narrow) hierarchy. This fragility notwithstanding, it remains the case that empires – not nation-states – typically formed the largest and most powerful forms of political association in world politics prior to 1945. Accordingly, explaining how empires emerged should rightly be central to advancing our understanding of international hierarchies. Within the specific context of this inquiry,

[21] Mann 1986, 27.   [22] Nexon and Wright 2007, 258–9.   [23] Nexon 2009, 72.
[24] Philpott 2001.

three popular explanations for the emergence of empires must be our point of departure.

The first and least satisfactory explanation for the emergence of empires consists of coercion-based arguments, which privilege military superiority as the preeminent foundation of imperial power. For proponents of coercion-based arguments, empires rest first and foremost on imperial elites' military superiority.[25] They moreover persist only so long as these elites maintain their military superiority over subject populations. There is no question that military power is a key to winning and keeping empires. And some forms of empire – especially forms of settler colonialism involving the genocide of indigenous populations – comport closely with this mode of explanation.[26] Nevertheless, for the empires I consider here, this explanation is unsatisfactory. Both Manchu and British empire-builders were hugely outnumbered by local populations and crucially lacked overwhelming military/technological superiority. An exclusively coercion-based explanation for imperial hierarchy is thus a weak empirical fit with my cases. More fundamentally, coercion-based explanations also overlook the central importance of legitimation strategies in generating the 'hybrid' military establishments[27] on which imperial rule rested.

In contrast to coercion-based explanations for empire, a second bargaining-based family of explanations sees empires as emerging from asymmetric bargains between imperial elites and local intermediaries.[28] Bargaining explanations recognize that rule can only rarely rely exclusively on coercion and that empires' costs are much reduced if empire-builders can win local elites' acquiescence.[29] The Chinese practice of tributary diplomacy – in which China engineered terms of trade that favoured its vassals to win their allegiance – is often cited as a historical example of hierarchies built at least in part on asymmetric contracting.[30] The advantage of this approach is that it takes local actors' agency into account when making sense of imperial hierarchies. Nevertheless, bargain-based explanations for empire run the risk of naiveté, airbrushing the hidden coercion that often underwrites bargains between imperial and local elites. More fundamentally, such explanations also take actors' interests and identities as given and prior to social interaction rather than being constituted through their participation in imperial hierarchies.

A final status-based mode of explanation for the rise of empires lastly conceptualizes empires arising and being importantly constituted as

---

[25] See e.g. McNeill 1982; Parker 1996.   [26] Belich 2011.   [27] Elliott 2001; Roy 2011.
[28] See the Introduction.   [29] See e.g. Hechter 2013.
[30] Kang 2010b, 111. Though Kang's larger argument is constructivist, he does acknowledge material benefits from the tribute trade as a key mechanism cementing subordinate polities' participation in East Asia's traditional Sino-centric hierarchy.

civilizational 'zones of prestige'.[31] This line of argument recognizes the immense power imperial elites often successfully claim in generating forms of symbolic capital that draw local intermediaries into active participation within imperial hierarchies as they seek to win social recognition and advancement within these hierarchies. To take one famous example, Europeans' promulgation of a nineteenth-century 'standard of civilization' powerfully shaped non-Europeans' reactions to the Western ascendancy, working often to reinforce imperial hierarchies as non-Westerners actively re-invented themselves to work their way up the 'civilizational ladder'.[32] This would point to a broad social hierarchy underwriting the constitution of a narrow hierarchy.

Of the alternatives considered, the status-based position I have just canvassed comes closest to the explanation for empires' emergence that I outline below in that it affords closest attention to ideational factors as being critical to the rise of empires. Nevertheless, for the cases I consider, this type of explanation tips the balance too far towards the universalizing aspects of imperial ideologies and away from the entrenched particularism informing the 'divide and rule' strategies that sustained Manchu China and British India. Both the Confucian 'civilizing mission' that the Manchus appropriated and British 'reform liberalism', which some Indians sought to emulate,[33] undoubtedly helped sustain Manchu and British imperialism. But these universalizing ideologies were subordinate to a more fundamental emphasis on diversity as empires' defining condition. Status hierarchies were an important feature of early modern empires. But the quest for recognition was subsumed within collective identity regimes that stressed difference rather than universality as the foundation of empire. It is to an explication of my alternative explanatory framework for empires' emergence – grounded in the idea of customization – that I now turn.

Imperial Statecraft, the Curatorship of Difference and the Constitution of Imperial Hierarchies

Empires are irreducibly composite systems. They are defined by their diversity and survive through imperial elites' ability to maintain their power through 'divide and rule' strategies. The central insight driving my argument is that empires do not form around asymmetric relations between the imperial centre and *pre-existing* subordinate communities.

---

[31] Collins 2004.   [32] Suzuki 2005; Zarakol 2011.
[33] On the Manchus' selective appropriation of Confucianism to sustain their rule, see e.g. Xiang 2013. On Indians' adaptation and reconstruction of liberalism, see Bayly 2011.

The communities to be divided do not stand as pre-constituted collectivities before their division. Instead, one of the most critical features of imperial statecraft is the construction of narrow hierarchies of rule through the organization and institutionalization of broad hierarchies of cultural difference.[34] Subordinate societies must be divided before they can be ruled.[35] Imperial hierarchies consequently take form through practices of customization that codify, inscribe and institutionalize cultural differences between subject peoples. These differences – once imagined and institutionalized – then form the basis for the heterogeneous contracts between imperial rulers and local intermediaries that collectively make up empires.

As vastly outnumbered cultural outsiders, empire-builders face a fundamental challenge in building and preserving imperial hierarchies. Specifically, they must find ways to channel patterns of collective identification and mobilization in ways that (1) maximize local intermediaries' integration into imperial structures[36] while (2) minimizing their inclination and capacity to identify and mobilize with each other and against the imperial centre.[37] Vertical incorporation (between centre and periphery) and horizontal segregation (between imperial segments) therefore form imperial statecraft's two interlinked imperatives.

Lord Elphinstone, one-time governor first of the Madras and then the Bombay Presidency in British India, pithily summed up the necessity of governing empires through 'divide and rule' strategies when he observed: 'The safety of the great iron steamers ... is greatly increased by building them in compartments. I would ensure the security of our Indian Empire by constructing our native army on the same principle.'[38] This 'compartmentalization' of subject peoples is, however, a formidable enterprise, for by necessity it entails extensive imperial intervention to modify existing collective identities to conform to imperial designs. *'Divide and rule' presupposes 'define and rule'*[39] *as its necessary precursor.* Consequently, the curatorship of collective identities – through customization practices involving the appropriation, adaptation and reorganization of indigenous ideational resources to shore up imperial authority – has historically been key to the business of empire-building.

---

[34] On cultural diversity as something that is socially organized rather than spontaneously given, see e.g. Hannerz 1989.

[35] Morten Andersen, also drawing from Nexon's conception of empires as polities defined by a combination of heterogeneous contracting and indirect rule, nicely captures this imperative in his observation that 'it is necessary to construct categories of differentiation to prepare for heterogeneous contracting.' Andersen 2011, 15.

[36] Barkey and Godart 2013, 85.   [37] Nexon 2007, 106.

[38] Lord Elphinstone, quoted in Omissi 1991, 9.   [39] Mamdani 2012.

Customization practices involve two processes. First, empire-builders systematically gather knowledge about subject groups to more clearly define and differentiate them. Far from being passive or neutral exercises in observation, these activities are fundamentally creative initiatives, which are productive of the categories of difference that will subsequently shape imperial administration.[40] Second, having articulated categories of difference in this way, empire-builders then institutionalize them by inscribing them into practices of imperial governance.[41]

Customization practices curate the collective identities on which imperial power rests. Once institutionalized, they then shape imperial hierarchies by working to identify and selectively empower 'traditional' local intermediaries. These intermediaries then become the critical brokers linking the centre to its dependencies, laying the basis for the narrow imperial 'bargains' between imperial elites and intermediaries that hold imperial orders together. Simultaneously, customization practices meanwhile also work to 'freeze' certain forms of collective identity in place, in ways that aim to minimize the scope for anti-imperial mobilization. Through this 'Medusa syndrome',[42] customization practices divide subject populations into controllable and mutually exclusive fragments, so securing the basis for imperial rule.

Customization manifested itself across the whole gamut of imperial governance practices in both the Manchu and British Empires. In this chapter I concentrate only on two of the most important: religious patronage and selective ethnic military mobilization.

In the early modern world, political power in most societies was thoroughly entangled with religious authority. Conquest elites could not afford to remain aloof from religious matters, even – indeed especially – where their own religious beliefs distinguished them from their subjects. Left ignored, religious difference provided a powerful vector for mobilizing indigenous opposition to alien rule.[43] Conversely, if managed effectively, the religious divisions among subject peoples could foster fragmentation among them, mitigating the risk of wholesale rebellion. Likewise, the targeted patronage of indigenous religious authorities within imperial segments could also bind powerful intermediaries to the imperial centre while granting conquest elites access to forms of symbolic capital crucial to legitimating their rule.

[40] *Ibid.*, 42.   [41] *Ibid.*
[42] Appiah 2010, 110. For an excellent application of this concept of the 'Medusa syndrome' to imperial Britain's management of difference on the Indian sub-continent, see Birnbaum 2015, 86.
[43] Philpott 2001; Nexon 2007.

Besides religious patronage, early modern empires also critically rested on practices of selective ethnic military mobilization. Both the Manchus and the British relied fundamentally on indigenous military resources to conquer and subsequently police their empires. Critically, the institutional mechanisms through which Manchus and Britons mobilized local military power exercised powerful constitutive effects on targeted communities. The Manchu 'banner' system – in which the Manchus organized Manchu, Han Chinese and Mongol soldiers in ethnically segregated units – proved crucial in consolidating the collective identities of all three groups.[44] Likewise, from the late nineteenth century especially, the British *Raj* rested on a military edifice that drew disproportionately from communities that imperial authorities identified as 'martial races'.[45] In selectively recruiting their soldiers disproportionately from formerly marginal frontier peoples (e.g. Sikhs, Gurkhas and Rajputs), the British sought to guard against a repeat of the Indian 'mutiny' of 1857, which had briefly threatened their rule.[46] Beyond its instrumental rationale, the practice of selective ethnic military mobilization nevertheless also powerfully shaped ethnic identities within the Indian subcontinent, compounding its diversity and so furthering British strategies of 'divide and rule'.[47]

Establishing control over both the means of salvation and organized coercion were both crucial to the success of Manchu and British imperial projects. Instrumental considerations clearly motivated policies of religious patronage and selective ethnic military mobilization. But these practices also exerted powerfully constitutive effects on subject peoples, working to coalesce the constituent communities that comprised the Manchu and British imperial hierarchies. Just as practices such as the census, modern cartography and the museum would later help entrench modular forms of modern nationalism globally after 1945,[48] so too did religious patronage and selective ethnic military mobilization help constitute the vertically incorporated but horizontally compartmentalized subject communities of Asia's largest and most powerful early modern empires. It is towards two empirical illustrations of this dynamic that I now turn.

Organizing Imperial Identities in the 'Manchu *Raj*'

The Qing Empire (1644–1912) was one of history's largest and most powerful empires. Arising out of China's north-eastern frontier from the late sixteenth century, the Manchus eventually carved out a vast

[44] Elliott 2001.   [45] Roy 2001; Streets 2004.   [46] Streets 2004, 11.
[47] See again Roy 2001.   [48] Anderson 1991, 163.

imperium, encompassing not only China but also large swathes of Mongolia as well as Manchuria, Tibet and Xinjiang. From their conquest of Beijing in 1644 to the mid-eighteenth century, the Manchus spearheaded conquests that doubled China's territory.[49] These conquests hugely increased the empire's ethnic and religious diversity.[50] The Manchus meanwhile also co-opted China's established system of East Asian tributary diplomacy.[51] This entrenched their status as eastern Eurasia's undisputed hegemons down to the era of Western encroachment after 1800.

A 'barbarian' dynasty, the Manchus were proudly self-conscious of their distinctiveness from subject populations. At the height of their power, the Manchus comprised a ruling elite of no more than two million, governing over 400 million – mostly Han Chinese – subjects.[52] Fearful that they might follow previous 'barbarian' dynasties in succumbing to 'Sinicization', the Manchus marshalled a range of practices aimed at preserving their 'ethnic sovereignty'.[53] These included residential segregation separating Manchus from subject populations, the maintenance of separate courts for Manchu and non-Manchu and retention of a separate praetorian guard of Manchu banner-men tasked with securing the regime from indigenous revolt.[54] Manchu rule could be brutal, and the Qing Dynasty was unsparing in its violence when threatened with separatism or rebellion. Nevertheless, the Qing Dynasty's system of 'Manchu apartheid'[55] did not rest on coercion alone. Instead, the Qing Dynasty's ruling ideology balanced Manchu supremacy and exceptionalism with a distinctive form of incorporative universal kingship. This latter system of beliefs affirmed and reified the empire's cultural diversity, and a brief consideration of it is key to contextualizing the practices of productive power that constituted imperial hierarchy within the Qing Empire.

As a foreign conquest dynasty ruling over hugely diverse populations, the Manchus 'had need of constructing categories of affiliation that would correspond to multiple, simultaneously expressed codes of legitimacy in the rulership'.[56] Given the importance of winning over the Han Chinese Confucian literati to help administer their empire, the Manchus early on appropriated Confucianism as an ideological resource to legitimate their rule. Nevertheless, what legitimized Manchu rule in the eyes of Han Chinese literati did not necessarily translate for Tibetans, Uighurs, Mongols and others. Instead, to cement the allegiance of these different groups, the Manchus had to embrace what historian Pamela Crossley refers to as 'imperial simultaneity'[57] – the practice of simultaneously

[49] Crossley 1990, 13.   [50] *Ibid.*   [51] Kang 2010b.   [52] Leibold 2007, 26.
[53] Elliott 2001, 130.   [54] *Ibid.*   [55] *Ibid.*, 93.   [56] Crossley 1999, 1.   [57] *Ibid.*, 12.

occupying multiple subject positions and relying on multiple codes of legitimation to uphold imperial rule. Expanding on the idea and practice of imperial simultaneity, Crossley explains

The Qing Emperorship was in its expression what I have called 'simultaneous' . . . That is, its edicts, its diaries, and its monuments were deliberately designed as imperial utterances in more than one language (at a minimum Manchu and Chinese; very commonly Manchu, Chinese, and Mongolian, and after the middle of the eighteenth century frequently in Manchu, Chinese, Mongolian, Tibetan and the Arabic script of many Central Asian Muslims that is called 'Uigur'), as simultaneous expression of imperial intentions in multiple cultural frames. *The simultaneity was not a mere matter of practicality. Each formally written language used represented a distinct aesthetic sensibility and a distinct ethical code.* In the case of each language the emperor claimed both, as both the enunciator and the object of those sensibilities and those codes.[58]

As a 'simultaneous' universal ruler, the Qing Emperor could be 'a Confucian monarch among the Chinese; a "divine lord" among the Manchus; "a great khan" among the Mongols and Manjusri, the Bodhisattva of Wisdom, among the Tibetans'.[59] To secure their rule, the Manchus adopted a chameleon-like strategy of legitimation, in which they tailored idioms of rule that they could simultaneously direct towards multiple constituencies. This strategy of simultaneity was far from unique to the Manchus and was indeed prevalent in other early modern empires, such as the Ottoman Empire and Tsarist Russia.[60] Its deeper theoretical significance for the study of hierarchy lies in the fact that imperial simultaneity did not merely reflect the empire as an already-existing multicultural mosaic. Rather, in critical ways, it helped make this mosaic in the first place, by fixing and institutionalizing collective identities on subject peoples and then dignifying these collective identities with a political significance they had not previously had. This production of difference was moreover hardly confined to the realm of court ritual. On the contrary, it was practically manifest in two critically important spheres of imperial rule – the governance of religion and the mobilization of military power.

One of the great early challenges the Manchus faced in consolidating their empire lay in pacifying potential challengers along their unruly frontiers. This proved particularly difficult in Mongolia – a region that had itself historically birthed some of Asia's mightiest conquest dynasties. Though the Manchus counted some Mongol tribes as their allies, refractory elements chafed against Manchu rule long after the Manchus had conquered Beijing. Eventually, the Manchus managed to subdue

[58] *Ibid.*, 11–12, emphasis added.   [59] Leibold 2007, 28.   [60] Crossley 1999, 40.

Mongolia through a combination of war, trade, marital alliances and religious patronage.[61] This last expedient is most relevant to this inquiry, for the Manchus' manipulation of Mongol religious identity reveals an important facet of the productive power underwriting hierarchy's consolidation in early modern Asia.

In the Qing Dynasty's first decades, Mongols primarily identified first and foremost with their own local tribal lineages rather than embracing a supra-tribal Mongol identity.[62] This localism was long-standing and helps explain Mongolia's historical propensity for fission and inter-tribal civil war.[63] As they consolidated their rule in Mongolia, the Manchus sought to re-engineer Mongol identities, reorienting them from a tribal to a supra-tribal (i.e. Mongol) basis. This promised to make the Mongols more legible to imperial authorities and so more manageable as well. Writing of Qing policy towards Mongolia, historian Johan Elverskog observes: '[T]he success of the Qing model [of colonial governance] resided less in brute military power and intimidation than within this process whereby they were able to redefine what it meant to be Mongol.'[64]

The Qing Dynasty's patronage of Tibetan Buddhism – a critical source of legitimacy for many of the eastern Mongolian tribes – was key to this process of identity redefinition. In particular, the Manchus worked hard to harness the sacred aura of the Buddhist idea of a universal ruler (*Cakravartin*) and to attach this legitimacy to the Qing Emperor. Successive Manchu rulers therefore systematically wove the iconography of Buddhist universal kingship into imperial rituals, art and monuments.[65] They also generously sponsored the growth of networks of lamaseries (Tibetan Buddhist monasteries) throughout their Empire, with a view especially towards redirecting Mongol loyalties towards the Empire and away from traditional holy sites in Tibet.[66] In forging a new alliance with Tibetan Buddhist lamas, and in claiming the title of *Cakravartin* for the Emperor, the Manchus sought to place the Emperor at the centre of the Buddhist world, in a manner Thomas DuBois has likened to the centralization of early Christianity on the city of Rome.[67] DuBois suggests that the resulting alliance between Manchu imperialists and Tibetan lamas led to a radical rationalization of Mongol religious belief. In particular, the Emperor harnessed Tibetan Buddhist monks to promote one school of Lamaism above all others.[68] This entrenched an orthodoxy that both localized and sacralized Manchu authority claims to make them palatable

[61] Elverskog 2006, 27.   [62] *Ibid.*, 20.   [63] *Ibid.*   [64] *Ibid.*, 38–9.
[65] DuBois 2011, 101.   [66] Farquhar 1978, 29.   [67] DuBois 2011, 103–4.
[68] *Ibid.*, 104.

to a Mongol audience. At the same time, it also elevated both Tibetan Buddhism and corresponding allegiance to the Emperor-as-*Cakravartin* as defining aspects of Mongol identity, casting them against the more local tribal allegiances that had formerly held sway.

Manchu attempts to harness Tibetan Buddhism, to solidify a coherent Mongol subjectivity on which stable relations of imperial hierarchy might rest, were only partially successful. Traditional accounts moreover overstate the importance of Manchu power relative to Mongol agency in consolidating the latter's identity reorientation as loyal Qing subjects.[69] These caveats aside, religious patronage did provide a powerful means of recasting Mongol subjectivities to consolidate imperial hierarchy. This was especially the case when it was reinforced with a second mechanism of acculturation – the Manchu banner system of military organization.

The Manchu banner system constituted one of the Empire's core institutions and was the main vehicle through which the Manchus had first organized a multiethnic confederacy to conquer China in 1644. The banner system mobilized military power by organizing warriors into companies (*niru*, meaning 'arrows') grouped into battalions (*jalan*) under the larger rubric of 'banners' (*gusa*).[70] Beyond simply being fighting formations, the banners encompassed entire communities, with each soldier and his family granted a plot of land and individual households tasked with provisioning warriors either with grain, horses and sheep or weapons and armour.[71] Historian Mark Elliot observes of the banner system that it was 'more than just an army, it was also a social formation and political structure. In fact, the Eight Banners was a hybrid institution in just about every sense. Along with its key military role, it discharged a range of governmental, administrative, economic, and social functions, and encompassed people of many different ethnic backgrounds within its ranks'.[72]

The banner system is relevant to this discussion because it represented a form of selective ethnic military mobilization that actively moulded the subjectivities that held the empire together. It was important not simply because it marshalled the coercive power the Manchus needed to conquer their Empire but also because it helped constitute the collective identities of imperial subjects. Manchu rule rested on an ideal of universal kingship 'based on the submission of divergent peoples, whose cultures would remain separate'.[73] This incorporative ideal was reflected in the banner system, which arranged imperial subjects in separate banners

[69] Elverskog 2006, 39.   [70] Narangoa and Cribb 2014, 25.
[71] Chang 2007, 21. See also Burbank and Cooper 2010, 207.   [72] Elliott 2006, 29.
[73] Rawski 1996, 835.

(e.g. Manchu, Mongol, Han Chinese) based on what we would now recognize as ethnic groups. These ethnic identities were not pre-given but took shape through institutions such as the banner system.[74] This was true even among the Manchus themselves, whose collective identity *as* Manchus was at best embryonic and inchoate in the lead-up to their conquest of China. As they organized themselves for conquest, the Manchu leadership created the banner system in part to weaken older lineage loyalties among the Jurchen, the group that formed the core of the modern Manchu ethnicity: 'The organization of Jurchen troops with their families into separate units, each with its own distinctive flag, broke up earlier lineage groups and provided the emperor with spoke-like connections to each of his armies.'[75] The banner system thus played a key role in moulding first modern Manchu identity and then later also Mongol and Han Chinese identity as the Manchus absorbed surrendering soldiers from these groups into their army. This template of ethnically segregated military units would persist for the Empire's duration, providing one of the most powerful institutional means for producing the system of collective identities that composed the Qing imperial hierarchy. So influential was this collective identity regime that it survived the Qing Empire itself, with the first flag of the Chinese Republic (the 'Five Races under One Union' flag, 1912–28), faithfully inscribing the Qing system of ethnic classification onto nationalist iconography, even following the dynasty's violent demise.

Organizing Imperial Identities in British India

Like Qing Dynasty China, British India was the product of a numerically tiny conquest elite who created imperial hierarchy through productive practices that generated distinct forms of collective identity among subject populations. The English East India Company (EIC) won recognition as a vassal of the Mughal Emperor Jahangir as early as 1619 and transitioned to large-scale territorial rule in India only from the mid-eighteenth century. Given their cultural distinctiveness from the Indians, and given that the vastly outnumbered British lacked decisive military-technological advantages over locals before the late nineteenth century, the EIC had to harness indigenous resources to build their empire. Once again, a consideration of practices of religious patronage and selective ethnic military mobilization helps us understand how this consolidation of imperial hierarchy took place.

---

[74] Elliott 2001.   [75] Burbank and Cooper 2010, 207.

The EIC secured the *diwani* (the right to collect land tax revenues on the Mughal Emperor's behalf) in Bengal, India's richest and most fertile province, in 1765.[76] In the following decades, the EIC slowly established hegemony throughout India, even while declaring their nominal fealty to the Mughal Emperor. As they grew in power, EIC officials faced key challenges in establishing and then legitimating their rule over subject populations. Like the Manchus, the EIC found a solution in allying with local religious authorities to help establish imperial rule. This was clear in the EIC's assumption of responsibility for control and management of the sub-continent's vast network of temples and other religious institutions. Historian Robert Frykenberg observes that the Company's creeping conquest of India 'involved a gradual takeover by the new Imperial state of all religious property, together with a systematic extension of State supervision and fiscal management of all charitable and religious institutions'.[77]

The Company's takeover of Indian religious institutions created 'a *de facto* Hindu Raj',[78] in that Company governance networks became deeply interwoven with indigenous religious institutions. More fundamentally, though, this entanglement drove important transformations in local collective identities. Most notably, Orientalist British scholars and bureaucrats helped for the first time to construct 'Hindu' as a coherent collective identity. As they sought to recover an ancient Indian civilization, Company officials (including both Britons and local Indian pundits) helped articulate an inclusive 'Hindu' identity to encompass the sub-continent's manifold local religious traditions. This codification involved the uneasy imposition of Western conceptions of religion onto local societies, which bore little relationship to Indian conceptions of the divine. Despite this disconnect, colonial officials institutionalized these understandings in governance practices. These ranged from the specific (e.g. the Hindu Religious (and Charitable) Endowments Board in the Madras Presidency) to the general, such as the inclusion of 'Hindu' as a category of identity in the Census of India, which was taken every decade from 1871 onwards.[79] The cumulative effect of these practices was to entrench more religiously exclusive forms of communal identity, on which the British Empire's strategies of 'divide and rule' subsequently rested.

To be clear, 'Hinduism' was not simply a unilateral British imposition, the product of purely Machiavellian calculation. British Orientalists did not come up with their ideas in isolation but in interaction with Indian reformers and intellectuals, who themselves often pushed for a more

---

[76] See Roy 2013.   [77] Frykenberg 1993, 535–6.   [78] *Ibid.*, 555.   [79] *Ibid.*, 537–9.

purified and homogeneous conception of 'Hinduism' than had existed before.[80] Still, a modern and monolithic 'Hinduism' did critically help to integrate the British *Raj*. 'In a continent so pluralistic, such a Hinduism helped to reinforce the construction of any single huge overarching political order.'[81] The institutionalization of communal cleavages (as, for example, in the creation of Muslim-only electorates with the Morley-Minto reforms of 1909) moreover entrenched religious division at the heart of Indian politics.[82] This, in turn, helped sustain British colonial understandings of India as irreducibly and irredeemably heterogeneous, a mere 'geographic expression'[83] that only the *Pax Britannica* could hold together.

Alongside religious patronage, selective ethnic military mobilization also helped produce the subjectivities that constituted the British Empire in India. From the mid-eighteenth century, the EIC relied intensively on India's incomparably large market for private military labour to man the armies that conquered its Empire. In these early decades of conquest, Company armies primarily consisted of high-caste northern Indian Hindus (*Purbiyas*).[84] Indeed, in the Bengal Presidency – the EIC's largest and most important power centre – the EIC explicitly restricted its recruitment to high-caste Hindus.[85] Company agents went to great lengths to foster a 'high-caste ethic' within the army, mandating that the army scrupulously respect Brahmin dietary, religious and travel preferences.[86] Not only did they strengthen the soldiers' esprit de corps, but they also differentiated them from the remainder of the local population, in keeping with classic 'divide and rule' imperatives.[87]

Company recruitment practices in Bengal were originally highly successful in building an effective fighting force. But the strategy of building esprit de corps through appeals to Brahmin caste identity disastrously backfired in May 1857 when mutineers harnessed religious fervour to mobilize elements of the Bengal Army in revolt against the EIC. The ensuing 'mutiny' nearly destroyed the Empire, forcing the British to mount what in effect constituted a 'second conquest' of India from 1857–9.[88] Following this re-conquest and the suppression of the mutiny, the British transformed their military recruitment practices.[89] From then on, the British recruited their troops disproportionately from previously marginal populations. Sikhs, Rajputs, Pathans and Gurkhas – the so-called 'martial races' – would come to dominate the Indian Army thereafter, down to the Empire's collapse in 1947. The invention of

---

[80] Pennington 2005, 20.   [81] Frykenberg 1993, 540.   [82] Birnbaum 2015, 86.
[83] Darwin 2013, 212.   [84] Rand and Wagner 2012, 237.   [85] Alavi 1998, 45.   [86] *Ibid.*
[87] *Ibid.*   [88] Darwin 2013, 257.   [89] Streets 2004, 11.

'martial races' – and its institutionalization within the Indian Army – provides another important example of the productive practices that constituted imperial hierarchy.

Colonial officials invented 'martial races' in the late nineteenth century. 'Martial races' thus emerged at a time when 'scientific racism' was gaining in popularity. The category also developed as British India was transforming into an 'ethnographic state',[90] in which pseudo-scientific ethnic categories increasingly suffused colonial governance practices. The intuition informing the 'martial races' idea was that certain ethnic groups – by virtue of a combination of physiological and cultural traits – were innately suited to the warrior vocation. On the basis of this understanding, imperial recruitment practices increasingly targeted these groups, producing a wholesale shift in the Indian Army's ethnic composition over time. By the outbreak of the First World War, for example, fully three-quarters of the Indian Army comprised recruits from the so-called martial races.[91]

Much like the EIC's sponsorship of a 'syndicated Hinduism',[92] 'martial race' recruitment practices did not simply mobilize pre-existing group identities for imperial ends. Instead, the colonial state systematically curated 'martial race' identities among targeted populations. 'Different "warrior" communities were constructed from the diverse groups which entered the Indian army by distorting the varied ethnic and religious strands in the sub-continent's society.'[93] To cite one example, the British contrived the ethnonym 'Gurkha' to encompass a subset of six Nepalese tribes they deemed suitable for recruitment into the Indian Army.[94] Much like the Manchu banner system, the Indian Army sought to dissolve existing lineage and tribal identities by subsuming them instead into constructed supra-tribal ethnic identities. 'The Indian army ... never went for mono-tribal units but mixed the various tribes to create a supra-tribal identity: the Gurkha community.'[95] To cultivate a sense of esprit de race among the Gurkhas, the British nudged their recruits towards religious homogeneity in the form of an idiosyncratic 'hill Hinduism' that nominally united the Gurkha regiments while still distinguishing them from the Hindus of north India.[96] The use of distinctive uniforms and headgear, supposedly evoking the Gurkhas' martial traditions, further consolidated their martial identity. Finally, the British made effective use of the existing regimental structure within the Indian Army to strengthen and institutionalize each Gurkha regiment as an 'imagined community'.[97] This further strengthened the regiments' affective bonds,

---

[90] Dirks 2001, 43.   [91] Rand and Wagner 2012, 234.   [92] Frykenberg 1993, 535.
[93] Roy 2001, 129.   [94] *Ibid.*, 132.   [95] *Ibid.*   [96] *Ibid.*, 134.   [97] *Ibid.*, 134–5.

enhancing both their combat effectiveness and their sense of distinctiveness from (and superiority to) the Empire's non-martial majority.

The Indian Army's reconfiguration through selective ethnic military mobilization was critical to the British Empire's re-foundation after the 'Indian Mutiny'. With its reconfigured army of 'martial races', Britain managed not only to hold onto India but also to use the Indian Army as an 'imperial fire brigade'[98] to police the vast new territories Britain conquered during the late Victorian and Edwardian eras. The key point here is that practices of productive power were irreducibly involved in generating the *coercive* power necessary to win and keep the Empire. The organization of violence and the organization of collective identity were two sides of the same coin. Imperial hierarchy, for Britons as well as Manchus, rested on an imbalance of military power that decisively favoured these conquest elites. But indigenous military recruits overwhelmingly provided the manpower that sustained British and Manchu imperial enterprises. And the mobilization of these indigenous armies demanded resort to productive practices of the kind described earlier, which laid the collective identity foundations on which imperial hierarchies ultimately rested.

Conclusion

This chapter has examined how agents constructed imperial hierarchies in Qing China and British India, two of history's most powerful empires. Through an examination of practices of religious patronage and selective ethnic military mobilization, I showed how conquest elites adapted indigenous ideational and material resources to build their empires. Imperial curatorship of distinct religious and ethnic identities provided the basis for divide-and-rule strategies that comprised imperial hierarchies. In their respective sponsorship of Tibetan Buddhism and Hinduism, the Manchus and the EIC shaped religious identities in ways that fortified their rule. Their approaches were very different. The Manchu Emperor directly claimed the mantle of *Cakravartin* to win the political loyalty of his (mainly Mongol) Tibetan Buddhist followers. Conversely, British Orientalist constructions of Hinduism did not imbue the imperial state with the direct aura of sacred legitimacy but did make India's population more legible and susceptible to alien rule. The Manchu banner system and the British recruitment of 'martial races' likewise provided distinct examples of the refashioning of ethnic identities to serve imperial military needs. Both, however, worked on a similar principle of mobilizing

---

[98] Jeffery 1982, 536.

military power through ethnically defined institutions, which profoundly shaped their empires' collective identities and patterns of stratified differentiation.

In teasing out these comparisons, this chapter makes three contributions to the study of hierarchy. First, this chapter emphatically demonstrates agents' capacities and ability to construct narrow hierarchies of rule within environments structured by broad hierarchies of difference. Indeed, my primary claim is that imperial statecraft fundamentally depends on the plasticity of broad hierarchies of difference and their susceptibility to being re-sculpted to support narrow hierarchies of rule. In this book's introduction, Zarakol asks: 'How are contractual hierarchies of legitimate authority created in a world of organized inequality?'[99] I have answered this question here by foregrounding the 'define and rule' practices of imperial curatorship that underwrite 'divide and rule' strategies of imperial governance. Though empires have historically been authoritarian and most often deeply exploitative of subject populations generally, they nevertheless depended on collaboration with local intermediaries to sustain themselves. This placed a premium on vertically incorporating these intermediaries within narrow hierarchies of rule while horizontally segregating them from one another through re-sculpting the collective identities composing broad hierarchies of difference.

My account of how imperial hierarchies emerge is thus unapologetically agency centred. It also clearly privileges the perspectives of rulers over the ruled. This simplifies a far more complex and interactive process of empire formation. Of course, both Manchus and Britons varied in their degree of sophistication and self-consciousness when curating the identities that upheld their rule. Equally, the productive effects of imperial curatorship were not simply top down. Rather, the experience of empire exerted transformative effects on Manchu and British identities, as well as those of their subjects.

In curating imperial religious and ethnic identities into existence, I must also note the bounded nature of imperial agency. Conquest elites drew promiscuously upon indigenous resources to curate imperial identities. But they were not free to invent new identities ex nihlio to serve imperial needs. Moreover, empire-builders rarely undertook this process unilaterally. Instead, practices of imperial curatorship frequently involved a complex play of contestation and collaboration with local intermediaries, whose responses profoundly shaped the forms of collective identity that empires produced.[100]

[99] See the Introduction.   [100] Andersen 2011, 19.

These essential caveats aside, the point stands that my treatment of empires still expressly foregrounds imperial agency. I also posit an intimate inter-relationship between one type of hierarchy (empire as legitimate authority anchored in asymmetric bargains between rulers and intermediaries) and another (empire as a broad hierarchy of difference comprising stratified communities divided around categories of religion, ethnicity and caste). This agency-centred conception of hierarchy undoubtedly differs from that of other contributors to this book, such as Sjoberg or Pouliot.[101] Both place greater stress on the constraining and constitutive effects of hierarchies and appear less optimistic about agents' capacities to shape or escape the broad hierarchies their chapters interrogate.[102]

To an extent, this difference in orientation follows from our different objects of analysis. Gendered hierarchies and diplomatic pecking orders constitute forms of hierarchy that are more global, more diffuse and more pervasive than imperial hierarchies. At the same time, however, the greater plasticity that I see in broad hierarchies is partially an artefact of my specific temporal focus on periods of unusual fluidity and change. Both the Manchus' conquest of China and the East India Company's conquest (and in 1857–9, re-conquest) of India marked seismic shifts in the respective regional orders of East and South Asia. They entailed the subversion of existing imperial hierarchies (Ming Chinese and Mughal Indian, respectively) and the establishment of new narrow hierarchies of imperial rule in their place. Patterns of collective identification and mobilization are likely to be especially fluid and susceptible to manipulation during such times of contested order transition.

For this reason, rather than aspiring to make general claims about the relationship between narrow and broad forms of hierarchy, it may be more fruitful for hierarchy scholars to pursue more contingent claims about this relationship, which pay greater heed to considerations of temporality. My analysis here suggests that actors' creative agency will be most visible when international hierarchies are first emerging or when actors are transitioning from one hierarchy to another. The boundaries between narrow hierarchy (conceived as a negotiated asymmetric bargain) and broad hierarchy (conceived as productive structures of organized inequality) will also likely be particularly permeable at these times. Conversely, the structural and productive effects of hierarchy will be more conspicuous during periods of relative stability, when hierarchies are in a phase of reproduction rather than either genesis or transformation. Given that change is a constant within social systems, this

---

[101] See Chapters 4 and 5.   [102] *Ibid.*

ideal-typical trichotomy between phases of genesis, reproduction and transformation is of course contrived. Nevertheless, a more explicit incorporation of considerations of temporality may provide some guidance as to where best to train our attention when studying hierarchies' evolution. This will, in turn, help us to develop more precise (albeit contingent) claims about the nature and operation of international hierarchies.

Continuing on the theme of temporality, my chapter's second contribution was to illuminate the dynamics of hierarchy emergence that were common to both Asian and Western empires at a particular historical juncture, from the early modern period through at least until the mid-nineteenth century. In comparing British India alongside Manchu China, I have shown that Western Orientalists held no monopoly on customization practices of imperial curatorship such as religious patronage and selective ethnic military mobilization. Whether Manchus or Britons, empire-builders confronted common challenges in establishing narrow hierarchies of rule over culturally distinct populations that vastly outnumbered them. Imperial elites in both contexts moreover resorted to similar practices of curatorship to address these challenges.

The similarities in Manchu and British imperial statecraft should not lead us to ignore their distinctive features. Nevertheless, their parallels remain illuminating, for they suggest that dynamics of hierarchy formation are importantly governed by historically particular conditions of possibility, at least as much as by the culturally specific beliefs of empire-builders themselves. Manchus and Britons came from different cultural universes. They furthermore thought about the purposes of empire in radically divergent ways. But before the mid-nineteenth-century 'global transformation'[103] at least, they confronted similar constraints and contrived similar solutions to the challenges of empire. Without the benefit of modern communication, transportation and administrative technologies, rulers of large-scale political forms depended on rule through local intermediaries. This imposed on them the dual imperatives of 'define and rule' and 'divide and rule'. Historically specific constraints on collective action thus substantially limited the form international hierarchies could take, regardless of imperial elites' cultural background or ideological preferences. Acknowledging these constraints gives us a better sense of the bounded agency of would-be hierarchy-builders, as well as potentially enhancing our ability to delineate the variations in forms of hierarchy likely to obtain in different historical epochs.

[103] Buzan and Lawson 2015.

Finally, though my analysis focuses on the age of empire, my argument has important contemporary implications for the study of hierarchy in global politics. In focusing on Manchu China and British India, I concentrated on a historical epoch that was conducive to the emergence of a particular type of international hierarchy, in the form of multi-ethnic empires. From the early modern period, Eurasia was transformed through the rise of territorially massive and internally heterogeneous empires. Within this world, political imaginations in both East and West remained deeply patriarchal and inegalitarian.[104] Hierarchy rather than equality was the presumptive norm underwriting most forms of collective association. And 'asymmetries in communicative prowess'[105] frequently favoured conquest elites, who could harness the high cultures of conquered peoples to develop the incorporative and ecumenical imperial ideologies needed to stabilize their rule.[106]

By contrast, it is comparatively far more difficult today to cultivate international hierarchies, especially of the imperial type. While Michael Barnett persuasively demonstrates paternalism's persistence as a key enabler of hierarchy in contemporary world politics,[107] the scope for leveraging this paternalism into formal empire is now almost completely foreclosed. Paternalistic ideals and practices, while still potent, grate against an increasingly entrenched global 'equalitarian' regime[108] predicated on ideals of sovereign equality. The globalization of nationalism and constitutionalism now also places immense barriers on empire-building projects.[109] Alien rule is now comprehensively stigmatized to a degree that would have shocked most people as recently as the immediate postwar era. As David Lake moreover demonstrates, today's global sovereign state system is undergirded by increasingly robust norms of non-intervention.[110] Certainly, persistent racism still compromises consistent adherence to this norm.[111] Nevertheless, strong states' rhetorical commitment to non-intervention significantly curtails their ability to subordinate (much less permanently extinguish) weak states' sovereignty. This again limits the forms international hierarchies can now take. Governments once saw possession of empire as a key marker of international prestige and a prerequisite for recognition as a 'civilized state'.[112] Now they widely regard it as an atavistic throwback to a less civilized age.

[104] On the role of Eastern and Western 'quasi-commensurable political imaginations', grounded in deeply hierarchical world views, in enabling Western expansion in early modern Asia, see Biedermann 2009, 266–7.
[105] My thanks to Janice Bially Mattern for this expression.
[106] I develop this argument further in Phillips 2014.   [107] See Chapter 3.
[108] Reus-Smit 2005, 71.   [109] See e.g. Armitage 2007.   [110] See Chapter 1.   [111] *Ibid.*
[112] Hobson and Sharman 2005, 87; Suzuki 2005.

Imperial hierarchy has been emphatically rejected as a legitimate means of organizing international life.

The global international system's current ordering principles thus expressly prohibit formal empire. At the unit level, transformations in the scope of state power also work against empires' resurgence. Today, even weak sovereign states typically have capacities for direct rule that eclipse those of historical empires. This has made it far less pressing for rulers to selectively empower local intermediaries through heterogeneous contracting, as empire-builders of an earlier age were forced to do. The advent of mass literacy and the proliferation of new media platforms have moreover both reduced the asymmetries of communicative prowess that once distinguished rulers from ruled. State-building elites still invest enormous resources consolidating the national imaginaries upon which domestic (i.e. intra-state) hierarchy depends. But rulers' capacities to curate collective identities are now increasingly contested, and their ability to do so between (rather than within) polities is greatly diminished in comparison to the early modern era.

None of this is to deny the importance of hierarchy in contemporary world politics. My point, rather, is that the conditions enabling international hierarchies' emergence and consolidation vary radically across historical epochs. The rise of immense international imperial hierarchies, such as the Manchu Empire or the British *Raj*, reflected distinct and ultimately transient historical conditions that are unlikely to recur. With this in mind, we should remain sensitive to the ways in which evolving modes of power both enable and limit the types of productive practices available to social agents seeking to construct international hierarchies. The demise of empires did not mark a definitive end to international hierarchy. But it did signify the end of narrow international hierarchy in its barest and most brutal form. Acknowledging the epochal significance of this shift is key if we are to properly contextualize – and thus properly understand – the nature and limits of international hierarchies in the contemporary world order.

3   Hierarchy and Paternalism

Michael Barnett

This chapter explores a kind of hierarchy – paternalism. Paternalism is the substitution of one actor's judgment for another's on the grounds that it is in the latter's best interests, welfare, or happiness. In global affairs, paternalism is evident in forms of intervention that are undertaken by actors who claim the authority to improve the lives of those who they judge to be unable to act in their own best interests. Colonialism's civilizing mission was the quintessential paternalistic relationship, but the end of colonialism and the internationalization of sovereignty have not meant the end of such interference. Those in the West spend a lot of time attempting to save those in the third world, but they often act before they receive an SOS signal, interfering first and asking questions (much) later.[1] The human rights community does not always wait for individuals to "discover" their rights and then ask for outside assistance – instead it often proceeds as if it has the moral authority and responsibility to spread and enforce "natural rights."[2] Paternalism is a constant and arguably growing presence in world affairs, richly deserving a place in any discussion of international hierarchies.

What makes paternalism a particularly interesting case of hierarchy is that a full understanding requires incorporation of both narrow and broad definitions. Many analyses of paternalism highlight how the ability of one actor to interfere in another's sphere of autonomy is premised on the distribution of authority between them. One actor has authority over another, and with that authority, the superordinate actor acts in a way that is intended to better the circumstances of the subordinate actor against his or her will or without his or her consent. Importantly, then, the superordinate actor has made the calculation that interference will lead to more benefits than costs for the paternalized actor. Because paternalism consists of interference that is against the will or without the consent of the subordinate party, paternalism would seem to be outside any sort of mutual agreement of the sort discussed by David Lake. In

---

[1] Abu-Lughod 2014.   [2] Hopgood 2014.

other words, it seems to be an act of domination. Perhaps, but it is not a standard act. Relations of domination frequently assume not just the existence of power but also the attempt by the more powerful actor to act against the interests of the less powerful actor for the former's benefit. Yet paternalism exists when the intent is to better the condition of the less powerful actor, and sometimes that can only be done if the more powerful actor is willing to make a sacrifice. Moreover, paternalism can exist even with "consent." The quintessential paternalistic relationship, parent and child, does not fit neatly into any sort of consent/no consent binary. And it is quite common to label traditional gender relations as paternalistic because the man decides what is best for the woman and often with her implicit acceptance. But does this mean that the woman has given "consent"?

To address these elements of paternalism requires moving behind the narrow to the broad understanding of hierarchy. Not only are relations of paternalism premised on stratification between actors, but they frequently produce and are produced by relations of inequality and roles of superiority and inferiority. If we want to understand the structural sources of inequality, why those in superordinate positions might feel a duty or responsibility to the welfare of the subordinate parties, and the possibility that subordinate parties might be willing to live with their position of inferiority, then we have to shift the level of analysis from agent interaction to structure. Structural approaches "begin with political relations rather than unencumbered individuals, emphasizing that paternalism is an authority relationship based on unequal status and power."[3]

Yet there are different approaches to structure, and these differences matter to different understandings of how relations of inequality are produced and reproduced. Some approaches to paternalism adopt a more standard definition of structure that presumes that each role-position has an attending set of objective interests – and these interests generally conflict with one another because these are relations of inequality that benefit those in positions of power and disadvantage the disempowered. These relations of domination are reproduced through some combination of coercion and consent – and ideology plays an important function in the latter. In order to continue to benefit from these relations of exploitation and sleep better at night, the powerful will adopt ideologies that explain why these inequalities owe to the inadequacies of the weak that generate some form of noblesse oblige. Why would the weak consent to their own domination? The answer is false consciousness of one form or another.

[3] Soss, Fording, and Schram 2011, 24–5.

A "post" approach to structure, of the sort used by Foucault and other students of discourse, makes three moves that have immediate implications for how we might understand relations of paternalism. First, instead of treating structure as coherent and directly productive of the roles that actors occupy, it treats structures as fragmented, historically contingent, diffuse discourses. Second, it rejects the language of objective versus subjective interests in favor of the more culturally contingent language of practices. And it rejects the idiom of ideology in favor of the more culturally contingent concepts of discourses, subjectivities, and self-understandings. Studies of paternalism that follow this approach to structure excavate the historically contingent social relations that produce the authority, sense of obligation, and legal, political, and cultural space for some actors to intervene in the lives of another for their benefit and why some actors have subjectivities and enact practices that are complicit in the making of their inferiority. For instance, Foucault's concept of pastoral power likens the relationship of the leader to the people as similar to the shepherd to the flock.[4] Gender relations are typically defined by roles of superiority and inferiority generated by sex difference, and historically, the presumption was that the male not only is superior to the female but also has a responsibility to act in her best interest (and the female is expected to defer). Studies of colonialism are replete with accounts of how various structures and practices produce some actors feeling superior and others with a sense of inferiority and even self-loathing.

There is one final reason why paternalism makes for such an interesting case of hierarchy, which has to do with normative propriety and legitimacy.[5] Liberal political theory and rationalist approaches, as exemplified by Chapter 1 (Lake), deem nonconsensual forms of hierarchy illegitimate. Yet scholars grounded in liberal political theory have spent considerable energy attempting to identify the restrictive conditions under which the suspension of another's liberty might be warranted – and these conditions usually orbit around moments when an actor is deemed unable to act in his or her own best interests. Paternalism might be illegitimate, but it can also be justifiable, especially when compared with the alternative. Scholars working with the broader perspective to hierarchy also take a dim view of it because of the general presumption that it is produced by domination, exploitation, and oppression. For many critical International Relations (IR) scholars, it is not enough to explain and unmask the relations of inequality; one must also imagine what kinds of human interventions might create the conditions for genuine emancipation. Could such interventions justify forms of paternalism?

---

[4] Foucault 2007.   [5] Le Grand and New 2015, 7.

My sense is yes. Much like the view from liberal political theory, critical theory might acknowledge occasions when paternalism is a necessary means to more desirable ends. Unlike liberal theorists, though, I am not aware of many sustained efforts by critical IR theorists to specify the conditions under which some actors should interfere in the lives of others to improve their long-term welfare, circumstances, and moral development.[6]

Paternalism raises a series of analytical and normative provocations for students of international relations in general and international hierarchy in particular. To begin, it arguably represents a distinctive *form* of hierarchy – no other form is so clearly constituted by principles of care and control. Moreover, despite its distinctiveness, it is quite common in world affairs. Paternalism was an overt and accepted hierarchical structure in pre-Westphalian politics, had an explicit justificatory ethos in colonial politics, and is present in many areas of global governance. In short, paternalism is not a historical curiosity but rather is a chronic presence in international affairs. Moreover, paternalism, like other kinds of hierarchy, is a form of rule.[7] As a form of rule, it also is a form of governance. And it is a form of governance that is distinct from the traditional power-saturated and voluntary-driven versions of global governance that dominate the field. Fourth, as a form of rule and governance, paternalism also exemplifies how different kinds of power operate in international affairs. There are forms of paternalism that characterize power as direct, visible, immediate, and coercive.[8] Yet there are forms of power that operate below the surface and at the level of social relations. To understand paternalism requires the incorporation of different kinds of power.

This chapter is organized as follows. The first section provides an overview of paternalism, beginning with a review of alternative definitions, and then it considers the boundaries between paternalism and other cognate concepts such as solidarity, institutionalism, persuasion, and hegemony. The second section unpacks the social relations of inequality, which demands attention to the discourses, institutions, and roles that generate positions of superiority and inferiority and give some actors the belief that they can and should interfere in the lives of others for their own benefit. The third section makes two moves in order to refine the concept for empirical analysis. Scholars of paternalism have identified a host of dimensions on which it might vary, but arguably six are most critical for interrogating paternalism in global and humanitarian governance: the

[6] Price (2008) lays down this challenge, but my selective reading of the responses is that they are better at offering a general defense of critical theory's possibilities than they are at offering a methodology and working through a concrete moral dilemma.
[7] Thompson 1990, 161–4.   [8] See Barnett and Duvall 2005.

tools used to restrict another actor's liberty (force versus information), the scope of the interference (wide versus narrow), duration (limited versus unlimited), purpose (means versus ends), the source of the paternalizer's confidence (faith versus evidence), and the mechanisms of accountability (internal versus external). Building on these six dimensions, the second move is to posit the existence of two ideal types of paternalism – strong and weak. Paternalism might be a constant feature of international affairs, but it also exhibits considerable diversity in its form and practice. To illustrate the continuing and constantly changing presence of paternalism in world affairs, I explore the possibility that the institutionalization of liberalism and discourses that favor principles of equality help explain the shift from strong to weak paternalism from the era of colonialism to the postcolonial period.

Paternalism Defined

How do we know paternalism when we see it?[9] The *Merriam-Webster Dictionary* defines it as "the attitude or actions of a person, organization, etc., that protects people and gives them what they need but does not give them any responsibility or freedom of choice." According to the *Oxford Dictionary*, paternalism is "[t]he policy or practice on the part of people in positions of authority of restricting the freedom and responsibilities of those subordinate to them in the subordinates' supposed best interest." Other definitions highlight not the attempt by one person to improve the circumstances of another but instead the intent to "prevent him from harming himself, either when he would harm himself voluntarily or when he would do so involuntarily."[10] According to another, frequently cited definition by Gerald Dworkin, paternalism is "the interference with a person's liberty of action justified by reasons referring exclusively to the welfare, good, happiness, needs, interests or values of the person being

---

[9] I use paternalism rather than maternalism for the following reasons. It has a level of familiarity that, for many, requires little explanation. It is the concept most closely associated with my central concern – the intersection of control and care. Maternalism does not have as clear an association. For some, maternalism represents an ethic of care in contrast to a masculine will to power; if so, then it does not capture the dynamics that concern me. In contrast to the essentialized notion of the maternal, there are discussions of maternalism that do try to recover the power that is present in an ethics of care. Some of these discussions, in fact, come quite close to the prevailing definitions of paternalism. That said, gender is important to paternalism for several reasons that go beyond the simple fact that the root of paternalism is "pater," or father. A considerable amount of paternalism in world affairs takes place in the area of gender and sexuality; this regularity probably owes to gender in general and the presumption that women are less able to make rational decisions and are in greater need of protection from themselves and others.

[10] Claassen 2014.

coerced."[11] In a recent review of the contending definitions, Dworkin marches through seven candidates, including Shiffrin's influential version, which emphasizes not the interference with another actor's interests but rather the interference in another actor's proper sphere of autonomy and judgment.[12]

Paternalism is the substitution of one actor's judgment for another's on the grounds that it is in his or her best interests, welfare, or happiness.[13] Definitions of paternalism are attempting to wrestle with this mixture of care and power, and the "care" part of the definition has proven much less controversial than the "power" side. Paternalism involves some form of power to the extent that there is interference in another actor's sphere of autonomy.[14] But how do we know when such interference has taken place? Many definitions of paternalism proceed to argue that absence of consent and the presence of coercion are the telltale signs. I omit these criteria for the following reasons. The substitution of judgment can occur through either coercive or other means. There are instances when one person's stated preference is overruled and countermanded by another; in these instances, power is immediate, direct, and visible, conforming to the classic Weberian notion of power. Yet there are other forms of power that are "hidden"; in these instances, the substitution of judgment occurs through indirect means and subjectivities. When individuals accuse someone of paternalism, sometimes they are objecting to the fact that their stated preferences and desires are being neglected or vetoed. Yet, at other times, they are suggesting that they should have been consulted but were not. While some definitions of paternalism want to exclude these noncoercive instances, I want to include them.

In part because of the influence of liberal political theory on the literature on paternalism, there is considerable attention to the concept of consent. But what counts as consent? Does consent have to be explicit? The medical field has had a revolution in patient's rights, which often means that no medical procedure or intervention can occur without the explicit, written, and informed consent of the patient. Consent, however,

---

[11] Dworkin 1972.
[12] Dworkin 2013; Shiffrin 2000. For a sampling of the definitional debate, see Thompson, 1990, Chapter 6; Archard 1990; Garren 2006, 334–41; Garren 2007, 50–9; Dworkin 1972, 64–84; Gert and Culver 1976; VanDeVeer 1986; Mead 1997; Husak 2003; Kelman 1981; and Grill 2007.
[13] For a similar approach, see Le Grand and New 2015, Chapter 2.
[14] There is the nontrivial matter of what constitutes an actor's sphere of autonomy. Some political theorists, especially those committed to liberal political theory and influenced by natural law, are likely to insist that all humans are entitled to the same sphere of autonomy. Other theorists, though, are more interested in the historically and culturally contingent forces that define the area of proper autonomy.

could be implied. It also could be inferred. It is because implied consent can camouflage subtle and not so subtle mechanisms of control, though, that many ethicists prefer to err on the side of caution, insisting that consent must either be explicit or "obvious" from what "most" people would want under the circumstances.[15] Consent does not mean the absence of constraints, but at what point do constraints become so severe that choice becomes, for all intents and purposes, no choice. What does consent mean in conditions of gross power asymmetries? Aid agencies arrive with considerable resources. Sometimes they make suggestions, but suggestions coming from the powerful with easy exit options can sound like commands, and recipients might prefer to keep quiet than bite the hands that feed them.[16] Structural theories of power raise an additional problem with the language of consent: preferences are formed in a social context, and those preferences might not represent the "true" and "objective" interests of the powerless but rather the interests of the powerful. Can individuals make informed decisions if they are, for instance, locked down by a culture that has taught them to blindly accept an outward and inward orientation that stifles their human development?

Paternalism Is Not the Same Thing as . . .

Paternalism is the substitution of one person's judgment for another's on the grounds that it is in the latter's best interest. Yet, as in all definitional exercises, what matters is where we draw the boundaries between one concept and adjacent concepts. If we tweak the motives from concern for others to self-interest, then we quickly move from paternalism to domination; if we accept that those who are in a position of inferiority might have voluntarily chosen their position, then we quickly move from paternalism to persuasion and voluntarily formed institutions designed to further individual and collective interests; and if we allow for the possibility that the person providing assistance is simply following the wishes of the recipient, then we can migrate from paternalism into forms of solidarity.

Solidarity is premised on a feeling of unity between people who have the same interests, goals, and objectives. If a labor union in France helps workers in Bangladesh, it represents an act of solidarity, not paternalism. When believers in one country help coreligionists in another country by providing aid for rituals, they are not engaging in proselytization but rather in fellowship and religious solidarity. When Amnesty International and other human rights agencies engage in letter-writing campaigns on

[15] Hartogh 2011.   [16] Harrell-Bond 1986.

behalf of political prisoners, they are typically acting in solidarity with the imprisoned. When aid workers scramble to help the victims of a natural or man-made disaster, they are acting in solidarity with those in need and in accordance with their belief in the unity of humanity. Solidarity, rather than paternalism, is the more accurate description of these acts because the benefactor is responding to the wishes and interests of the beneficiary.

Yet it is common for those who profess to be acting in solidarity with others to be accused of sliding into paternalism because they have failed to properly listen to the views of those they want to help and unilaterally substituted their judgment for theirs. Those in solidarity might assume that they know the interests of those they want to help without ever asking. Those in the West spend a lot of time attempting to save those in the third world, but it is not always clear that those in the third world feel as if they need to be saved, at least not in the way perceived by Westerners. Those living under oppressive conditions are quite likely to want to better their human rights but might have a very different idea about what those rights are and which rights should be prioritized. Additionally, outsiders might be attempting to further the interests of those in need in ways that the latter defines them but be interfering in a manner that the recipient finds inefficient or even harmful. Western-based nongovernmental organizations (NGOs) that attempt to defend the interests of underage workers being subjected to slave-like factory conditions have pursued policies that have left the children jobless, home-less, and forced into an even more dangerous situation on the streets. Sometimes those suffering under oppression welcome economic sanc-tions as a way to pressure their governments to enact serious political reforms, but at other times they have asserted that such sanctions do more harm than good and that other kinds of interventions are preferable. In these situations, acts of "solidarity" can feel demeaning and disrespectful.

Paternalism is also not synonymous with persuasion. Paternalism is the substitution of one person's judgment for another. Persuasion suggests that there has not been the forced substitution but rather the attempt to offer reasons, evidence, and arguments to convince another person to decide for himself or herself, based on the merits of the case, to alter his or her direction.[17] Persuasion typically includes most, if not all, of the following elements: a belief that another is thinking or acting in a wrong-headed manner, the attempt to steer them in a different direction because

---

[17] Tsai 2014, 79. Tsai's assertion is not that all forms of persuasion count as paternalism but rather that "not all instances of rational persuasion are morally on a par" and that some acts of persuasion exhibit paternalism because they are guided by a distrust of someone's ability to make a reasonable judgment and might, in the process, intrude on someone's agency.

of a concern for their welfare, an approach that communicates respect for the other's autonomy and capacity for making an informed decision, the avoidance of coercion, and the right of refusal by the person being persuaded. Once again, our emotions provide a guide to the distinction between persuasion and paternalism. When someone attempts to sincerely convince me to change my mind for my own good, he or she has recognized my dignity, autonomy, and ability to judge for myself what is in my best interest.

A critical way in which solidarity and persuasion differ from paternalism is that the former two are presumably reflective of relations of (relative) equality and not relations of hierarchy. However, there are relations of hierarchy that generate superordinate and subordinate positions that nevertheless might not qualify as paternalism. Specifically, there are instances when an actor has voluntarily delegated the authority to another to act in ways that the authority believes is in the best interest of the actor in the subordinate position. Why would anyone do such a thing? Presumably because he or she believes that it is in his or her best interest to enter into an arrangement where another actor has the authority to restrict or guide his or her choices in the future. We might do so when experiencing collective-action problems, a self-awareness that we are sacrificing long-term gains for immediate gratification, or to improve our welfare by seeking out another's assistance. For instance, William Talbott distinguishes between legal paternalism, which "overrules the targets population's judgment about what is good for them," and a legal solution to a collective-action problem, which "gives effect to the target population's judgments about what is good for them by bringing about an overall outcome they general regard as better for them than the outcome that would eventuate if there was no law."[18] To perform this welfare-enhancing role, the agent must be relatively autonomous from the (most powerful) members. Critical to this arrangement working out the way the principals imagined, of course, is that the decision to yield some authority is truly a result of consent and not coercion, the agent or institution is truly interested in acting in the best interests of the principals, and the transfer of authority is temporary or can be retrieved if the principal decides that the agent or institution is pursuing an alternative agenda that is not in his or her best interests. Institutionalist and principal-agent approaches capture this logic and have been used to understand why states might voluntarily surrender some part of their sovereignty to a third party.

If so, then the question is not whether there are factors that interfere in an actor's choice but whether those factors can and should be influenced

---

[18] Talbott 2010, 277 (italics in original).

by a third party to produce an outcome that is prospectively closer to the interests of the actor and Pareto improving. This role can be played by institutions.[19] In this spirit, Robert Thaler and Cass Sunstein advocate for "libertarian paternalism."[20] Institutions are supposed to help "nudge" people to make choices that are good for themselves and good for society. As they forthrightly state

> The paternalistic aspect consists in the claim that it is legitimate for private and public institutions to attempt to influence people's choices and preferences, even when third-party effects are absent. In other words, we argue for self-conscious efforts, by private and public institutions, to steer people's choices in directions that will improve their own welfare. In our understanding, a policy therefore counts as "paternalistic" if it attempts to influence the choices of affected parties in a way that will make choosers better off.[21]

They call their approach "libertarian paternalism" because it "preserves the freedom of choice but … encourages both private and public institutions to steer people in directions that will promote their own welfare."[22] A critical part of their defense of preserving freedom of choice is the assumption that these arrangements are being made in a liberal democratic context, in which the political institutions have significant legitimacy and the "planners" who are called to guide decisions are accountable to the public.

Solidarity, persuasion, and voluntary self-binding share an interest in the needs of the target object and the use of noncoercive tools to further its interest or change its behavior. However, the moment we judge that the motives are primarily self-interested, then we have moved away from paternalism and into domination. Many scholars object to the very possibility of paternalism on the grounds that actors care about no one but themselves. This is a powerful critique. Actors are constantly presenting their private interests as beneficial to others and in the public interest.[23] And even if actors sincerely believe that they are intervening on the benefit of others, they might be ignorant of either their true motives or how their actions serve the interests of the powerful. Whether or not actors can have a compassionate bone in their body, to my mind, should be treated not as an axiom but rather as an empirical matter. To further complicate

[19] Sunstein 2013; Levy 2014.
[20] See Sunstein and Thaler 2003; Thaler and Sunstein 2003, 2008; Sunstein 2006; Cohen 2013; Sagoff 2013; Qizilbash 2011; Ben-Porath 2010; and Le Grand and New 2015, Chapter 7.
[21] Sunstein and Thaler 2003, 1162.
[22] *Ibid.*, 1201. Also see Ben-Porath 2010; Conley 2013.
[23] Yet the central issue is not whether individuals understand their "true" motives or even whether acts of caring might advance the interests of others; instead, it is whether actors are motivated by the sincere desire to aid another.

matters, motives are often mixed, and care is often a part of this mixture. Consider nineteenth-century British and French civilizing missions: whereas some scholars see such civilizing discourses as mere ideology that masks the existence of interests, others suggest that discourses of responsibility were genuinely felt.[24] Aid workers are often treated as the paragon of virtue, but they are often described as "selfish altruists" because of the mixture of care and interest.[25] Precisely when the proportions justify the label of "paternalism," though, is another debate.

The Social Relations of Paternalism

Paternalism is the substitution of one actor's judgment for another's on the grounds that it is in the latter's best interests, welfare, or happiness. To simplify matters, in this section I want to decompose these social relations into two elements: the belief by the would-be paternalizer that an actor's rationality and reasoning processes are deficient and could lead to self-harm and the sense by the would-be paternalizer that it possesses the authority and has the obligation to intervene in the lives of another. These two elements produce discourses of superiority and inferiority and the backbone of hierarchy. Although there are individual judgments that are involved in both the self-assessment and the assessment of another's competence, following the logics of positionality and productivity, I want to focus on the social roles that exist prior to the actors that occupy them, which, in turn, distribute differential social capacities, authority relations, and felt responsibilities by some to others.

Before proceeding, though, I want to address briefly a concept that figures prominently in many studies of hierarchy and paternalism – authority. Authority is the ability by one actor to use institutional and discursive resources to get others to defer to the actor. I want to stress several features of this definition. First, authority is a social construction and, therefore, is produced in and through enduring social relations. Second, authority works through a combination of command and consent; it is the very mixture of the two that makes it such an essential but elusive category of analysis. Third, those in authority often are able to draw from institutional resources to get others to listen to and obey their commands. Fourth, and related, authority does not make compliance automatic, but it does provide a significant advantage for those attempting to change the behavior of others at drastically lower cost. Fifth, and perhaps most important for any discussion of hierarchy and paternalism,

---

[24] Kinsella 2011.   [25] Vaux 2001.

authority relations generate relations of inequality and positions of super-ordination and subordination.

The distinction between being "in authority" and "of authority" is useful to this discussion.[26] Actors whose authority derives from the institutional roles they occupy can be said to be "in authority"; these roles grant them the right to speak and perhaps even enjoy enforcement mechanisms to make sure that the audience does what they say. Those who hold public office have authority that comes from the institution, and when they leave office, those rights and powers disappear. In contrast, to be "an authority" is to be conferred the right to speak because of creden-tials, education, training, and experience. In other words, authority of this kind adheres to the individual who has it, regardless of changes in the institutional role. Those who have this kind of authority often feel entitled to offer an opinion on subjects they claim to have mastered (and some-times even subjects they know nothing about).

There also are different kinds of authority. Four kinds of authority arguably cover the possibilities in international affairs. There is "dele-gated" authority, whereby the authority possessed by one actor is trans-ferred or delegated to another agent. This is the sort of authority that is typified by rationalist/institutionalist approaches to world affairs and consistent with the logic of tradeoffs. There is "rational-legal" authority, whereby authority is derived from seemingly impersonal and objective laws, procedures, standards, and rules that are applied evenly and without discrimination. Third is "moral" authority, whereby authority is derived from various kinds of transcendental appeals and discourses; actors who link themselves to theological and humanist claims are generally based on this form of authority. In the humanitarian sector, faith-based and humanist organizations draw from these distinct sources of authority. And finally, there is "expert" authority, whereby authority is claimed and conferred on the basis of specialized knowledge.[27] As we will see, authority, the distinction between in and of authority, and the different kinds of authority are useful for understanding the theory and practice of international paternalism.

Inferiority, Incompetence, and Incapacity

Paternalism is motivated by a desire to help – not just anyone, but those who are deemed unable to act in their own best interests. Consequently, implicit in paternalistic acts is a judgment about the competence and capacity of the subordinate actor. These judgments can be treated case by

---

[26] Friedman 1958.   [27] Barnett and Finnemore 2004.

case, as a part of the human condition, or by categorical analysis. In many societies, it is when individuals turn eighteen years old that they are considered to be sovereign, autonomous agents – unless proven otherwise. There are individuals who are involuntarily committed because they have been deemed a potential harm to themselves and others. My wife is constantly monitoring my behavior for evidence of the early onset of Alzheimer disease; presumably, the moment of discovery will be the moment I am forbidden from making any decisions on my own. There are laws that prohibit individuals from committing suicide or electively amputating a healthy limb on the grounds that anyone who wanted to do so was, by definition, not of "sound mind and body." Many international campaigns are designed to outlaw certain behaviors on the grounds that an actor, even if of the age of consent, would never "voluntarily" agree to such an action. For instance, one argument in favor of banning the movement of individuals across borders for the purposes of selling sex is that anyone who ever engaged in such behavior must have been coerced or had never consented.

Another emerging line of thinking is that all of us are lacking in judgment. It begins with a simple question: what if individuals do not have stable preferences or there are factors that interfere with a rational decision-making process? Psychology, experimental economics, and behavioral economics offer considerable empirical evidence that individuals do not make choices as economic textbooks portray. There are various factors that might lead to impaired choice: preferences over options can be shaped by framing, preferences can be affected by individuals' psychological state at the moment preferences are expressed, preferences might be affected by irrelevant information, and preferences might be different if experts had a chance to present the information.[28] The 2015 World Bank Development Report acknowledges that everyone exhibits biases in the processing of information, but individuals who suffer from constant deprivation, a lack of education, and hardship will be particularly hard hit and least able to afford the costs of a poor decision because they have no margin for error.[29] Development experts, including the World Bank, should take such matters into consideration as they provide their advice and design their programs (and should also become more self-aware of their own biases in reasoning).

And then there are categories of actors who are deemed to be deficient until proven otherwise – children. Because they lack emotional and cognitive maturity, children are best "seen but not heard."[30] The godfather of

---

[28] See Tversky and Kahneman 1974, 1981.   [29] World Bank 2015; Duflo 2014.
[30] White 2000, 5; Soss, Fording, and Schram 2011.

antipaternalist sentiment, John Stuart Mill, argued that all should be pre-sumed capable and competent – except for children and barbarians. There are negative assessments that are based on prejudice. Sexism typically includes the claim that women are unable to make rational decisions because they are too emotional. Racists believe that some races are naturally and genetically superior to other races and that the inferior races are incapable of higher-order reasoning processes and sound deci-sion making. Various kinds of binaries in international affairs – civilized/uncivilized, modern/premodern, advanced/traditional, secular/religious, well-governed/failed – are productive of roles of superiority and inferiority[31] and discourses of responsibility and care by the former for the latter.

Superiority, Competence, and Responsibility

The possibility that actors might genuinely possess an ethics of care does not explain why they might. Simply put: why do some actors feel as if they have short- and long-term responsibilities to others? Perhaps there is a compassion gene. Perhaps it is because of anxiety and a sense of guilt. Hobbes is reported to have defended giving to a beggar on the street on the grounds that he was trying to relieve not the distress of the beggar but rather his own. Perhaps it was because of good (or bad) parenting. Perhaps it owes to diffuse reciprocity. While this explanation might be plausible when discussing small-scale communities or societies that have an existing social contract, diffuse reciprocity stretches believability when considering most instances of transnational care and compassion. Do those from the West who donate to emergencies in the global south imagine that the recipients will reciprocate if the situation is reversed at some point in the future? And if so, do such expectations exist because of the same sort of social contract that constitutes the domestic sphere?

Rather than looking at individual-level characteristics, other approaches examine structures and underlying social relations. It might be because of blood and belonging, which is particularly pronounced when considering a sense of obligation one family member feels for another. It can be because of a sense of humanity. It might be that events that shock the human conscience are tests of our own morality; the failure to respond represents a failure of our own humanity. Religion also might play a role. For many evangelical Christians, democracy and proselytization were (and continue to be) a central part of political theology. Many religious doctrines have codes of charity and compassion, and to be a good Hindu, Jew, Christian, or Muslim requires caring for the less fortunate. The

---

[31] See e.g. Zarakol 2011.

crucial point is that an individualistic ontology is generally insufficient to explain why people go out of their way to help others, sometimes at considerable hardship and risk to themselves, requiring reference to discourses, beliefs, and senses of self that produce an ethics of care and compassion.

Authority relations offer another explanation for why some actors feel as if they have the insight and duty to help others. To be an authority of any kind often comes with a job description that includes the right and duty to interfere for the good of others. Authorities, as authorities, often have superior knowledge and insight relative to those who are defined as nonauthorities. Authority, though, not only designates superiority, it also comes with responsibilities to use that authority for the betterment of others. The parent has authority and a responsibility for the welfare of the child, which include looking after its immediate and long-term welfare; when parents fail or neglect their responsibilities, then the child becomes a ward of the state, which has the authority and a responsibility to protect.

The sense of superiority that inheres in authority can derive from two different kinds of epistemes. The first is based on preternatural commitments whose core principles cannot be challenged by empirical evidence. These quasi-foundational claims help orient the self in relationship to humankind and the cosmos. Religious theology has this characteristic. "Theological propositions are unverifiable because the existences they posit – God, immortal souls, and so forth – do not, even if they exist, intrude on human experience in such a way as to provide compelling evidence for their verification."[32] Some secular thought has these very qualities as well. For instance, many statements on human rights are founded on nonverifiable claims regarding the entitlements that all individuals possess because of their status as human beings; these claims cannot be proven or disproven but rather are a matter of faith. In terms of its effects, then, belief in God is not that different from a belief in humanity.[33] Claims to operate in the name of the values of "international community" or transcendental and universal values have faith-like qualities.

Relatedly, the substitution of judgment can also be produced by the very discourse of compassion and an ethic of care. Hannah Arendt's observation that modernity has made possible a "passion of compassion" represents one such approach.[34] It begins with what she calls the "social question," that is, the existence of poverty and deprivation. Although compassion has a long pedigree, it was not until the eighteenth century

[32] Westerbrook 2000, 194.   [33] Hopgood 2009; Feldman and Ticktin 2011.
[34] Arendt 1965.

that compassion became part of politics. At this moment, she argues, the repugnance of suffering became a mark of one's humanity and moral character, and, importantly, became part of a revolutionary zeal and a reformist politics. "Necessity" becomes the rallying cry, and liberty becomes a necessary casualty. As a "social" revolution is carried out in the name of the "people" and a "general will," in other words, an anti-democratic spirit takes hold. Elites operating in the name of compassion and for the "people" now see themselves as having the authority to act in their name without actually having to solicit their views. The general will, Arendt argues, replaces the notion of consent and stands superior to the aggregation of private interests. Furthermore, this passion of compassion both corresponds to the sentiment of pity and is bound up with a politics of domination. It is, in her words, a perversion of genuine compassion. What is pity's apposite? Solidarity. But solidarity requires more than one person taking pity on another. It also requires that the "other" be granted authority and voice and that the fortunate and powerful also be aware that they might be implicated in the conditions of the poor. Revolutionaries, those who are in the vanguard of the social question, can become insensitive to the very people who they want to assist.

Arendt's analysis can be extended to humanitarianism.[35] Humanitarian organizations also address the social question, use the language of needs, and arguably exhibit similar effects. Although not all humanitarians count themselves as part of a revolutionary class (indeed, many are suspicious of all kinds of utopian politics, which is why they stick to saving lives), they are motivated by the discourse of necessity. And while humanitarians claim to operate in the name of the "people" and to be in solidarity with the oppressed, the language of needs also arguably comes at the expense of "liberty." Humanitarians rush at the sight of suffering to attend to the needs of the victims; at such a moment, they can easily treat the act of consultation and consent as disposable. Much like Arendt's revolutionaries, humanitarians speak vaguely in the name of the people and the dispossessed but are frequently accused of allowing their "passion of compassion" to generate a politics of pity that creates structures of domination.

The discourse of needs also can play out in another way: it creates two categories of actors – those with urgent needs (victims) and those who have the capacity to provide them (saviors). Each of these roles comes with specific characteristics. As many scholars have pointed out, the discourse of victim in the context of humanitarianism produces an image of an individual who is vulnerable and whose vulnerability is

[35] Barnett 2011; Kapyla and Kennedy 2014; Wilkinson 2015; Fassin 2011.

often the result of circumstances and character. Specifically, victims are victims because they are lacking certain kinds of material resources and cognitive abilities that translate into poor decision making and an environment of deprivation. Saviors are not just those with the capacity to help but also have certain characteristics that help explain the presence of these capacities, which, coupled with a self-image of compassion, can lead them to believe that they have a responsibility to help those who cannot help themselves.[36]

Alternatively, confidence can be founded on claims to superior knowledge. Such knowledge can come from experience. It is simply a matter of living long enough and having enough experiences. Sometimes it is because of learning through doing, that is, "experiential" or "practical" knowledge. In modern society, though, the presumption is that evidence-based knowledge, obtained through scientific methods and stamped by certifications of advanced and superior training, trumps lived knowledge.[37] Those who possess such superior knowledge have expert authority and are known as experts. The sociological category of expert is a modern creation, emerging in the late nineteenth century with the expansion of capitalism, the growth of a more specialized division of labor, the heightened importance of services in the modern economy, and ultimately, the emphasis of modernity on knowledge obtained by formal training. The "gold standard" in modern society and the knowledge economy is specialized and advanced training, backed by certificates, credentials, and other symbols of achievement, and this "gold standard" is now a global standard as experts have become a familiar and powerful feature in modern global governance.[38]

Expert authority and expertise have several characteristics that are particularly relevant for any discussion of paternalism.[39] Expert authority derives from the possession of specialized knowledge that is highly valued in modernity. Relatedly, knowledge is not only specialized but assessments and decisions are also based on analytical reasoning, evidence, and science. Because of the objective character of this knowledge, experts are seen as better able to work for the public interest, overcome private interests, and keep politics at bay. Expertise, in this way, contains depoliticizing effects that contribute to the public welfare. These are some of the attributes that give the rule by experts, that is, technocracy, such a

---

[36] Barnett 2011; Fassin and Rechtman 2009.
[37] Boswell 2009, 23–4; cited in Schrefler 2014, 63 fn.1; Collins and Evans 2007.
[38] For various statements on these issues, see Sunstein 1997, 128–50; Brint 1996; Goldman 2001; Ambrus et al. 2014; Kennedy 2004; Barnett and Finnemore 2004; Klabbers 2014; and Best 2014.
[39] Haskell 1984; Sunstein 1997, 128–50; Brint 1996.

good name – they are supposed to listen to what the facts tell them and not anyone else, including the people. Such expert authority, therefore, generates a sphere of autonomy. As Larson aptly states, "because such crucial decisions are both assisted by expert advice and esoteric technologies, and increasingly involved with matters of great scientific and technological complexity, the average person is ... disenfranchised by his [or her] lack of expert knowledge."[40] These qualities – reliance on objective knowledge and acting in the public interest – provide the space for experts to intervene in the world. Indeed, not only do they have the authority to intervene in the world, but they also have an obligation to do so. Simply put, they would not be doing their job, or enacting their identity, if they were not constantly attempting to intervene to improve the world.[41]

In general, these different sources of authority are likely to generate different kinds of hierarchical relationships, including different understandings of why some actors are superior to others and different reasons why some are more likely to defer.

Variations of Paternalism

Paternalism comes in different kinds. In an effort to capture variations in the practices of paternalism, scholars have nominated various dimensions on which they might pivot.[42] These analytical exercises are essential for considering paternalism historically. The paternalism that characterized the relations between the state and the urban poor in nineteenth-century Victorian England differs from the "new paternalism" in the contemporary American welfare state.[43] The paternalism associated with the humanitarian governance in the nineteenth century differs from the prevailing forms of paternalism in contemporary humanitarian governance.[44] Not all paternalisms are alike. To better discriminate between different kinds, I want to briefly outline six critical dimensions: tools of influence, scope, purpose, projected duration, source of confidence, and source of accountability.

As in all forms of power, the means of imposition can vary from outright physical violence that leaves the object little or no choice to the existence of formal and informal institutions that limit (and might even preserve the illusion of) choice. There can be the threat and use of force. During natural disasters, states will physically and forcibly remove individuals

---

[40] Larson 1984, 39; also see Rayner 2003; Nowotny 2003; Liberatore and Funtowicz 2003.
[41] Mosse 2011, 4; Boström and Garsten 2008; Branch 2008.
[42] See e.g. Mead 1997; Archard 1990; VanDeVeer 1986; also Le Grand and New 2015, Chapter 3.
[43] See e.g. Mead 1997; Soss, Fording, and Schram 2011.   [44] Barnett 2012 and 2017.

from their homes if they believe that remaining is too dangerous. The United Nations High Commissioner for Refugees (UNHCR) has joined with states to forcibly repatriate refugees on the grounds that it is in their best interests. Great powers and international organizations have coerced states to change their behavior for their own good and for the good of the international community.

Control also can be exercised through institutions, information, and knowledge. Formal and informal institutions are designed to limit choice by setting the agenda, removing some options from consideration, creating incentives and disincentives for some kinds of actions, and manipulating information. Their choice-constraining properties are justified on the grounds that they will improve individual and collective welfare, and they are able to perform this valuable function if they are relatively autonomous from (the most powerful) members. Simply put, institutions can function effectively and legitimately if they are free from the demands of principals that might not have the knowledge, self-discipline, or prudence to act in ways that are consistent with their individual short- and long-term interests and collective welfare. Institutions often are created and expected to serve this fundamental objective. For some, this can imply something close to a benevolent dictatorship.[45] For others, it is limited to the manipulation of information in a way that "preserves the freedom of choice but . . . encourages both private and public institutions to steer people in directions that will promote their own welfare."[46] But at what point does influencing choice become giving the illusion of having choice? And if they truly know best, but because of political correctness have to cleverly design information to manipulate people into doing what they should, then why not spare the pretense and simply invest these institutions with greater coercive ability?[47]

Imposition can vary in terms of scope: from surgical interventions to wide-ranging supervision. What are the range of areas and activities that are subject to oversight? The liberal democratic state does not exhibit regulatory and paternalistic power over all aspects of public and private life; it is selective. The World Health Organization (WHO) and medical relief agencies such as Doctors without Borders routinely engage in immunization programs in rural areas and refugee camps without the formal or full consent of the patients. Other trustees claim broad supervisory functions. Parents, for instance, claim jurisdiction over nearly all aspects of their children's lives, more so when they are younger than when they are older (in part because children are supposed to be increasingly

[45] Conley 2013.   [46] See Sunstein and Thaler 2003, 1201.
[47] This is one implication of Sarah Conley's *Against Autonomy*.

competent and in part because learning by doing is one way that children become competent). In international affairs, trusteeships, transitional administrations, and peace-building operations involve themselves in all areas of life.

Scope often correlates with the third and fourth criteria. The purpose of paternalism can be distinguished between means and ends. There are forms of interference that are intended to alter the choices, options, strategies, policies, and tactics that are adopted by an actor on the grounds that they represent a less effective or efficient alternative to a predetermined objective. If the goal is to save for retirement, then it might be smarter to put money into a 401k than to play the lottery. There are forms of interference, though, that are intended to change the very goals. The hope, in other words, is to increase the capacity of individuals for reason, rationality, and emancipation. The purpose of parenting is not only to help their children avoid immediately self-destructive behavior but also to guide their moral development. The League of Nations' trusteeship system was informed by a similar logic.

The disjuncture between what is possible and what currently exists produces a tension between a "moral legal standpoint," or moral universalism, and an "anthropological-historical standpoint," or belief that human development happens unevenly.[48] Many otherwise autonomy-defending liberals resolve this tension by justifying interference on the grounds that the trustee has a duty to help with both short-term shortfalls and the longer-term goal of creating the conditions for liberty and the capacity for reasoned choice. "As a result, historical events and tendencies that are unacceptable from a moral legal perspective" can be defended from a "developmental perspective as a means to the perfection of our rational nature."[49] Sometimes the line between means and ends, though, can be blurry. For instance, theorists of human development and human capabilities often disagree over whether education is a means or an end; for some, education is an end because it is simply intrinsic to moral development and emancipation, and for others, it is instrumental to opening up future opportunities.[50]

The fourth is projected duration of the interference. There might be no explicit or projected expiration date, which might be justified on the grounds that there is no reason to believe that the paternalized actor will develop the capacity and competence to make informed choices. Some opponents of decolonization argued that the colonies were unlikely to develop the capacities required for independence until far in the future. If

[48] See McCarthy 2009, 169.   [49] *Ibid.*, 170.
[50] Mozaffar Qizilbash 2011; R. Claassen 2014.

Table 3.1 *Strong and Weak Paternalism*

Elements	Strong	Weak
Tools	Force	Information
Scope	Wide	Narrow
Purpose	Ends	Means
Projected duration	Unlimited	Limited
Source of confidence	Faith	Evidence
Accountability	Internal	External

the goal of the interference is to improve the long-term capacity and rationality of the target, then it might be impossible to set a specific date for the expiration of responsibilities. If the goal is to affect the means that are adopted by an actor, then it is probably much easier to identify a point of termination.

I have already discussed the fifth factor, the paternalist's confidence, which can be either faith based or evidence based. Accountability is the final feature that helps distinguish between kinds of paternalism. This is not the place to review the debate on the multiple meanings of accountability; for my purposes, what matters most is whether the affected populations have the ability to check those who claim to be their trustees.[51] Paternalists typically bristle at being fully accountable to those they want to help; it will be hard to do what needs to be done if they have to seek the advice and permission of those who do not know enough. That said, paternalists tend to be subject to one of two kinds of accountability mechanisms. Internal accountability mechanisms are typically sown by self-doubt and a crisis of confidence; in other words, they are dependent on the conscience of the paternalizer. External mechanisms, however, allow affected populations to register their opinions, to punish the abuse of power, and to sanction officials who are guilty of too much slack or slippage. Competitive elections are the standard tool for holding politicians accountable in modern democracies, yet global and humanitarian governance is not run according to democratic principles and does not claim to be.

These different kinds of paternalism combine to produce, stylistically, strong and weak variants (Table 3.1). A strong paternalism exists when force can be entertained, interference is wide ranging, the paternalizer's confidence is metaphysical rather than epistemic, and the paternalizer's actions are immune to redirection by the paternalized. A weak paternalism

---

[51] For broader discussions regarding the globalization of accountability, see Ebrahim and Weisband 2007; Kim 2011; Lloyd 2008; Chesterman 2008; Steffek 2010.

exists when force is severely proscribed, interference is relatively restricted, the paternalizer's confidence has epistemic roots, and the paternalized possess mechanisms that potentially allow them to make their views known and hold the paternalizer accountable.

By way of illustration and experiment, I want to briefly entertain the possibility that changes in the discourses of equality and autonomy in global affairs have had an impact on the pattern in the practices and kinds of international paternalism. Specifically, my speculation is that the deepening of liberalism over the last century has shifted the prevailing form of paternalism from strong to weak. I do not want to suggest that liberalism owns and operates discourses of equality and autonomy, but it is widely credited with enabling, producing, and legitimating identities, practices, and institutions that orbit around these principles in international affairs. These principles, moreover, are at the core of various global institutions and practices, including the United Nations, sovereignty, and human rights. The impact of liberalization, I want to further suggest, can be seen in three questions of global life that are at the heart of paternalism: When should others be entitled to rule their own affairs? Who has the ability and responsibility to intervene when actors are judged incompetent? And what kinds of practices are deemed more or less acceptable? In order to simplify how degrees of liberalism affect these questions, I want to contrast the colonial and postcolonial worlds.

How do we know who is and is not qualified for self-governance? In the era of colonialism and empires, it was the standard of civilization – a measuring stick constituted by a mixture of race, religion, technology, and wealth. Under this regime, non-Western peoples were often judged to be "unfit" unless proven otherwise. At what point did they become fit for independence, self-governance, and sovereignty? Theoretically at least, this occurred when they had crossed some arbitrary threshold of institutional development, education, wealth, and rationality.

The internationalization and institutionalization of liberalism after World War I undermined these justifications because all peoples became deemed competent unless proven otherwise (a process hastened by the sense that the same powers that were responsible for colonialism and the horrors of the world wars were not in a position to judge the civility of others). How do a people or state demonstrate an inability to exercise mature judgment and self-rule? Sovereignty and legitimate authority depend not only on external legitimacy but also on domestic legitimacy. In other words, a state's sovereignty depends on popular sovereignty, and popular sovereignty, in today's world, is best guaranteed through democratic institutions and the rule of law. Consequently, illiberal states cannot convincingly claim to represent the people and are therefore in no position to refuse or give consent to external interference.[52] This position connects John Stuart Mill to John Rawls. For Mill, the principle of noninterference does not extend to barbarian peoples. For Rawls, the law of peoples includes "the duty of non-intervention" but only for "well-ordered states" that possess some unidentified measure of legitimacy and representativeness. Principles of noninterference do not apply to "outlaw states," situations of grave violations of human rights, and less well-ordered states.[53] One contested implication is that it is possible to paternalize a people only after there exist legitimate political institutions; accordingly, paternalism is not a problem in situations in which those institutions do not exist.[54]

If a people or state is judged to be unable to self-govern, then whose job is it?[55] In the pre–World War I period, prior to the invention of the "international community," such duties and responsibilities fell to those self-anointed purveyors of superior judgment – that is, the colonial powers. Armed with standards of civilization, the colonial states were expected to engage in civilizing missions. During the colonial period, well-meaning and not so well-meaning imperialists, missionaries, and liberal humanitarians frequently operated with the belief that they were an upgrade over the backward despots who exploited their own people. Although this might be seen as nothing more than swapping one absolutism for another, they justified their absolutism on the grounds that it was benevolent, enlightened, and genuinely interested in improving the welfare of the population.[56] John Stuart Mill defended British imperialism in India on the grounds that it would help the Indians develop the mental capacities and social institutions to become free-thinking, reasoning people who were capable of self-governance (which, it just so happens, would benefit the British).[57] Given the presumption that the Western states were the parents and the colonial peoples were childlike, the latter was not recognized to have the moral or legal authority to give or withhold consent. If they did object initially, hopefully they would come to see the wisdom of colonial rule. In this spirit, the great abolitionist leader William

[52] On modern international sovereignty and the conditions under which states might confer or expect recognition from other states, see Koskenniemi 2002; Crawford 2006, 45–86; Anghie 2005; and Osiander 2001.
[53] Rawls 2001. For a discussion of this Rawlsian-centered analysis and the general question of interference in postwar situations, see Recchia 2009.
[54] Applbaum 2007.
[55] I will set aside for the moment the obvious question of who gets the authority to play judge.
[56] McCarthy 2009,171.
[57] *Ibid.*, 175; Long 2005, 76–7. Stanley 2001, 170–2. For three excellent intellectual histories of the leading thinkers on the subject of the relationship between liberalism and imperialism, see Muthu, Pitts, and Mehta 1999.

Wilberforce proclaimed at a dinner in 1816 that freed slaves would come to appreciate their protected position: "Taught by Christianity, they will sustain with patience the suffering of their actual lot ... [and] will soon be regarded as a grateful peasantry."[58]

Conversely, accusations that colonial administrators and commercial elites were exploiting the colonial peoples could unleash a torrent of outrage. In one famous instance in the mid-nineteenth century, the British public put on trial a British colonial administrator in India on the grounds that he had failed to be a proper trustee.[59] The outcry against King Leopold of Belgium's rule over the Congo in the early twentieth century was not that he was a colonialist but rather that he was acting in an un-Christian-like manner. He was eventually stripped of his personal fiefdom, and authority over the territory and its people was handed by the other European powers to Belgium with the explicit mandate to rule for the benefit of the population and prepare them for independence.

With the end of colonialism, the states that were deemed to be unfit for rule or that had demonstrate a serious lapse of competence could end up being placed under the authority of the "international community." Similar to the colonial period, the underlying claim is that the "international community" is a better representative of the people than is the state and is more likely to have the population's interests and welfare in mind. Sometimes the "international community" was nothing more than a new name for the former colonial power that remained in control. The League of Nations' mandatory system institutionalized the idea that the international community has a responsibility to help the backward populations develop the skills for self-governance; in most cases, though, the former colonial power continued to be the governing authority, though with a new set of instructions delivered by a European-dominated League of Nations. Over the last century, the development of the international community has grown substantially, arguably becoming more amorphous because more and more actors claim to operate in its name and for the purpose of improving humanity. The United Nations, accompanied by a flotilla of states, international and nongovernmental organizations, and contractors, descends on "failed states" that are trusteeships in all but name and the UN is, for all intents and purposes, the pro-consul.[60]

Importantly, the international community has a responsibility not just to protect failed states from themselves but also to resurrect them so that

---

[58] Hochshild 2006, 314.   [59] Dirks 2006.   [60] Skendaj 2014.

they are no longer a harm to their neighbors of their own peoples post-cold war humanitarian intervention goes beyond wanting to save lives to include wanting to save failed states.[61] Contemporary peacebuilding aspires to do more than stop wars from happening; it also wants to remove the causes of war. How? By bringing markets, the rule of law, and democracy to conflict-prone societies.[62] The Responsibility to Protect (R2P) doctrine includes both short and long-term responsibilities: it proclaims a responsibility to save populations that are in immediate danger and a responsibility to prevent and rebuild – which can include anything from "regime change" to constructing a liberal peace.

Although it is tempting to suggest that the institutionalization of liberalism produced a change in the language of justification and nothing more, it did have an effect on the practices of paternalism, shifting them from the strong to the weak variety. As typified by colonialism, liberal empires saw themselves as being superior because of their breeding, education, and religion; saw the uncivilized as lacking these qualities and thus undeserving of personhood; believed that they had a responsibility to bring light to the darker parts of the world; were prepared to use the stick if needed; imagined that raising colonial children to be sovereign adults was a decades-long commitment; leaned on both God and science for their confidence; and listened only to themselves for understanding right and wrong. The institutionalization of liberalism over the last century, though, has meant that all humans are seen as deserving autonomy and liberty, incapacities and incompetence are not sweeping but limited, interventions are to be limited in duration and intensity, expert authority becomes seen as the legitimating discourse, and the paternalized are supposed to have some mechanisms to limit the possible abuse of power.

The comparison between the colonial and postcolonial orders is instructive – but also potentially misleading. On the one hand, the institutionalization of liberalism, especially its effects on the practices of sovereign states, arguably not just shifted paternalism from its strong to weak varieties but also reduced its frequency. On the other hand, global governance has evolved from a Westphalian to a post-Westphalian architecture, and authority is no longer concentrated in the state but rather has become rationalized, fragmented, and splintered. If the practice of paternalism is any clue, the old hierarchies are gone – replaced by new hierarchies of "paternalism-lite."

---

[61] Keohane 2003; Krasner 2005; Krasner 2004; Fearon and Laitin 2004.
[62] Paris 2004; Ponzio 2007; Chandler 2006; Duffield 2001.

Conclusion

Hierarchy, much like paternalism, is more than a concept of analysis – it also is a concept of judgment. Hierarchy, like paternalism, carries considerable normative weight. The mere mention of international hierarchy conjures images of empires, colonialism, superpowers pushing around lesser powers, the strong doing what they can and the weak suffering what they must, enduring relations of inequality, and forms of domination. There is a case to be made for hierarchy and its order-generating and welfare-enhancing properties, but, except for Chapter 1, it cannot be found in this book.

Paternalism also has a public relations problem. Paternalism violates many sacrosanct principles of the modern age. John Stuart Mill, the patron saint of the antipaternalism camp, famously wrote that

[t]he sole end for which mankind are warranted, individually or collectively, in interfering with the liberty of action of any of their number, is self-protection. That the only purpose for which power can rightfully be exercised over any member of a civilized community, against his [or her] will, is to prevent harm to others. His [or her] own good, either physical or moral, is not a sufficient warrant.[63]

Thus Mill laid down his "harm principle." The reason for his vitriol on the subject was because of his passionate belief in the virtues of liberty – and even when liberty might be exercised in ways that cause self-harm. Autonomy and liberty are central to human dignity. No one can know better than us what we want, and we can never know what is best for another. Even if individuals act in ways that appear to be irrational or demonstrating poor judgment, to stop them from acting on their perceived interests would violate their dignity. It also denies them an opportunity to learn from their mistakes. Nor can paternalism be defended on the grounds that the interference improves the welfare of the individual – ends do not justify means. Paternalism presumes that an individual is incompetent or inferior. It is infantilizing and demeaning. No one wants to be paternalized or accused of being a paternalist.

Yet liberal political theorists, who have argued vehemently against paternalism, have not gone so far as to recommend its banishment from modern society. Instead, they concede that it might have some redeeming features and, under certain restrictive conditions, might be a relative blessing (when contrasted with the alternatives). What should bystanders, observers, and authorities do when they see an actor about to make what could be a disastrous and self-injurious decision? Should they take a

[63] Mill 1975, 10–11.

laissez-faire libertarian stance? If they do act, though, they might offend the paternalized, who will suffer a loss of autonomy. Is there anything as bad as losing one's dignity? Sometimes. It is precisely because there might be occasions when paternalism can be warranted that autonomy-respecting theorists, scholars, and policy analysts attempt to identify the restrictive conditions under which the right authority is both enabled and perhaps even expected to make decisions that properly belong to another.

But paternalism in international affairs seems to cause greater offense and have fewer defenders than does paternalism in family and domestic affairs. We expect parents to have the last word regarding what their children can and cannot do, and we defend their authority to do so on the grounds that because of their immediate biologic bond, they will know what is in their children's best interests, will allow their decisions to be guided by what is in the best interests of the child, and have the immediate responsibility to protect their children from potential harm and to guide them from childhood to adulthood. The relationship between the dissertation advisor and the advisee is not supposed to be one of equality but is expected to contain elements of paternalism; dissertation advisors advise, but sometimes they must do more than merely advise, and they probably would not be doing their job if they took a hands-off approach for every circumstance. Paternalism in domestic governance is a daily happening, and while there are lots of cries about a future "nanny state," even the most fearful critics would concede that, at times, the state can and should forcibly intervene when individuals show poor judgment in areas that are critical to their welfare and well-being.

Once paternalism crosses a border, our objections multiply and our outrage amplifies. Why? The concept of legitimacy offers some insight. Legitimacy has two dimensions – procedural and output. A legitimate process corresponds to the correct procedures. A standard claim, for instance, is that modern institutions are legitimate when they have followed democratic procedures and an inclusive decision-making process; conversely, institutions lack legitimacy when they don't. The other side of legitimacy is output legitimacy, where the ends (improved welfare) justify the means (the lack of liberty, choice, or autonomy). Paternalism does not attempt to legitimate itself according to following the correct procedures but rather according to the results. It operates, in other words, according to an ethic of consequences – it improves the welfare of the paternalized. Indeed, the presumption is that allowing some actors to determine their own fate will lead to a substantially reduced quality of life. Paternalists are not necessarily out to win popularity contests but rather to reduce the suffering and improve the welfare of others. Of course, they would rather be liked than resented, and their popularity rating can be an important factor in the success of the program, but popularity is secondary to results.

Although paternalism rests its claim to legitimacy on the results, it is not dismissive of the procedural dimension. We are more likely to accept paternalism from those who are the right authorities, and the right authorities are often those who are viewed as intimately tied to the community, a *gemeinschaft*, in which members feel a thick sense of belonging to each other, to the point that their identity derives from the collective, and they feel a deep sense of obligation for each other's welfare and fate. In other words, paternalism is most easily justified and defended when there is a strong sense of community that convincingly informs the decision-making process and goals. Those who defend forms of libertarian paternalism, for instance, generally argue against the backdrop of a liberal democracy that is embedded in a community and has a social contract. Consequently, the presumption is that those in positions of authority are tied to the local community. Moreover, there is the sense that if those in positions of power go too far, there are always mechanisms of accountability, including courts and elections that might discipline them. And even when such accountability mechanisms are absent, sometimes just knowing that the authorities in charge are culturally proximate to governed makes a difference. It can be easier to suffer orders from one of your own than from an outsider. In general, the variation in a sense of community is generally related to the perceived legitimacy of the community's institutions – the more the sense of community is imprinted on, and guides, the institutions of governance, the more the institutions are imbued with legitimacy.

However, as paternalism scales up from the intimate and continuous interaction to the itinerant and the imaginary, the sense of community declines.[64] IR scholars use the language of community advisedly and cautiously and almost always restrict it to bounded transnational spaces that are constituted by ongoing and layered networks of interactions.[65] All these attributes that can justify associating the concept of community in the domestic sphere are absent in the international sphere. There is no deep sense of community. There is an absence of representative institutions. There is considerable cultural difference between those who govern globally and those who are affected by their decisions. There is a dispute over who might be the "right" authority to make decisions. There are few, if any, accountability mechanisms to guide the governors or punish them if they abuse their power. Indeed, IR scholars often surround

---

[64] Tönnies 2011.
[65] For its adoption in international relations, see Adler and Barnett 1998; Buzan 2004.

"international community" with scare quotes. Not only is there skepticism of the concept, but it deserves the scare quotes because it can be a dangerous fiction, appropriated by evil-doers and do-gooders to intervene in all kinds of places where they are not wanted. In general, there is no international community. At best, there is an international society, a *gesellschaft*, in which individuals are bound together not by identity but rather by interests, and group association is instrumental rather than intrinsic to the self.

It is because of the absence of a genuine sense of international community that the weight of legitimacy continues to be invested in the sovereign state. As the principal unit of authority, identity, and security, the state trumps the "international." And the continued organization of the international system around the principle of sovereignty severely restricts the development of a sense of international community, the creation of genuinely representative institutions, and the manufacture of legitimacy. If global actors want to enter the sovereign state, they need its consent and permission. As a general rule, our objections to paternalism seem to increase as we migrate from the interpersonal to the global because we are more suspicious of authorities the more distant they are from the object of concern.[66]

Like hierarchy, paternalism in global affairs will have a legitimacy problem for the foreseeable future. But that is unlikely to stop the continued presence of paternalistic behavior. Nor, arguably, should it.

[66] This is a subtle but significant undercurrent in the essays in the special issue [50(1)] on the "Good State" in *International Politics* (2013).

4   Revealing International Hierarchy through Gender Lenses

Laura Sjoberg

The Independent in the United Kingdom reported on May 23, 2015, that a Hampshire police and crime commissioner "has said that girls as young as five in Portsmouth are expressing a desire to become jihadi brides" for Daesh in Iraq and Syria. The commissioner was met with a significant backlash, with parents, schoolteachers, and political leaders doubting the empirical validity of the his claims.[1] *Newsweek* Europe reported on March 16, 2015 that Daesh members "are using similar online grooming tactics to paedophiles to lure western girls to their cause." The story characterizes female recruits as victims of "exploitation and abuse" where the ISIS "abusers" engage in "identifying vulnerabilities" in young girls.[2] Stories of (especially Western) women migrating to join Daesh/ISIS constitute between 15 and 20 percent of the news reports about Daesh/ISIS in Western media.[3]

Many people reading these stories (and even some of the stories themselves) note that it is important to consider gender subordination in Daesh/ISIS and possibly even gender subordination in the depiction of "jihadi brides" as without agency in their choices to join the radical organization.[4] In other words, gender-based critiques of ISIS/Daesh are widespread, and gender-based critiques of the simplicity of those critiques are also common. Yet a Google search for "gender hierarchy" and "jihadi brides" turns up four results of two unique blog posts.[5] In the scholarly literature as in the news media, the membership, operation, foreign relations, and fighting forces of Daesh/ISIS are rarely talked about in terms of gender *hierarchy*, even though they are frequently talked about in terms of gender.

---

[1] Bolton 2015.   [2] Richardson 2015.
[3] Result of three separate Google News searches for March, April, and May of 2015.
[4] E.g., Aly 2015; Vinograd 2014.
[5] Search run May 23, 2015. A search for "gender hierarchy" and "Daesh" found less than ten results, with seven unique sites. Replacing "Daesh" with "Islamic State of Iraq and the Levant" still finds fewer than ten results; using "Islamic State of Iraq and Syria" finds twenty-eight results. All but one of these results refers to gender hierarchy *within* the organization.

This chapter explores the utility of the terminology of "gender hierarchy" for thinking about Daesh/ISIS in Iraq and Syria while using that situation as an example to demonstrate the different ways in which it is important to use gender lenses to study hierarchy in global politics. The central contention of this chapter is that gender is implicated in and implicates all hierarchies in global politics. To substantiate this claim, the chapter explores three key relationships between gender and hierarchy in global politics. First, it explores gender hierarchies that explicitly order actors on the basis of associations with sex and gender, which *are* hierarchies. Second, it engages hierarchies *as gendered* that deploy associations with sex and gender to signify organization of actors along other distinctions, including, but not limited to, race, class, religion, culture, and nationality. Third, it investigates hierarchies in global politics as gendered institutions.

In deploying the typologies of gender hierarchies, hierarchies as gendered, and hierarchies as gendered institutions, this chapter looks to make the argument that a deep structure of gender stratification manifests and is manifest in other kinds of hierarchical systems in global politics. In so doing, it uses a broad, structural understanding of hierarchy[6] to explore gender as a foundation for hierarchies in global politics, which are, through gendered power, productive of both outcomes and significations in the global political arena. This chapter looks to make this contribution through explicative sections dealing with gender hierarchies, hierarchies as gendered, and hierarchies as gendered institutions, concluding with an exploration of what a feminist approach to hierarchy in global politics might look like.

Gender Hierarchies

In some ways it is easy to understand that gender hierarchies exist in global politics. Violence against women causes more death and injury to women worldwide than war, cancer, malaria, and traffic accidents. It is estimated that one in three women worldwide have been beaten, forced or coerced into sex, or otherwise physically or sexually abused. Globally, women make up less than 20 percent of all parliamentarians, and parliaments are the branch of government in which women's representation is the strongest. Less than 4 percent of development aid globally is allocated to gender equality, as well as less than 8 percent of postconflict needs assessment and reconstruction budgets. Maternal mortality rates, despite being largely preventable, remain high, where a woman dies every minute

[6] See the Introduction.

from childbirth. More than 10 million more girls fail to get a high school education compared with school-aged boys, and 41 million girls world-wide *right now* are being denied a primary education. Women are nearly two-thirds of the people in the world who cannot read. Women produce more than three-quarters of the food in many countries but are more likely than men to be hungry or malnourished. Many women in the world still do not have the right to own land.

Most workplaces in the world are sex unequal. Almost everywhere in the world there is both a general wage gap for women and a "glass ceiling" at the top of the professional world. Women are traditionally associated with particular types of work, which causes that work to be paid less well (whoever does it) and women to be paid less well (whatever sorts of work they do). In many places around the world, women have limited mobility – in some places, women are not allowed to drive cars or ride bicycles on public roads. Everywhere in the world, poverty is feminized – most of the very poor people in the world are women, and while women do a strong majority of the world's work, they have less than 10 percent of its income and own less than 1 percent of its means of production. Women have a number of difficulties accessing healthcare both generally and as compared with their male counterparts. In many places in the world, women do not have the freedom to marry or divorce of their own choosing.

Every single one of these sex-based gaps exists somewhere in the world, and most of them exist most places in the world. While places that consider themselves gender liberal often measure better along a number of these indicators than places that retain restrictive policies about the things women are allowed to do, I repeat from earlier, in no place in the world are women held equal to men politically, economically, socially, or culturally. Still, on face, this is sex inequality rather than gender inequality and sweeping but not necessarily structural. Asking why all these things are true of women, however, demonstrates the link between institutions of sex inequality and structural gender hierarchy.

Women are not disadvantaged to men in almost all areas of social and political life because of something inherent about women that makes them different from, or less capable than, men. Instead, women are disadvantaged to men because women are associated with femininity and because femininity is devalued politically, socially, and economic-ally – globally. When women are paid less in the workplace, it is because they are associated with feminized labor, which is understood to be both procurable for less money and potentially free. When women are denied access to education, it is because it is assumed that women are either less capable in the classroom than men are or are destined for a division of labor in life for which their education is not required. When women are raped in war and conflict, it is because there is a particular expression of gendered power (over both the women and the men who are charged with their protection) that a belligerent is engaging in that manifests itself in gender-based violence. In other words, women are not necessarily feminine and men are not necessarily masculine, but the association of women with femininity (and men with masculinity) and the concurrent valorization of masculinity and devalorization of femininity means that women are structurally disadvantaged to men in almost every area of the practice of (local and) global politics.

Association with masculinity and association with femininity differently situates people in global politics, but feminists have also suggested that it differently situates groups, states, organizations, and other actors in global politics. In fact, they have associated various interstate processes, such as trade patterns, manifestations of nationalism, military interactions, and the like, with gendered interactions and gendered posturing. In other words, traits traditionally associated with masculinity – such as strength, autonomy, rationality, competitiveness, bravery, aggression, provision of protection, sexuality, and dominance – remain associated with masculinity when they are associated with leaders, with military commanders, with companies, and even with states in the international arena. Traits associated with femininity – such as passivity, dependence, emotionality, weakness, timidity, cooperation, need for protection, chastity, and submission – remain associated with femininity when they are associated with leaders, with military commanders, with companies, and even with states in the international arena. Both behaviors that exhibit traits associated with masculinities and the actors that engage in those behaviors are valorized, whereas both behaviors that exhibit traits associated with femininities and the actors that engage in those behaviors are devalued.

In other words, I am arguing that gender hierarchies in global politics are reflective of gender *as a hierarchical structure* in global politics. Decades of research on gender hierarchies in global politics have drawn attention to "the political nature of gender as a system of difference construction and hierarchical dichotomy production that constitutes virtually all contemporary societies."[7] In so doing, feminist work has suggested that gender is both *a principle used to order* global politics and *a principle that orders* global politics, mapping onto hierarchies of associations with sexes and genders.

In this understanding, gender is the social expectation that people associated with biologic sex categories will have certain characteristics –

---

[7] Runyan and Peterson 2013, 6.

that people understood to be women will have traits associated with femininities and people understood to be men will have traits associated with masculinities. The social construction of gender is complex because gendering is not static or universal in its *content* but is always present *ontologically*. Genderings, while diverse, "constitute a shared cognition and consensus essential in shaping our ideas and relationships, even when we are unaware of their role in our thoughts, behaviours, and actions."[8] In this way, genders are inscribed and lived in people's daily lives and in processes among individuals, states, and other actors in the international system. These inscribed genders are not only inscribed differences but inscribed inequalities, where the perceived differences between those people, states, and other actors understood as masculine and those understood as feminine create a self-reinforcing inequality of power between the (valorized) masculine and the (subordinate) feminine. Gender, then, is a socially constructed power differential between persons based on their perceived membership in sex categories and/or their perceived relationship with masculine/feminine characteristics and categories. This use of the word "gender" is as "a noun, a verb, and a logic that is product/productive of performances of violences and security."[9]

It is the logic of gender that, in my view, suggests that gender can be characterized both *as a hierarchy* in global politics and as productive of a wide variety of gender hierarchies across global politics. When I suggest that gender *is* a hierarchy, then I am understanding hierarchy broadly as distributive of position in global social and political life. This approach sees gender as an ordering principle that sorts the relative and absolute positions of actors in the global political arena. Associations with masculinities and femininities influence relative and absolute position.[10] Gender hierarchy's distribution of position, however, I argue, is endogenous to the performative nature of gender hierarchy in global politics. In other words, gender not only *is a hierarchy* but also is a structural ordering principle of global politics. In this view, gender *as a hierarchy* produces gender hierarchies in global politics, from the individual level to the international level. As discussed earlier, the argument that gender hierarchy exists on the individual level in global politics is relatively uncontroversial – most, if not all, scholars would accept the premise that women are held unequal to men in many places in global politics and that those inequalities are power laden.

The argument that gender as a hierarchy manifests in structural gender hierarchy in global politics, which produces those individual-level gender hierarchies, however, is both more controversial and less frequently made

[8] Sjoberg 2013.   [9] Shepherd 2008.   [10] See Sjoberg 2012.

explicit. Still, I contend that it is important to see the international system as *ordered gender hierarchically*. Acker has argued that labeling an organization or structure gendered "means that advantage and disadvantage, exploitation and control, action and emotion, meaning and identity, are patterned through an in terms of a distinction between male and female, masculine and feminine."[11] Combining Waltz's understanding of international structure[12] with Acker's understanding of gendered organizations,[13] in previous work I have made the argument that gender hierarchy is a structural feature of global politics. I suggested that the international system is a gender hierarchy, meaning that states' identities have gendered components, states' positions and power distributions are distributed on the basis of associations with masculinities and femininities, and interstate interaction is premised on gender hierarchy between states.[14]

My argument is that state identities have gender components built on feminist research on the gendered dimensions of nationalisms, which rely on women as biologic and cultural reproducers of states while building states' reputations on their abilities to protect and defend their feminized others.[15] I argue that these gender dynamics are reflected in unit capability distribution as well. By "distribution of capabilities," Waltz means the organization of states or "units," positionally, in relation to each other, on the basis of their relative power.[16] State relative power relies on gender-based traits and perceptions among states, relying on feminist research that has provided evidence of states' associating gender identities and relative positions among states.[17] If gender plays a role in relative position among states, I argued that it also plays a role in how states relate. This work, together and parsed with Acker's theoretical framework, demonstrates that gender hierarchy is a structural feature of global politics in the Waltzian sense – an argument that means that one cannot assess system-, state-, or substate-level interactions accurately without taking account of the structural nature of gender hierarchy in global politics. These gender hierarchies vary in type, size, and scope but have the similarity that they are based on (perceived or actual) associations with masculinities and femininities.

For example, one can see a number of gender hierarchies at work in the operation of, news coverage of, and opposition to ISIS/Daesh. First, much like almost everywhere else in the world, there is evidence that women are held unequal to men in a variety of ways under the rule of ISIS/ Daesh. Second, though, while the axis of hierarchy (sex and gender) is the

---

[11] *Ibid.*   [12] Waltz 1979.   [13] Acker 1990.   [14] Sjoberg 2012, 2013.
[15] Pettman 1996; Tickner 1992; Niva 1998.   [16] Waltz 1985, 93.
[17] E.g., Banerjee 2012; Weber 1999.

same in this situation as it is elsewhere in the world, the particular dimensions of the hierarchy differ. In other words, the current ISIS/ Daesh situation is a manifestation of gender hierarchy in global politics, but the specific gender hierarchies involved are context unique.

There is no debate that there is significant oppression of women by Daesh/ISIS. A *Haaretz* report presents details of a sexual slavery market.[18] *Newsweek* reports that the organization published a pamphlet on how to treat female slaves, including permission to rape and beat and punish them for attempts to escape.[19] *The Independent* describes a case where a woman was "burned alive because she refused to perform an extreme sex act."[20] In addition to the reports of the mistreatment and torture of captive women, there are a number of reports of sex-specific killings.[21] From available reports, much of this torture and killing is directed at women perceived to be opposed to Daesh/ISIS and/or perceived to be members of religious, ethnic, or political groups to which the organization is opposed; in other words, a significant amount of the abuse seems to be directed toward women understood to be enemies. That said, a number of human rights advocacy groups and media outlets have expressed concern, backed with enough first-hand testimonials to suggest some veracity, that women *within* the organization are also treated as secondary to, or less than, men.[22] In other words, there are a number of gender hierarchies *within* (sex-based treatment of "member" women) and *around* (sex-based treatment of "other" women) that are related to general gender hierarchies in global politics (in that they are gender-based hierarchies) but take context-specific shape.

The treatment of women in and by ISIS/Daesh, though, is not the only gender-based hierarchy around the organization. The discussions of the group's recruitment of women members show *not only* gendered recruitment strategies by ISIS/Daesh but also gendered understandings of agency, citizenship, and political capacity by onlookers to and opponents of the organization. For example, many of the stories depict the women and girls from the Western world who are joining ISIS/Daesh as hapless victims, attracted by the pedophilic tactics of the organization. This view organizes Western women and men along a gender hierarchy where women are seen as more susceptible to the lure of such tactics and therefore weaker links in the political chain. These significations also position Western masculinity (as protector) as superior to the masculinities in ISIS/Daesh, understood to be predatory. These gender hierarchies are based on the perceptions of women recruits *as women*, ISIS/Daesh leaders

---

[18] Bar'al 2015.   [19] Smith 2014.   [20] Tharoor 2015.   [21] E.g., Pickles 2015.
[22] Shubert and Naik 2014; Abdul-Alim 2015.

as men, and Western political leaders as men/masculine. In other words, there are gender hierarchies in the global political *relations of* and *readings of* ISIS/Daesh and those actors with which they interact in international politics.

The gender hierarchies between ISIS/Daesh and other actors in the global political arena, as well as other gender hierarchies *among states and other international actors*, are gender hierarchies in the meaning discussed earlier – they are organized at least in part on perceived associations with certain traits identified as masculine or feminine. But, as I will discuss below, they are also *gendered* hierarchies – hierarchies that involve, or are even founded on, differences other than perceived associations with sexes or gender but are still articulated, reified, and enforced by the production and repetition of those associations.

Gender*ed* Hierarchies

The main contention of this chapter is that limiting the contribution of gender theorizing to understanding inequality between genders in global politics would be both a theoretical and empirical mistake. This is so because gender hierarchy is only one of the three sorts of hierarchy that feminist research reveals in global politics. The second sort is the ways in which hierarchies in global politics are gendered. If gender hierarchy is hierarchy ordered fully or mainly by associations with gender (where things that are seen as masculine are held above things that are seen as feminine), seeing hierarchies in global politics as gendered is recognizing that hierarchy structured by another principle of differentiation (be it race, religion, class, nationality, or something else) is often nonetheless framed in gender terms and enacted at least in part through gender-associated valorizations and devalorizations.

This understanding builds on Peterson's understanding of feminization as devalorization. Peterson suggests that "not only subjects like women and marginalized men can be feminized, but also concepts, desires, tastes, styles, and ways of knowing ... [this feminization has] the effect of reducing the legitimacy, status, and value [of the feminized object]. Importantly [in Peterson's terms] this devalorisation is simultaneously ideological *and* material – that is discursive, cultural, structural, and economic. It normalizes the marginalization, subordination, and exploitation of feminized practices and persons ... which comes to be a taken-for-granted 'given' of social life."[23] In these terms, the process of devalorizing people *by* feminizing them can happen to people who are

---

[23] Peterson 2010.

neither women nor traditionally associated with femininity. MacKinnon has observed that feminization can happen to anyone – it is just to women that it seems natural. But what is the applicability of the understanding that feminization happens to others in global politics? As I suggested briefly earlier, it is the ability to see and understand the ways in which many hierarchies in global politics are gendered.

In these terms, feminization takes place across hierarchies, where the dominant actor or actors use feminization as a "strategy of power." Feminist work[24] has identified three sorts of power in the political arena: power-over (the power to enforce an actor's will on another actor), power-to (power to resist power-over), and power-with (the power that weak actors can have when they act in concert). Most hierarchies in global politics are instantiated by and sustained by the use of power-over: the power to coerce another actor into bending to the dominant actors' will. This coercive power can be *instituted* (i.e., coercive force can be used) or threatened (i.e., the threat of coercive force combined with a mutual understanding of the result that would happen if that force was used). Strategies of the use of power-over (whether instituted or threatened) often involve causing and enforcing fear.[25] For this reason, feminists interested in the stratification of the international arena have urged scholars to take *gendered power* seriously.[26]

It is the argument of this section that it would behoove scholars of hierarchy in global politics to take gendered power seriously, particularly how feminization can be deployed to push people and/or other actors down in interstate, interrace, interreligion, interclass, internationality, or other relations structured hierarchically. Valorization or honor of masculine traits and values, or devalorization or dishonor of feminine traits and values often serves to as signification, highlighting positions of either dominance or subordination along hierarchies that do not look like they have anything to do with gender. The process of the use of feminization *to wield* power-over and *to assert* dominance is a gendered process at work as hierarchies in global politics work.

Gendered hierarchy wields gender words, gender values, and gendered put-downs to enact subordination on those on the lower side of many hierarchies. In these gendered discourses, those associated with femininity are constituted as weak, violable, docile, silenced, and humiliated.[27] This association of those "low" on hierarchies with traits associated with femininity happens in class hierarchies, in race hierarchies, and in

[24] E.g., Allen 2000.   [25] Young 2003; Pain and Smith 2012; Pain 2014, 2015.
[26] E.g., Enloe 1990; True and Mintrom 2001; Kirby 2013; Stachowitsch 2012.
[27] Hawkesworth 2003.

hierarchies of national identities. Hawkesworth suggests that this is also a constitutive feature of hierarchies in colonial and post-colonial interstate relationships, where the (former) colonized is feminized.[28] Feminization, then, is a mechanism of gendered power used to subordinate enemies, firm up hierarchies, and communicate messages of dominance and superiority.

This is not to make the argument that hierarchies in the international arena are reducible to gender hierarchy. But it is an argument that the nature and constitution of many particular hierarchies in the international arena can be read as gendered. *Gendered* hierarchies use gender-based mechanisms in the creation and enforcement of relationships of dominance and subordination, including gendered power, masculinization, and feminization. Those mechanisms can be seen in a wide variety of hierarchies that are primarily across other axes of dominance and subordination.

Seeing gendering as a part of the instantiation of hierarchies can be theoretically useful – it can add a more complex understanding of what hierarchies in the international arena are and how they function. But it can also be practically useful – it can help explain a wide variety of sex and gender elements of "other" hierarchies. There are a plethora of examples in the global political arena where gender subordination is used *within* hierarchical relationship *as an expression of subordination of the enemy*. Expressions of gender subordination of the enemy include gendered conflict sexual violence, gendered unemployment patterns during exonomic crises, and gendered enforcement of social, religious, or even state law. These are, of course, a few simple examples of many complex ones – but they provide insight into the potential explanatory value of understanding a gender dimension to hierarchies in global politics. In this way, global political hierarchies can be understood as gendered processes, produced and then also producing associations between perceived sex/gender and relative capability, relative position, and relative power.

Moving from the abstract to the concrete, then, it is possible to see the gendering of hierarchies around ISIS/Daesh that are not primarily about maleness and femaleness. In ISIS/Daesh, and in the organization's relationships with other organizations, states, and superstate actors in global politics, there are gender hierarchies – the hierarchies discussed earlier, where people's relative positions (and sometimes even identities) are drawn explicitly and primarily on (perceived or actual) sex- and/or gender-based characteristics. Still, talking about those gender-based

---

[28] Hawkesworth 2006.

hierarchies only tells part of the story of the role of gender *in* hierarchies around ISIS/Daesh. Instead, there are a number of ways in which hierarchies *around* ISIS/Daesh that are primarily *about* other things (e.g., the terrorism/counterterrorism debate, territorial control, race, religion, nationality/nationalism, forms of government, and cultural value) are often talked about in sexed/gendered terms and enacted by masculinization and feminization. For example, a number of news stories about the mistreatment of women in ISIS/Daesh are *both* about the mistreatment of women and about the suggestion that the mistreatment of women is a signifier of inferiority. In other words, implicitly,[29] there is a standard by which civilized men treat "their" women, and failing to live up to that standard merits *both* emasculation *and* the general inferiority that such emasculation signals.

Another example is the enactment of sexual abuse by ISIS/Daesh and the reporting of that sexual abuse by media outlets.[30] Feminist scholars have studied the frequent occurrence of conflict sexual violence, both as a strategy and/or as a tactic, or when soldiers take it on themselves to engage in such violence.[31] Lene Hansen has explained[32] that strategic or tactical rape "works to install a disempowered masculinity as constitutive of the identities of the nation's men" through abusing its women. In these situations, rape "becomes a metaphor for national humiliation … as well as a tactic of war used to symbolically prove the superiority of one's national group."[33] In this way, "raping women is a symbolic attack on men's virility and their ability to protect their women, as well as a material attack on [the enemy]."[34] Because "women are seen as precious property of 'the enemy,'" conflict sexual violence is the communication of a message of dominance on, and through the use of, gendered bodies. In these dynamics, the rape victim, the men expected to protect her specifically, and the group of which she is a symbol are feminized both in terms of gender/sexuality and in terms of ethnic/religious/political identity.[35] In this view, sexual abuse as a strategy or tactic is both a direct act of abuse, disempowerment, and feminization to the victim of the abuse *and* an indirect strategy of dominating, and communicating domination to, an enemy.

The sexual abuse perpetrated by ISIS/Daesh seems to fit this logic. The majority of sexual abuse that ISIS/Daesh perpetrates seems to be against those whom they see as inferior and/or the enemy, particularly Iraq's Yazidi community.[36] Akbar suggests that Daesh/ISIS fighters (including women) see that defeating the enemy comes with "capturing

---

[29] And sometimes explicitly; see, e.g., Hudson et al. 2012.   [30] E.g., Akbar 2015.
[31] See the discussion in Sjoberg and Peet 2011.   [32] Hansen 2000, 60.
[33] Wilcox 2009, 233.   [34] Sjoberg 2013, 221.   [35] Skjaelsbaek 2001, 225.
[36] Akbar 2015; Dearden 2015.

their women, and enslaving their children."[37] ISIS/Daesh fighters speak with pride about their ability to violate women seen as belonging to the enemy – "I write this while the letters drip of pride … We have indeed raided and captured the kafirah women, and drove them like sheep by the edge of the sword."[38] If the message of ISIS/Daesh to its (female) victims of sexual abuse is defilement of their bodies and of their cultures, there is evidence that that message is being understood by those who are victims as well.[39] Deardon explains that women and girls who escape ISIS/Daesh receive a chilly reception after their escape, where "those managing to reach safety, mostly in Iraqi Kurdistan, face being ostracized by their community and even by their family because they have been raped."[40] This stigma comes from a notion that women who have been raped by the enemy are impure because they have had sex outside of marriage. The involuntariness of that sexual contact is not a mitigating factor; if anything, it makes the impurity worse because it is a reminder to the men who were charged with the women's protection of their inability to provide it.[41]

In these situations, acts of gendered sexual violence (and gendered statements about that sexual violence) are used to instantiate, enforce, and reify hierarchies between ISIS/Daesh and the local populations that they look to conquer or defeat. That is one layer of gendered hierarchies in the ISIS/Daesh context – the gendered hierarchies between the organization and its opponents and/or victims. Another group of hierarchies that are gendered are between ISIS/Daesh and its international opponents and/or detractors. Significant media coverage of the sexual abuse committed by ISIS/Daesh uses graphic descriptions of the gender subordination that the organization commits in order to condemn its values more broadly.[42] Characterizations of the organization as pedophiliac, as sexually brutal, and as "sexually extreme" are certainly popular in the media and policy circles because they are of concern in themselves. But they also are characterizations that are only possible *within* and as an expression of an extant condemnation if ISIS/Daesh as an organization. In other words, gender-based claims about the inferiority of ISIS/Daesh are *both* gender based in intent and a mechanism of the expression of a more general sense of the inferiority of the organization, its values, and its way of life.

ISIS/Daesh is not seen as lower on the international hierarchy than its critics largely or exclusively *because* of its abuse of women. That abuse is a *part* of the complaint that the organization's opponents have with it. But the disproportionate attention that it receives and the sensationalization

---

[37] Akbar 2015.   [38] *Ibid.*   [39] E.g., Dearden 2015.   [40] *Ibid.*
[41] See, e.g., Sjoberg and Peet 2011.   [42] See, e.g., Marcus 2014.

of it suggest that the function of that sexual violence is not fully characterized by understanding it as a part of the problem that ISIS/Daesh's
opponents have with it. Instead, I argue, it suggests that the repeated
discussion of the abusive nature of ISIS/Daesh masculinity as sexually
abusive is *both* an expression of an actual problem with the abuse *and*
a signification of the overall evil with which ISIS/Daesh is to be associated. The hierarchies between ISIS/Daesh and those who would condemn its actions, then, are not gender hierarchies per se but are gendered
in two ways: the understood inferiority of the organization and its members is in part based on sex/gender expectations and behaviors, and sexed/
gendered shortcomings are expressed, sensationalized, and used as general tools of derogation of the organization. These hierarchies, I suggest,
are much like many other hierarchies in the international arena: even
when they are not primarily or exclusively about sex/gender, they have
sexed/gendered elements and are often expressed, reified, enforced, or
instantiated in sex/gender terms. Such hierarchies are *gendered* whatever
axis they are primarily or mainly structured around.

Hierarchies in Global Politics as Gender*ed*

If hierarchies are often expressed, reified, enforced, or instantiated in
sexed/gendered terms, then it is appropriate to raise the question of
whether all hierarchies are gendered and all gender relations are hierarchical. This section answers both of those questions in the affirmative but
looks to understand the relationship between gender and hierarchy in
a more complicated way than equating gender and hierarchy, hierarchy
and gender. Rather, because gender is itself a hierarchical social relation
and hierarchies are themselves gendered, hierarchies are institutionalized
in the international arena in gendered ways. One way that hierarchies are
gendered is featured in the 'gendered hierarchies' section of this chapter –
that many hierarchies that are constructed around other stratifications are
represented in gendered terms. Put another way: most hierarchies
(including but not limited to those that are explicitly about women)
have gender *in* them.

Still, the argument that hierarchy in global politics is itself gendered is
not reducible to the places that gender can be found in most hierarchies.
Instead, I mean that hierarchy in global politics *works on gendered logics*.
In particular, I am arguing that gendered hierarchy in global politics is
a performed forcible and reiterative process of recognition, where gender
is signifier of position and signified in the process of positioning. To make
this argument, I model an account of the materiality of hierarchy on
Judith Butler's account of the materiality of the body – suggesting that

the performed reiteration and recognition of hierarchies in the international arena functions on gendered logics.[43] Butler's *Bodies that Matter* engages the question of the relationships between the significations of gender and the materiality of the sexed body – answering those who had challenged her assertion in *Gender Trouble* that gender is performative.[44] Then what of the body? Of its materiality? When asked whether or not the body *exists*, Butler shoots back that the body's existence is intricately linked to the power relations that construct it as what it is. In other words, Butler[45] suggests that the performativity of gender cannot be theorized apart from the forcible and reiterative process of regulatory sexual regimes. By "regulatory sexual regimes," Butler is referring to the circumscription of materiality through the substance of sexual hierarchy.

Bodies *exist*, Butler argues, but are readable through and only through the sexualized hierarchy in which they are performed. As she explains, "to invoke matter is to invoke a sedimented history of sexual hierarchy and sexual erasures."[46] Bodies are created in, and inscribed on, the gendered hierarchies that make them possible and comprehensible. In my reading, this is an argument that bodies do not exist without sex/gender, which does not exist without the bodies to read it onto. In other words, the very *foundation* of material existence (and hierarchy among materially existing people and/or things) is the performative reading of those material things – the reification of "the force of authority through the repetition or citation of a prior, authoritative set of practices."[47] In this sense, "it is no longer possible to take anatomy as a stable referent that is somehow valorised or signified through being subjected to an imaginary schema."[48] Instead, anatomy is *performed*, where "performativity cannot be understood outside of a process of iterability – a regularized and constrained repetition of norms."[49] Butler is interested in "how the criteria of intelligible sex operates to constitute a field of bodies."[50] In the case of bodies, "although the referent cannot be said to exist apart from the signified, it nevertheless cannot be reduced to it."[51]

This account of materiality has something to offer both for the constitution of hierarchies in global politics directly and as a logic for the production of hierarchies in global politics. For the constitution of hierarchies in global politics directly, I suggest that hierarchies' material manifestations are intrinsically linked to the power relations that construct hierarchies as what they are. In other words, hierarchies are, at their basis, a forcible and reiterative process of regulatory regimes. These regulatory regimes go beyond and complicate, but are built on, the

---

[43] Butler 1993.   [44] Butler 1990.   [45] Butler 1993, xxiii.   [46] *Ibid.*, 22.   [47] *Ibid.*, 172.
[48] *Ibid.*, 35.   [49] *Ibid.*, 60.   [50] *Ibid.*, 27.   [51] *Ibid.*, 38.

sexualized regulation of bodies in global politics. In other words, materialized hierarchies among people and states in global politics *exist*, but they do not exist and are not readable without "a specific modality of power as a discourse" – gendered power.[52] The foundation of *material difference* is in the force of authority through the repetition of authoritative practices. It is not that the utterance of hierarchy *makes it* but instead that the continued, repetitive, reified utterance of hierarchy *is* it.

In this view, thinking about the performance of authority, then, Butler means to equate materiality with "power in its formative or constituting effects" where "the boundary, forming, and deforming of sexed bodies is animated by a set of founding prohibitions, a set of enforced criteria of eligibility."[53] In other words, material hierarchies are constituted with/by power *as a formative force*. The formative effect of power is in the disciplining impact that it has – enforcing a criterion of eligibility to "count" as being worthy of recognition.[54] As such, material "superiority" and "inferiority" cannot be understood as stable referents signified through the imaginary schema of masculinities, femininities, or shame, honor, valorization, or devalorization.[55] Instead, the hierarchies and the discursive/symbolic politics around them are coconstituted, where their materiality is performed, iterated, regularized, and constrained. In this understanding, the discourses of gendered power that play a role in the construction of hierarchies and the gendered materiality of the bodies that are affected by and subjected to hierarchies are coconstituted.

Even if gender were not a key force in the direct production of hierarchies, as I claim, Butler's understanding can be understood to support a feminist understanding that hierarchies in global politics operate by logics that can be understood to be gendered. In previous work[56] I have asked the question of why dominance is preferable to parity for actors in global politics. In a very simple definitional sense, actors who engage in either formal or informal hierarchies are (implicitly or explicitly, consciously or unconsciously) rejecting parity. The realist story is that only superiority guarantees survival, but many, if not most, hierarchies in global politics are so far removed from questions of survival that an alternative logic must be in play as well. My suggestion is that an alternative logic would also account for the prioritization of power-over logics in global politics at the expense of power-with and power-to logics.

The story Butler tells about discourse as a modality of power can provide insight into these questions. A missing link in the account of the

---

[52] *Ibid.*, 139.   [53] *Ibid.*, 9, 27.
[54] See Butler's later work on grievability, e.g., Butler 2003.   [55] See, e.g., Steele 2008.
[56] Sjoberg 2013.

need for hierarchies – the need for dominance/subordination in global politics – is the valorization of a particular sort of masculinity in ideal-typical constructions of not only states but also their leaders. This sort of masculinity associates men's honor with the provision of protection to their (imagined or real) feminized others *and* with the ability to convince the enemy of their ability to provide such protection in the face of efforts to attack.[57] The dominance of this notion of masculinity instantiates gendered hierarchical logics not only among states, but also among families and other groups in the international arena.[58] This gendered logic does not only *shape* hierarchies, it incentivizes the creation of hierarchies – which makes it important to understand hierarchies as gendered political institutions.

The stakes of this discussion may seem semantic until it is brought into focus by engagement with other analyses of hierarchy. Seeing hierarchies in global politics as gendered would prompt the asking of the question: how do hierarchies rely on gendered logics? For example, Chapter 3 tells a detailed and painstaking history of hierarchy in global politics and the political theory of that hierarchy *as paternalism* with little acknowledgment of the gendered nature of the concept and operation of paternalism. Paternalism is named such derived from the gendered word for "father" – it is *paternal* not *maternal*, and, despite Barnett's claims to the contrary, *maternalism* would, in discourse and in practice, signify a very different sort of relationship between and among states. In popular discourses, fatherhood is seen as an aloof, guiding-by-example, no-room-for-error sort of leadership that comes with the assumptions that masculinity is independent, strong, and regimented. Motherhood is seen as an engaged, guiding-by-interaction, forgiving sort of leadership that comes with assumptions about femininity as caring, interdependent, and emotional. While these are oversimplifications, and comparisons that may vary across time, space, and culture, the basic *differentiation* of gendered logics of masculinities and femininities holds. *Paternalistic* hierarchies are different than *maternalistic* ones; these differences derive from and are inseparable from the sexed and gendered logics that permeate *both* understandings of hierarchy.

Seeing hierarchy as gendered has much more abstract, and much more far-reaching, implications for the current situation of ISIS/Daesh in Iraq and Syria. Feminist work in International Relations (IR) so far has suggested that gendered logics and gendered power are a condition of possibility of the existence of and competition among states. I suggest here that they are also a key component of the existence of hierarchy and the

[57] See, e.g., Peterson 1977; Young 2003.   [58] See, e.g., Peterson 1992, 2010.

function of hierarchy in global politics. In this view, the gender subordination in ISIS/Daesh and the gendered condemnation of it by the organization's Western opponents are not just gender-based hierarchies and gendered expressions of other claims to superiority (though they are both). They are constituted by a gendered logic of social hierarchy and performed through the wielding of gendered power. As such, it is not only the axis of measurement and the logic of enforcement of these hierarchies that are gendered. It is also the very constitution of their subjects and objects and their organizations.

In other words, it is not just that ISIS/Daesh both has and is situated in gender hierarchies and hierarchies based on other differentiations that are expressed through feminization, it is that the hierarchies around ISIS/Daesh function on gendered logics of recognition, subordination, and valorization. Seeing this might help us to understand the layers of signification that go into the adversarial relationship between actors who otherwise might not be involved in the conflict in Iraq/Syria and ISIS/Daesh and its messaging to attract the support and participation of people in societies that perceive themselves to be opponents and/or above ISIS/Daesh. At the same time, the denaturalization of this hierarchical relationship (or others) is not necessarily an answer to the problem of its practice/performance. As Butler suggests, that denaturalization "does not imply a liberation from hegemonic consent" because denaturalization can augment the hegemony of dominant ideas by reifying their ideal-state even in the suggestion that they are "unnatural." In other words, it would be the wrong message to take away from this analysis that these hierarchies, or others, in global politics "do not have to be" and therefore can be deconstructed.

Instead, the realization that hierarchies in global politics function by gendered logics might allow for a rearticulation – "the question of subversion, of working the weakness in the norm, becomes a matter of inhabiting the practices of rearticulation."[59] The conclusion that ISIS/Daesh could/should be rearticulated, that the hierarchies in and around the organization could/should be rearticulated, and that the racial, cultural, religious, national, and interstate hierarchies that are directly and indirectly related to those relationships could/should be rearticulated is, in my view, the easy part of this sort of analysis. The hard part is finding the theoretical, ethical, and everyday political foundations on which to base such a rearticulation. This sort of rearticulation, though, will not end hierarchy generally or the hierarchies surrounding ISIS/Daesh specifically. And it is not a magic answer to the conflict, the brutality, or the

---

[59] *Ibid.*, 181.

human rights problems. But it might allow for a disruption of the flow of the gendered logics, gendered instantiations, and gendered structures that characterize hierarchy and hierarchies in global politics.

A Feminist Approach to Hierarchy

As this chapter has argued, there are three ways to see a relationship between gender and hierarchy in the international arena. The first is to see some hierarchies in global politics that are organized around gender – gender hierarchies. The second is to see other hierarchies in global politics that are organized around some other factor, but are either expressed in gendered language or enforced with gendered tactics – gendered hierarchies. The third is to see hierarchy in global politics as itself always and everywhere gendered – gendered hierarchy. Looking at these through gender lenses can provide a value added to understanding what hierarchy is and how it works in global politics.

Seeing these relationships, of course, is only possible with a broad view of hierarchy as vertical relations, unbounded by direct legal authority. While these understandings of the structure and function of hierarchy *apply to* formal institutions, they are *themselves* informal institutions, where gendered discourses and gendered power are coconstitutive of the materiality of hierarchies in global politics. In this sense, it matters to use the language and theoretical construct of hierarchy rather than some other expression of inequality *both* in defining gender and in understanding global politics for two main reasons. First, the language of hierarchy makes it possible to see gender *as* hierarchy, gender hierarchies, gendered hierarchies, and gendered hierarchy as interrelated instantiations of gendered power. Second, the use of the language of hierarchy helps to combat the fundamental assumption that, in a *formal* anarchy, there is no disciplinary authority and therefore no hierarchy. Instead, the gender analysis in this chapter has suggested that *formal* anarchy is *structured* by *informal disciplinary power* – gendered disciplinary power, among other forms – the totalizing impact of which can only be fully understood when it is named as anarchy's *opposite* within it – hierarchy.

5   Against Authority
The Heavy Weight of International Hierarchy

*Vincent Pouliot**

The growing body of research on international hierarchy is remarkably vibrant. A lot of its strength has to do with the intellectual diversity of its participants, which – to use theoretical pigeonholes – include realists,[1] institutionalists,[2] English School scholars,[3] constructivists,[4] critical theorists,[5] and eclectic scholars.[6] Today we find ourselves with not only a rich variety of contending perspectives but also a relatively broad analytical scope in terms of the many forms that hierarchy may take at the global level, from hegemony to the post-colony through normative stratification, special responsibilities, international pecking orders, and several others. By fostering cross-theoretical dialogue, this book contributes to the development of this promising pluralist research program in International Relations (IR).

In order to engage meaningfully, however, scholars must be able to specify not only where they agree with one another – that hierarchy matters, for a start – but also the key points of contention among them. In this chapter I focus on one major area of disagreement in the existing literature: the relationship between hierarchy and authority. In the two dominant IR approaches, it is either contracts (agreed upon through rational calculations) or compacts (hinging on normative approval) that explain international hierarchy.[7] The connection with authority is critical

---

* For useful comments on earlier versions of this chapter, I am thankful to fellow contributors to this book, especially Michael Barnett, Jack Donnelly, David Lake, Janice Bially Mattern, Jason Sharman, and Ayşe Zarakol. Parts of this chapter borrow from Pouliot 2016a.
[1] Gilpin 1981; Krasner 1999; Wohlforth 2009; Stone 2011.
[2] Lake 1996; Weber 1999; Cooley 2005; Ikenberry 2012.
[3] Clark 1989; Dunne 2003; Hurrell 2007; Keene 2013.
[4] Rumelili 2003; Suzuki 2005; Hurd 2007; Zarakol 2011; Barnett 2012; Bukovansky et al. 2012; Towns 2012; Sharman 2013.
[5] Enloe 2000; Doty 1996; Barkawi and Laffey 2006. The complete list here would be very long because critical theory, whose key objective is to unmask power relations, has hierarchy built into its core analytical interests.
[6] Donnelly 2006, 2009, 2012a, 2012b; Kang 2004, 2010a; Nexon and Wright 2007.
[7] Both of these approaches belong to what Zarakol calls the "narrow conception of hierarchy"; see the Introduction.

in both cases: contracts generate delegated authority, whereas compacts produce normative authority. I argue that the narrow understanding of equating hierarchy with consent-based authority produces too light a notion of hierarchy. For one thing, it flies in the face of the empirical record: if hierarchy could be upset through renewed calculations (given a changing structure of power, say) or through the withdrawal of consent (in the event of normative contestation), then should we not see much more upheaval – at least instability – in vertically differentiated systems than what history actually shows? What is more, given that for several IR scholars authority hinges on consent, is the authority-based notion of international hierarchy not at risk of misrepresenting the subaltern experience of social stratification?

We thus find ourselves in need of a different kind of social-theoretical micro-foundation – one that can account for the resilience of hierarchy, on the one hand, without presuming acceptance or choice on the part of subordinates, on the other. This alternative I find in the notion of embodiment, which I draw from Bourdieu's political sociology as well as Goffman's social dramaturgy. To Zarakol's first guiding question – "What is the nature of hierarchy?"[8] – I provide the following answer: hierarchy is made of an embodied relationship to international practice that makes social stratification a seemingly immanent feature of the world. The key insight is a rather simple one: instead of agents pre-existing hierarchy (and "embarking" on it, so to speak), hierarchy generally predates agents and thus produces constitutive effects on them. To put it in different terms, people are born in, and with, multiple hierarchies. Most of the time there are no (apparent) ways around them; social stratification simply is the order of things. From this perspective, social stratification lies within ourselves, in the form of what Goffman calls the "sense of place." In the second section of this chapter I briefly illustrate how this plays out in the realm of multilateral diplomacy. Stripped of any reference to consent-based authority, hierarchy becomes heavier as a social system of vertical differentiation. As contested as its organizing principles may sometimes be, I conclude, in general social stratification is much harder to shed than what the existing IR literature often suggests.

"Hierarchy-Lite": Problems with Consent-Based Authority

Most scholars who conceive of hierarchy as authority fall in one of two camps. First, authority (and by implication hierarchy) may be *delegated*;

---

[8] See the Introduction.

this is the contract view. Second, authority (qua hierarchy) may be *norma-tive* – what I call the social compact view. In this section I argue that what these two accounts have in common is not only an authority-based notion of hierarchy but also a similar conception of authority as *consent based*, that is to say, as involving some form of choice or approval on the part of actors (both dominant and subordinate). It is important to note that at the definitional level, there is no necessary connection between authority (i.e., rightful rule) and consent. It is quite possible to have effective authority short of explicit agreement, such as when we follow laws promulgated by people for whom we did not vote. Rightful rule need not reflect (let alone arise from) consent.[9] Yet, key figures in IR, from both the contract and compact views on hierarchy, seem to espouse a decisionist view of authority. By critically reviewing a few landmark works, I want to suggest that such a conceptualization produces too weak a notion of hierarchy. It often seems as though hierarchy may be relatively easily overturned as a new set of structural incentives comes about (prompting revised calculations) or when its legitimacy becomes contested to the point of withdrawing consent. By contrast, the empirical record and the view from below rather suggest that hierarchy is generally enduring – and rather difficult to overturn.

The Contract View

The contract theory of international hierarchy is most associated with Lake's influential work. Lake conceives of hierarchy in terms of dyadic relationships of authority. In tune with institutional economics, he equates hierarchy with a contract. One of the great benefits of this con-ceptualization is to bring to the fore the relational dimension of hierarchy: "Obedience springs not from A's assertions," notes Lake. "Rather, A's ability to expect compliance derives from B's conferral of the right to rule."[10] Cooley's "logics of hierarchy," also inspired from firm theory, similarly posit this contractual explanation in order to explain distinct forms of hierarchy in world politics.[11]

In Lake's scheme of things, the micro-mechanism of hierarchy is rational interest. The assumption is that repeated cost-benefit calculations by parties to the contract explain their continued adherence over time: "[b]oth dominant and subordinate states have to be better off in hierarchic than in strictly anarchic relations for the contract to be fulfilled."[12] Rational calculations operate at two particular points in the establishment and

---

[9] Thanks to Jack Donnelly for helping me formulate this point.
[10] Lake 2009, 20. See also Chapter 1.   [11] Cooley 2005. See also Chapter 7.
[12] Lake 2009, 93.

sustenance of hierarchy. First, the mechanism sets in at the moment of entering the contract: "the decision of one state to subordinate itself to another is a profound act."[13] Second, calculations are then continually made, as structural incentives change and parties decide whether to keep on acting under the contractual parameters: "[i]n an authority relationship, individuals *choose* whether to comply with a ruler's command."[14]

Ikenberry relies on similar contract logic, even though his own brand of institutionalism is more historical than purely rational. In his 2001 book, Ikenberry contends that international orders rest on a kind of deal between dominant and subordinate states: the former agrees to curb its use of power in order to obtain from the latter participation to, and compliance with, the institutions it sets up to its own benefit.[15] As he further elaborates in *Liberal Leviathan*, "[i]nternational order takes the shape of a hierarchy. Superordinate and subordinate relations are established between the leading state and weaker and secondary political entities that are arrayed around it."[16] To an extent, the same kind of deal between the strong and the weak occurs in Stone's (realist) understanding of "informal governance": "[t]he puzzle for a power-politics interpretation of international institutions is explaining why weak states *consent* to participate. Why should weak states participate in an arrangement skewed towards the interests of the strong, and why should secondary powers tolerate an arrangement that disproportionately favors the leader of the system?"[17] His answer clearly follows contractualist logic: "[i]nformal governance rests on an implicit contract: the leading state will participate if it is allowed to exert informal influence, and the member countries consent to grant informal influence if it is not absurd."[18]

Various criticisms have been raised at the contract notion of hierarchy, but here I focus on what I think is the most important one: its excessive voluntarism. Lake and consorts exaggerate the room for choice in hierarchy. Indeed, the contract view seems to presume that the terms of a hierarchical relationship are always at stake and up for grabs (in theory at least). As soon as environmental conditions change, prompting a new structure of incentives, rational parties may opt out of the contract should costs outweigh benefits. In Sharman's apt critique, "if parties are free to bargain, transact or break off negotiations as best suits their individual interests, this suggests a 'horizontal' market interaction on the basis of formally equal parties, rather than one premised on super- and subordination."[19] By consequence, the space for agency, especially on the

---

[13] *Ibid.*, x.   [14] *Ibid.*, 18 (emphasis added).   [15] Ikenberry 2000.
[16] Ikenberry 2012, 55.   [17] Stone 2011, 16 (emphasis added).   [18] *Ibid.*, 41.
[19] Sharman 2013, 190. See also Chapter 7.

subordinates' part, is blown out of proportion: "contractualist accounts in IR confuse the distinction between markets and hierarchies in explicitly assuming that subordinate actors can always walk away."[20] Sharman's point is certainly on target, yet, as I show in the next section, the power of his critique is somewhat blunted by the fact that the alternative framework, based on legitimacy, also relies on forms of approval.

The Social Compact View

Several scholars coming from the constructivist and English School perspectives espouse a notion of hierarchy as social compact. To begin with the latter, Hurrell is concerned with the normative acceptability of the contemporary international order, including the inequalities that pervade it.[21] For his part, Clark conceives of hegemony as one of the fundamental institutions of international society, rooted in notions of social legitimacy.[22] Closer to constructivism, Bukovansky and her colleagues theorize "special responsibilities," which describe a set of hierarchical practices, as resting on a compact between great powers and others: special rights in exchange for special duties. The specific terms of this compact are infused with historically contingent legitimacy battles and normative principles. Finally, Phillips criticizes purely constructivist accounts and insists that international order rests on a combination of coercive force and social purpose.[23] Where rationalists à la Lake see cost-benefit calculations in the making of international hierarchy, then, constructivists observe a politics of legitimacy.

Problematically, however, a number of scholars who conceive of legitimacy as the basis of authority fall back on similar logic of agreement as their rationalist peers. One may imagine a continuum of approbation here, ranging from consent to recognition. At one extreme, Goh argues that "hierarchical relations depend upon the *consent* of the subordinates."[24] Accordingly, her study of East Asian hierarchy focuses on "the processes by which *agreements* about the particular social compact that determines the nature and mechanisms of international order are forged discursively and normatively."[25] Hurd's study of the Security Council's authority (as a form of international hierarchy) would seem to subscribe to a similarly decisionist account of authority. As he puts it, "[w]hen an actor believes a rule is legitimate, the *decision* whether to comply is no longer motivated by the simple fear of retribution or by

---

[20] Sharman 2013, 197.   [21] Hurrell 2007. See also Keene 2013; and Chapter 12.
[22] Clark 2011.   [23] Phillips 2011. See also Chapter 3.
[24] Goh 2013, 216 (emphasis added).   [25] *Ibid.*, 10–11 (emphasis added).

a calculation of self-interest but, instead, by an internal sense of rightness and obligation."[26] At the other end of the spectrum, Hobson and Sharman put the matter in terms of recognition: "[h]ierarchical authority means ... that some are entitled to command and some are required to obey, and that both sides *recognize* as legitimate the social logic of this unequal situation."[27] But even such recognition, as a thinner form of approval, still requires some acknowledgment on the part of actors. This stands in contrast with Bourdieu's notion of authority, for instance, which rests on "misrecognition" and seeks to evacuate reflexive agency from the equation (more on this below).[28]

To variable degrees, then, several adherents of the social compact view also equate hierarchy narrowly with a form of agreed-upon authority. This point takes us back to the relational argument advanced by Lake. Recall that the basic conceptual difference between coercion (or brute domination) and consent-based authority is that the latter implies some kind of choice (beyond strict subjection) on the part of subordinates, whether through cost-benefit calculations (contract) or social agreements (compact). By putting authority (and more specifically consent) in the driver's seat of hierarchy, the contract and compact views generate a concept that is too light and voluntaristic. Is hierarchy really something that people bargain or even deliberate over? Students of international hierarchy appear at serious risk of being "paternalistic" (in Barnett's sense[29]) by presuming consent where there is none to be obtained.

Beyond Authority I

In the preceding renditions, international hierarchy hinges on consent-based authority, obtained either through rationally agreed delegation or normative legitimation. In fact, even realists have an authority-centric understanding of what hierarchy consists of. Per Krasner, for instance, "Westphalian sovereignty has never been taken for granted. The exercise of informal authority has been pervasive in the international system."[30] Arguably, the reason why the IR literature overwhelmingly defines hierarchy in terms of authority has to do with the way in which Waltz defined anarchy in his defining book, which he conceived of as the lack of a central authority.[31] By mirror logic, hierarchy is taken to mean the presence of authority.

[26] Hurd 2007, 30 (emphasis added).
[27] Hobson and Sharman 2005, 69 (emphasis in original).   [28] See Bourdieu 2001.
[29] Barnett 2012. See also Chapter 4.   [30] Krasner 1999, 50.   [31] Waltz 1979.

Prevalent conceptions articulated around forms of agreement are problematic in at least two ways. First, theorizing hierarchy in terms of authority tends to tell an incomplete story – one that privileges the perspective of the dominant. To say that subordinates abide by a given domination structure out of choice or decision (whether rationally delegated or normatively legitimated) implies that they somehow approve of it. And yet, if we take seriously the experience of subalterns, it quickly becomes obvious that, in general, a central part of being a subordinate precisely consists of not having any real options but to work from within the existing hierarchy. This is a key lesson I learned through interviewing diplomats from poorer countries on their experience of "international pecking orders."[32] From the bottom point of view, most hierarchies are neither rational nor legitimate; they are just there, seemingly unmovable. Contrary to the IR literature, it is not because subordinate practices reproduce the hierarchy that they necessarily consent to it, in the sense of exerting a choice. As Barnett notes, for instance, paternalistic humanitarian intervention, as a hierarchical form, often negates the very need for consent in the name of one's superior good.[33]

In theoretical terms, there is almost a functional necessity at work here: in order to have social and political relationships, subordinates are forced into reproducing the structure. Hierarchy is sustained through "faking it."[34] Even the most autistic actors on the margins of a group still need to behave in ways that make sense to the rest in order to have intercourse. As Reus-Smit suggests, "functional imperatives compel outlier states, along with others, to reproduce basic institutional practices."[35] Sending and Neumann give the example of the World Bank's Country Policy and Institutional Assessment (CPIA), a set of practices that recipient countries must comply with in order to obtain development aid. To argue that subordinates find this social structure legitimate would obviously be a stretch: they essentially have no choice. As Barnett puts it: "implied consent is a slippery slope, especially once the absence of a registered dissent becomes taken as an indicator of consent."[36] And if their behavior may be said to follow a rational interest (e.g., mimicking good governance practices in order to obtain funding), then again it is hard to see what alternatives they actually had. And yet, the notion of consent entails the possibility of following another course.

Ultimately, then, the reproduction of hierarchy by subordinates is less a question of legitimacy or rationality than of practicality. The logic is one of making social relations possible in the first place. As Swidler puts it,

---

[32] See Pouliot 2016a.   [33] Barnett 2012.   [34] Weber 1999.   [35] Reus-Smit 1999, 35–6.
[36] Barnett 2012, 495.

"[t]he crucial thing about social practices – and the feature that differentiates them from most habits – is that they are the infrastructure of repeated *interactional* patterns. They remain stable not only because habit ingrains standard ways of doing things, but because the need to engage one another forces people to return to common structures."[37] This is a key departure from the standard constructivist framework centered on norm internalization, which focuses on "transformative effects on basic actors' properties."[38] In my view, one cannot infer either a positive cost-benefit calculus or "third degree internalization"[39] simply from compliant behavior. On the contrary, most of the time subordinates reproduce hierarchies because this is how the world goes round. Actors perform the prevalent script because there is apparently no other way to play. In a sense, the logic here is reminiscent of "social influence" or "public conformity without private acceptance," although contrary to Johnston I do not see a "rationalist logic" at work here.[40] The practical logic of being part of the game operates on a different analytical plane than delegated authority and normative legitimation.

For this reason, we should try to find ways to think about hierarchy in other terms than authority. There already exist promising examples in the literature. For example, in Barkawi and Laffey's relational account of North-South dynamics, hierarchy is nowhere presumed to be a form of rationally or normatively consented authority system.[41] It rather is a historically inherited, post-colonial domination structure that feeds on mutually constitutive oppositions, from race to economic and political development. Subordinates are less consenting than they are sucked into reproducing the hierarchy precisely because it is so powerful. Likewise, Zarakol's notion of stigma does not suggest that stigmatized actors view such social stratification as rational or legitimate; it rather is the political effect of a pervasive system of vertical differentiation.[42] The same could be said of Towns' argument to the effect that "international norms necessarily both generate and draw on social rank (the ordering of states as superior and inferior)."[43] Subordinates reproduce hierarchy not because of its rationality or legitimacy but because of its powerful structuring effects on social relationships. If you cannot overturn the system, the subordinate logic goes, then you better work at it from within.

In sum, hierarchies are heavy historical structures whose weight cannot be shed by whim – a premise that runs counter to existing micro-mechanism of hierarchy based on rational cost-benefit calculation or

[37] Swidler 2001, 85.   [38] Lewis 2005, 938.   [39] Wendt 1999.   [40] Johnston 2008.
[41] Barkawi and Laffey 2006.   [42] Zarakol 2011.
[43] Towns 2012, 181. See also Chapter 10.

normative deliberation. According to these frameworks, both dominant and subordinate players agree upon a contract or social compact. As a result, hierarchy ends up being something quite light. Empirically, the expected pattern should be one of instability: after all, both the international environment (i.e., material incentives) and the politics of legitimacy tend to shift, that is, not even to mention agency itself (and domestic politics, in the case of states), which may be another reason to alter choices. This is the second major weakness in consent-based notions of hierarchy: the occurrence of fragile and short-lived domination is not what a cursory look at the historical record suggests. To be sure, hierarchies do come and go over long periods of time, but much less often than what should happen if subordinates could simply withdraw their consent when they feel like it. Actual cases rather indicate that escaping from domination structures short of violent means is easier said than done. We thus find ourselves in need of an alternative theoretical framework that can better account for this resilience than the contract and social compact views, pointing us in the direction of a broad understanding of hierarchy.

Born with(in) Hierarchy: Embodiment

One of the deeper puzzles that animate Bourdieu's political sociology is what he calls the "miracle of social order." Throughout his career, he was obsessed with "the ease (which in the end really is amazing) with which, throughout history but for a few crisis situations, dominant agents impose their domination."[44] By what kind of social magic does the world remain so orderly despite so many inequalities? How is it possible that individuals occupying vastly unequal positions within a social configuration still come together in performing practices that maintain their hierarchical interaction pattern orderly? As I argued earlier, existing answers in the IR literature – that hierarchy exists because actors have an interest in it or deem it legitimate – can hardly explain the durability and pervasiveness of the phenomenon. Missing, I want to argue, is an account of the deeper effects that hierarchy produces.

The Constitutive Effects of Hierarchy

The main difference between the conceptualization that I advance and those currently on offer in IR may be summed up thusly: instead of individuals pre-existing hierarchy and erecting hierarchies as institutional

---

[44] Bourdieu 2003, 257. All translations from French are by the author.

solutions to problems of order, I posit that hierarchy precedes agents. This is obviously not always the case: new hierarchies do form once in a while. In the grand scheme of things, however, I argue that domination structures usually come first, in the sense that people are born in already existing schemes of social stratification. Except for rare founding moments, analysis is better served by presuming that there is no t_0 in hierarchy. The social world always and inevitably presents itself as already structured and unlevelled. To borrow Bourdieu's words, "one does not embark on the game by a conscious act; one is born into the game, with the game."[45] The key implication is that hierarchy produces much deeper, constitutive effects on agents than what both the contract and compact views account for.

Indeed, the contract theory of hierarchy problematically assumes pre-existing units that embark on the authority relationship at a given point in time. In this scheme, there is no hierarchy at t_0; then a contract is rationally consented at t_1, followed with obedient acts at t_2. This allows Lake to define interests at t_0 outside of – or prior to – hierarchy, in some kind of fictional foundational moment in which the world is flat and agents are akin to blank sheets with exogenously given preferences. This premise does not withstand closer analysis, though, because the social playing field at any given point necessarily arises out of past games played. As such, preferences never come out of thin air; they are, in significant part, constituted by past interactions and structures. Interests at t_0 are in large part defined by what happened at t_1. And to the extent that the relationship was already stratified in some way at t_1, chances are that this unequal condition helped to determine the political patterns that follow.

Still, one could agree with Lake that hierarchy persists only so long as agents feel an interest in acting accordingly. As he puts it, "[b]oth dominant and subordinate states have to be better off in hierarchic than in strictly anarchic relations for the contract to be fulfilled."[46] Arguably, Lake's additional argument that hierarchy may become sticky because of "vested interests" accounts for the lighter constitutive effects of domination. It suggests that part of the interest in maintaining hierarchy may not be defined independently of, or prior to, hierarchy but as part of hierarchy itself. But the implication of my argument is much more radical, I believe: the room for choice, which Lake needs to preserve for his rationalist framework to apply, gets reduced to the point that it often disappears from sight. Thus, while it may be true that agents comply with a hierarchy so long as they feel an interest in doing so, most of the time that interest knows of no alternative courses of action. Social stratification takes on a self-evident

[45] Bourdieu 1990, 67.   [46] Lake 2009, 93.

dimension of routine and taken-for-grantedness, so patterns of subordination are less the result of instrumental calculations than of established ways
of doing things. Thanks to the practical sense, domination and subordination become the "done things" that somehow go by themselves.

The key implication is that hierarchy plays a fundamental role in sustaining itself by constituting actors with an innate sense for it. The "interest"
that agents follow in complying with a hierarchy is the habituated result of
the hierarchical relationship itself. From a practice perspective, and contrary to rational choice and other representational theories of social action, it
is not only agents who invest in a game (e.g., states in multilateral diplomacy). Agents are also invested (or taken) by the game. In other words, the
game constitutes agents with a seemingly innate interest in playing it. Thus
the constitutive effects of hierarchy are much deeper than Lake is willing to
concede. Because it pre-exists agents, hierarchy transforms those who are
born within it. This is what Bourdieu calls "illusio," a socially induced
disposition to play the social game within which agents happen to be
involved. As a "basic membership to the game," illusio describes "the
enchanted relationship to the game which is the result of the ontological
complicity between mental structures and the objective structures of social
space."[47] Agents come to embody the necessity of the social world and
develop an innate sense of playing the game as an end in itself.

Recall that for Bourdieu, practices are "the encounter of two histories":
"[t]he principle of action," he argues, "lies in the complicity between two
states of the social, between history in bodies and history in things, or, more
precisely, between the history objectified in the form of structures and
mechanisms (those of the social space or of fields), and history incarnated
in bodies, in the form of habitus."[48] In other words, practices form at the
confluence of dispositions – ingrained and mostly inarticulate proclivities
and tendencies accumulated through personal exposure and collective
history – and positions in a field – defined by the distribution of valued
resources within a social game. These two spaces, importantly, are inter-
connected yet distinct. Overall, "there is a strong correlation between
social positions and the dispositions of the agents who occupy them."[49]
This "homology" stems from the fact that an agent's habitus comprises
historical traces of his or her occupying various positions in the past.

In Bourdieu's sociology, then, social order stems from "the pre-
reflexive fit between the objective and the embodied structures,"[50] that
is, the homology between habitus and field. The micro-mechanism of
social hierarchy lies with habitus and its many embodied dispositions,

---

[47] Bourdieu 1994, 151.   [48] Bourdieu 2000b, 150–1.   [49] Bourdieu 1984, 110.
[50] Bourdieu 2003, 256.

which, by being the product of social structures, come to naturalize existing conditions as the normal state of affairs. Acquired in and through practice, habitus generates aspirations and practices that generally correspond to field positions. And when agents' dispositions mirror the social hierarchy of which they are part, the practical sense becomes a self-regulating mechanism. Under such conditions, necessity makes virtue, so to speak: the (structurally) impossible is (subjectively) unthinkable and the (structurally) plausible is (subjectively) inevitable.[51] This "orchestra without a conductor," as Bourdieu called it, is the engine of social order and domination patterns.

Under circumstances of homology, then, history somehow communicates with itself, with field positions aligned with habitus dispositions and reciprocally. In terms of hierarchy, subordinate players become complicit[52] in maintaining the domination pattern. Despite the disadvantage conferred by their position in the distribution of capital and especially by the rules of the game (field), subordinate players partake in their domination insofar as they are inclined (habitus) to play the game of their own exploitation. Hierarchy becomes the natural or obvious way to go, as part of taken-for-granted reality. A habitus that is homologous to the field's structure essentially reproduces domination patterns as part of the order of things. Social distances become inscribed in bodies, feeding on a doxic "relationship of immediate adherence" to the world as it experienced.[53] In this practical logic, embodied hierarchy is akin to a second nature, operating axiomatically as part of the order of things. Revisited through the concepts of illusio and habitus, then, the practical relationship to hierarchy is a very different one from what frameworks based on rationality and normativity would suggest.

Hierarchy within Ourselves: The Sense of Place

In practice theory, agents tend to reproduce social structures, including hierarchical ones, within their bodies. This premise privileges the

---

[51] *Ibid.*, 332–3.

[52] In Bourdieu's usage, complicity does not require consent. His interest is in *ontological* complicity, which captures the match (or mismatch) between social structures and embodied dispositions. This kind of complicity produces practices, but it is emphatically *not* the product of reflexive agency. As such, Bourdieu's view stands in contrast to Goh's, for instance, who argues that "hierarchical orders, especially hegemonic ones, are crucially constituted by complicity: without the consent and acquiescence of all states in the system, hierarchies cannot be sustained"; Goh 2013, 211. I agree that subordinates partake in their own domination, but given embodiment, such complicity does not involve consent.

[53] Bourdieu 1990, 68.

subjective experience of international hierarchy – that is, what social stratification *feels like* for practitioners of world politics. Building on Goffman, I suggest that at the level of practice, hierarchy takes the form of what Goffman calls the "sense of place," a socially acquired feel for one's possibilities and limits in a given interaction setting. In his words, "[s]ocial life is an uncluttered, orderly thing because the person voluntarily stays away from the places and topics and times where he is not wanted and where he might be disparaged for going. He cooperates to save his face, finding that there is much to be gained from venturing nothing."[54] Thanks to the sense of place, players are able to figure out where they stand in a social configuration and relate their position to that of others. The key insight here is that social structures operate through our very practices. In other words, hierarchy lies not above our heads, but within ourselves.

Bourdieu borrowed Goffman's concept and articulated it with his notion of habitus. He defines the sense of place as "a practical, corporeal knowledge that agents have of their position in a social space … which expresses itself through gestures … or the unconscious adjustment of practices."[55] Once deposited within us, social structures operate through our very practices, "making virtue out of necessity, refusing the refused and liking the inevitable."[56] Players go on with their lives in a way that conforms to patterns of influence and standing. Understood in this way, the sense of place does not negate the possibility of strategy and choice but rather forms the practical baseline from which these forms of agency become possible.

At the level of experience, the sense of one's place is a largely inarticulate feel for the game. "The sense of one's place is a practical sense," argues Bourdieu, "a practical knowledge that does not know itself, a 'learned ignorance' … The knowledge that stems from the incorporation of the necessity of the social world, for example in the form of a sense for limits, is very real, as is the submission that it implies and which often expresses itself under the imperative observations of resignation: 'this is not for us.'"[57] In tune with what I call the "logic of practicality,"[58] the sense of place stems from a stock of tacit know-how acquired from experience. It designates a kind of second nature that skillful practitioners have about the local interaction order and the pattern of practices upon which it rests. The sense of place stems from a stock of tacit know-how that is bound up in competent performance. In everything that people do,

---

[54] Goffman 1967, 43.   [55] Bourdieu 2003, 265–6.   [56] Bourdieu 2000a, 260.
[57] Bourdieu 2003, 267.   [58] Pouliot 2008.

there is always a practical substrate, learned through experience in the world, from which strategic action and intentionality become possible.

The socially integrative effects of the sense of place are worth emphasizing because it is through such embodied dispositions that groups may stick together despite deep internal inequalities. As Bonham notes, "[h]abitus is supposed to explain how it is that agents come to share a culture and its practices, even when there are asymmetrical positions and relations of domination. Bourdieu solves the Parsonian problem of social order not through the internalization of norms, but through the 'inculcation' of dispositions that come not only from being socialized into a culture generally, but also into a particular subordinate or dominant position within it."[59] The sense of place helps to make sense of the miracle of social order, by which unequal competitors face off and play by the same rules of the game.

By way of illustration, take the case of "international pecking orders," that is, the informal hierarchies of standing among permanent representatives and their teams posted to major IO headquarters.[60] The miracle of social order is in full display in the world of multilateral diplomacy. While this practice generates patterns of interaction that exhibit variable degrees of orderliness, it is striking how its everyday unfolding remains rather smooth and functional on the whole. The miracle stems from the fact that diplomatic players, despite unequal standing and influence, come to the multilateral table equipped with a similar notion of the international pecking order and a willingness to play by the local rules of the game. As Hurd perceptively notes, "[o]ne cannot be offended by another's rejection of protocol, or by a rival being well treated by a third party, unless one shares a common definition of what appropriate protocol requires and what constitutes a step up or down on the ladder of status."[61] Multilateral diplomacy thrives on social stratification, as both dominant and subordinate players reproduce the local pecking order in and through practice.

Never fully spoken out but always present on the minds of multilateral diplomats, the international pecking order is a mostly inarticulate yet key organizing structure of world politics. Thanks to their sense of one's place, socially competent diplomats develop "reasonable" expectations, set "realistic" objectives, calibrate "rational" tactics and maneuver "efficiently" in the thick of negotiations – all social attributions related to how well attuned practices are to existing patterns of stratification. While the sense of one's place is a key driver of social order in any kind of

---

[59] Bonham 1999, 174.   [60] For more on this, see Pouliot 2016a, 2016b.
[61] Hurd 2007, 3.

configurations, it is solicited with a particular intensity in multilateral diplomacy, which forms a rather conservative social realm. For example, the practice of holding a bracket risks disrupting the working consensus around the multilateral table if not properly calibrated to the configuration of influence, whereas the practice of joining the consensus generally consolidates the interaction order by making virtue out of necessity. Permanent representatives must navigate fast-changing waters, and their practical sense of limits and possibilities is at the root of their competence – and standing.

Taking the sense of one's place seriously is, in this sense, an invitation to study the subjective experience of hierarchy – something missing in parts of the existing literature (with the exception of post-colonialism and feminism, most notably). For example, one diplomat whom I interviewed as part of my book expressed how the pecking order feels for those at the top: "[t]he difference between being high in the pecking order is that people can call and say that they are pissed off, and you can say: 'too bad.'" The possibility to ignore objections and, conversely, the incapacity to have one's objections taken into account are practical instantiations of pecking orders. Under such circumstances, those at the bottom will see no point in voicing disagreement, while those at the top will axiomatically ignore views from below. According to my empirical research, these mechanisms are often inarticulate, part of embodied routines in tune with the sense of place. As one interviewee put it, "[t]hat is something that, if you're doing it, you know it. I cannot quantify exactly how you come to know ... It's a complex wave."

As such, the sense of place is a social skill – arguably the most important one that a competent multilateral diplomacy should master – thanks to which agents adapt more or less seamlessly and successfully to different social configurations. It allows them to figure out their place, as well as that of others in a group's pecking order. Thus, the sense of place is not only constraining but also enabling. It is a knack for the working order and the social logic by which ranks and roles are distributed. Here Ambrosetti's ethnography of the UN Security Council is particularly illuminating: "[f]inding out what action is expected or appropriate is a practical process, based on a non-rationalized, non-verbalized, quasi-certainty that such and such words, or such and such arguments, will meet the group's expectations and obtain its acquiescence."[62] Such an account helps to resolve a key puzzle in Lake's argument (and other existing works). Lake writes that "[i]n equilibrium, rulers will typically command only what they *know* their subjects will accept, and the ruled

[62] Ambrosetti 2009, 56.

will usually do that which they are asked."[63] But just how do rulers know or feel what their subjects will accept and what they will not? The sense of place provides a useful solution.

The matter is all the more complicated that in multilateral diplomacy, the sense of place relates not only to individuals but also to the corporate entities that they represent – states. Ambassadors speak not in their own personal name but as the embodiment of their country and government. In the everyday, diplomats seamlessly mix the two levels, referring to each other not by personal names but as countries: "France said this," "India objected."[64] At the level of practice, representatives come and go as rotations in posting dictate – yet states remain put. Ultimately, when permanent representatives square off at the multilateral table, it is also states that do, and that process forms the structural background against which the actual performances of diplomacy occur. The sense of place, then, is a practical understanding of the roles and ranks that different countries play through their ambassadors.

Furthermore, the sense of place is a feeling not only for how much power one *has* but also for what power *is* in the first place[65] – that is, the locally defined markers of standing. These markers are "situationally specific,"[66] to borrow Baldwin's language. Recall that in Bourdieu's sociology, resources (or capital) need to be socially valued in order to have currency in the field and produce structural effects. In certain fields, a resource may be determinant in structuring power relations, whereas it may be ineffective in other social realms. For instance, one may own huge stocks of economic capital in the form of money, yet in the academic field that will only take one so far. It is rather the accumulation of a specific form of cultural capital, notably publications and professional titles, that can move the agent toward the top of this hierarchy. What counts as a valuable resource, thus, is never immanent and objective but always historically contingent and socially defined. As Guzzini puts it, "measures of power are agreed to and constructed social fact: diplomats try and need to agree first on what counts before they can start counting."[67]

The implication is that at the level of practice, hierarchy hinges on a limited set of organizing principles of social stratification: economic development, race, "soft power," technological prowess, and so on. These organizing principles are historically and culturally contingent.[68] Contrary to the social compact view, however, I argue that players do not have to "truly believe" in these yardsticks or find them morally

[63] Lake 2009, 165 (emphasis added).   [64] Adler-Nissen 2014, 62. See also Chapter 11.
[65] Pouliot 2010, 244.   [66] Baldwin 1989, 138.   [67] Guzzini 2006, 127.
[68] See Pouliot 2014 for more on this.

appropriate or legitimate to set them in motion. In fact, actors don't even have to be conscious about contingent markers of standing. This is so because the sense of place instantiates, in and through practice, the organizing principle(s) of hierarchy. There is no consent-based authority involved in this scheme, in the sense that players would agree to a contract or compact. The only authority that there is, here, attaches not to individuals but rather to practices, which are established ways of doing things. Ultimately, then, what matters is the fact that social markers get publicly instantiated as part of the order of things as players go on with their trade.

Beyond Authority II

How might we conceive of hierarchy if we strip it of any reference to the notion of authority? Perhaps the best starting point is to remember that hierarchy may be decomposed into form and content. It is standard knowledge that the form of hierarchy is vertical differentiation or stratification.[69] The content, for its part, varies from one historical instantiation to the next, but the generic idea is constant: hierarchy rests on a set of organizing principles of difference. These evolving principles rank order participants in function of selected attributes. Thus, hierarchy is socially organized around norms, identities, practices, rules, standards, responsibilities, duties, privileges, entitlements, and so on. This is the social load of hierarchy, which demarcates the concept from pure coercion or brute domination. Yet, this social load need not be normatively approved or rationally consented in order to produce social stratification. It suffices that it is there in the form of established practices, as a pre-existing and heavy social structure that produces far-ranging social effects. This is the basic condition of the social world, as Phillips correctly notes: "[p]olitics necessarily entails relations of organized domination."[70]

When it comes to definition, I cannot improve on Towns', who similarly conceives of hierarchy outside the bounds of authority: "[s]ocial hierarchy, which I use synonymously with social rank, concerns the ordering of actors as superior or inferior to one another in socially important respects."[71] The payoff of keeping hierarchy and consent-based authority conceptually distinct should become clearer now. Authority is a legitimate, that is, socially acceptable (and generally accepted), form of stratification. There are commanders in authority and followers who defer to them (through some form of approval ranging from consent to recognition). By contrast, hierarchy as a social concept denotes socially *organized* stratification. Hierarchy need not be agreed upon in order to

---

[69] Donnelly 2012a. See also Chapter 11.   [70] Phillips 2011, 26.   [71] Towns 2012, 188.

produce practices of deference or discipline. In most cases, actors who are part of a hierarchy were never asked to join anyway; the structure is rampant enough to maintain itself short of consent because it forms an inescapable social infrastructure. The implication of this conceptualization is that hierarchy occupies a qualitatively distinct terrain from authority, where those at the bottom cannot withdraw from the structure by putting an end to a delegated or normative authority relationship. In other words, when hierarchy is embodied, cost-benefit calculations and normative agreement may still occur, but they operate *from* the baseline of existing social stratification. Embodied hierarchy is a much weightier form of social domination than consent-based authority.

Even short of authority, however, hierarchy remains a fundamentally social concept, capturing something eminently more complex than brute coercion or domination maintained through force. The organizing principles that structure hierarchy in the form of strata are socially constructed and politically generated. The distribution of material capabilities, to take a classic example, does not create a hierarchy in and of itself unless it is meshed with a set of social rules. A good example of this is the hierarchical system of "special responsibilities" in world politics, in which capability differentials cohabit with normative structures.[72] In fact, as soon as we veer away from the authority-centric view, then the opposite of hierarchy becomes not anarchy (or lack of a central authority) but the absence of a social system of vertical differentiation (or social stratification). Theoretical possibilities here would range from a flat world to brute coercion – but these asocial forms can hardly be found in actual world politics.

As such, hierarchy refers to social wholes that are not reducible to dyads. Lake's focus on dyadic relationships of domination and subordination problematically leaves aside the more holistic issue of system-wide hierarchy and its organizing principles. In his masterpiece, *Homo Hierarchicus*, Dumont defines hierarchy as the "principle of gradation of the parts of a whole in reference to the whole."[73] What matters here is that the principles by which a dyad is hierarchized are not confined to its two members but defined "in reference to the whole." In other words, the organizing principles of hierarchical orders are to be found in the whole of relationships. These are usually complex, changing, and ambiguous – contrary to Wohlforth's view that "[t]he social system in which states operate is dramatically simpler than the domestic social settings much of the research seeks to capture."[74] In that sense, Donnelly is certainly right that the concept of hierarchy "is too blunt an analytical tool." "Society,"

---

[72] Bukovansky et al. 2012.   [73] Dumont 1966, 92.   [74] Wohlforth 2009, 36.

he continues, "may be multiply ranked ('heterarchic')."[75] Layers of social stratification coexist in what might be termed, *pace* Bull, the heterarchical international society.

Conclusion

This chapter has made the case for a weightier understanding of hierarchy, compared to the contract and social compact views, as an embodied social structure. In this rendition, social stratification is a much more enduring and resilient phenomenon than what cost-benefit calculations and normative deliberation would otherwise suggest. Because of illusio, agents (including subordinate ones) develop a vested interest in playing the game, and because of the sense of place, they tend to reproduce the organizing principles of vertical differentiation in and through practice – even when they seemingly work against them.

The question that this account raises, then, regards the amount of reflexive agency and transformative capacity that are possible in a world of embodied hierarchy. On the face of it, it may seem as though my argument is taking away any space of contestation for subaltern players. But my view is actually slightly less pessimistic. As structurally derived as it may be, habitus and the sense of place do not determine practices but rather define their scope and repertoire. Improvisation and deviation abound in practice theory, even as players are inclined to resort to certain ways of doing things that associate with their position in society. The social orchestra may indeed be playing without a conductor, but this does not suppress the possibility of subversive practices or even overt challenges to the order of things. As Bourdieu put it, "[h]abitus is a *structuring mechanism* that operates from within agents, though it is neither strictly individual nor in itself fully determinative of conduct."[76] I do not argue that hierarchy "bring[s] social beings into being"[77]; instead, my point is that hierarchy *works through* social beings.

In fact, in many ways my account falls in line with the research that Zarakol describes in the Introduction as agreeing "that hierarchies are relatively durable; that an actor's position within an existing hierarchy is not (just) a choice or the result of a bargain; that an actors' identity, role, interests and/or expectations are constituted by, or an effect of, their position in the existing system; and that it is through these socializing dynamics that existing hierarchies create effects in world politics."[78] In fact, in my book I argue that social stratification emerges out of the

---

[75] Donnelly 2012a, 157.   [76] Bourdieu and Wacquant 1992, 18 (emphasis in original).
[77] See Introduction.   [78] See Introduction.

ordinary process of practice.[79] The performance of practice generates vertical differentiation through a never-ending struggle for competence or practical mastery. As practitioners perform their trade, they also stake a claim as to how things are done. Thanks to its social productivity, practice tends to generate collective notions of what it means to be an able player at the game, which grant certain players more standing than others. As a social structure, then, hierarchy rests on practice, which is nothing else than the process of agency itself.

As noted by Zarakol and explored more thoroughly in Part II of this book, though, "disagreements exist over the degree of agency actors enjoy within hierarchical systems."[80] Indeed, this is where the embodied notion of hierarchy that I developed in this chapter departs from more optimistic accounts, such as those found in Part II. For Adler-Nissen, to use one example, diplomats can play games within international hierarchies in order to substantially alter their positions.[81] My account leads to less positional movement and voluntarism. Of course, subaltern strategies of "braconnage" and subversive "weapons of the weak" do exist.[82] But given the structural forces against which such occurrences are pitted, it seems important not to overstate their probability. Hierarchy stacks the deck against such scenarios. The room for resistance is, indeed, always contained in practice; its actualization, however, remains rather extraordinary. Once again, a cursory look at the empirical record suggests that the overwhelming majority of social processes go toward the reproduction, not the transformation, of existing structures. This empirical observation is reinforced by Goh, for example: "[t]his type of upward resistance, which I term 'revolt,' is noticeably absent in the survey of post-Cold War East Asia conducted in this book."[83]

The reason for such social stability and reproduction is a simple one: born into an already existing social world, actors cannot change established ways of doing things out of whim. When subordinate diplomats enact pecking order practices, for instance, they are reproducing socially meaningful patterns of interaction from which they can hardly deviate, whether they like it or not, because these patterns are the precondition for social existence and actorhood. The sense of place is both a propeller (enabling) and a cage (constraining). It is a skill in that a diplomat who behaves in tune with his or her country's standing (shutting up when needed or speaking up when expected) will gain recognition in his or her

---

[79] Pouliot 2016a, 2016b.

[80] In this quote, Zarakol seems to equate agency with freedom or at least the capacity to deviate from structure. By contrast, I conceive of agency as the process of practice, which often ends up reproducing structure (although not necessarily).

[81] See Chapter 11.   [82] De Certeau 1980; Scott 1985.   [83] Goh 2013, 222.

peers' eyes. But it is also self-limiting precisely because it takes away some of the wiggle room that a practitioner may seek in subverting the social expectations that flow from the pecking order.

This is where the tragic hits. In order to be competent diplomats, practitioners must act in sync with their sense of place (and that of others). In so doing, however, they end up "skillfully" reinforcing the pecking order and hierarchy of standing. The practical logic of competence, in order words, is tilted toward social reproduction. Standing must be acquired from within, by playing along the rules. The sense of place is a sense of possibility, which also implies a sense of limits. Transcending one's standing is easier said than done: it requires a rare kind of subversive competence that plays social rules against themselves. Generally speaking, such processes produce change but mostly at the margins and in an incremental fashion. Bigger transformations are not impossible to achieve, as virtuosos remind us from time to time, but, as a general rule, diplomats rather find themselves acting in tune with the hierarchy of standing in order to stay a part of the multilateral game. And the "miracle" of enduring international hierarchy goes on and on.

Part II

How Actors Experience Hierarchies

6   Hierarchy in an Age of Equality
Micro-States and Dependencies

J. C. Sharman

This chapter takes a conceptual middle road to investigate how hierarchy works from the bottom up, from the perspective of subordinates, by examining a group of tiny polities, a combination of sovereign micro-states and self-governing dependent territories. The main point of the chapter is that hierarchy (defined narrowly) is surprisingly scarce in the contemporary international system. This scarcity is both relative to presumed functional need and compared with past international systems. In all probability this reflects a historically novel norm (or related norms) of sovereign equality and associated international institutions such as conditional sovereign lending that provide a safety net for weak states.[1] Whether it is sovereign states or individuals' human rights, we live in an age defined by its unprecedented commitment to equality.[2] Hierarchy was historically the rule but is now the exception, even in circumstances where functional imperatives would seem to strongly favour hierarchical solutions over a principled and practical commitment to sovereign equality. All other things being equal, the smaller the state, the less self-sufficient it should be in security terms and with reference to economic viability, and thus the more likely it should be to subordinate itself within a hierarchical relationship. Yet, even in these most propitious circumstances, for micro-states, hierarchy is the exception rather than the rule. Even self-governing dependencies, by definition subordinates in a hierarchical relationship, have also tended to claim more and more autonomy.

The chapter begins by arguing that some definitions of hierarchy raise the danger of concept stretching and the prospect that the prevalence of hierarchy will be empirically over- or understated. If as per the 'narrow' understanding[3] hierarchy is fundamentally premised on authority, then generally neither brute coercion nor market transactions can establish hierarchy. But the former position is contradicted by a wide range of historical evidence of hierarchy via imperialism and occupation, whereas the latter is conceptually incoherent. Conversely, 'broad' views

---

[1] Jackson 1990.   [2] Meyer et al. 1997.   [3] See the Introduction.

of hierarchy must nevertheless be bounded by a focus on relations and be careful not to simply re-package the commonsense observations that some states are bigger than others, that perfect equality is rare, that differences between actors are ubiquitous, and that power is pervasive. This chapter is an example of a middle ground or intermediate view of hierarchy located between the narrow and broadest conceptions.

Evidence is drawn from eight tiny polities with populations between 10,000 and 150,000: the Cayman Islands, the Cook Islands, Curaçao, the Faroe Islands, Liechtenstein, Nauru, the Seychelles and St Kitts and Nevis. On one view, sovereignty is an all-or-nothing affair, and in this sense, the group divides into four sovereign states, Liechtenstein, Nauru, Seychelles and St Kitts and Nevis, and four dependencies, the Caymans (British), the Cooks (New Zealand), Curaçao (Dutch) and the Faroes (Danish). Another conception held by Krasner, Donnelly and Lake sees sovereignty as a bundle of attributes or authority claims that may be disaggregated, delegated and exchanged.[4] According to this notion, the bright line separating the micro-states from the dependent territories softens and blurs.

A caveat on what this chapter does not do: given the focus on hierarchy, it does not systematically discuss the norm of sovereign equality.[5] Also, it asserts that hierarchy was much more common in previous eras, including the European empires and indigenous arrangements in East Asia and the Indian Ocean littoral, but no evidence is adduced to support this claim.[6]

The Concept of Hierarchy

Trail-blazing scholars such as Clark (1989), Lake (1996), Cooley (2005), Donnelly (2006) and others have rendered the field a great service by putting hierarchy back on the map in International Relations (IR). As stated in the Introduction, 'hierarchy is any system through which actors are organised into vertical relations of super- and subordination.' Scholars from a variety of different viewpoints have converged on the idea that hierarchy is above all to do with authority, the 'narrow' conception, though most also agree that in practice it is often difficult to separate authority from coercion.[7] Waltz speaks of hierarchy as 'relations of super- and subordination' whereby 'actors are formally differentiated according to the degrees of their authority, and their distinct functions.'[8] Lake sees hierarchy as

---

[4] Krasner 1999; Lake 1996, 2007, 2009; Donnelly 2006.
[5] See Jackson 1990; Philpott 2001; Reus-Smit 2013.
[6] For historical evidence on this point, see Buzan and Little 2000; Nexon 2009; Kang 2010b; Johnston 2012; Reus-Smit 2013; Phillips and Sharman 2015.
[7] Lake 2007, 51–3; Donnelly 2009, 63.   [8] Waltz 1979, 81, 114.

a continuum 'defined by the extent of authority exercised by the ruler over the ruled', in the context of the international system, the superior state over the subordinate.[9] Cooley explicitly draws on an earlier formulation of Lake's definition.[10] Writing specifically about the East Asian historical context, Kang refers to hierarchy as 'a rank order of prestige and, just as importantly, the legitimacy of the rank as accepted by secondary states'.[11] There is thus some general, though certainly not unanimous, support for the narrow view of hierarchy spanning rationalist and constructivist scholars: an authority relationship constituted by a superior and subordinate, recognised as legitimate by both. Yet, this narrow hierarchy has difficulty accommodating relations premised on coercion and contracting.

Transaction cost economists such as Douglass North have argued that even highly lopsided relationships may be thought of as bargaining or contractual exchange. Monitoring and supervising convict labour, for example, are expensive, so convicts and guards may be said to reach an implicit or explicit deal over productivity whereby guards can minimise the costs of monitoring and convicts can maximise their privileges. While this does capture some of the subaltern agency of even the most subordinated, repressed populations, it also tends to obscure a fundamental analytical difference between relationships based on consent and those based on coercion.[12] Thinking of convicts as independent contractors bargaining with wardens over their perks and conditions to reach a mutually acceptable and Pareto-improving deal gives us a very misleading picture of forced labour.

So too presuming that all international hierarchical relations must rest on consensually negotiated, mutually acceptable deals that leave both sides better off as a result seems to confuse some fundamentally different analytical categories, not to mention run against a huge range of historical evidence. Where were the contractual benefits to those countries subordinated to the Japanese, German, Italians or Soviets in the 1930s and 1940s or, for that matter, most other historical empires? Thus, an incisive review by Patrick Thaddeus Jackson has noted the general shortcoming of this kind of theorising: 'it cannot effectively deal with the exercise of coercive power and must therefore transform coercive situations into more or less voluntary instances of compliance.'[13] Surely a theory of politics that cannot distinguish between consent and coercion, or tyranny and democracy, has major conceptual problems.

The second caveat relating to hierarchy as Pareto-improving bargains between superiors and subordinates is that it fundamentally

---

[9] Lake 2009, 9.   [10] Cooley 2005, 5.   [11] Lake 2010, 594.   [12] Scott 1990.
[13] Jackson 2002, 743.

misunderstands the transaction cost economics that it claims to be based on, specifically the analytical separation of markets and hierarchies. Economists of the firm such as Coase and Williamson explained that transactions could *either* be co-ordinated through contracting in the market, as conventional economics assumed, *or* co-ordinated hierarchically within the firm.[14] Contracting in the market was explicitly seen as analytically distinct from hierarchy, as the title of Williamson's most famous work, *Markets and Hierarchies*, clearly communicates. He poses the central problem of this research programme as explaining the use of the market to handle some transactions and recourse to hierarchy for others.[15] If hierarchies are just another form of market based on contracting between independent actors, then the whole point of hierarchies as a concept within this tradition disappears. Empirically, there are many economic arrangements that fall in between,[16] but this does not change the fundamental conceptual difference between the two. One could still somehow maintain that hierarchy is a form of market-based contracting, but this would then be outside and directly opposed to the tradition of transaction cost economics.

A further point that supports Williamson's conclusion that contracting and markets are antithetical to hierarchy is the broader conclusion that contracting depends upon a basic equality between the parties involved. Unless both are free to bargain, and to reject an unsatisfactory deal, then there is no contracting in the proper sense of the term. If I wash your car because you pay me $100, this is a market transaction, a mutually agreeable exchange of benefits, and not an example of hierarchy. If I wash your car because you are a lord and I acknowledge your superior social station, then this is a hierarchical relationship.[17] A further possible objection might be that rational choice accounts see the actors involved in hierarchy as constitutively independent of each other, whereas at least as strong a claim may be made that hierarchy is at bottom a relational concept: that the relationship constitutes the actors rather than vice versa (Jackson 2002; Jackson and Nexon 1999). Such a reading is very much in line with what this book refers to as the broad view of hierarchy.

However, the major positive contribution of the narrow view of hierarchy is to avoid reducing this concept to any and all differences in size, wealth, social standing or power between actors. Playing his usual role as synecdoche for the IR mainstream, Waltz maintains the clearest division according to which, for all the difference in their relative capabilities, the

---

[14] Coase 1937; Williamson 1975.   [15] Williamson 1985, 16, 2002, 176.
[16] See e.g. the literature on value chains; Gereffi et al. 2005.
[17] And note Elster's (2000) and Green and Shapiro's (1995) caveats against trying to turn this into a market exchange by imputing some sort of psychic pay-offs for the subordinate.

United States and Nauru are formally equal as sovereign states, with neither having authority over the other. Alliances between states and other international collaborative arrangements do not change this conclusion. Saying that big and powerful states are in a hierarchical relationship with others merely because they are big and powerful, or because they are allied with each other, drains away all the conceptual novelty and utility of hierarchy.[18]

At a much higher level of abstraction, converting all differences of social status to hierarchy, or all situations where power or its effects are at play, threatens to turn the concept into one that 'explains' everything and hence nothing. Here the potential pitfall is analogous to that identified in Motyl's scathing, thorough-going demolition of much of the recent work on empire.[19] To paraphrase this piece, it would be a pyrrhic victory for the nascent hierarchy research programme if the conclusion were to be that hierarchy is everything, and everything is hierarchy. The broad perspective is invaluable in pointing out that hierarchies are at least as likely to produce actors as the other way around. Similarly, claims about the ubiquity of power differentials are impossible to dispute. The challenge is to harness and bound this insight in such a way as to convince the rest of the discipline that broad views of hierarchy can generate specific advances in our understanding of world politics, as the other chapters in this book do.

If the narrow view of hierarchy leaves too much empirical content out, especially hierarchies based on coercion, some broad views may sweep too much in. The position taken here largely excludes contracting, simple material differences and varied social attributes and identities that do not constitute a system of stratification but includes coercion. Hierarchy is a vertically stratified relationship constituted by at least one superior and subordinate, with no requirement that the relationship is based on authority, legitimacy or consent. James Scott, among others, has written persuasively on hierarchy as social relations of domination.[20]

Case Studies: The Relative Scarcity of Hierarchy

The remainder of this chapter presents evidence from four sovereign micro-states and four dependencies to argue that there is less hierarchy than we would expect. This conclusion can only be tentative, as there is no definite benchmark that enables us to judge how subordinated subordinate states should be. Nevertheless, if functional imperatives are important in motivating states to trade authority for some combination

---

[18] Goh 2013.   [19] Motyl 2006.   [20] Scott 1990.

Table 6.1 *Micro-states and Dependencies*

Polity	Region	Ruler	Population	GDP per capita
Liechtenstein	Europe	Austria-Hungary until 1918	37,000	$89,400
Nauru	Pacific	Australia until 1968	10,000	$5,000
Seychelles	Indian Ocean	UK until 1976	92,000	$24,500
St Kitts and Nevis	Caribbean	UK until 1983	52,000	$20,300
Cayman Islands	Caribbean	UK	55,000	$43,000
Cook Islands	Pacific	New Zealand	10,000	$9,100
Curaçao	Caribbean	Netherlands	147,000	$15,000
Faroe Islands	Europe	Denmark	50,000	$30,500

of military or economic security or economies of scale, these micro-states should be most likely cases of such. The perspective is very much 'from the bottom up', that is, from the viewpoint of the prospective subordinate micro-states and dependencies, to balance the conventional IR fixation with top-down international politics.[21]

Table 6.1 gives a brief overview of these eight relatively obscure polities.

In determining how hierarchy works, there are a number of policy areas in which such a relationship could manifest itself. The empirical section here concentrates on defence and security; economics, including currency and customs unions, monetary policy and financial supervision; and diplomatic, constitutional and legal affairs.

Defence and Security

If the basic imperative for sovereign states is ensuring their own survival, micro-states would seem to be least able to satisfy this requirement on their own and thus perhaps most likely to subordinate themselves to enhance their security. Indeed, much of the literature on small states has worried about their presumed susceptibility to outside predation and conquest.[22] Historically, the need to ward off outside predation is perhaps the main reason polities have subordinated themselves to superior powers as protectorates or similar semi-sovereign arrangements. At the same time, it is important not to make the category error of assuming that all alliances and mutual defence agreements create hierarchical relationships. The fact that France, Japan and Britain have alliances with the

---

[21] Neumann and Gstohl 2006.   [22] Mosser 2001; Bartman 2002; Wivel and Oest 2010.

United States does not constitute a hierarchical relationship, along the lines of the argument about avoiding concept-stretching presented earlier.

None of the dependencies considered earlier have anything more than police forces, and each has a formal security guarantee from the metropolitan power (Britain, Denmark, the Netherlands and New Zealand). Dependencies with their own substantial forces have been common in history, for example, the more than a million troops from British Empire dominions serving in World Wars I and II. Yet, if dependencies do not now maintain armed forces, many small sovereign states from Costa Rica to Iceland to perhaps thirty others also have no militaries.[23] Of the sample here, Liechtenstein has not had an army since the nineteenth century, whereas Nauru simply never saw the need for one at independence or any time thereafter. The approximately 400 members of the St Kitts and Nevis Defence Force are tasked with fighting drug traffickers, civil unrest and natural disasters, as well as ceremonial duties, and thus perhaps serve a paramilitary or gendarme function.[24] At the time of independence in 1976, the Seychelles had no armed forces, with the country's first government considering a military unnecessary.[25] However, a left-wing coup the following year saw the creation of the Seychelles People's Liberation Army.[26] This fought off an attempted invasion in November 1981 by a mercenary force masquerading as a South African rugby club (they posed as 'Ye Ancient Order of Froth-Blowers', having earlier rejected the team moniker the 'Male Chauvinist Pigs'; see Hoare 1986). After the return to multiparty democracy in the early 1990s, the armed forces were sharply reduced to their current strength of around 1,000.[27]

If these dependencies and micro-states either have token militaries or none at all, it would seem that there is a strong rationale for them to trade off sovereign prerogatives with stronger states in order to meet their security needs. Although dependencies all have a security guarantee from the metropolitan power, there is less evidence of hierarchy than might be expected. Even the dependency arrangements are perhaps a truism, as a dependency might be defined as a polity with self-government that delegates its security to a super-ordinate state. Only Curaçao has voiced fears of international predation, thanks to long-standing territorial claims by Venezuela.

What of the micro-states which could plausibly be expected to be most likely cases for hierarchical security arrangements? Confounding

---

[23] Farrell 2005.   [24] Author's interview 2013.   [25] Author's interview 2013.
[26] Shillington 2009.
[27] www.defenceweb.co.za/index.php?option=com_content&view=article&id=32423:sey chelles-peoples-defence-forces&catid=119:african-militaries.

expectations, none of the four is in a hierarchical security relationship. Liechtenstein has consistently pursued a policy of unarmed neutrality through both world wars up to the present.[28] Nauru refused an Australian defence guarantee at independence,[29] hosts no bases, has no allies, and (as noted earlier) has no military forces. The Seychelles sought a British security guarantee in the run-up to independence, but this was refused as part of the United Kingdom's retreat from all defence commitments East of Suez.[30] The Seychelles then invited the United States to set up a naval base, an invitation that was declined on the grounds that Diego Garcia was sufficient. The country did, however, host a US satellite tracking station on the main island of Mahé, even during the time of one-party Marxist rule, concurrent with the presence of 'fraternal support' from Tanzanian troops.[31] The Seychelles has no formal alliances. A number of foreign militaries have had some sort of temporary presence on the island as part of the international campaign against Somali pirates.[32] Yet, taking into account that many countries host some sort of temporary military presence on their soil, even the United States, it seems unwarranted to conclude that a hierarchical relationship exists on this basis alone.[33] St Kitts and Nevis does maintain an alliance: the Eastern Caribbean Regional Security System, the most powerful member of which is Barbados, an unlikely great power patron. Looking at the functions of this alliance, they all relate to policing and natural disasters, with no equivalent of NATO's famous clause about an armed attack against one being considered an attack against all.[34]

Thus, in sum, there is much less evidence of hierarchy in military affairs even among the countries where we should be most likely to find it, tiny defenceless micro-states. Though there may be other micro-states that have extensive foreign military presence and do seem to fit the hierarchy template (e.g. the Marshall Islands), there are more that do not. Most micro-states have no armies, no allies, no bases and hence no hierarchical security arrangements. Their behaviour, supported by interview evidence from all four countries, strongly suggests that currently they do not take the threat of military invasion seriously. Quantitative evidence backs up this point, in that 'state death' (being conquered) is surprisingly unrelated to size or military power.[35] The idea that micro-states are too small to be worth conquering completely fails to account for the fact that each has been bitterly fought over in the past, while, of course, the political situation of the dependencies, which are no bigger, is a direct product of earlier

---

[28] Beattie 2004.   [29] Viviani 1970.   [30] Scarr 1999; Mancham 2009.
[31] Shillington 2009.   [32] Author's interview 2013.   [33] See Chapter 7.
[34] www.rss.org.bb/about-us/functions-of-the-rss.aspx.   [35] Fazal 2007.

invasion and annexation. The claim that because conquest is no longer a danger in most parts of the world, the security realm is not a fair test of the hierarchy hypothesis would be a rather contrived attempt to explain away disconfirming evidence by artificially constricting the domain of application of the argument. After all, technological progress has made these places more vulnerable to invasion rather than less. Changing norms about the permissibility of conquest have obviated the functional need to adopt hierarchical security solutions, while norms of sovereign equality have dulled the desire for such measures.

Hierarchy and Economies of Scale

If micro-states can be seen as most likely cases for military security via hierarchy, broadly the same logic applies for the institutions that underpin economic viability. Given their tiny physical and demographic size, the corresponding lack of economic diversification, often coupled with remoteness from major markets, micro-states face daunting diseconomies of scale. While many of these are brute facts, others could potentially be addressed through the institutions of hierarchy, specifically by delegating what are conventionally sovereign economic privileges to larger states. Examples might be customs unions, dollarisation or equivalents and delegating financial supervision, commercial law and monetary policy to larger patron states. As discussed below, there are indeed important examples of just these sorts of institutional responses to the challenge of smallness, but once again, these are less common than we might expect.

An interview with the Seychellois Foreign Minister (and former economic advisor to the president) in 2013 fleshes out the nature of the problem. He pointed out that as a middle-income country the Seychelles has a per capita gross domestic product (GDP) that is far higher than most sub-Saharan countries and has had much more political and legal stability over the last twenty years. However, the Seychelles still faces higher borrowing costs than these countries because foreign commercial lenders are worried about the lack of diversification in the economy, dependent as it is on fish and tourism. But, despite this challenge, the Seychelles has opted to retain its own currency, central bank, monetary policy and commercial courts and has not joined any customs union. In this sense, the economic sovereignty of the Seychelles is roughly the same as that of the United States despite the vast difference in the size of the two economies. The Seychelles has, however, drawn extensively on the concessional lending facilities open to it as a sovereign state from the Bretton Woods institutions. The government's response to an economic crisis in 2008, when public debt reached almost 150 per cent of GDP, is a fairly conventional story of structural adjustment that would be reasonably familiar from the perspective of Asian countries in the late 1990s or Greece, Ireland or Portugal in the Euro Crisis.[36]

As with the case of alliances discussed earlier, arguing that receiving conditional loans from a multilateral development bank constitutes hierarchy seems to represent the same sort of concept-stretching. Though multilateral development banks have at various points exercised a great deal of influence over micro-states like the Seychelles, St Kitts and Nevis[37] and Nauru,[38] and in the case of dependencies the Cook Islands too, conflating this influence with the formal authority necessary for hierarchy seems to confuse two very different concepts. The fact that some states practically have more freedom of manoeuvre than others is trivially true but is not evidence of hierarchy.[39] There is more evidence of hierarchy for economic than for security purposes, but even so, it is hierarchy à la carte. Perhaps not surprisingly, subordination is more in evidence among the dependencies than the micro-states, but there are many exceptions.

In the second half of the nineteenth century, Liechtenstein was within the customs area of the Austro-Hungarian Empire and used the same currency. After the dissolution of the Empire, the Liechtenstein authorities unilaterally adopted the Swiss franc and left the Austrian customs union to join the Swiss one, also winning agreement that the Swiss would represent Liechtenstein in foreign diplomacy.[40] As a result of this delegation of foreign representation, Liechtenstein joined the European Free Trade Association (EFTA) largely by default when Switzerland did so in 1960. By the time of the negotiations between the rump of EFTA and the now European Union in the early 1990s about forming the European Economic Area (EEA), Liechtenstein was able to negotiate on its own behalf. As a result of separate referendums, Switzerland rejected EEA membership a few weeks before Liechtenstein's citizens voted to join it. The current situation is thus that Liechtenstein is still in a customs and currency union with Switzerland while also being bound by EFTA rules, including EFTA trade deals with such countries as China and having access to EU markets through the EEA.[41] The Principality has thus delegated a whole range of sovereign economic prerogatives to another state (Switzerland) as well as international organisations with some binding supra-national authority. Members of Liechtenstein's twelve-person Foreign Ministry maintain that in so doing the Principality has actually increased its sovereignty relative to the earlier situation where it was exclusively bound to the Swiss.[42]

---

[36] African Development Bank 2011; Kothari and Wilkinson 2013. See also Chapter 9.
[37] International Monetary Fund 2013.   [38] Asian Development Bank 2007.
[39] Waltz 1979.   [40] Duursma 1996.   [41] Beattie 2004.   [42] Author's interview 2013.

The experience of Curaçao shows some important contrasts in how hierarchy works. Until October 2010, Curaçao was the dominant island in the Netherlands Antilles, which jointly constituted one country within the Kingdom of the Netherlands until the other islands either became countries in their own right within the Kingdom (Aruba in 1986 and Sint Maarten in 2010) or were re-integrated into the Netherlands-in-Europe (Bonaire, Saba and St Eustacius). Prior to their dissolution, the Antilles government was repeatedly able to exploit its hierarchical ties with the Netherlands by over-spending domestically until the point of fiscal crisis, before then repeatedly being bailed out by the Dutch.[43] Despite the Antilles having their own currency (the Antilles guilder), their own central bank and the power to tax and spend, they were able to have the best of both worlds. The local government was able to fend off repeated Dutch attempts to impose fiscal discipline, in the name of self-government, while also passing on their losses to the Dutch taxpayers rather than their own. In despair, the Hague attempted to enlist the International Monetary Fund (IMF) to impose a structural adjustment program on the Antilles, a ploy which ultimately failed. The negotiations in 2007–9 to split the Antilles were only secured with yet more Dutch money, with their officials wryly admitting that their 'no more bail-outs' bluff had been called so many times that this line no longer had any credibility (some of the same stereotypes as discussed in Chapter 9 apply here).[44] Clearly, in this instance, hierarchy paid dividends for those at the bottom. More broadly, that this hierarchical relationship still existed at all was despite the failed efforts of successive Dutch governments during the 1970s and 1980s to push their Caribbean dependencies towards independence as sovereign states.[45]

A brief comparison with the Faroe Islands and the Cook Islands shows some marked parallels but also some notable differences. The Faroes suffered a deep recession in the first half of the 1990s that saw GDP fall by up to a fifth, leading to a bail-out by the Danes. Archival records show that like the Dutch in relation to the Antilles, the Danes tried to persuade the IMF to administer the harsh economic medicine. The IMF, however, had no desire to play the enforcer in what it saw as a domestic matter. Yet, unlike the Antilles, the Faroes did undergo wrenching reforms. A vital escape valve was provided by the fact that the Faroese have the freedom to live and work in the metropole, and something like 10 per cent of the population left to look for work in Denmark.[46] The same logic obtained when the Cook Islands fired around half of its government workforce

---

[43] Oostindie and Klinkers 2003; author's interview 2009.   [44] Author's interview 2009.
[45] Oostindie and Klinkers 2003.   [46] Author's interview 2008.

during its own economic crisis in the mid-1990s,[47] leading to a spike in emigration to New Zealand. In these cases, the small size of the dependency, coupled with the option of de-camping to the metropole to work, claim welfare and send back remittances, has provided an invaluable buffer during hard economic times. It has, however, also posed a longer-term threat in terms of a brain drain and more general de-population.[48] Significantly, freedom of movement only works one way: Faroese can work in Denmark and Cook Islanders in New Zealand, but it is difficult for residents of the metropole to work in the dependency.

Thus, in general, both sovereign micro-states and dependent territories have entered into some important hierarchical economic relationships. Despite their uniformly small size, they have responded to this challenge in a variety of ways. The Seychelles runs its economic affairs along broadly the same institutional lines as a state with a thousand times its population in accord with the expectation of sovereign equality and independence and with no concessions to hierarchy. The Cayman Islands needs permission from the United Kingdom to borrow but otherwise maintains its own currency and fiscal, monetary and regulatory policies. The Faroes, the Cooks, Nauru and Liechtenstein take the clearly hierarchical approach of adopting a super-ordinate state's currency, though they otherwise vary in their economic subordination, with the Faroes having alienated the most sovereignty in this realm.[49] St Kitts and Nevis and Curaçao take an intermediate approach of adopting a regional solution to currency, monetary policy and regulatory supervision. The former shares the Eastern Caribbean Dollar and Central Bank with six other states and two UK Overseas Territories, and the latter has joint arrangements with Sint Maarten (of the other Dutch Caribbean Islands, Aruba has its own currency and central bank, whereas the remainder use the US dollar). In principle, these regional shared sovereignty arrangements seem no more (or less) hierarchical than their much better known EU equivalents. Given the overall variation, the delegation or alienation of sovereign economic perspective again seems to have been done on a fairly bespoke basis.

Diplomacy and Constitutional Affairs

This final empirical section examines evidence on hierarchy in international law, diplomacy and constitutional structure. Practices such as diplomatic recognition are the essence of sovereignty and presumably therefore also of deviations from the classic model of such, such as hierarchy.

---

[47] Larmour 2002; author's interview 2009.
[48] Skaale 2004; author's interviews 2008, 2009.   [49] Skaale 2004.

If sovereignty and hierarchy are both centred on authority, then these subjects are fundamental. Again, what might be expected to be a sharp line between sovereign and non-sovereign polities blurs in practice.

With regards to the dependencies, by definition, they do not have generalised diplomatic recognition as sovereign states, and none is a member of the United Nations. However, the Cook Islands, for example, has a Ministry of Foreign Affairs, despite having constitutionally delegated responsibility for foreign affairs to New Zealand under the association agreement (author's interview, 2009). In July 1997, China and the Cook Islands established diplomatic relations at the ambassadorial level 'on the basis of the principles of mutual respect for sovereignty and territorial integrity'.[50] Various dependencies have either sought to join or actually joined specialised inter-governmental organisations such as the International Maritime Organisation. The Cayman Islands plays an important role in international bodies dealing with securities (International Organisation of Securities Commissions), insurance (International Association of Insurance Supervisors) and tax (OECD Global Forum on Taxation). It has signed a mutual legal assistance treaty with the United States and tax treaties with a range of countries, including the United Kingdom.

For Nauru, the period leading up to and immediately after independence posed questions of sovereign authority in particularly stark form, with the prospect of moving the entire jurisdiction with all its population from one island to another. Something approaching 90 per cent of the surface area of the island had been rendered uninhabitable by the phosphate mining that was the island's only source of economic viability.[51] Acting on the advice of a visiting UN delegation, the pre-independence Nauruan local government considered abandoning the island and re-establishing the country on one of Australia's coastal islands. Any prospect of a deal broke down, however, because the Nauruans wanted full self-government in the new location excepting only defence, foreign affairs and quarantine, whereas the Australian government was only prepared to give very limited powers of local government.[52] Thus, in 1968, the Republic of Nauru obtained independence on the territory of the island of Nauru. At the time mustering a population of 4,000 people, Nauru declined to delegate any sovereign prerogatives or enter into hierarchical relations (with the exception of the currency, as noted earlier) but also essentially opted out of the international system. It declined to join the United Nations and all other international organisations (barring

[50] www.chinaembassy.org.nz/eng/kkqd/t39446.htm.   [51] Hughes 1964, 2004.
[52] Viviani 1970; Hughes 2004; author's interview 2012.

the Commonwealth and South Pacific Forum) despite invitations and did not maintain ambassadors. The logic was that since the country was the size of a small town, it should act like a municipal government.[53] This position only changed once Nauru's phosphate ran out in the 1990s.

The experiences of the Seychelles and the Netherlands Antilles demonstrate the power of the norm of sovereign equality, though with different outcomes. The last pre-independence election in the Seychelles was won by an anti-independence party that wanted some sort of associated state or dependency status link with the United Kingdom.[54] Stung by charges of imperialism in the United Nations and the Organisation of African Unity, however, the British were having none of this hierarchy and insisted on full sovereignty.[55] The Dutch were just as keen to cut their ties with the Caribbean but were much less successful. From the early 1970s, the Dutch worked hard to push Surinam to independence, after which the country suffered a military coup, massive economic decline and correspondingly large exodus to the Netherlands (even the original independence leaders emigrated). Noting this precedent, the Dutch Caribbean islands refused various inducements for independence. The Netherlands-in-Europe was constitutionally hemmed in, only having the extreme option of itself seceding from the Kingdom of the Netherlands and starting a new country. In 1986, the Hague convinced Aruba to accept independence in 1996, but immediately after the deal was done, the Arubans worked to subvert it, ultimately succeeding in the early 1990s.[56] Thus, in these examples, the pressures to replace international hierarchy with sovereign statehood came from anti-colonial colonisers and were resisted by the pro-colonial colonised.

Some echoes of this dynamic were present in the British three-island associated state of St Kitts-Nevis-Anguilla after 1967. The latter two smaller islands feared domination by the (relatively) more numerous Kittitians, and each strongly preferred to be a dependency in direct association with London.[57] This paralleled the attitude of the Cayman Islands at the time of Jamaica's independence in 1962, the Caymanians strongly preferring to remain a dependency linked with Britain than becoming part of an independent Jamaica.[58] The governments in London and especially Basseterre (St Kitts) were adamantly against splitting the three islands. The Anguillans chased out the local police and held a referendum which overwhelmingly endorsed the option of being a British dependency separate from the other islands. The template was to have internal self-

[53] Author's interviews 2008, 2012.   [54] Mancham 2009; author's interview 2013.
[55] Scarr 1999; Mancham 2009; Shillington 2009.
[56] Author's interview 2005; Oostindie and Klinkers 2003.   [57] Abbott 1983–4.
[58] Roberts 1995.

government while the United Kingdom handled foreign affairs and defence. The British rejected the decision. The Anguillans then held a second referendum, this time on independence, again garnering a huge majority in favour. At this point, the British lost patience and decided on a military solution, sending several Royal Navy ships and a detachment of paratroopers. This operation was dubbed the 'Bay of Piglets', as the troops stormed ashore to the derision of a sizeable media contingent.[59] In London, the opposition sarcastically congratulated the Prime Minister in the House of Commons for at last having taken on an opponent his own size. Yet, in the end, victory belonged to the Anguilla, which remains a UK Overseas Territory to this day.[60]

The Anguillan debacle further reinforced the difficulty for Britain in convincing Nevis to accept independence as part of a federation with St Kitts. Eventually in 1983 the Nevisians agreed to the deal, but only on the condition that they retained self-government and had the right to secede as a separate state after obtaining a two-thirds majority in a referendum on the matter. Nevis came very close to achieving this goal in a 1998 referendum that would have made the 13,000 people on the island the western hemisphere's smallest state. The independence blue-print was to maintain a customs union and free movement of people with St Kitts, stay within the Eastern Caribbean dollar and eschew any armed forces.[61] Independent Nevis would also have had the Privy Council in London as its supreme appellate court, as St Kitts and Nevis does today. Currently, Nevis has its own legislature, cabinet and premier and separate corporate law (see Table 6.2).

Hierarchy à la Carte in Micro-States and Dependencies

Although much of the preceding discussion has dealt with exceptions to the standard template of sovereignty, what stands out is nevertheless the relative rarity of hierarchy. It would seem that by any objective functional standard, the massive diseconomies of scale faced by all of these tiny polities would have militated in favour of far more hierarchy than is actually observed. In most respects, micro-states are institutional clones of other states, irrespective of the vast disparity in material capabilities. This fact would seem to reflect the direct and indirect power of the norm of sovereign equality and related shared beliefs about legitimacy in the contemporary international system. Although addressing much larger nations, Jackson's classic work about how 'quasi-states' persist not only due to the lack of competition for survival but even more so because of the

---

[59] Abbott 1971.   [60] Mawby 2012.   [61] Author's interview 2013.

Table 6.2 *Micro-states, Dependencies and Sovereignty*

Polity	Army	Alliance	Currency	Local Supreme Court	Financial Supervisor
Liechtenstein	No	No	No (Swiss franc)	Yes	Yes
Nauru	No	No	No (Australian dollar)	Yes	Yes
St Kitts and Nevis	Yes	Yes (Eastern Caribbean)	No (East Caribbean dollar)	No (Eastern Caribbean and UK)	No (Eastern Caribbean)
Seychelles	Yes	No	Yes (Seychelles rupee)	Yes	Yes
Cayman Islands	No	Yes (UK)	Yes (Cayman dollar)	No (UK)	Yes
Cook Islands	No	Yes (New Zealand)	No (New Zealand dollar)	No (UK)	Yes
Curaçao	No	Yes (Netherlands)	No (Caribbean guilder)	No (Netherlands)	Yes
Faroe Islands	No	Yes (Denmark)	No (Danish kroner)	No (Denmark)	No (Denmark)

normative, legal and logistic safety net established to support such states seems very relevant here.[62]

Perhaps the purest incarnation of this sovereignty norm is in the UN Committee on Decolonisation. According to the Committee, ridding the world of the scourge of colonialism requires that all seventeen of the remaining recognised Non-Self-Governing Territories be given independence, including Pitcairn Island (population fifty).[63] Apparently, in this context, self-determination should proceed regardless of the actual wishes of the populations involved, since many (like Anguilla and the Falkland Islands) have consistently expressed their wish for continued dependency rather than sovereign independence.

Conclusion

In concluding that there is a surprising lack of hierarchy in the contemporary international system, this in no way undermines the value of studying international hierarchy. Leaving aside the virtues of studying a concept in the abstract, the current lack of hierarchy is probably very much the exception rather than rule historically. Over the centuries,

[62] Jackson 1990.   [63] www.un.org/en/decolonization/.

hierarchy has dominated, and the situation of like units under anarchy is very rare, especially outside IR's native habitat of Western Europe. Recent studies of historical hierarchy in East Asia[64] and the Indian Ocean littoral strongly endorse the idea that hierarchy was the norm for centuries.[65] Even the European empires that dominated the world until the last fifty years were organised along hierarchical lines.[66] Thus, perhaps one of the most important findings is that if we are left with only small fragments of hierarchy today, this gives us a better appreciation of the un-representativeness of the current international system of formally equal sovereign states.

[64] Kang 2010b; Johnston 2012.   [65] Phillips and Sharman 2015.   [66] Reus-Smit 2013.

7 Command and Control?

Hierarchy and the International Politics of Foreign Military Bases

Alex Cooley

Foreign military bases have long been viewed as both symbols and sites of international hierarchy. Scholars and commentators regularly refer to the US basing network as an "empire," whereas overseas bases are considered to be markers of enduring foreign influence, control, and coercion.[1] David Lake uses the numbers of foreign troops in any subordinate country (divided by national population) as a measure of security hierarchy in developing his arguments about authority and security patronage in the international system.[2]

But scholars of US base politics themselves differ over what precisely is hierarchical in relations between a troop "sender" and a basing host.[3] Some accounts argue that foreign troop deployments, like imperial settlements, inevitably bring extensive foreign influence, exploitation of local areas and populations, and unwanted interference in local politics.[4] More recently, from a structural perspective, Daniel Nexon and I have argued that the architecture of the US global basing network combines both elements of empires – heterogeneous contracts and indirect rule – with features of multilateral order (e.g., NATO commitments and standardized Status of Forces Agreements).[5] As a result, the United States increasingly faces many of the pathologies of imperial systems, but it usually lacks the capacity to exert control over the policies of its base hosts, rendering it vulnerable to periodic bargaining failures, the disruptive entrance of alternative security patrons, and even evictions by base hosts.[6] And some other researchers, consistent with Sharman's

---

[1] For an overview, see Cooley and Nexon 2013. On hierarchy and order, see Lake 1996, 2009; Weber 1999; Nexon and Wright 2007; Nexon 2009.

[2] Lake 2009, 68–9. [3] Cooley 2008.

[4] Gerson and Birchard 1991; Johnson 1999, 2000, 2004; Lutz 2009. Kaplan (2005) views the empire analogy as a positive.

[5] Cooley and Nexon 2013.

[6] US forces have been evicted from their bases in Uzbekistan (2005), Philippines (1991), Thailand (1976), Libya (1970), France (1966), and (Morocco 1956). More recently, the United States has been forced to withdraw after unsuccessful renewal negotiations from Ecuador (2007), Iraq (2011), and Kyrgyzstan (2014).

skepticism in this book (see Chapter 6), explore how, over time, basing agreements can shed their initial hierarchical character and embed themselves in a broader security community or "enduring partnerships."[7]

Looking beyond the structural imperatives of the US basing network, for this book I am interested in uncovering the range of issues that inform basing relations between a sender and basing host and relate them to the forms and characteristics of international hierarchy laid out in the Introduction. Following the Introduction's distinctions about different types of hierarchy, I explore how military bases embody both a functional/bargained tight concept of hierarchy and also invoke changing social connotations embedded in broader social structures. These different understandings inform not only varying theoretical approaches to understanding the purpose and political dynamics of overseas military bases but also inform policymakers' views of basing dynamics once they are enmeshed in the contractual arrangements that govern their legal standing and operation.

Interestingly, identifying how different actors respond to the basing relationship and its hierarchical features is both complicated and compelled by the current normative taboo that surrounds the term "military base." Over the last two decades, the topic of foreign military bases has acquired a distinctly pejorative connotation in international public diplomacy, signaling foreign domination or coercive influence, much like the evolution of the International Relations (IR) term "hegemony." Both US defense planners and host country officials seem to dread the political ramifications of using the term "military base" to describe US overseas facilities, especially when referring to a short-term or campaign-specific forward deployment; instead, installations that once were routinely referred to as "bases" are now termed "host country installations," "rotational presences," "coalition facilities," or simply "access agreements."

Further, IR scholars of different theoretical predilections (e.g., realists, liberal institutionalists, and constructivists) often assume away the political dynamics generated by basing relations by subordinating them analytically to the overall broader security relationship, multilateral security architecture, or normative foundations of a "security community." Lake's own theory of hierarchy, beyond his use of foreign troops as an indicator of security hierarchy, posits that in exchange for deference to the authority and order provided by a dominant state, subordinate states (such as base hosts) receive the benefit of spending less on their security. This argument captures the functional logic of several important US overseas basing relations and prevails in the assumptions of US policymakers and

[7] Duke 1989; Sandars 2000; Calder 2007; Yeo 2011; and Pettyjohn and Vick 2013.

analysts.[8] However, bases are used for a variety of purposes, with these roles implicating the United States and other senders in different types of contractual, security, and symbolic conceptualizations of hierarchy.

I begin this chapter by outlining the classic organizational or functional logic of US basing as embedded in Williamsonian theory about the logics of markets and hierarchies, especially the bargaining dynamics generated by relationally specific assets. Next, I overview how bases were central to decolonization bargains, effectively embedding a mode of continuing hierarchy at the very point of independence and sovereignty, and I then discuss the evolution of the legal regimes governing basing relations. I then take up the question of the changing normative significance of "military bases" and illustrate how these different contractual and social understandings of bases actually reflect the US and Russian positions, respectively, about foreign military bases in contemporary Eurasia. Finally, I overview the emerging move toward "hidden hierarchy" in the US security network. Although most of the theoretical work on the politics of basing remains overwhelmingly focused on the United States, comparisons with France, the United Kingdom, and the Russian Federation yield important insights into the varying roles and functions of overseas bases. Understanding them seems even more pressing as we enter an era of probable US global retrenchment and the rise of "emerging powers," where multiple security patrons increasingly vie for basing rights within the same regions.

Bargaining Logic: Bases as Relational Contracting

The first perspective on basing is that offered by relational contracting and theories of firm organization and institutional adoption pioneered by Oliver Williamson – a classical functional logic of hierarchy. The Williamsonian model posits that in situations where transactions among firms are frequent and there are no readily available substitutes on the open market, firms will opt for vertical integration rather than market-based contracting with suppliers of the specific asset in order to avoid the "holdup problem."[9] In the international political setting, asset specificity has been explored as a key determinant of whether dominant states might opt for formal hierarchy – colonialism or formal institutions – in their dealings with subordinate states.[10] The model's central insight for basing

---

[8] This basic bargain convincingly characterizes US relations with Japan, South Korea, and the Gulf States, which all greatly subsidize the presence of US facilities so that they have their security needs met by an outside patron.

[9] Williamson 1975 and 1985.

[10] Frieden 1994; Lake 2009 and 1999; and Cooley and Spruyt 2009.

relations is that for installations acquired by the sender via contracting, as opposed to military occupation or conquest, the relative bargaining power of a sovereign base host vis-à-vis the sender will be determined more by the specificity of the assets involved rather than by the relative military power balance between host and sender. In this way, even small and weak states can exert significant bargaining leverage over sending powers if they host basing assets that are difficult or too expensive to substitute.[11]

US Basing Network as the Organizational Equivalent of a Global Multinational Company

Though political analogies to economic environments must always be qualified, the US basing network shares certain important features with a large multinational company with a global footprint. First, the United States has hundreds of "holdings" in its network that are scattered over a hundred countries. Administratively, the United States governs its network of bases and overseas assets through both functional units responsible for network-wide tasks and roles (e.g., logistics and transport, special forces, and intelligence gathering) and the regional commands assigned to specific areas of operations.[12] As with any large organization, these cross-cutting imperatives spawn a whole set of coordination challenges, organizational rivalries, and redundancies across the network.

Applying relational contracting to US basing relations, the determinants of a particular installation's "asset specificity" will hinge on a number of factors that shape the overall organization of the US basing network, including the importance of any given asset to a priority theater, the availability of alternative sites for the same role, the timing of a military operation, particular doctrinal innovations that emphasize or deemphasize the asset's role, and overall technological change that may suddenly increase or decrease the importance of certain installations (i.e., shift from bombers to ballistic missiles).[13] Thus, in purely material terms, a base's or installation's relative position and value within the network *should* be relatively straightforward to calculate,[14] though for other political reasons (e.g., diplomatic norms, domestic politics, and interservice rivalry), US officials may overplay or downplay the asset's positional value within the broader basing network.

---

[11] Cooley and Spruyt 2009, Chapter 4.   [12] Blaker 1990.
[13] See Harkavy 2005; and Lake 2013, 84–85.
[14] Annual US Base Structure overviews report the Plant Replacement Value or PRV of each officially designated base.

Political Consequences of Hosting Relationally Specific Assets

Important theoretical caveats about relational contracting aside – for example, its neglect of sociocultural context and firm conventions, incomplete contracting's insights that property rights can be split or shared, and the importance of overall network effects on the nested dyadic relationship – Williamsonian theory provides important insights into basing relations between sender and host. First, all else being equal, sending states will be more likely to assume the high costs of direct rule (formal hierarchy) and governance over a periphery that hosts a relationally specific military base. Or, according to the model's logic, when choosing among possible overseas sites for new assets (say, a missile defense radar or interceptors), sending states are more likely to locate them in nonsovereign territories already under hierarchy.

Anecdotally, we some evidence of this across multiple sending countries – the United States redeploying politically controversial assets from Okinawa to the unincorporated territory on Guam or France recently designating New Caledonia as its consolidated Pacific basing hub.[15] Hansen has argued that throughout decades of formal hierarchy exerted by the United States over the Guantánamo Naval Station in Cuba, US officials have deliberately taken advantage of the facility's nonsovereign status to avoid extending US and international legal protections to political asylum seekers, such as Haitian boat refugees, or, most recently, indefinitely detaining a group of "enemy combatants" captured in the global war on terror without affording them US Constitutional protections.[16] However, in situations where imposing formal hierarchy is not an option and sender and host are not bound by a security commitment, US planners must contract for these basing rights with a sovereign host. Negotiating for basing rights, in turn, generates hard-bargaining dynamics and empowers host states to hold up renewals, especially after expiration of the initial agreements. In such contracting situations, rational base hosts will demand quid pro quo that approaches, but does not exceed, the cost of the United States replacing the asset with the next-best alternative.[17]

Accordingly, the compensation packages or quid pro quo paid by the United States generally has tracked changes in the specificity of facilities to the overall US posture. In the 1970s and 1980s, the peak of "base bidding wars" during the cold war, even formal allies such as Greece, Turkey, Portugal, and the Philippines demanded substantial aid packages

[15] Vine 2009.   [16] Hansen 2011.
[17] Cooley and Spruyt 2009. This reasoning appears in US defense planners thinking about bases as early as Nash 1957.

for renewing US basing rights.[18] The aftermath of the cold war saw the "basing rights market" effectively dissolve as the United States retrenched from many overseas positions and saw no reason to continue paying its basing hosts when it enjoyed the dominance of the post–cold war liberal order. However, following the onset of the global war on terror and new US interventions in Afghanistan and Iraq, the United States, albeit reluctantly and often tacitly, found itself having to compensate new base hosts in Central Asia, the Middle East, and Africa to establish and maintain access.

Regarding domestic politics, countries hosting specific assets, regardless of their relative power, will be in strong positions to use the holdup threat to stem political criticism of the regime – say, on issues of democracy or human rights – and pare down conditionalities that otherwise might be demanded by the sender. The awkwardly muted US reaction to Bahrain's post–Arab Spring crackdown on democracy activists and Shia demonstrators is a good case in point, as was the general silence that US officials showed when Kyrgyzstan's President Bakiyev escalated his political crackdown in years 2007–9. In both instances, US officials tempered political criticisms because of the underlying threat that these small states could curtail basing rights.[19] None of this is particular surprising or unique to the United States – great powers have always made expedient political bargains with countries that hosted strategically important assets (energy producers are another classic set of cases) – however, these wide inconsistencies are more routinely pointed to by global media outlets as examples of US cynicism and double standards, substantially raising broader US hypocrisy costs when it makes such political concessions.[20]

Institutionalizing Hierarchy within Anarchy: Bases as Imperial Legacies

A second strong connection between international hierarchy and foreign military bases lies in the actual decolonization or sovereign bargains that have legalized and institutionalized basing rights in hosts that were former colonies or previously occupied by the sender.[21] Here, inserting hierarchical bargains as institutional solutions to decolonization actually informs the very establishment of nominally sovereign polities. In a host of cases of imperial disengagement, former metropoles struck deals to retain the use of strategic military and economic assets in former colonies by employing

---

[18] Clarke and Daniel O'Connor 1993.
[19] On these cases, see, respectively, Cooley and Nexon 2011 and Cooley 2014.
[20] Cooley and Nexon 2013. On hypocrisy costs, see Farrell and Finnemore 2013.
[21] This section draws on Cooley 2013.

hybrid forms of governance such as territorial leases.[22] Basing rights were often at the core of these "conditional decolonization" bargains – hosts had to acquiesce to granting basing rights to the former metropole and military occupier in order to actually formally secure their juridical independence.[23] These acts constituted single points of consent that established the legal framework on which basing rights were accepted and subsequently renegotiated. In some cases these basing carve-outs were written into the very nascent constitution of the newly independent host country, whereas in others they were governed by a lease or bundled into a bilateral security agreement. Hierarchy therefore endured in the form of basing rights, though it did so under a new legal rubric.

US Imperial and Wartime Basing Acquisitions

In the case of the United States, two main waves of "conditional sovereignty" bargains helped to establish many of the sites that endure in its global basing network. The first wave followed US imperial expansion in the late nineteenth century and early twentieth century, netting the US facilities in the Philippines, Cuba, and Panama, as well as Hawaii and territories across the Pacific.[24] In the first three cases, the guarantee of generous US basing rights was actually inscribed in these countries' nascent constitutions. The second major group of acquisitions took place in the aftermath of World War II, where the United States concluded basing deals with wartime allies and conditioned deoccupation and from Japan, Germany, and Italy on the retention of basing rights. The Japanese case is especially striking because not only did the United States obtain rights to a network of permanent bases through the 1952 Peace Agreements, but under Article III it also lopped off the island prefecture of Okinawa – Tokyo being awarded a new legal designation of "residual sovereignty" – which was formally administered by the US military until its reversion in 1972 to Tokyo.[25] This foundational sovereign bargain itself was skillfully maneuvered by Japanese Prime Minister Yoshida Shigeru, who invoked Japanese political fragility and pending collapse to limit Japan's concessions to granting post-treaty basing rights, avoiding an expensive and politically difficult acquiescence to initial US requests that Japan rearm.[26] Not surprisingly, this differential experience of the US military presence between the main islands of

[22] Cooley and Spruyt 2009. On the political dynamics of decolonization see Spruyt 2005.
[23] As Halperin and Palan argue in the same project, transitions from empire to independence are usually incomplete.
[24] Lafeber 1998; Kramer 2011 and 2006; and Burnett 2005.   [25] See Eldridge 2001.
[26] Samuels 2003, 203–209.

Japan and Okinawa, which along with its direct experience of US military rule continues to host 75 percent of all US military facilities in Japan, also explains the diverging political attitudes in Tokyo and Naha toward US military bases today.[27] In Okinawa, regional officials invoke a more direct link between imperialism and the US basing presence than the various bureaucracies in Tokyo, where US facilities are more broadly accepted as serving the mutual security of the two countries.[28] For many Okinawans, in contrast, US bases are also direct symbols and contentious sites of the prefecture's unequal relations with Tokyo and the "unfair" military burden that it shoulders on behalf of Japan.[29]

European Conditional Decolonization Bargains

The European cases of decolonization frequently were structured along the "bases for independence" formula, though this was more a feature of France's decolonization bargains than Britain's. Most notably, "conditional sovereignty" base bargains were critical to French disengagement from the entire African continent. In North Africa, France granted Tunisia its independence in 1956 and agreed to withdraw all troops except for those at its base Bizerta, which was leased and whose precise sovereign status was left undecided.[30] In the famous Algerian Evian Accords of 1962 that followed the seven-year Algerian war, Algeria was granted its independence but ceded basing rights to the naval station of Mers-el-Kébir for fifteen years. The formula was widely used in sub-Saharan Africa, where in 1960 France systematically granted independence to fourteen former colonies, securing postindependence basing rights in seven of those new states.[31] Except for Chad, these agreements were all renewed in the early 1970s.

Unlike France, Britain's more gradual retreat from its Empire created a more mixed pattern of voluntary relinquishment of overseas basing sites and conditional independence. In the interwar period, Britain demanded basing rights from the Irish Free State in 1922 and negotiated eventual "conditional decolonization" bargains in Iraq (1932) and Jordan (1946), but by the 1950s it was very much an "empire in retreat," ceding many of its overseas facilities voluntarily. In a twist on the "conditional

---

[27] On US military administration, see Yoshida 2001.

[28] For this reason, in Cooley 2008 I devote different chapters to explaining the respective domestic politics of US bases on Okinawa and on the main islands of Japan.

[29] See Johnson 1999.   [30] I rely on Cooley and Spruyt 2009, 58–68.

[31] Senegal (Dakar), Madagascar (Diego-Suarez), Cameroon (Fort Lamy), Chad (Ndjamena), Côte d'Ivoire (Port Bouet), Gabon (Libreville), and Central African Republic (Bangui). In 1977 Djibouti - host to a major set of installations - was also granted "conditional independence." See Chipman 1989.

sovereignty" pattern, Britain also transferred basing rights from former colonies to the United States. The most well known of these cases was that of the Mauritius and the creation of the British Indian Ocean Territory (BIOT), host to the US base of Diego Garcia. In exchange for its sovereignty, Whitehall forced Mauritius to relinquish the Chagos islands chain, which, immediately after, was named as the BIOT and leased to the United States as a site designated for base construction, also precipitating the forced ouster of 1,500 to 2,000 of the island's residents.[32] Nevertheless, the United Kingdom did grant two more classic cases of conditional independence to the Mediterranean island states of Cyprus and Malta in exchange for maintaining basing rights.[33]

Unlike these previous cases, the legal agreements that facilitated the sovereign apportioning and transfer of Soviet-era military assets to the Russian Federation and its former satellites were established after the Soviet dissolution in December 1991; they were not central to the actual process of decolonization. Having rapidly collapsed under the centrifugal forces unleashed by Gorbachev's decentralizing reforms, political experimentation, and the rise of nationalist elites at the republic level, the apportioning and governance of Soviet-era assets and basing installations were achieved post hoc, because Moscow concluded a number of bilateral leasing arrangements with the post-Soviet states in the 1990s. These installations included early-warning radar stations (Latvia, Belarus, and Azerbaijan), the Baikonur Cosmodrome (Kazakhstan), and several missile-testing sites.[34] The most important of these leasing deals, until 2014, was the 1997 agreement to partition the Black Sea Fleet between Russia and Ukraine, with Kyiv also agreeing to lease to Moscow harbor facilities in Sevastopol for twenty years for an annual $100 million rental payment. In 2010, newly elected Ukrainian President Viktor Yanukovych extended the agreement for a further twenty-five years in exchange for Russian energy subsidies. The deal was revoked by Moscow in March 2014 following its annexation of Crimea.

[32] Vine 2009. The base now is perhaps the most important single overseas US military facility, hosting a harbor that can accommodate an aircraft carrier task force, a large runway that can host heavy bombers and refuelers, surveillance and intelligence facilities, and, by some accounts, a "black site" detention facility used by the CIA. On the base's immense strategic value, see Erickson et al. 2010.
[33] The UK granted Cyprus independence in 1960 only after it had secured the 99-square-mile carve-outs of Dhekelia and Akrotiri, basing sites that became sovereign UK territory and have remained under UK control throughout the island's turbulent postcolonial history, including bouts of intercommunal violence, the 1974 Turkish military intervention, and Cyprus' accession to the EU. See Constantinou and Richmond 2005.
[34] For an inventory and discussion, see Cooley 2001.

Importance of Bases as Hierarchical Legacies

In sum, the extent to which decolonization and deoccupation have been facilitated by basing agreements has been severely underappreciated by IR scholars. A significant share of modern sovereign states had their origins in "conditional sovereignty" agreements that were tied to accepting, at least initially, an enduring basing presence by the former metropole. In other words, hierarchy was embedded within the emergence of these new nominally sovereign units in the anarchical system. In Western Europe, the onset of the cold war and the development of the US-led multilateral security order resolved most of these occupation legacy political tensions, but in the European decolonization cases, as well as select hosts of US facilities, basing rights are still understood as a direct colonial legacy, not as facilities acquired for an enduring partnership or a mutual security purpose.

Hierarchical Contracts and Basing Rights: Reactions and Issues

Beyond considering the role of bases as specific assets and their roles in sovereign bargains, the formal contracts and agreements that govern bases themselves are important hierarchical legal institutions. All peacetime foreign military installations are subject, under international law at least, to host-country consent.[35] Basing agreements come in many different forms – treaties, executive agreements, technical annexes, security cooperation agreements, and so on – but taken as whole, they must specify the types of assets that can be deployed and delineate the rights and obligations of the sending country. Importantly, the degree of hierarchy embodied in this agreement varies across base hosts and over time.[36] Thus their exact provisions are frequently the subject of renegotiations and contentious base politics, as well as comparisons made with the terms secured by comparable base hosts.

Use Rights in Basing Contracts

The most important provisions of basing contracts specify the situations and purposes for which the bases can be used, as well as the procedures (i.e., consultations, notification, and formal consent) for sender–host interactions. Bases can be used to maintain the mutual defense or,

[35] Woodliffe 1992.
[36] Structurally, the heterogeneous nature of these basing contracts lends them the properties of an imperial hub and spokes system. See Cooley and Nexon 2013.

exclusively, to enable the sender to project power into a third area without a defense guarantee extended to the actual host. For example, the Madrid Pacts of 1953, under which the United States obtained basing rights in Franco's Spain, did not extend a security guarantee to the Spanish dictator, though Franco himself publicly trumpeted the deal, concluded at a time when he was ostracized by other Western European countries, as Washington's public acknowledgment of his regime's legitimacy.[37] In Europe during the 1970s and 1980s, even NATO ally base hosts routinely denied basing rights for US out-of-area missions in the Middle East and North Africa. The now dramatic 2003 vote by the Turkish Parliament that failed to grant US forces the right to transit through the country for Operation Iraqi Freedom was necessitated by the fact that the mission was neither of NATO origin nor had been authorized by the United Nations.[38]

At the most hierarchical extreme, sending countries might be granted unrestricted rights to use the bases for any operations without prior specification or host-country consent. For example, early US basing agreements with the Philippines, Cuba, Japan, West Germany, and Italy ceded to the United States the right to use bases to interfere in their domestic affairs in order to promote stability or guarantee the nascent constitutional status quo. These domestic intervention clauses, such as the infamous Platt Amendment inserted by US officials into the Cuban constitution in 1903 or Article 136 of Panama's new constitution proved deeply unpopular and were usually the first items demanded by base host governments to be renegotiated.[39] In the cases of the French sub-Saharan bases, between 1962 and 1995, Paris used its African facilities for nineteen different domestic interventions within these hosts, exclusive of UN operations, including operations to prop up ruling regimes, put down antigovernment protest and riots, defend French nationals, and suppress rebellions.[40] And in a stunning contemporary example, Russia's swift and decisive use of special forces and troops from refer its Sevastopol facilities in February and March 2014 to capture key strategic installations in Crimea was critical for its rapid annexation of the peninsula. After doing so, the potential for overseas Russian troops to

[37] Cooley 2008, 57–62.   [38] *Ibid.*, 130–4.

[39] Platt granted the United States an open-ended right to intervene "for the preservation of Cuban independence, the maintenance of a government adequate for the protection of life, property, and individual liberty, and for discharging [of concluded bilateral] obligations." This amendment was used to justify the so-called second occupation for the country from 1906 to 1909 and was revoked only in 1943 in exchange for the Cuban government accepting a perpetual US lease over Guantanamo. See Hansen 2011; Pérez 1991.

[40] For a list up until 1986, see the chart in Chipman 1989, 124. To these I've added interventions in Gabon (1990) and Djibouti (1991).

intervene in the domestic affairs of their base hosts in Armenia, Belarus, Tajikistan, and Kyrgyzstan seems far more plausible.

Beyond delineating the sender's rights to use the installations, basing contracts may limit the number of troops that can be stationed at the facility and the types of military hardware or assets that can be stationed and deployed. Some of the most controversial of "use rights" restrictions in the US case occurred when base hosts wished to restrict the stationing or transit of nuclear weapons through their territories in violation of US policy to "neither confirm nor deny" their existence. In the case of New Zealand, in 1985, US officials suspended their security commitment under the ANZUS Treaty after the New Zealand government refused port visits to the US Navy for a ship that refuse to deny transiting nuclear weapons on board. Interestingly, the two well-known cases of base hosts that the US granted the nonnuclear transit concession to were Spain and Denmark, both of which in the 1960s experienced a crash involving US bombers that carried actual nuclear warheads.

SOFAs as Use Rights

One other noteworthy category of "basing contracts" is the Status of Forces of Forces Agreements (SOFAs). SOFAs, frequently but often erroneously equated with pure US extraterritoriality, delineate the legal procedures and standing that govern the stationing of foreign forces abroad, where the laws of the sending and host countries must be reconciled. The most contentious of these issues in US cases has been the question of which country retains legal jurisdiction over US service personnel accused of crimes committed within the host country.[41] Until the early 1950s, US troops enjoyed wartime-like immunity and absolute extraterritorial protections – true "legal hierarchy." Under the NATO framework, the United States concluded a set of agreements with its allies that introduced a unique system of "concurrent jurisdiction," where legal jurisdiction was apportioned to sender or host depending on the nature of the crime and the "on or off-duty status" of the service member accused.[42] Nevertheless, the terms and provisions of SOFAs can vary considerably across the US basing network. US officials are particularly reluctant to cede any legal jurisdiction or pretrial custody to countries that are not established allies and lack similar legal protections to those found in the United States, while basing hosts consider the NATO-style SOFA to be the "least hierarchical" standard.

---

[41] See Cooley 2008; Cooley and Nexon 2013.   [42] Delbrück 1993.

In short, even hierarchical basing contracts can vary quite extensively in their legal provisions. From a comparative perspective, French and Russian SOFAs with their overseas base hosts veer more toward the extraterritorial model (pure hierarchy) than the NATO model (mixed jurisdiction). Accordingly, it is inaccurate to blanketly refer to US-negotiated SOFAs as "immunity agreements" for the US military, though practically they are often experienced in this way by certain base hosts.[43] Certainly, these agreements are asymmetrical, and weak states are often pressured into accepting more hierarchical terms than established allies. Tellingly, however, in many hosts it is the actual content of the SOFA and these unequal legal provisions – not the actual stationing of US forces – that is the main focus of antibase activists and protests. As Kathy Moon has pointed out in the South Korean case, most of the Korean antibase campaigns of the early 2000s termed the SOFA unfair and demanded not US withdrawal but rather the renegotiation of the US–Republic of Korea SOFAs so that criminal jurisdiction procedures could be harmonized with equivalent agreements that the United States has with Japan or NATO.[44]

Hierarchy within Hierarchy: Bases as Symbols of Subordination and Foreign Influence

A fourth form of hierarchy associated with military bases is their symbolism and social connotation, which can be thought of as pointing to social hierarchies more broadly understood. Over the years, the term "military base" has itself become associated as a marker of differential status between the host and center, even as a site of actual foreign influence and bilateral hegemony. In general terms, the overall norms associated with foreign military bases have tracked with the overall institutionalization of the norm of sovereignty in international relations. For example, though American imperial acquisitions at the turn of the twentieth century and ensuing "conditional decolonization" bargains during the interwar years were acutely hierarchical, they were not beyond prevailing great power norms of colonialism, extraterritorial legal regimes, and/or the mandate system. However, as decolonization accelerated through the 1950s and 1960s, the norm of national sovereignty strengthened, and foundational neoimperial basing rights agreements were redefined,

---

[43] On this issue, Johnson (1999, 2004) analytically misses the mark. Similarly, Kayaoğlu's (2010) otherwise fine analysis of the rise of Western extraterritorial legal regimes in Japan, the Ottoman Empire, and China also makes this flawed comparison with US military SOFAs, generally characterizing them as "extraterritorial."

[44] Moon 2012.

renegotiated, and more narrowly specified by more assertive and legally capable base hosts.[45] Symbolic issues, such as which country's flag would be flown on the facility or which forces would patrol the entrance, were also deemed centrally important in these revised agreements.

Emerging Foreign Basing Taboo

As a result, in the post–cold war era, the very term "foreign base" carries overtones of undue influence and incursions on a host country's sovereignty. Interestingly, even as states have recognized, accepted, and ultimately accommodated a number of other international practices that routinely violate state sovereignty – such as human rights treaty obligations, arms control inspections, the responsibility to protect, and international election observation missions[46] – attitudes toward foreign bases, even given the more equal renegotiated treaties and SOFAs, appear to have become decisively more negative.

The antibasing norm is so strong now that it is almost a taboo. US and local officials go out of their way to insist that new US base access agreements are forms of "security cooperation" and not a type of "foreign base." The Department of Defense's own official Overseas Base Structure Report from 2012 lists only thirty-nine overseas hosts of officially designated US military installations, though the network of access and stationing agreements far exceeds this around the world.[47] For example, in announcing the new ten-year US-Philippines access deal in Manila in April 2014, President Barack Obama said, "I want to be very clear: the United States is not trying to reclaim old bases or to build new bases. At the invitation of the Philippines, American service members will rotate through Filipino facilities."[48] Even so, the deal allows the United States to both construct new facilities and preposition equipment in designated areas.

However, for other powers, having a network of "foreign bases" may itself be considered a marker of great power status and therefore desirable. This is especially the case with official Russian views about foreign bases and consistent with Russian foreign policymakers' broader emphasis on the importance of international status and status-conferring

---

[45] Cooley and Spruyt 2009.   [46] See Simmons 2009 and Hyde 2011.

[47] Department of Defense 2013, 79–96. The DOD's own criteria for inclusion in the inventory are that a site occupy at least ten acres and be valued at over $10 million plant replacement value (PRV).

[48] Remarks by President Obama and President Benigno Aquino III of the Philippines in Joint Press Conference. Available at www.whitehouse.gov/the-press-office/2014/04/28/ remarks-president-obama-and-president-benigno-aquino-iii-philippines-joi.

agreements.[49] Pushing the argument, it may well be cognitively impossible for Russian officials and security analysts to view "foreign bases" as anything but enduring symbols of international great power status, influence, and hegemony – social logics will always trump pure functional ones. In part, this explains the Russian obsession with the buildup of US military bases in Eurasia and Eastern Europe, though by no means should this detract from seriously considering Russian arguments about the threatening posture created by multiple waves of NATO expansion. But it is also clear that for Russia, securing a network of foreign military bases is both consistent with and constitutive of its reclaimed great power claims.

The point seems to have been underscored by the Russian Defense Minister's statement, in the midst of the Ukrainian crisis in February 2014, that Moscow was currently negotiating a range of new agreements to secure "military bases" in Vietnam, Cuba, Venezuela, Nicaragua, the Seychelles, and Singapore. Yet, as one analysis points out, the actual "military bases" allegedly under negotiation, such as Vietnam's Cam Rahn Bay Port, seem more like "access agreements" that would grant rights for port visits, refueling, and repair for Russian Navy vessels rather than actual new deals to establish sovereign Russian spaces.[50] Nevertheless, the symbolic value of such an international network seems to be of enormous significance to the Kremlin for both domestic and international purposes.

Case Example: Differing US and Russian Views of Bases in Eurasia

The contrasting public diplomacy of the United States and Russia over their respective overseas bases in Eurasia emphasizes both the current prevalence of the US basing taboo and Moscow's view of bases as status markers. In short, contrasting US and Russian policymakers' views of each other's military bases in the region suggest how different governments can act with very different understandings of hierarchical institutions. For the United States, its military bases in Central Asia, in Uzbekistan and Kyrgyzstan, were established in the fall of 2001 to support military operations in Afghanistan.[51] Following the "color revolutions," in whose aftermath the United States was evicted from its K2 base in Uzbekistan, and increasingly critical statements by Russia and China regarding the purpose of the US's military presence in Eurasia, US officials have been at pains to emphasize that the US effort serves an international coalition in Afghanistan, rejecting any accusations that

---

[49] Tsygankov 2016.   [50] Keck 2014.   [51] Cooley 2012.

these bases are used to project power or influence in Central Asia itself.[52] Along these lines, Manas Transit Center in Kyrgyzstan, previously referred to as Manas Air Base and Ganci Air Base, was renamed in 2009 as part of a new "rename and raise the rent" agreement between Washington and Bishkek that sought to publicly deemphasize its "basing functions" and raised the rent from $17 million to $63 million annually.[53] Quite incredibly, the Manas Transit Center was never listed in the Department of Defense's Overseas Base Structure Reports, despite continuously hosting KC-135 refueling operations for Operation Enduring Freedom for nearly thirteen years and staging about 50,000 US service personnel each month during the peak of the Afghanistan "surge."[54] Similarly, across other sites in Central Asia, such as Uzbekistan's newly refurbished Navoi Airport (upgraded by Korea's Hanjin Group under a contract solicited by DOD), US logistics planners have set up a network of base-like facilities that are mostly operated by contractors or other third-party commercial parties, in large part so that US officials can formally deny that they actually operate any Central Asian bases.[55]

By contrast, Russia primarily views and labels its facilities on former Soviet territory as "bases" because it emphasized the social connotations of the term, the implied Russian higher rank order and designation as the region's primary security guarantor. Its own establishment in 2003 of an air base in Kant, Kyrgyzstan, only thirty-five kilometers away from Manas, was a clear reaction to the US presence at Manas. This also gave Kyrgyzstan the distinction of simultaneously hosting separate US and Russian airbases for over a decade. In the wake of the "color revolutions," Russian officials became increasingly obsessed with Manas as a US-backed challenge to Russian regional influence, even offering in February 2009 the regime of Kurmanbek Bakiyev a $2.1 billion aid package to effectively close the base.[56] Moscow was subsequently double-crossed by Kyrgyz President Bakiyev, who took the first installment of $300 million from the Kremlin but then renewed with the United States for a higher rent. But the Kremlin finally got its wish by pressuring the government of President Almazbek Atambayev to refuse to further renew the Manas lease beyond July 2014, prompting the United States to withdraw and relocate its Afghanistan transit flights to facilities in Romania.

Consistent with the social connotations of hierarchy, Moscow has shown a clear preference for securing very long leases for its renegotiated

---

[52] *Ibid.*, Chapter 3.   [53] *Ibid.*, Chapter 7.

[54] Anecdotally, during each of the author's five different site visits to Manas from 2005 to 2012, the facility itself has been referred to as a "base" by the commander or public affairs officer.

[55] See Cooley 2012, Chapter 3.   [56] See Cooley 2012 for details.

agreements in the post-Soviet space. Since 2010, Moscow has concluded separate basing rights renewals extending its presence for an additional twenty-four years with Armenia (extending the 1995 deal until 2044, thereafter with automatic five-year extensions), thirty years with Tajikistan (until 2044), and fifteen years with Kyrgyzstan (until 2032). In 2010, Moscow extended the Black Sea Fleet agreement with President Viktor Yanukovych for an additional twenty-five years beyond its original 2016 deadline (until 2042), though after Moscow's annexation of Crimea in March 2014 the Kremlin declared the previous deal void, thereby also absolving itself of the obligation to provide Kyiv with a discount on future gas sales. In 2011, three years after its recognition of the independence of the Georgian breakaway territories of Abkhazia and South Ossetia, Moscow concluded forty-nine-year basing agreements with the territories. Interestingly enough, during these negotiations, Abkhaz officials acknowledged the inevitable "hierarchical nature" of the draft deal but complained that they had not even been given similar nominal rights of sovereignty as conferred to Armenia, which they regarded as the second most hierarchical of all of Russia's "bilateral" basing deals.[57]

Summary of Bases as Hierarchical Symbols

In sum, the social connotations of foreign military bases and how they intersect with more structural or bargaining logics are critical aspects of basing politics. Not only do we see the emergence of a "foreign military basing taboo," but we also see such contrasting public diplomacy from US and Russian officials regarding the negotiation, role, and function of "foreign bases." In the US case, defense officials, with the important partial exception of allies with defense treaty commitments, are loathe to label facilities as "bases" and/or might even deny their existence altogether to avoid international scrutiny and domestic political attention.[58] However, Russia cannot but regard US facilities in areas of interest such as Central Asia as actual sites of hegemony and instruments of influence because it itself aspires to acquire such a network in order to enhance its own status, hierarchy, and prestige.

[57] Author's interviews with Abkhaz parliamentarians and de facto Ministry of Foreign Affairs officials, Sukhumi, 2010. Abkhazia's independence is recognized only by Russia, Nicaragua, Venezuela, and Nauru.
[58] Most recently, see the coverage of the United States owning up to the fact that it operates the Al Udeid Air Base in Qatar, a facility that US defense planners deliberately and erroneously referred to routinely as a facility "somewhere in southwest Asia." See Barnes 2013.

From Bargaining to Social Logics to New Modes of Action: Hidden Hierarchy and Unofficial Basing

Over the last decade, another notable feature has emerged in US overseas basing – what we might call "hidden hierarchy." Thus far I have explored modes of hierarchical politics and basing issues that have been mostly observable by both hosts and senders and grounded in formal agreements, contracts, and technical agreements that govern the origins and use of bases. But partly as a result of the growing "foreign basing taboo" and its positional connotations and partly as a result of the legal and strategic shifts introduced by the global war on terror, a new set of actors and purposes has emerged that has made the status and use of US overseas facilities more informal and less transparent and has heightened their legal ambiguity. Briefly, consider the importance of military contractors, black sites, and drone bases to this emerging network of "hidden hierarchy."

First, the spectacular emergence of security contractors has both complicated the questions of who comprises the overseas US military and how they might be held legally accountable. The rise of private security companies and contractors (PSCs) has been a striking feature of the post–cold war security landscape.[59] Different countries have adopted different types of governing relations with PSCs, but in the US case they have been integrated into a wide range of military and security services, including maintaining force protection and site security, operational support, managing logistics, gathering intelligence, and providing advising and training services to target countries.

Whatever their utility, the heavy use of contractors has been useful politically to the US executive branch in several ways. Avant notes how the increase in contractors renders congressional oversight more difficult and de facto shifts power away from the legislature to the presidency.[60] But the use of contractors also can counteract some of the more overt or visible signs of hierarchy associated with overseas basing. Using contractors on bases depresses the official number of troops on any facility or arena (good for US domestic politics), even though host countries, in practice, may hardly distinguish between military personnel and contractors. For example, according to one CENTCOM inventory in its area of responsibility in 2012, the regional command employed 113,766 contractors in Afghanistan (more than official troops in the country) and an additional 7,336 in Iraq.[61] Overall in 2012 there were an estimated 13,500 contractors serving all US agencies in Iraq, despite the fact that

---

[59] See especially Avant 2005; Singer 2003.   [60] Avant 2005.
[61] http://nation.time.com/2012/10/09/contractors-in-war-zones-not-exactly-contracting/.

the official mandate authorizing a US presence had expired at the end of 2011, and US forces had officially withdrawn. We should also note that in the Iraq case, arguably, the very immunity of contractors, emphasized by the Nisour Square massacres of 2007 perpetrated by Blackwater contractors, complicated official basing negotiations and was a major stumbling block in the unsuccessful attempt by the United States to extend the US-Iraqi SOFA beyond 2011. In sum, the reliance on contractors allows the United States to continue to perform security-related services in overseas hosts without official acknowledgment of the extent of its footprint or, in cases where contractors almost exclusively staff a security facility, admit to the presence of a US installation.

Second, the global war on terror itself precipitated the use of foreign bases and sites for covert or extralegal operations. According to an Open Societies Foundation report, US extraordinary renditions targeted 136 identified individuals with the complicity of fifty-four foreign host governments.[62] The issue of complicity within this "hidden hierarchy" is especially interesting, for despite severe criticism from investigators such as Council of Europe's Dick Marty, with only a few exceptions, the European host countries identified as enabling US renditions have yet to conduct comprehensive internal probes on the matter.[63] This is all the more important for the question of basing use rights because in many of these cases, under legal agreements, the airfield and sites in question should not have been used without explicit authorization from the host.[64]

Third, the increasing use of unmanned aerial vehicles (UAVs) and the expansion of a supporting basing infrastructure constitute another type of hidden hierarchy in the US security network. Over the last several years, armed drones have launched strikes against targets in Afghanistan, Iraq, Libya, Pakistan, the Philippines, Somalia, and Yemen. Sarah Kreps and Michael Zenko indicate that the United States has launched over 1,000 strikes in Afghanistan since 2008, 48 strikes in Iraq between 2008 and 2012, and 145 strikes in Libya in 2011.[65] Drones have also been launched from allied facilities in Turkey, Italy, Saudi Arabia, the United Arab Emirates, and the Philippines. These operations require both basing and overflight rights, which are more likely to be granted by countries such as Saudi Arabia for the covert drone program than they are a US Air Force or other official basing presence. A series of *Washington Post* investigative stories reveals that the United States is in the midst of expanding its drone base network across Africa, with facilities hosting UAVs

[62] Singh and Berry 2013.
[63] Council of Europe, Parliamentary Assembly and Dick Marty 2006. On the renditions program, also see Grey 2006.
[64] See Tóth 2008.   [65] Kreps and Zenko 2014.

appearing in Mauritania, Burkina Faso, Ethiopia, Djibouti, Kenya, Seychelles, and Niger.[66] These new drone bases are relatively small, requiring 100 to 200 contractors and military personnel, yet they are sanctioned at the highest levels. In the cases of both the Seychelles and Uganda, host-country presidents requested that their use be kept secret and the US presence low profile. Strikingly, of these new African hosts, only Djibouti has the status of an official forward operating base and actually shows up in the annual Department of Defense Overseas Base Structure Report.

Without explicit contracts and publicly known terms of these basing agreements, the regular checks on a sender's "use rights" that we see in formal basing agreements are weaker in these cases of drone basing while questions of "violations of sovereignty" can be avoided altogether. As Kreps points out in the case of Pakistan, "[d]rones allow both countries to maintain the convenient fiction that the United States has not encroached on Pakistani sovereignty, which would be impossible with ground troops This is even more relevant if something goes wrong with an operation, where the prospect of an American pilot shot down or soldier injured in a country with whom the United States is not at war would produce grave diplomatic fallout."[67]

Together with the status of contractors and black sites, the expansion of drone bases seems to give US planners the operational flexibility of hierarchical arrangements, but without the legal accountability of domestic political constraints that arise in formal basing agreements. In some ways, this new mode of state action is a direct result of the social connotation of formal military bases that bring unwanted domestic political and legal scrutiny to both host and sender. The emergence of these forms of hidden hierarchy in basing practices also coincides with attempts in the early 2000s by US planners to fundamentally alter the global base posture of the United States (Global Defense Posture Review [GDPR]) and shift from an emphasis on cold war–era large forward basing hubs to a more flexible, adaptable mix of smaller facilities – known as "forward operating locations" and "cooperative security locations" – that could be expanded in the case of a local or regional emergency. One of the key doctrines driving the GDPR has been the idea of securing "operational flexibility" from base hosts or the right to not designate a facility's functions and purpose a priori.[68] Though much of the GDPR remains incomplete, already the changes in US posture in areas such as Africa, the Middle East, and the Black Sea suggest that the future of US basing lies more in

[66] *Washington Post* articles.   [67] Kreps 2013.
[68] See Pettyjohn and Vick 2013; Cooley 2008.

creating GDPR-like informal networks, incorporating features of "hidden hierarchy" rather than maintaining high-profile formal bases with clearly defined strategic purposes and delineated use rights.

Conclusions

This chapter has explored the multiple ways in which analytical logics of international hierarchy and their different theoretical approaches apply to the study of foreign military bases and how different states react to them. Bases certainly can serve the common defense of sender and host, but bases also function as specific assets, as hard conditions for decolonization, as hierarchical contracts, and as markers of international social status. In terms of the framing project, a distinct trend has emerged in the use of these logics. While US planners primarily look at basing agreements as institutional solutions to their bargaining and planning needs, the international political and normative environment has increasingly associated "military base" with an incursion of the host state's sovereignty, attempts at foreign influence by the sender, and a site of actual social hierarchical practice.

Accordingly, a taboo has emerged on the labeling of US bases as such, even though, in practice, the United States continues to regularly use and negotiate about the use of hundreds of installations worldwide.[69] Interestingly, as the Eurasian case shows, Russian officials, in contrast to US counterparts, overwhelmingly view bases through a social status lens rather than an institutional one, especially in their self-designated regional sphere of influence. This global normative shift and basing taboo, however, is also generating more hidden forms and practices of hierarchy by the United States across an increasingly diffuse, informal, and legally ambiguous global network. The use of contractors, extraterritorial secret sites, and drone facilities erodes many of the legal foundations on which formal overseas basing agreements have been founded. They also constitute a distinct new set of hidden state practices and political actions that challenge the more formal and legal logics of hierarchy that have been the hallmarks of both the study and policy planning surrounding overseas military bases.

---

[69] It is possible that Chapter 6 by Sharman is missing similar hidden dynamics.

8   Leading Authority as Hierarchy among INGOs

*Sarah S. Stroup and Wendy H. Wong**

In the two decades since the end of the cold war, the number of international nongovernmental organizations (INGOs) has almost tripled,[1] and the scholarly literature on INGOs has experienced similar expansion.[2] Yet, in much of the International Relations (IR) literature, INGOs are treated as a homogeneous group, more or less interchangeable in a larger story about the loss of state-led governance. In this chapter we show how using hierarchy as a framework illuminates the fact that INGOs as a class of actors are as varied and ordered as states. These variations have important implications for understanding *who* speaks for civil society and *which* norms circulate globally.[3] Our goal in this chapter is to establish empirically that social hierarchy permeates the INGO population and demonstrate the value that a hierarchy framework brings to the study of INGOs.

Nongovernmental organizations (NGOs) or civil society organizations (and, by extension, INGOs) are defined by the United Nations[4] as "a not-for-profit group, principally independent from government, which is organized on a local, national, or international level to address issues in support of the public good."[5] The "international" adds a "going abroad" dimension: the *Yearbook of International Organizations* defines INGOs as those that work in three or more countries.[6] Such definitions are very

---

* We thank the other participants in the Hierarchies workshops, but especially Ayşe Zarakol and Jack Donnelly, for making thoughtful suggestions for this chapter.
[1] The Union of International Associations counted 20,063 in 1989 and 54,977 in 2009. See Anheier et al. 2012.
[2] A fairly restrictive search on JSTOR (8/6/2013) for "nongovernmental organization" yields 1,755 articles from 1922 to 2013. Seventy-seven percent of these articles on NGOs were written after the end of the cold war (117 from before 1970, 119 from the 1970s, 160 from the 1980s, 332 from the 1990s, 793 from the 2000s, and 234 from 2010 to 2013).
[3] Stroup and Wong 2017.
[4] United Nations Economic and Social Council (ECOSOC) offers an eight-point definition of INGOs eligible for consultative status and, as such, recognition before the United Nations and its member states. ECOSOC Resolution 1296 (XLV), May 23, 1968, available at www.un-documents.net/1296.htm.
[5] From United Nations Rule of Law Website and Document Repository, www.unrol.org/article.aspx?article_id=23 (accessed April 29, 2014).
[6] Union of International Associations, *Yearbook of International Organizations*, various years.

inclusive, which makes the basic task of identifying the relevant population challenging. As we will argue, the social recognition of an actor as an INGO by other actors (INGOs or otherwise) is critical. As with states, mutual recognition constitutes this actor, and while there may be great variation within the INGO category, two distinguishing features stand out: private status and a commitment to serving a public good.[7] Importantly, this public good is often defined by the INGO as it responds to a perceived need for which there is often no direct demand (such as saving the whales or feeding neglected populations). INGOs decide what to work on, for whom, in accordance with priorities that they themselves construct.

We argue that the position an INGO occupies within a hierarchy determines the set of choices that that organization might make. Identifying "a hierarchy" necessarily involves choosing one dimension on which to evaluate INGOs across the board, and we opt to evaluate the deference they receive from different actors ("authority").[8] Our conception of hierarchy is broad because we are foregrounding the authority relationships that those in the hierarchy have with external audiences rather than relationships among INGOs. Because we are interested in explaining the effects of this hierarchy, however, we also consider how hierarchy pushes some actors to institutionalize these rankings among themselves (i.e., we look at how broad hierarchies are sometimes institutionalized as narrow ones).[9]

Highlighting hierarchy allows us to examine the relative social status in terms of authority of INGOs and how it shapes their strategic choices, and as such, using a hierarchy lens will help future INGO studies to articulate the inequalities among INGOs. However, unlike other contributions in this book (e.g., Chapters 5, 6, 9, and 10), our hierarchy is external to the actors in question and therefore more akin to conceptualizations where hierarchy can be implicit (e.g., Chapters 3 and 4). We see a hierarchy on INGOs based on their varying levels of authority in global politics. INGOs differ in myriad ways, including substantive focus, budget, geographic location, organizational structure, and tactics, and they appeal to different audiences. Nevertheless, by arranging INGOs on a hierarchy based on a systematic evaluation of their deference from different audiences, we make explicit the assumptions about the roles of various INGOs

---

[7] We avoid the term "nonprofit" because it is a legal one related to tax status, and many INGOs, such as Amnesty and Greenpeace, have different legal designations depending on the national environment in which they operate. Also, we note Bob's (2012) reminder that the "public good" needs to be construed from all possible sides, not just ideologically progressive or conservative.
[8] See Avant et al. 2010.   [9] Following Lake 2009a.

and what actors, including INGOs themselves, presume about their peers. While we are confident in this approach, we also acknowledge that this is not the *only* way to think about hierarchy among INGOs and that different measurements could arrive at altogether different hierarchies. Ultimately, we see our construction of hierarchy as constituted by authority as one of many ways to systematically sift through INGOs and their many relations among different types of actors.

We assume that INGOs compete for audiences, and while there might be audiences specific to certain issue areas (e.g., the Human Rights Council is most likely a target audience for only human rights INGOs), most of the time INGOs compete with other INGOs for audience deference, whether that is deference from legislatures, international bureaucrats, or individual and organizational funders. Because an individual INGO's status can vary before multiple audiences, we can think about variation among INGOs by evaluating the breadth and level of attention they receive from different political audiences. We show here how audience reception creates a de facto hierarchy among INGOs, identifying a set of "leading INGOs" that have deference from multiple audiences. In short, these differences in authoritative status create a hierarchy that is at once externally imposed, by our evaluative criteria, but also implicitly acknowledged by INGOs within the hierarchy when they act differently depending on their positions. This way of viewing order among INGOs is not the only form of hierarchy, but it is an important one if we are interested in how certain INGOs become high status and then use that status to prioritize their preferred issues.

INGOs and Their Audiences

As actors seeking to change state policy and social practice, INGOs target particular audiences. Not all audiences will listen, however; only some INGOs will be deferred to as the audience recognizes their right to speak or unquestioningly accepts the claims they make. We evaluate three audiences here: other INGOs, public opinion, and the media.[10] These are broad categories, but they allow us to explore the span of INGO influence across various targets.[11] Herein we distinguish between leading INGOs – INGOs that receive the most deference from the most audiences – and others and identify a clear hierarchy in the INGO population.

[10] In the larger project from which this chapter draws, we also examine the reception of INGOs by states and multinational corporations as audiences.
[11] Because INGOs are rarely involved in policy implementation and enforcement, the depth of authority (the intensity of an audience's commitment to that INGO) may be less important than for other actors. INGOs advise, advocate, and may even perform tasks that other actors do not do, but they are authorities, not in authority.

First, INGOs seek deference from their peers. High standing in the eyes of one's colleagues can allow an authoritative INGO to set standards for performance, narrow the range of acceptable practices, and set (and vet) the agenda.[12] INGOs that hold one another in high esteem may be more likely to collaborate in service delivery and in collective policy campaigns.[13] Network ties can reinforce or bolster the status of a networks' members.[14] Even for prominent INGOs, low status within the INGO community can be very problematic. The World Wildlife Fund (WWF), for example, has had to go to great lengths to defend its reputation when faced with criticisms from other NGOs, including Global Witness, that it is enabling the "greenwashing" of environmentally irresponsible corporations.[15]

Second, INGOs can seek to influence public opinion in particular countries. The public can act as valuable leverage in shaping the preferences of national policymakers, such as when evangelical Christians in the United States helped the INGO World Vision make the case for debt relief in the Jubilee 2000 campaign.[16] Alternately, the public can be a direct route for INGOs that seek to change social practices; for example, citizens interested in helping with the humanitarian relief effort after the 2010 Haiti earthquake were encouraged to send cash, not goods.[17] Many INGOs use the for-profit language of "branding" to describe their strategies for advancing their public image.[18] A strong brand can help INGOs, particularly less well-established ones, establish their credibility among their INGO peers and attract partners.[19]

Finally, the international media, especially eminent outlets such as the *New York Times* and *The Economist*, can also serve as an important audience. High levels of attention and favorable treatment from media outlets can be a source of political leverage for INGOs, and sometimes may appear to be an end in itself.[20] The public attention that results from media coverage can generate grassroots pressure on policymakers. INGOs can also use the media to bring new issues into the public arena,

---

[12] Wong 2012; Carpenter 2014, see also Chapters 5 and 9.

[13] Chung, Singh, and Lee 2000; Podolny 2001; Shumate et al. 2005.

[14] Hafner-Burton and Montgomery 2006.

[15] Tom Zeller, Jr., "Companies Not Alone in Image Issues; Green Inc.," *International Herald Tribune*, April 6, 2009; "Greenpeace and WWF Anniversaries Highlight Wildly Different Tactics," *The Guardian*, September 14, 2011; "Campaigners Accuse WWF of 'Greenwash,'" *Daily Telegraph*, July 27, 2011. Available at www.panda.org/wwf_news/press_releases/silence_pact_pandas_wwf.cfm.

[16] Jayawickrama and McCullagh 2009.

[17] www.nytimes.com/2010/01/21/us/21charity.html?_r=0.

[18] See www.propublica.org/article/the-red-cross-secret-disaster (accessed November 6, 2014).

[19] Branding concerns can also impede cooperation among INGOs. See Kylander and Stone 2012.

[20] Ron et al. 2005.

setting the agenda for policymakers.[21] In a political system that is hostile to direct confrontation, INGOs can use media coverage to create indirect pressure for policy change, an approach adopted by many environmental NGOs in China.[22] Online advocacy via new social media may allow INGOs to disseminate more information to a wider audience as a complement to their core political strategies.[23] Finally, media attention can result in new donors or new volunteers joining the organization.

In sum, we evaluate the response of three audiences to INGOs to explore whether a hierarchy of more or less prominent INGOs exists. Our ranking of INGOs vis-à-vis peers and the public offers a new analysis of existing data, and we gathered original data on coverage of INGOs by the media. While casting a broad net to evaluate audiences, we remain cognizant that INGO status is determined in particular social relationships – for example, there is no "global public opinion" but rather an aggregation of different publics in different contexts.[24] INGOs are well aware of this and thus maintain multiple offices around the globe to reach audiences in multiple countries and institutional settings.

Peers

We begin by looking inside the INGO community – a place where the exercise of power is an uncomfortable but important subject. Organizations held up as effective become models for other groups to emulate. INGOs perceived as powerful or effective are more likely to receive invitations from others to collaborate. This standing within the INGO community may then serve as political support as INGOs seek to influence other audiences. Peer organizations are particularly well placed to evaluate the effectiveness of other INGOs because they are most familiar with the functional requirements of an INGO's work.

We draw on survey data from Syracuse University's Transnational NGO Initiative (TNGO) to examine the perceptions of "effectiveness" among INGOs.[25] From 2006 to 2008, researchers conducted interviews with leaders from 152 US-based INGOs from five sectors – environment, human rights, humanitarian relief, sustainable development, and conflict resolution.[26] Among the range of questions, interview subjects were asked

---

[21] Wong 2012; Bob 2005; Carpenter 2007.   [22] Yang 2005.

[23] Kingston and Stam 2013.

[24] See Grant and Keohane (2005) for a discussion of the challenges of "global public."

[25] Many thanks to George Mitchell for help with these data. A more extensive discussion can be found in Mitchell and Stroup 2016.

[26] "The Transnational NGO Study: Rationale, Sampling and Research Process." TNGO white paper, last updated January 2010. Available at www.maxwell.syr.edu/moynihan/tngo/Data/.

Table 8.1 *Peer Perceptions of Effectiveness*

Name	No. of Times Mentioned as Effective by Peers
World Vision	24
CARE	16
Oxfam	12
Catholic Relief Services	10
Amnesty International	8
Save the Children	8
Food for the Hungry	7
International Rescue Committee	7
World Wildlife Fund	6
Doctors without Borders (MSF)	6
Mercy Corps	6
Human Rights Watch	5
Red Cross/ICRC	5
Heifer	5
Natural Resources Defense Council	4
UNICEF	4
World Relief	4
Global Fund for Women	4
Conservation International	3
Nature Conservancy	3
Rainforest Action Network	3
Food for the Poor	3
Freedom from Hunger	3
Salvation Army	3
Samaritan's Purse	3
Center for Global Development	3
Habitat	3
Opportunity International	3
Rotary	3
International Crisis Group	3

Source: TNGO data.

to name five organizations within their field that they considered particularly effective. On average, respondents named 3.18 organizations, and a total of 298 different organizations were mentioned. This fact alone demonstrates that only a few INGOs are "known" by their peers. If each respondent had named five separate organizations, then a possible 760 organizations could have been named, out of a total population of almost 7,000.[27] Table 8.1 displays the thirty organizations mentioned more than

[27] There were 6,986 US-based INGOs in 2006 (nccs.urban.org).

twice, collectively accounting for 36.6 percent of the total mentions of "effective" organizations. INGOs from the humanitarian relief and sustainable development sectors account for 63 percent of the TNGO sample and roughly 64 percent of the total US-based INGO population[28]; this helps account for the high number of relief and development organizations mentioned.

The TNGO data offer a first cut at how American INGOs across a range of sectors view their peers. World Vision, CARE, and Catholic Relief Services are relief and development organizations with sizable budgets, technical proficiency, and low levels of policy work that stand out as effective organizations in the eyes of other US-based INGOs. Amnesty International and Human Rights Watch (HRW), the two organizations that are dominant in financial size and media coverage in their sector, rank high among their INGO peers in effectiveness. Interestingly, relatively low numbers of mentions appeared for two publicly prominent environmental INGOs, Friends of the Earth (FoE) (2) and Greenpeace (1). For these US-based INGOs that are reporting on their effective peers, public salience seems less important than expertise and capacity.

Public Opinion

Influencing public opinion is an important grassroots strategy for INGOs across various issue areas. In order to influence the public, INGOs must first be known. To understand the prominence of various INGOs, we look to data on direct interest in INGOs by the American public. Charity Navigator (CN) has a public website where it shares its ratings of approximately 7,000 domestic and international charities, and it collects data on how those ratings are used. Since launching its website in 2002, CN has allowed registered users to create individual portfolios with specific lists of charities they can follow, and CN also tracks the number of times that an individual charity has been viewed in the past thirty days.[29] The total followers of the top-ranked US-based INGOs are shown in Table 8.2.

The data on viewing patterns of CN's users reveals that there are substantial differences in the political salience of particular organizations. There are a relatively high number of internationally oriented charities in this list – seven of the top ten followed charities. This is surprising because Americans pay relatively little attention to international events,

---

[28] TNGO white paper, 8; author calculations based on data from Reid and Kerlin 2006, 8.
[29] We do not claim that CN users are representative of the broader American public, but they are likely to be informed about INGO practices and recommendations. In 2012, the website had 6.2 million visitors. www.charitynavigator.org/index.cfm?bay=content.view &cpid=1602#.UwTc2c4z2vk.

Table 8.2 *Public Perceptions: Followers of US Charities on Charity Navigator*

Charity name	Followers on Charity Navigator (total, 2002–14)
Doctors without Borders, USA	13,628
American Red Cross	11,519
The Nature Conservancy	9,664
World Wildlife Fund	8,016
United States Fund for UNICEF	7,158
World Vision	7,130
CARE	7,088
Save the Children	6,521
Oxfam America	6,420
Natural Resources Defense Council	6,338

and American donors are relatively less generous toward international charities.[30] One interpretation of the high ranking of international charities is that for American donors, uninformed about daily life in other countries or about differences between INGOs, it may be even more important for them to rely on an authoritative INGO. This aggregate figure on a twelve-year period covers up some additional variation in public attention to charities. We examined CN data on the most viewed charities in two thirty-day periods, in February 2014 and October 2014. Four prominent INGOs – Doctors without Borders (MSF), the American Red Cross, the US Fund for UNICEF, and World Vision – were also among the ten most viewed charities in those two periods. Two other types of charities made appearances on these lists – a charity for US veterans, the Wounded Warrior Project, was among the most frequently viewed in these two periods, and in October, two ALS/Lou Gehrig's disease–focused charities were frequently viewed during the height of the Internet-based "ice bucket challenge." These monthly rankings reinforce our assumption that CN's data accurately reflects public interest in particular charities and that only a few INGOs enjoy durable public prominence.

Media Attention

We follow common practice in assuming that media coverage is a critical avenue by which INGOs seek to influence public opinion.[31] This is

---

[30] Stroup 2012.

[31] Castells 2008; Ron et al. 2005. Of course, media coverage may also shape the way that other audiences view an INGO.

a more indirect way than measuring public reception, as mentioned earlier, but the data on media mentions are still useful for two reasons: they are more extensive and searchable, and media mentions are also a way for INGOs to become prominent in the eyes of other targets such as states and firms. In exploring reception by the media as an audience, we go beyond US-based audiences to assess English-language world news publications indexed by Lexis-Nexis. We build on the methodology employed by Thrall et al. to understand media coverage of INGOs in a single sector, namely, human rights. Using a sample of 257 INGOs drawn from the Union of International Associations (UIA), Thrall et al. found that from 2010 to 2012, three INGOs – Amnesty International, Human Rights Watch (HRW), and Oxfam – accounted for 50 percent of all news appearances in major world publications, and the top twenty-six groups (10 percent of the sample) accounted for 91 percent of news appearances.[32] Social media (Facebook, Twitter, and YouTube) reflect similar patterns of concentrated attention to certain human rights INGOs.[33]

Building on this methodology, we searched two different groups of INGOs: a random sample and a short list of those most likely to enjoy deference from multiple audiences. To establish a baseline of INGO authority, we drew a random sample of INGOs from three populations. First, we sampled from the population of NGOs holding general consultative status with the United Nations Economic and Social Council (ECOSOC). As of September 2010, 171 INGOs enjoyed this status; we drew a random sample of thirty organizations, including groups such as the Association of Medical Doctors of Asia, the World Alliance for Citizen Participation (CIVICUS), Soroptimist International, and the World Federation of UN Associations. We then drew samples from two other populations, INGOs based in the United States and United Kingdom. INGOs headquartered in these two countries account for more than 20 percent of the total INGO population according to the UIA.[34] In 2013, there were roughly 8,000 internationally oriented charities in the United States and approximately 3,000 INGOs based in the United Kingdom.[35] We do not claim that British and American INGOs are representative of the INGO community, but they are most likely to possess the resources and global reach that give them the capacity to reach

---

[32] Thrall et al. 2014, 9.   [33] Kingston and Stam 2013.

[34] Anheier et al. 2012: 20. In 2010, INGOs headquartered in these two countries numbered 8,395 (United States) and 3,258 (United Kingdom) out of 55,853. Other top-ranked host countries are Belgium, France, and Germany.

[35] Figures from National Center for Charitable Statistics and Charity Commission (United Kingdom).

many different audiences.[36] In addition, the two host countries are powerful; the foreign policies of the two states and the global activities of their firms have global ramifications.

In the United Kingdom, the key regulatory agency, the Charity Commission of England and Wales, provided a comprehensive list of all charities (2,794) that operate overseas on issues related to health, poverty alleviation, famine relief, environmental conservation, economic development, and human rights.[37] From this list, we drew a random sample of 140 organizations (5 percent). In the United States, we used the charities evaluated by Charity Navigator (CN), a private ratings agency. CN has reports on over 7,000 US charities, both domestic and international, equivalent to about one-fifth of the total number of US charities.[38] CN is one of the most prominent charity rating agencies in the United States, and its ratings systems shape broader organizational practices within the charitable sector.[39] CN only evaluates charities that receive more than $500,000 annually in private donations, so its sample (and thus ours) is skewed toward larger organizations. Again, these are the organizations most likely to have the capacity to reach multiple audiences. This sample is helpful in identifying the leading INGOs but is biased upward as a baseline for assessing INGO authority in general. Following the categories used in the United Kingdom, we identified 894 organizations rated by CN and active in international and environmental affairs; our sample includes forty-six organizations (5 percent).[40]

Our second sample attempts to identify a group of INGOs likely to be leading INGOs. Creating such a list is fraught with difficulties. If we could search the entire population of INGOs, we would use these metrics to identify a category of leading INGOs and then identify their shared characteristics. Such an endeavor is prohibitively time-consuming, however, and the organization-level data on INGOs is decentralized and

[36] Stroup 2012; Tarrow 2005.

[37] Provided on request, June 2014. This number is slightly lower than that reported by the UIA; we rely on the national agency rather than the UIA.

[38] CN data as of February 2014. CN evaluates organizations with total revenues greater than $1 million and who have filed forms with the Internal Revenue Service (IRS) for at least seven years or more. According to the NCCS, as of December 2013, there were 358,034 charities that filed Form 990 with the IRS; organizations with incomes of $1 or more account for 20.25 percent of that number. This top fifth accounts for 97 percent of the total revenue of the charitable sector. http://blog.charitynavigator.org/2014/02/an-update-on-our-charity-data.html; http://nccsweb.urban.org/tablewiz/pc.php.

[39] Lowell et al. 2005.

[40] The US Tax Code does not have a specific category for international environmental charities. Using CN's search function, we selected all those environmental charities with international or global activities.

somewhat haphazardly kept.[41] Yet any random sample will not capture the group of INGOs at the top of the hierarchy.

We constructed a sample of fifty likely leading INGOs based on the following assumptions. First, organizations that are well regarded with one audience may be better positioned to access new audiences. Thus we include the fifteen INGOs that, according to the UIA, had the highest number of incoming ties from other INGOs in 2001–2.[42] Second, larger organizations are more likely to have the capacity to build their reputation and prominence. Because this is a search of English-language world news, we identified thirty-five of the largest environmental, human rights, and relief and development INGOs in the Anglophone world using data from CN, the National Center for Charitable Statistics, and the Charity Commission (United Kingdom).[43] The full list of these organizations is presented in Table 8.3.

We emphasize that these fifty organizations are a sample of INGOs that are most likely to be leading INGOs in English-language media or Anglophone countries. We offer two important caveats. First, we emphasize that our "most likely" list is not exhaustive and is generated using a second-best methodology because, ideally, one would search media mentions *first* to yield a comprehensive list. Second, the list of "most likely leading INGOs" will vary by the national or institutional context; thus, for example, a number of French INGOs are not included in our most likely sample but may be leading INGOs in Francophone countries or French-speaking media.

[41] Since many INGOs are actually separately registered national-level NGOs, along with an international headquarters registered in a country of choice, there are necessarily duplications in the way that INGOs are counted. For instance, Amnesty International is registered twice in the United Kingdom as Amnesty International UK and Amnesty International, as well as separate organizations in the United States (Amnesty USA), Mexico (Amnesty Mexico), and so forth.

[42] This list is based on data from Murdie and Davis 2012. There are forty organizations that have thirty-five or more incoming ties; we only include those that fit our definition of INGOs and exclude industrial associations, foundations, and (most) campaign groups. In rank order, these are EarthAction, the International Campaign to Ban Landmines, IUCN, Amnesty, ICRC, Oxfam, CIVICUS, International Commission of Jurists, International Council of Voluntary Agencies, International Institute for Environment and Development (IIED), Christian Aid, HRW, International Planned Parenthood Federation, Friends of the Earth, and the International Federation of Human Rights Leagues (FIDH).

[43] For more on this sample and various audiences, see Stroup and Wong (2017). There are a number of organizations that meet these criteria but that were not included because their names are too generic, including the environmental group RARE and the relief groups Feed the Children and International Relief and Development. In addition, using tax codes to limit the search excluded a number of likely leading INGOs (WWF, for example, is categorized as an animal charity rather than an environmental one in the United States).

Table 8.3 *Mentions of INGOs in World News Publications, 2010–12*

Name	Total news appearances
Amnesty International	14,047
Human Rights Watch	13,519
Oxfam International	9,803
Greenpeace	9,202
Salvation Army	8,771
Save the Children	8,057
Friends of the Earth	5,323
CARE	4,640
ICRC	3,457
World Vision	3,417
International Crisis Group	3,313
WWF	3,060
Reporters without Borders	2,557
International Planned Parenthood	2,459
Doctors without Borders	2,383
Committee to Protect Journalists	2,102
Habitat for Humanity	1,857
Christian Aid	1,681
ActionAid	1,666
Natural Resources Defense Council	1,566
Freedom House	1,502
Carter Center	1,099
Rotary	890
International Commission of Jurists	707
Environmental Defense Fund	615
BRAC	523
Conservation International	497
CAFOD	470
Physicians for Human Rights	465
IUCN	452
International Rescue Committee	405
Center for Global Development	404
Catholic Relief Services	390
Human Rights First	368
Heifer International	349
Action against Hunger	273
Ceres	273
MDM/Doctors of the World	262
Mercy Corps	258
International Institute for Environment and Development	239
Samaritan's Purse	226
Food for the Poor	205
Handicap International	194

Table 8.3 (*cont.*)

Name	Total news appearances
FIDH	183
Compassion International	108
Rainforest Action Network	69
International Campaign to Ban Landmines	54
CIVICUS	49
Earth Action	21
International Council of Voluntary Agencies	4

Having constructed these two samples, we analyze the same time period (2010–12) and publications as Thrall et al. (2014) for a wider set of organizations. First, we combined our three random samples of UN, US, and UK organizations into a total random sample of 207 organizations.[44] Our findings for environmental, human rights, and relief and development INGOs almost exactly mirror those in the human rights sector alone. Over half (54 percent) of the sample had no media mentions, and 96 percent of the media mentions covered only 10 percent of our sample. Four INGOs in our random sample – Oxfam, the World Economic Forum, Friends of the Earth, and the Rotary Club – account for 50 percent of the total media mentions (59,252). Of the organizations that had any mentions, the median number was 13.5 and the average was 378, reflecting a skewed distribution of media attention to INGOs. Next, we used the same methodology to examine the media appearances of a subset of most likely leading INGOs. Recall that this list includes INGOs that have the most resources or have high numbers of incoming ties.[45]

First, even within this skewed sample, one-third of the organizations have fewer mentions than the average for the random sample. US-based relief groups such as Samaritan's Purse and Mercy Corps have enjoyed little public salience during this period despite their substantial material resources. The southern-based civil society support group CIVICUS averaged about one story every three weeks during this three-year period, whereas a group such as Oxfam averaged about nine stories a day. Second, the five organizations in this sample with the fewest media mentions are

---

[44] There are 216 organizations in the combined sample; we did not count searches for nine organizations whose names are too broad (e.g., one INGO is named Empower).

[45] The peer data and network data draw from the UIA and TNGO earlier rankings. For US-based INGOs, we selected the wealthiest INGOs based on Reid and Kerlin (2006) and list of the wealthiest international environmental INGOs from Charity Navigator. Because this is a search of world news, we included several of the largest French and British relief organizations.

networking organizations or campaigns. We see this as support that the authority of networks rests in the individual members of those networks rather than their collective weight. Third, a short list of INGOs clearly enjoys status as leading INGOs with media outlets: in human rights, Amnesty and HRW; in environmental protection, Greenpeace, Friends of the Earth (FoE), and the World Wildlife Fund (WWF); and in relief and development, Oxfam, Save the Children, CARE, and World Vision. While these results may not surprise regular INGO watchers, there are a few revelations here. For example, despite an "ethos of direct intervention and media involvement"[46] and a reputation as a media darling, Doctors without Borders (MSF) receives less attention than a number of other relief and development groups. This could be a reflection of the English-language search but is more likely due to the fact that other humanitarian relief INGOs engage in a much wider range of relief and development activities.

These sorts of raw counts of media mentions are used by INGOs themselves to assess their salience and the success of their campaigns.[47] These advocacy evaluations are costly, however, which presents a vicious cycle for small INGOs – media coverage could improve their bottom line, but they cannot get attention without spending more money (which they do not have). These count data have limitations, of course. One is that they do not separate out favorable from unfavorable mentions, though we are agnostic as to whether this matters for evaluating the salience of INGOs. In fact, there is no such thing as bad publicity for leading INGOs, since critiques of leading INGOs demonstrates that these actors at the top of the INGO hierarchy are prime targets for others because discrediting them is key to establishing an alternative view as legitimate. A second limitation is that comparing the rates of media coverage over time is desirable but difficult with limitations to full-text archives.[48] Still, the media coverage data show an ordering of INGOs in the public eye. Certain INGOs are sought for quotes and facts; most are not.

Identifying Leading INGOs

Drawing on both new and existing sources, the aforementioned analysis demonstrates ways to conceptualize the varied reception of INGOs by a select set of important audiences. Our analysis does not present results over time across all audiences but can use the aforementioned rankings to construct a visual representation of the hierarchy of more and less

---

[46] Redfield 2005, 331.

[47] For an example, see Otero 2010. For a discussion, see Hudson 2002 and Tsui 2013.

[48] The Lexis database is limited in its full text coverage. Thrall et al. (2014) compared news coverage data in nine elite global newspapers from 2000 to 2009 and found similar results.

authoritative INGOs. We refer to INGOs that receive considerable deference across multiple audiences as "leading INGOs."

Before identifying leading INGOs, we highlight two points. First, these leading INGOs are well regarded in the eyes of *multiple* audiences. This is a hefty strategic challenge for even the largest of INGOs. There are clear tradeoffs for organizations choosing among different audiences; for example, in the environmental realm, INGOs that partner with corporations may be accused of helping with "green-washing" and lose credibility with their INGO peers or with the general public. Yet, in other ways, an INGO's deference from one audience may positively feeds into its authority with another; INGOs that receive substantial media coverage may be more likely to be receive public donations.

Although "leading INGO" status can change over time, we expect a virtuous cycle for these groups: organizations that have had political victories in the past then achieve the sort of prominence that allows access to future political debates.[49] This may be true with regard to a single audience or multiple audiences. Overall, this positive-feedback loop suggests that INGO power is sticky over time but also raises questions about how newer organizations such as the International Crisis Group or 350.org break through to achieve prominence. Over time, we expect the exact composition of leading INGOs to shift as technology, issues, and political environments shift but also expect that those at the top of the hierarchy have every incentive and many resources to hang onto their positions. No matter *which* INGOs are leading INGOs at any given time, some will occupy that status, and the vast majority will not.

Different Authorities

We aggregate the preceding metrics across different audiences and display them in Table 8.4. It is worth repeating that this is not a claim about a single INGO hierarchy but rather a heuristic device for understanding positions of super- and subordination within the INGO community. Looking across the different audiences from the data in the table, there is a clear top tier, a few groups that stand out as authoritative in the eyes of multiple audiences: in human rights, Amnesty International and HRW; in environmental protection, FoE and WWF; in relief and development, CARE, ICRC, MSF, Oxfam, Save the Children, and World Vision. Our sample drew from INGOs that are salient in the United States, which explains the appearance of several NGOs that are more aptly considered to

[49] Grant and Keohane (2005) suggest that these strong INGOs are difficult to hold accountable.

Table 8.4 *Leading INGOs across Three Audiences*

INGO	Effective (US-based peers)	Media mentions, 2010–12 (1,000+)	Followed by US public
First tier			
Amnesty International	X	X	
CARE	X	X	X
Doctors without Borders	X	X	X
Human Rights Watch	X	X	
ICRC	X	X	
NRDC	X	X	X
Oxfam	X	X	X
Salvation Army	X	X	
Save the Children	X	X	X
US for UNICEF	X		X
World Vision	X	X	X
WWF/ World Wildlife Fund	X	X	X
Second tier (aspirants)			
Carter Center		X	
Christian Aid		X	
Committee to Protect Journalists		X	
Friends of the Earth		X	
Freedom House		X	
Greenpeace		X	
Habitat		X	
Int'l Crisis Group		X	
Int'l Commission of Jurists		X	
Int'l Planned Parenthood		X	
Reporters without Borders		X	
Catholic Relief Services	X		
Heifer	X		
Int'l Rescue Committee	X		
Food for the Hungry	X		
Mercy Corps	X		
Nature Conservancy			X
Bottom tier			
Conservation International			
Environmental Defense			
EarthAction			
Human Rights First			
IUCN			
Ceres			
CIVICUS			
FIDH			
Physicians for Human Rights			

be domestic groups with some international operations (including NRDC) rather than INGOs. Surprisingly, Greenpeace may be a "brand name" INGO, but its substantial prominence in global news is not met by high regard by American donors or American INGOs. The organization's confrontational strategies and principled claims may garner it more authority in other national environments.[50] The high ranking for the US Fund for UNICEF says more about the intergovernmental organization than it does about the charitable arm that does fundraising and advocacy.[51]

Beyond leading INGOs, there is a second tier of INGOs that receive considerable deference from one audience. Groups such as the Carter Center and Habitat do well with the global media, are relatively young, and are seeking to expand their global influence.[52] Catholic Relief Services and the International Rescue Committee are well respected by American peers but may struggle with non-American audiences. Christian Aid, Greenpeace, the International Commission of Jurists, and the International Planned Parenthood Alliance all perform well with global media and well may be leading INGOs in other national or institutional contexts. The final row at the top of the hierarchy includes organizations that do not receive deference from the three audiences examined here but may possess substantial authority in the eyes of other audiences – they have authority, but it is narrowly based. Finally, we include a category of specialists. These are groups well regarded by one audience. CIVICUS and EarthAction are viewed with high esteem by other INGOs.[53] Groups such as EDF and Conservation International develop strong partnerships with corporations but have a weak principled reputation with the public and peers.

These three levels of INGOs are still at the top of a vast population of INGOs, all struggling to receive deference from one or more audiences. Data on our random sample reveal that the median INGO receives zero coverage by the media. In the surveys of leaders of US-based INGOs, 298 different organizations were named as particularly effective – out of a total population of US-based INGOs of about 6,000.[54] There may be very low barriers to entry into the INGO community, but most INGOs become part of a vast bottom of a rather stable pyramid. Order within the community is socially constructed rather than explicitly defined, and this order is based on who is deferred to as an authority by multiple audiences.

---

[50] Stroup 2012.
[51] UNICEF receives an average 20 percent of its funding from private donors around the world; www.globalhumanitarianassistance.org/wp-content/uploads/2012/04/Private-funding-an-emerging-trend.pdf.
[52] See Hyde 2012.   [53] See Murdie and Davis (2012) and sampling discussion above.
[54] Mitchell and Stroup 2016.

Why Hierarchy Is a Useful Lens for INGOs

While the INGO community can sometimes appear fragmented or competitive, it is not anarchic. There is substantial stratification among the tens of thousands of INGOs active in global politics today. Our research shows clear gaps among INGOs in terms of the attention they receive from the different audiences they seek to influence. If hierarchy is defined as having order in terms of superordination and differentiation[55] – that is, in contrast to anarchy, where there is an absence of government or governing order – then we show here that hierarchy is a persistent feature of relationships among INGOs. Leading INGOs are at the top of an INGO status hierarchy. An INGO's status – high or low – plays a key role in shaping its practices and influence. In this chapter, the status hierarchy is constructed as external audiences defer to different INGOs.[56] Within the INGO community, as for other actors, "social hierarchy is an implicit or explicit rank order of individuals or groups with respect to a valued social dimension."[57] For INGOs, status plays an important role in their abilities to be build networks, advance policy goals, and promote new norms because (relative to most states and many multinational corporations) their material power is weak.

Consistent with the middle-ground position, status *within* hierarchy can have important consequences for what individuals do with their positions. More authority may not equal more latitude because "social status matters for behavior, but precisely *how* it matters depends on positionality."[58] Leading INGOs face different opportunities and constraints and may develop vastly different interests than other INGOs; more is not more. As with other actors, their positions within hierarchy define activities and the terms of their participation.[59] For example, for the past decade, leading INGOs have focused on building more robust international structures to facilitate coordination among their different global offices. In doing so, an INGO such as Save the Children is not focusing on making their individual country offices (e.g., Save the Children Mozambique) more competitive with other local NGOs; they see themselves as competing for attention (and deference) against other leading INGOs such as Oxfam, CARE, and World Vision.[60] These INGOs define their interests as developing coherence and demonstrating global reach, in contrast to the concern over securing funding, which is so central to many INGOs.[61] INGO positionality shapes INGOs' interests and their distinctive competitive behaviors.

---

[55] Waltz 1979; Donnelly 2006.   [56] Magee and Galinsky 2008.   [57] *Ibid.*, 354.
[58] See the Introduction.   [59] Kang 2010a.   [60] Stroup and Wong 2012.
[61] Cooley and Ron 2002.

Positions within a status hierarchy are relatively sticky because those with higher status generally have the capacity and the incentive to remain there. One important lesson from the logic of positionality is that actors do not necessarily "choose" to engage in hierarchy, which is a prominent vein in the logic of tradeoffs. In the hierarchy we have identified here, status is defined by deference from external audiences as much as by deference from other INGOs. There is no one to which "consent" to a hierarchy must be given – there simply are audiences that defer (or not) to INGOs as a result of the limited time and resources that *they* have to entertain the claims of INGOs. No INGO chooses to be middling or irrelevant, but given low status, most INGOs learn to play their roles within the hierarchies. Status is not static, however, and the positions of individual INGOs can change – MSF, the International Crisis Group, the Carter Center, and 350.org are all INGOs that had meteoric ascents as newcomers to the INGO community and have received substantial deference from multiple audiences.

Facing this structure, INGOs make different choices about how to respond to the opportunities and constraints they face. Their positions within a hierarchy may limit their choices, but INGOs occupying similar statuses do not all make the same choices; in fact, they work to differentiate themselves. The INGO status hierarchy does not have a single dominant player; there are hierarchies across different issue areas and political contexts. For example, an INGO such as the environmental group WWF may elect to work with corporate partners, earning it greater deference from businesses but scorn from other environmental INGOs. The logic of positionality suggests that socialization may deter certain behaviors but does not prevent them. INGOs that enjoy different statuses across multiple audiences may choose to pursue gains before some audiences but losses before others.

As Donnelly[62] points out, stratification can be multiple and layered, and hierarchies among INGOs will vary depending on the qualities evaluated. Some hierarchies may be formal and constructed within the INGO community. For example, the voluntary NGO Code of Conduct has hundreds of signatories but is housed at the International Federation of the Red Cross. A handful of high-status INGOs participated in the design of the Code of Conduct, but the stratification of NGO members into host, participants, and signatories was a useful tool for NGOs that were seeking recognition of the code inside and outside the NGO community. Most hierarchies among NGOs will be less formalized. Assessments and evaluations of social ranking are malleable and subject to the era in which

---

[62] See Chapter 11.

they arise[63] as well as the values of the audience(s).[64] At the same time, audience deference can reinforce the status hierarchy by enabling high-status NGOs access to money, policymakers, and media outlets. Yet, because NGOs seek deference from multiple audiences with sometimes conflicting values and preferences, there is no single INGO hierarchy, and an INGO's high status is not fixed. For instance, Save the Children is a high-status INGO in both the United States and Britain but has much greater public recognition in the United Kingdom. The British public tends to favor more radical and activist-oriented INGOs in comparison with the Americans.[65] Balancing the sometimes conflicting demands of these audiences can be challenging, and there was an enormous public outcry in Britain when the American chapter of Save the Children gave a "global legacy" award to former British Prime Minister Tony Blair.[66] In the face of challenges to their credibility, all INGOs work to defend their reputations.[67] The NGO status hierarchy is contested, reproduced, and defended in the many interactions that INGOs have with their multiple audiences.

The middle ground is useful in understanding the hierarchy's effects on INGOs, but the perspective of hierarchy as institutional tradeoffs can also help to explain the functional bargains among INGOs and how these create and reinforce hierarchies.[68] First, the roles that INGOs play in global politics may be the result of an implicit or explicit allocation at the global level of the functions of representation and interest articulation. Hierarchical relations define the borders of "us" versus "them" – status needs to be conferred by others who also hold a particular (or better) status.[69] For example, the International Monetary Fund (IMF) sees engagement with NGOs and civil society organizations as serving an important function – a way to demonstrate its accountability to recipient countries and their citizens.[70] INGOs that serve this function may be rewarded with high status (and access to IMF staff and officials). In short, a global logic of tradeoffs may determine the subordinate position of INGOs in global governance; they are rarely rule enforcers that govern,

---

[63] Neumann 2014.

[64] A major theme in Paul et al. (2014) is difficulty of arriving at the "right" status evaluation, but this speaks to the need to evaluate how different audiences view the same actor.

[65] Stroup 2012.

[66] Sam Jones, "Save the Children Head Apologises for Upset over Award to Tony Blair," *The Guardian*, March 3, 2015. Available at www.theguardian.com/global-development/2015/mar/03/save-the-children-head-apologises-for-upset-over-award-to-tony-blair (accessed October 30, 2015).

[67] Gourevitch et al. 2012.   [68] See Zarakol Introduction.

[69] Larson, Paul, and Wohlforth 2014; Neumann 2014.

[70] www.imf.org/external/np/exr/facts/civ.htm.

but the status of superordinate states and international organizations is partly determined by their legitimacy in the eyes of INGOs.

Second, thinking about tradeoffs helps to explain the construction of orderings within subgroups of INGOs, particularly collective campaigns.[71] If hierarchy provides order and predictability, conferring status to individuals within it, it can lead to opportunities for coordination and incentives for organizations and individuals to perform in certain ways[72] that may include both cooperative and competitive elements. Consider the International Campaign to Ban Landmines, formed in 1992. As with many other INGO campaigns, the success of the campaign rested on centralized agenda setting combined with decentralized implementation.[73] But equally important to the campaign's success was which INGOs were at that center – high-status INGOs such as HRW, well-regarded specialist INGOs such as the Mines Advisory Group and Handicap International, and a long-standing campaign against antipersonnel landmines by the International Committee for the Red Cross.[74] As more INGOs (and NGOs generally) have formed, a de facto hierarchy has created roles for different types of organizations to participate in political efforts. While Bob (2005) adopts a critical tone of the role of high-status INGOs as gatekeepers, his research reveals differentiation among INGOs, with smaller local organizations bringing new causes to light while high-status INGOs package and disseminate (some of) those causes to wider audiences. This "division of labor" among INGOs involves different roles for north and south, for activist and professional, for entrepreneurial and establishment groups.[75] A hierarchy perspective gives us a chance to systematically document, explain, and drive home the fact that INGOs are not just free floating out in global political space, and we should not treat them as such. Furthermore, they are not equally situated. Some are higher in a given hierarchy, and some are lower, and these positions help us to distinguish between and among INGOs in their quests for social and political change. While the INGO field is too nascent to have committed some of the more egregious assumptions of anarchy in other parts of IR, to date many have assumed that INGOs are basically interchangeable and that differences among them do not matter significantly for analysis.[76] Hierarchy among INGOs may not be evident in explicit structures of super- and subordination, but as we have shown here, there are ways to think about implicit hierarchy[77] once we relax the need to have explicit recognition of and consent to hierarchical arrangements.

[71] See Moyes and Nash 2011.   [72] Magee and Galinsky 2008.   [73] Wong 2012.
[74] Price 1998.   [75] Siméant 2013.   [76] Carpenter (2014) is a recent exception.
[77] Which is not "informal" hierarchy because that involves some kind of negotiation between actors; see Magee and Galinsky 2008; Diefenbach and Silince 2011.

Our contribution demonstrates how actors with varying levels of authority interact in accordance with the roles that are given to them based on their positions within a hierarchy. Some actors might explicitly recognize that others are "higher" or "lower" than them in a particular hierarchy, but others may not. Nonetheless, INGOs will still be affected by this hierarchy, even if it is not explicitly recognized, because the hierarchy is based on what authority other audiences confer on them. In many ways, they have very little control over their positions in the hierarchy, akin to Chapters 5 and 9 in this book. Where some might actively try to do things to change the deference they receive from audiences or to actively limit the number of audiences to whom they speak, generally speaking, the ability of INGOs to shape their positions in the hierarchy is limited at best, which contrasts our analysis from that of others, such as Chapters 2 and 10 in this book, which emphasize the agency that those who are lower on or excluded from different social orderings can press for new recognition.

In terms of the contribution of using the metric that we do to evaluate INGOs across issue area, the identification of leading INGOs differentiates our view from previous analyses of what it means to have power or authority as an INGO in global politics. Our focus on audiences points to the fact that to gain authority, INGOs need to pursue a wide variety of audiences and that, ultimately, many of the key audiences that confer authority at the global level are the same, no matter what the particular issue area to which an INGO is committed. The hierarchy perspective accentuates the "collective" nature of the INGO identity, across issue area, while also highlighting the diversity of strategies and breakthroughs to audiences that INGOs have had in recent history. We apply the lens of hierarchy, which has largely been limited to studies of states in this book and beyond, to demonstrate its utility in analyzing nonstate actors and discuss the implications of this move.

Conclusion

Our new evidence of the varied status of INGOs reveals an ordering of relations among INGOs and between INGOs and the other audiences they seek to influence. Alongside this new research, our claims about the effects of hierarchy on INGOs should be familiar to more state-centric theorists in international relationship. Being at the top of a hierarchy reflects an INGO's authority and gives it flexibility to make choices. Leading INGOs, referred to by other INGO scholars as "gatekeepers," have the opportunity to choose campaign themes and define agendas for external audiences; subordinate INGOs have no such opportunity.[78] Thus a high-status actor's preferences matter more in determining systemic outcomes. At the same time, high status, socially conferred based on the expertise and principles of an INGO, comes under attack and must be defended. Finally, actors occupying different positions within a hierarchy take on different types of roles that we can constitute a rough division of labor. Hierarchy among nonstate actors such as INGOs reflects implicit logics of tradeoffs and results in particular behaviors based on the position of the INGO.

We end by reflecting on how hierarchy shapes cooperation among INGOs, a constant subject of interest for INGO scholars. While a hierarchical ordering among INGOs that resulted in functional differentiation might yield extensive inter-INGO cooperation, such an outcome is unlikely for several reasons. First, INGO hierarchies are implicit rather than explicit. The delegation of tasks could be impeded by other INGOs that nevertheless want to reject certain tasks as "beneath them" in an attempt to create the perception that they are leading INGOs or by high-status INGOs asked to commit substantial resources to achieve a public good but under no requirement to do so. Second, an effective division of labor requires agreement on the goal being sought, and such agreement is elusive in a diverse global community of INGOs pursuing the complex and lofty goal of social change. Hierarchy is thus not a better or a worse condition for INGOs; it is a collectively determined social structure that creates order but also results in the uneven distribution of authority among them.

---

[78] Bob 2005; Carpenter 2011.

9 Are We 'Lazy Greeks' or 'Nazi Germans'?
Negotiating International Hierarchies in the Euro Crisis

Rebecca Adler-Nissen *

This chapter argues that to understand international hierarchies, we need to examine not only forms of hierarchy but also processes of internalisation of – and resistance to – hierarchies. We will then discover that many hierarchies are not simply imposed from above but that subordinate actors are often complicit in the ongoing production and negotiation of hierarchies. I begin this argument with the simple observation that some international hierarchies are taken for granted. Today it seems obvious that there is a hierarchy in the Eurozone with Germany at the top and Greece at the bottom. Scholars, politicians and media see Germany as the leader and economic power-house of Europe, while Greece is represented as 'bankrupt' and 'dysfunctional' with high levels of unemployment. What we often overlook, however, is that it was not inevitable that these particular countries would occupy these positions in the hierarchy. Why Greece and not Italy, Spain or Ireland? We cannot explain why Greece became the poster boy for the Eurozone crisis based purely on its economic troubles – because Spain and Italy share similar debt problems as Greece and are just as closely monitored and subordinated to the austerity measures imposed by the International Monetary Fund (IMF), the European Union (EU) and international lenders.[1] Likewise, while the German economy has been doing relatively well, it suffers from structural problems, including a growing number of working poor.[2]

The Euro Crisis has pushed national leaders to adopt policies and deepen European integration in ways that they would not otherwise have

* Research for this chapter was carried out as part of a project entitled, 'Images and International Security', directed by Lene Hansen and funded by the Danish Council for Independent Research – Social Sciences, grant number DFF–1327–00056B, and a project entitled 'DIPLOFACE', funded by the European Research Council, starting grant number 680102. I am grateful to Cleio Katsivela and Johan Spanner for research assistance with the data collection. I wish to thank Ayşe Zarakol, David Lake and Neil Dooley for excellent and detailed suggestions. And thanks to all the contributors to this book for their stimulating comments in San Diego and Cambridge.
[1] Dooley 2014; Tzogopoulos 2013.   [2] Grahl and Teague 2013.

done.[3] Why? Economic scholarship has largely adopted what Zarakol calls an agentic/institutional understanding of hierarchy, focusing on the causes of the global financial crisis or the flaws in the architecture of the Economic and Monetary Union (EMU).[4] The problem becomes one of institutional design needing adjustment. In contrast, scholars in international political economy, sociology and anthropology have adopted a structural under-standing of hierarchy, arguing that the Euro Crisis cannot be understood by economics and the institutional setup of the EMU alone. They have addressed the way in which the crisis is also ideologically constructed, focusing on the dominance of monetarism, ordo-liberalism and a particular idea of austerity.[5] Along these lines, scholars such as Fourcade, Antoniades and Hertzfeld have analysed the stigmatisation of Greece and the other 'PIGS' (this derogatory term refers to the economies of Portugal, Ireland, Greece and Spain; sometimes Italy is also included, leading to the acronym 'PIIGS').[6] It has even been demonstrated that repetition of the acronym 'PIIGS' in public debates shaped the behaviour of market actors towards these countries, such that increased media usage of the term 'PIIGS' was followed by increased changes in Irish bond yields.[7]

However, a focus on the character of the hierarchy – be it agentic/institutional or structural – only brings us some way in explaining the relative positions of Greece and Germany. In this chapter I adopt a broad view of hierarchy, focusing on the interplay of mediatised discourses in the Eurozone, but contrary to a structuralist approach, I suggest that the ranking of states is an *interactive*, not unidirectional process, leaving more room for agency within international hierarchies. Self-labelling, including low self-esteem and anxiety about national status, is just as important (if not more important) than discourse emerging from top positions in the hierarchy. In other words, the Euro Crisis gains its public meaning through interactive dynamics that rank states by labelling them. It is the public naming and shaming in national and pan-European debates that not only construct, sustain and destabilise particular national stereotypes but, as I will show, also shape a self-reflexive struggle over hierarchy in Europe. Both Greek and German public debates are deeply concerned with how 'the others' view 'us'.

This first part of this chapter explores why hierarchy appears awkward in multilateral institutions emphasising sovereign equality. It shows how hierarchies are produced, upheld and challenged through stigmatising and stereotyping labels. The second part presents a survey of how

---

[3] See the Introduction; Beach 2014; Tzogopoulos 2013; Schimmelfennig 2015.
[4] Soros 2012; Pisani-Ferry 2012; De Grauwe 2012.   [5] Ryner 2012; Blyth 2013.
[6] Hertzfeld 2013; Antoniades 2013; Fourcade 2013.   [7] Brazys & Hardiman 2015.

German and Greek newspapers label – and thereby also rank – Germany
and Greece and react to the way in which their countries are ranked
themselves in a period of three months during the height of the Euro
Crisis. The labels include Germany as 'Nazi oppressor and coloniser',
'strict teacher' and 'naive victim' and Greece as 'colonised and
oppressed – and possible neo-Nazi resistant', 'immature pupil' and
'moral sinner'. Each label positions the state very differently. Based on
an in-depth analysis and contextualisation of the stereotyping of self and
other, the chapter suggests that rather than merely consolidating
Germany's (and Northern Europe's) economic and political superiority
and sustaining the subordination of Greece (and other southern states),
the Euro Crisis generates a series of more complex, self-reflective national
debates and political gestures of repair and embarrassment. These
dynamics reveal a deep concern in both Greece and Germany about
how they are perceived on the international scene. The chapter concludes
with reflections on how international status struggles are more interactive
and self-reflective than usually assumed, suggesting different ways in
which hierarchies may change from within.

Interactive Labelling and the Production of International Hierarchy

This section develops two theoretical claims about hierarchy in International
Relations (IR). First, I suggest that that the norm of sovereign equality,
which helps legitimise multilateral cooperation, requires a concealment of
international hierarchy. Second, I propose that international hierarchies are
produced through interactive processes of self- and other-labelling where
subordinate states contribute to their own subordination.

Hierarchy in a World of Sovereign Equality

Hierarchy comes from the Greek *hierarchia* (ἱεραρχία), which means
'leader of sacred rites' – or 'sacred sovereignty'.[8] It is an arrangement of
items (objects, names, values, categories, etc.) in which the items are
represented as being 'above', 'below' or 'at the same level as' one
another. We find social hierarchies in all societies, but hierarchy clashes
with most assumptions about international anarchy that have dominated
realist and much of liberal IR theory.[9] Yet, the important observation for
this chapter is that if hierarchy is about stratification, its logical opposite
must be equality rather than anarchy. This is important for IR theory

---

[8] Grint 2010, 90.   [9] For a discussion, see the Introduction and Chapter 11.

because of the assumption that sovereign states are formally equal under international law irrespective of their military power, economic size and so on.[10] For the same reason, hierarchy is also awkward for the functioning of multilateralism, including the European Union, which gives its members – large and small – a promise of sovereign equality.[11] The principle of sovereign equality is written into the European Union's treaties and is reflected in the rights and privileges that all member states enjoy. In principle, this makes it possible for the Danish Prime Minister to have just as much voice in the nomination of a new European Council President as the French President during a European Council Meeting. Also, the Economic and Monetary Union (EMU) is attached to sovereign equality. All members of the Eurozone sit on the board of the European Central Bank and have equal voting rights.[12] Yet, although sovereignty is a marker of equal status in multilateral fora, it does not put all states on a level playing field. The difference in voting weights between big and small EU member states suggests that some states are more equal than others.[13]

Yet, even a closer look at the distributions of formal rights and privileges in the Eurozone, that is, the institutional form of hierarchy, tells us little about how hierarchies actually play out. The degree to which 'objective' systems of measurement of power (e.g. voting weights or length of membership) feed into the negotiation of the Euro Crisis depends on different labels that are attached discursively to the different member states. Perceptions of relative status flow from the ways in which nations define themselves and are defined by their place in the international pecking order.[14] This symbolic and mediated struggle affects the relative positions of states.

---

[10] See Reus-Smit 2005. Sovereign equality was formally recognised as the basis of diplomacy and international law at the Congress of Vienna (1814–15). See Osiander 2001.

[11] This promise is historically contingent: before state sovereignty was established as a universal principle, polities could not (and did not) necessarily expect to be treated as equals. There were great formal differences in status, rights and privileges between, for instance, colonies, protectorates and free cities and empires. See e.g. Nexon 2009; Nexon & Wright 2007; Krasner 1999.

[12] On January 1, 1999, the third and final stage of EMU commenced with the fixing of the exchange rates of the currencies of the eleven member states initially participating in monetary union and with a single monetary policy under the responsibility of the European Central Bank. It was not until German unification that a European Monetary Union became politically possible. During the Maastricht Treaty negotiations in 1991–92, Germany sacrificed its strong Deutschmark for a common European currency and was allowed unification (Berger 1997, 57).

[13] The practical experience of statehood can differ dramatically, but sovereign equality remains a guiding principle for how states talk to each other in diplomatic relations (Adler-Nissen & Gad 2013).

[14] Pouliot 2011, 2016a.

Social Labels as Markers of Hierarchy

How do we know hierarchy when we see it? IR scholars have adopted insights from sociology, particularly from Norbert Elias and Erving Goffman, to show how stigmatisation plays a crucial function in international relations by shaming states, displaying normality and clarifying the boundaries of acceptable behaviour.[15] This literature suggests that labels single out particular socially constructed attributes, whether related to religion, geography, race, gender, class or language or something else.[16] These attributes are used to homogenise the nation discursively. Sometimes the label in question connotes that a particular state has or is assumed to have a presumed positive or negative attribute of some kind – a superior quality or a 'handicap' or perceived cultural, social or racial difference. For instance, labels such as 'Europeanisation'[17] and 'gender equality'[18] locate states in international hierarchies. Stigmatising labels' negative connotations become manifested in discriminatory practices that in turn designate the nation's status in international society. In world politics, labelling is often directly linked to the distribution of resources and opportunities. For example, the Corruption Perception Index, which orders the countries of the world according to the degree to which corruption is perceived to exist among public officials and politicians, has an impact on the allocation of development aid to many countries. While the index, provided annually by the international non-governmental organisation (INGO) Transparency International, has been criticised for reducing the complex political and economic challenges facing a state to problems of corruption, it provides an efficient means of rating states according to one feature.[19]

International hierarchies are often moral ordering tools. They help to decide when a state is 'guilty' or 'innocent', when it has to pay for war crimes, when it can be sanctioned and when it is allowed to defend itself. After World War II, Germany and Japan were occupied by the Allies and were punished not just as military but also as moral losers.[20] Such processes involve an inter-state dramaturgy that produces, upholds and challenge hierarchy. By their very political and social usage, stigmatising labels confirm the existence of distinctions between full rights and rights as social privileges extended to certain groups and denied to others. Thus, labels become part of the struggle of both the 'higher' and the 'lower'

[15] Zarakol 2011; Adler-Nissen 2014.
[16] See Lippmann (1922) for one of the first analyses of the importance of stereotypes for public opinion.
[17] Rumelili 2003.   [18] Towns 2012.   [19] Lancaster and Montinola 1997.
[20] Buruma 1994; Zarakol 2011; Adler-Nissen 2014.

nations alike. When it comes to economic transactions and debt, hierarchies are often naturalised on the state level so that the moral worth of a state – and resultant moral ordering of states – is simply taken to be a direct reflection of its sovereign debt.[21] As Fourcade puts it, 'economy is always and everywhere a morality play, where actors – individuals, corporations, countries – are apprehended not only through numbers, formulas and charts aiming at precision, but also through rather coarse moral categories of virtue and vice, good and bad, high and low'.[22]

Hierarchies in international relations depend on constant recognition by both those that are above and below in ranking. As Subotic and Zarakol explain, states' 'sense of self' or cultural intimacy may be linked to sense of shame, guilt or embarrassment rather than positive traits or characteristics.[23] In other words, states' international positions are not just a result of their struggle for a better status vis-à-vis other states as social identity theory[24] would have it but also a result of their dealings with their own past and domestic conflicts (which again are shaped by the outside world). This does not mean that hierarchies are legitimate or accepted by everyone – often they are not. But in struggling to manage their international status, states sometimes end up reproducing their own subordination.

Negotiating Hierarchies in Europe

Many Europeans have held exaggerated beliefs about how 'entering Europe' would impact on the relative status of their nation. As Giurlando shows, Italy's entry into the EMU in 1999 is an example of this. Italy (as all EU members) had to make many sacrifices to enter the EMU, and to build support for these sacrifices, Italian political leaders explained that EMU membership would mean that Italy would rise in status.[25] Even before the Euro Crisis, the adoption of the particular path of economic reform and the construction of EU-level governance helped to rank EU member states. Examining Italian newspapers from 1996 to 2004, Giurlando shows that even though Italy was one of the founders of the European Union, adopting the euro was framed as something that would solve Italy's marginalisation in Europe, as Italians had continued to identify themselves and were identified by others as a 'second tier' country compared to Germany, France and the United Kingdom. Italians understood EMU membership as a chance to allow external forces to re-shape them as 'modern' and 'mature' Europeans.

---

[21] Fourcade 2013, 622; Dooley 2014.   [22] Fourcade 2013, 262.
[23] Subotic and Zarakol 2013.   [24] Larson and Shevchenko 2010.   [25] Guirlando 2012.

Giurlando argues that this constant comparison with other member states is a form of 'associative evaluation' revealing a 'perceived hierarchy' in Europe.[26] Associative evaluation helps to explain the hopes and aspirations in Italian support for the euro. Therefore, when Italy joined the Eurozone, there was a widespread sense that the country had indeed entered the league of European elite countries. Later, following the Euro Crisis, populist discourses developed, leading to what some observers see as an emerging 'intra-European neo-racism'[27] and neo-colonial politics,[28] which discursively infantilises the periphery in Europe.[29] The correction of PIIG immaturity has been viewed as a 'civilising mission', a paternalistic Eurocentrism directed within Europe itself.[30]

However, contrary to a structuralist understanding of hierarchy, this dominant civilising narrative and its resultant ranking of states were not the logical result of inevitable pressures that dictated austerity as the only answer to the Euro Crisis. As Matthijs and McNamara convincingly show, the response to the crisis that arose out of public and economic debates privileged certain definitions and solutions over others.[31] Austerity and structural reform became the respective cures for member states' national problems of 'fiscal profligacy' and 'lack of competitiveness' over more federal diagnoses.[32] Swift implementation of those policies, the argument went, would produce both fiscal discipline and labour market flexibility, and the crisis would gradually go away.[33] Yet, this winning narrative and subsequent set of policy prescriptions are puzzling since they did not fit the situation in Ireland, Portugal and Spain and only partly did the 'fiscal sin' logic materialise in Greece. 'Plausible systemic counter-narratives of what went wrong'[34] included the Eurozone's lack of supporting economic governance institutions and the pressures of persistent trade and financial imbalances, yet neither of these would end up driving the debate nor the solutions offered. How did the disciplining austerity narrative become dominant?

The most convincing answer so far is that the 'myriad explanatory narratives of the Eurozone debt crisis' emerged in a split between a EU- and a national-level account.[35] Both EU-level and national-level narratives reflected largely an institutional approach to hierarchy. EU-level accounts of the Euro Crisis pointed to the euro's flawed institutional design at Maastricht in 1991 and the many missing unions (economic, fiscal, political, financial, debate and banking) that were never constructed.[36] National-level accounts, however, focused on failings within the individual

[26] Giurlando 2012.   [27] Kouvélakis 2012, xix.   [28] Verovšek, 2014.   [29] O'Neil 2014.
[30] Marder 2012.   [31] Matthijs and McNamara 2015.
[32] Matthijs and McNamara 2015, 235.   [33] Matthijs and Blyth 2015.
[34] Matthijs and McNamara 2015, 230.   [35] *Ibid.*, 235.   [36] *Ibid.*, 230.

member states and thereby turned the Euro Crisis narrative into a 'morality tale' of northern 'saints' and southern 'sinners'.[37] As Matthijs and McNamara write, 'Hard work, prudent savings, moderate consumption, wage restraint, and fiscal stability in Germany were seen as Northern virtues and were juxtaposed to the Southern vices of low competitiveness, meagre savings, undeserved consumption, inflated wages and fiscal profligacy in the Mediterranean.'[38] The solution to the crisis accordingly became one of 'necessary' reforms in the periphery.

The national-level account won. This meant that the sinners needed to start behaving more like the saints. If they did, all would be well with the single currency's future. Instead of rebuilding the Eurozone from the top down (with supra-national solidarity mechanisms) as the EU-level account prescribed, this strategy tried to transform Europe from the bottom up. Arguably, as critics adhering to a structural understanding of hierarchy explained, this strategy would force the Eurozone onto a path towards some kind of 'model *Deutschland* writ large', by making wage and price flexibility in the periphery into the main shock absorbers during future crises.[39] As Matthijs and McNamara explain 'German thinkers, opinion writers and policymakers played a pivotal role in making the diagnosis of the euro's ills as well as stipulating its cure, framing and ultimately "resolving" the crisis' (Matthijs and McNamara 2015, 236).

While a structural understanding of hierarchy in the Euro Crisis takes some way in accounting for the role of public debate and stereotyping, it glosses over important interactive processes and reifies states. Blyth, Fourcade and others[40] point at the homogenisation of nations resulting from the moral tales of 'sinners' and 'angels', but they fall into trap of claiming that 'Germany' is doing something – or rather that German political leadership is uncontested within or outside Germany. Yet, to fully understand why a particular narrative about the Euro Crisis became dominant and how this enabled Greece to be situated at the bottom of the reform agenda, we need to analyse the complicity of Greek voices in this debate. We need to look at the self-reflexive and highly interactive responses that led to the construction of Germany and Greece as in a hierarchical and antagonistic relationship. This requires changing the question from 'What or who put Greece in this position?' (where Greece becomes a passive victim due to Germany's domination) to the question, 'How is the hierarchical relationship produced?'.

[37] Fourcade 2013.   [38] Matthijs and McNamara 2015, 235.
[39] Matthijs and Blyth 2015, quoted in Matthijs and McNamara 2015, 235.
[40] With Matthijs and McNamara (2015) as an important exemption.

Searching for Labels of Greece and Germany

To capture the process that produces hierarchy, we need to investigate not only dominant narratives (i.e. hierarchy as a structure) but also how subordinates perceive their own position and that of the rest of Europe – and their mutual resonance. With this purpose in mind, publicly available material within the Germany and Greece – the two countries that came to represent two extreme positions in the Euro Crisis – was analysed. To select the periods for data collection, a parallel search was done on Google Trends. Google Trends analyses a percentage of Google web searches to determine how many searches have been done for the terms entered compared to the total number of Google searches done during that time. A search was done for the country name ('Greece', 'Germany'/ 'Greek*', 'German*') and the word 'euro' (specified as the currency). This was done in both Greek and German languages. The search period was limited to January 2008 to March 2014 to identify peaks on the resultant curves. Correlating peaks in the two countries were identified, and a selection was made for the largest search peak and a three-month period around this peak: April, May and June 2010.

Newspapers were selected not by the criteria of top circulation but with a view to the newspapers' agenda-setting qualities and to represent different political views and ways of stereotyping in tabloids, broadsheet and intellectual newspapers. The aim was to cover as broad a spectrum of domestic public opinion and debate as possible. For Germany, this resulted in the choice of *BILD*, Germany's largest tabloid; *Tageszeitung (TaZ)*, a Berlin-based intellectual newspaper; and *Frankfurter Allgemeine*, a centre-right broadsheet.

For Greece, selection of newspapers proved more difficult because the economic crisis has dramatically changed the media landscape. Some newspapers have been closed permanently or have limited their circulation to Sunday editions, confining to Internet version on weekdays. Moreover, new newspapers have appeared as well as a series of online papers, magazines and blogs. There is a major difficulty in accessing archives. Greek newspaper archives are generally not accessible online.[41] On this basis, the decision was made to cover four newspapers, two of which represent the mainstream – *Kathimerini* (centre right) and *To Vima* (centre left). Both newspapers are highly agenda setting, especially in their Sunday versions. The other two Greek newspapers are *Proto Thema*, a tabloid style newspaper (mostly) in circulation on weekends, and *Avgi*, a left-wing newspaper

[41] One has to go to each newspaper site and search through that or do a Google search with 'site: (Internet address of newspaper) (search words)' and then limit the search through Google tools.

representing mainly the left-wing party *Syriza*, which the has been the main opposition party since 2010, a serious challenger of shifting Greek governments and winner of the 2015 general election.

With this selection of German and Greek newspapers, the key patterns in public opinion are captured, although the most extremist or populist stances were not covered, which were either low in circulation and/or did not have online archives. The types of articles were limited to editorials, which were known to shape public opinion and produce labels. Despite the increased digitalisation of media, major newspaper editorials continue to influence national and international politics and events, as well as provide insight into social and broader cultural issues. A search was done with two keywords 'Euro' and 'Griech*' in German editorials and 'Germany' (and derivatives) and 'euro' in Greek editorials. This resulted in a total of 221 editorials, of which 152 were Greek and 69 were German. An open coding process was used, adding labels along the way to ensure that all possible labels were included in the analysis. This open coding was subsequently reduced to ten labels. For Germany, this resulted in 'oppressor', 'teacher', 'victim', 'other' and 'none'. For Greece, it was 'cheater', 'tragedy', 'child/pupil', 'patient', 'resister', 'other' and 'none'. Distinction was made between who or what is labelled ('the other', 'oneself', 'both' or none) and whether the label is positive or negative.

Results

The survey of the editorials makes it possible to correct the story of 'sinners' and 'saints' and the unidirectional force of hierarchy as a structure. First, labels of nations and nationalities used in the Greek and German newspapers refer to different ranking principles with different policy implications. Second, German and Greek media produce not only negative but also *positive* labels of 'the other'. For instance, one Greek editorial in the main conservative newspaper argues that 'we can learn from the well-tuned and disciplined Germans.' Third, and perhaps most interestingly, there is a considerable degree of self-stereotyping or self-blame taking place. Twenty-five per cent of German editorials are stereotyping Germans, and the majority of these labels are negative. The number of 'pure' self-stereotyping was significantly lower in Greek newspapers (12 per cent), but 30 per cent of the Greek editorials labelled both Germans and Greeks, and over 70 per cent of these were negative or mildly negative of Greece, arguing that the crisis is Greece's own fault (due to mismanagement, an intrinsically corrupt political establishment, a spoiled culture, etc.) (see Table 9.1).

This widespread Greek and German self-bashing based on crude generalisations indicates that states do not just seek positive identities with

Table 9.1 *Labelling 'Other' and 'Self'*

Labels	Greek newspapers		German newspapers	
	Number	Percentage	Number	Percentage
Other	56	37%	16	23%
Self	18	12%	17	25%
Both	44	30%	9	13%
None	30	19%	27	39%
Others/not categorised	4	2%		
Total	**152**		**69**	

a view to maintaining or improving their relative positions. Through public debates, they also internalise international criticism and develop various forms of shame. In fact, as I will demonstrate, there was a remarkable degree of interaction and responsiveness in the Greek and German debates on the Euro Crisis and their own roles in it. Both Greek and German editorials are deeply concerned with how 'the others' view 'us'. Controversial depictions of Greeks or Greece in German debates (and of Germans in Greek media) are quickly picked up, circulated and widely discussed. This suggests a European – or trans-national – dimension of a domestic debate about morality and responsibility for the Euro Crisis. This concern is also apparent in the many blogs by Greek journalists and opinion makers, frustrated with the ways in which foreign media display Greek as moral hazard and stereotype all Greek citizens[42] (see Figure 9.1).

The sections that follow explore how the different labels invoke particular positions in the international hierarchy, how they are in dialogue or respond to news outlets in the other member states and how these labels suggest different responses to the crisis.

Dominance: Negotiating the Trope of Nazism

One of the most dramatic performances of hierarchy in the Euro Crisis is linked to German Chancellor Angela Merkel. The chancellor figures regularly in protests in the streets of Athens and Thessaloniki – with fangs dripping with blood and dressed up as the leader of a new Reich. The Nazi version of the German chancellor was staged first in a public protest in Greece in the summer of 2011, about the same time that Merkel made two provocative statements: that Greece was in need of more

[42] See e.g. 'Keep Talking, Greece', available at www.keeptalkinggreece.com.

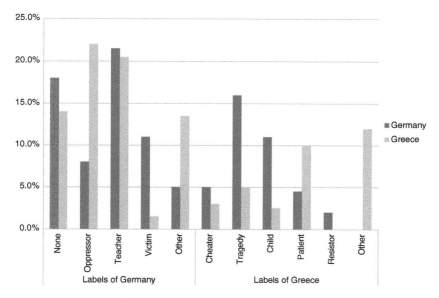

Figure 9.1 Distribution of Labels

permanent 'supervision' and that its default could lead to the dissolution of the euro and the collapse of European unity.[43] In Greek newspapers, no person is more identified than Merkel with the punitive measures.[44]

Yet, when examining the Greek and German coverage of the trope of Nazism in the three-month period of 2010, references to the Nazi past turns out to be more complex. Many traits that are ascribed to 'the other' are traits that Greek society struggles with domestically. Two patterns of labels relating to Nazism can be identified in the survey of Greek and German editorials: (1) Germany trying to dominate Europe as it did during the Nazi regime, making Greece a victim or resistant to German occupation, and (2) Greek neo-Nazism as the underdog's response to German hegemony and EU technocracy.

The German Oppressor

Several Greek editorials draw parallels between modern-day soup kitchens and the 'hungry country' under German occupation. More than

---

[43] *Bild*, October 2010; *FAZ*, April 2010.
[44] Other European countries have also dusted off their Nazi imagery during the Euro Crisis, including Cyprus (which was spared from German occupation), Spain and Italy.

500,000 Greeks died between October 1940 and October 1944, more than half of that figure is put down to hunger and malnutrition.[45] As one Greek editorial explains, 'Germany does not pay its war compensations even though courts have ruled so, and the German government is politically pressuring Greece not to enforce the legal decision of its courts.'[46] The question of war compensation pops up in numerous Greek editorials. In a controversial July 2012 issue of the Greek left-wing magazine *Crash*, journalists placed a photo of the German chancellor in orange prison uniform (à la Guantanamo) on the cover. *Crash* suggested sending Merkel to the International Criminal Court on charges of crimes against humanity (arguing that the chancellor has 'made Greece a modern concentration camp, in which the Greeks were isolated like lepers').[47] With this labelling of Germany as oppressor, Greece becomes an innocent victim.

Yet, the Greek (historical) subordination to German occupation and later dictatorship are not just a story of victimhood. It is also a story of humiliation and self-blame. As anthropologist Michael Herzfeld notes, the Greek capacity for self-criticism is also 'an expression of political subordination, when some Greeks "accepted" the military junta of 1967–1974 on the grounds that they "needed" discipline or bowed before repeated Nazi claims that they were "degenerate"'.[48] This Greek narrative of subordination and need for external discipline generates a sense of shame, but it also paves the way for a possible active role: that of resistance. The newspaper *To Vima* quotes Navy reservist Giorgos Drakopoulos: 'All the Greek people must rally together to rid the country of all those who oppress and humiliate us.'[49] This trope is present in the streets of Athens with demonstrators holding banners saying, 'Don't buy German products, resistance against fourth Reich', and the Greek unions have big banners saying '*Merkel Raus!*' ('Merkel Out!'). The idea of collective self-defence is seen as loyalty or bravery from the underdog's point of view.

The Greek image of Germany as a (neo-)Nazi oppressor is ambiguous and contested. Greek editorials are keenly aware of the sense of shame and guilt that German leaders carry with them. *Kathimerini* reports that this means that 'the country, plunged into its guilt, is trying with agony to prove that all her actions are necessitated out of pure idealism.' According to this reading, Germany necessarily tries to mask its dominance as a form of 'euro-nationalism'. Interestingly, several Greek newspapers embrace

---

[45] Lynn 2010, 5.   [46] *Kathimerini*, 2010.
[47] *Crash* only appeared around that period and was highly marketed. Then the printed version stopped, and now it is online only and not widely circulated.
[48] Hertzfeld 1987, 36.   [49] *To Vima*.

and quote sociologist Ulrich Beck's criticism of German economic dominance. While Merkel has never spoken up against the Nazi references in accordance with German stigma acceptance,[50] some German media have objected to the Greek accusations. On October 10, 2012, the *BILD* front cover reacted directly to the Greek criticism of Germany with the heading 'Germany hasn't deserved this.' German tabloid newspapers picked up the use of Nazi symbols in Greek protests and were appalled. One cover reads 'The Greeks Shame Europe ... and Still Gets New Millions'.

Related to the Nazi trope is the notion of 'colony'. Demonstrators in Athens use banners reading 'Merkel Out, Greece Is Not Your Colony' and 'This Is Not a European Union, It's Slavery'. The image of a colony is repeated in many editorials of *Kathimerini*, seeing the bailouts as colonial strategies. Interestingly, the colonial metaphor became almost literal in the German press when in October of 2010 *BILD* controversially suggested that Germany or German citizens bought Greek islands as a compensation for the bailout. The heading read, '*DIE REGIERUNG IN ATHEN WILL JETZT KRÄFTIG SPAREN – ABER WAS, WENN DAS NICHT REICHT? Verkauft doch eure Inseln, ihr Pleite-Griechen ... und die Akropolis gleich mit!*'[51], suggesting that Germans should simply buy Greek islands and the Acropolis from the 'bankrupt-Greeks'. The tabloid quotes CDU leader Josef Schlarmann as saying, 'Greece owns buildings, companies and uninhabited islands that can be used for debt repayment.' Yet, far from all German newspapers rallied behind this proposal. German journalists are carefully watched by the rest of the world and by their each other in the on-going self-reflexive debates about Germany's position in Europe.[52] For many Germans, upholding credibility after the atrocities committed during the Nazi regime still requires that Germany must live up to the highest moral standards and even outperform them; this does not involve colonising or buying up Greek islands.

The Complexities of Golden Dawn

The reference to Nazism in the Euro Crisis comes full circle with the neo-Nazism of the Golden Dawn movement, which received 6.3 per cent of votes in the general election in Greece in January of 2015. Golden Dawn is staunchly Eurosceptic, opposing Greece's participation in the European

[50] See also Jackson 2010; Adler-Nissen 2014.
[51] Bild, www.bild.de/politik/wirtschaft/griechenland-krise/regierung-athen-sparen-ver kauft-inseln-pleite-akropolis-11692338.bild.html.
[52] Adler-Nissen 2014.

Union and the Eurozone. Its members are frequently responsible for anti-Semitic graffiti, and their logo resembles a swastika. Officially denying that it has any connection to neo-Nazism, even though it openly admits 'heiling' and selling World War II Nazi propaganda at rallies, the party admires Ioannis Metaxas, the Greek general who established the fascist dictatorship between 1936 and 1941.[53] Ilias Kasidiaris, a spokesman for Golden Dawn, wrote an article that was published in a Golden Dawn magazine on 20 April 2011 in which he said

What would the future of Europe and the whole modern world be like if World War II had not stopped the renewing route of National Socialism? Certainly, fundamental values, which mainly derive from ancient Greek culture, would be dominant in every state and would define the fate of peoples. Romanticism as a spiritual movement and classicism would prevail against the decadent subculture that corroded the white man. Extreme materialism would have been discarded, giving its place to spiritual exaltation.[54]

In the same article, Adolf Hitler is characterised as a 'great social reformer' and 'military genius'. According to Greek cultural theorist Paul Cartledge (1994), this return to classical heritage (combined with references to Nazi myths) can be interpreted in part as a take-over from the West's desire for the modern Greeks to live up to their ancestors' supposedly glorious past. Greek antiquity as a form of supreme society is in this sense constituted as a 'huge burden' on Greek self-understanding.[55] This combination of Nazi-era rhetoric to spite a German politician does lend itself to a perverted sense of irony. It underscores anthropologist Michael Hertzfeld's point that German Nazi propaganda, on the one hand, condemned modern Greeks as fit for only 'servitude and death' and, on the other hand, insisted that 'present-day Germans and the ancient Greeks [are] the twin pillars of the Aryan race'.[56]

The usages of Nazi regalia in demonstrations in Greek cities and the rise of the extreme right and left have given rise to much self-reflection in Greek newspapers about how the rest of Europe and, in particular, Germany view Greece. When polls showed that Syriza was not on the rise in 2010, one editor concluded

The news is better. First: we are no more the only black sheep in the white European herd ... the polls show that the Greek public opinion is not only neo-fascists who want to burn the parliament but also people who think.[57]

[53] Ellinas 2013.
[54] 'Ο Κασιδιάρης εξυμνεί τον Χίτλερ, 17 September 2012.' Tvxs.gr. 2013–06–20, author's translation.
[55] Cartledge 1994, 4.   [56] Hertzfeld 1987, 66.   [57] *To Vima*, 2010.

With Syriza now in power, this 'black sheep' image has become stronger in the Greek discourse, further strengthening an obsession with status, hierarchy and resistance of international shaming.

Subordination: Negotiating Victimhood

The most predominant image of Greece in German newspapers is that of 'liar', 'cheater' and 'sinner'. These labels are linked to crime, decadence and lost virtues. These labels also refer explicitly or implicitly to a better Antiquity where Greece was a 'superior civilisation'. From this perspective, Germany is 'naive' to support the Greeks. For the German tabloid *BILD*, the bail-outs (which are in fact mostly guarantees rather than transfers of funds) is called *'Griechenlandhilfe'*. *BILD* adopts the perspective of the 'ordinary German tax-payer' at the bottom of German society. Accordingly, Germany becomes the victim of a 'careless' and 'selfish' Greek society that drains the pockets of German tax-payers. One *BILD* headline reads, *'Bundies gegen Lüge'* ('Alliance against Lies') and argues that journalists must now pose uncomfortable questions and 'dig out the truth'. *Bild* continues, '[T]hey must ask why Greece tricked the EU and falsified statistics and say stop.'[58]

Falsified statistics refer to the time when the euro was launched in 1999. Italy was allowed in, despite doubts about whether it was ready. Greece was turned down because of the budget deficit and outstanding debts in a crushing blow for the political and economic establishment in Athens. By fiddling with the debt and deficit numbers, the Greek government later managed to convince the other EU members to allow Greece to join the Eurozone in 2001, signalling a landmark moment in the national aim to 'increase our standard of living' and 'bolster our national self-confidence', 'based more on knowledge and modern structures' as Minister of Economy and Finance Yiannos Papantoniou explained.[59]

While he secured Greece's membership in the Eurozone, Papantoniou did not manage to convince the rest of Europe that Greece had modernised and become a well-behaving member state. In November 2010, the German magazine *Focus* released a front page with Aphrodite showing the middle finger and the headline, 'Swindlers in the Euro Family'. The *Focus* cover was picked up by many Greek newspapers. In an instance of self-bashing, Greek journalists cultivated the 'nasty' comments in the German press, arguing that the German press had demonised Greece, making the crisis worse. As one editorial put it, 'The riots in the streets

---

[58] *BILD*, May 2010.   [59] Lynch 2011, 54–5.

and the bad press [are] driving away tourists; we are not doing enough to attract FDI and to privatise.'[60]

An interesting comparison is how Germany views Ireland, another of the PIIGS.[61] Ireland has been playing the 'good pupil' card in relation to developments in Greece. This has led Angela Merkel to urge the Greeks to follow the Irish example.[62] Also within Ireland, the hierarchy looks different. In terms of the causes of the crisis, the Irish have their own moral version of the immaturity thesis, as Power and Nussbaum highlight: 'Several people we spoke to believe that the Irish public acknowledges they are partly responsible for their own misfortune and are prepared to reap what they sowed.'[63] German public debate considers the PIIG countries quite differently. A 2014 poll in Germany showed that 60 per cent of those interviewed believed that Ireland 'took austerity lying down'.[64] This is not the case for Greece.

Greek Tragedy

A second and related image is that of the Greek tragedy, which suggests that Greek suffering is inevitable and that there is little that Greece or any other state can do about it. The sense of tragedy has also been reflected in situations of tension between Athens and Berlin. For instance, Greek President Carolas Papoulias accused German Finance Minister Wolfgang Schäuble of insulting the country by likening Greece to a 'bottomless pit' (later, Schäuble refrained from using the term, but it was repeated by German media and German government members). As one German journalist wrote, 'The terrible scenes of Greece make us all deeply affected. But they should not lead to hasty relief efforts ... Where are the billions going anyway?'. The tragedy trope lead to the conclusion in several German newspapers in 2010 (repeated in May of 2012 on the front page of *Der Spiegel*) that the Greeks must inevitably leave the Eurozone. 'Grexit' became a common term and with that the idea that Greece had tricked itself into an exclusive club to which it did not belong and inevitably would have to leave.

Interestingly, several Greek editorials re-circulate this idea of an inevitable tragedy, which reduces the complexities of the Euro Crisis to a Greek problem. As one editorial in *To Vima* reads, 'We are not serious: we are not willing to work to get out of the mess where we led ourselves, acting immaturely.' Interestingly, the editorial adds: 'This is impossible to change.' In addition, Greek reports of its 'brain drain' of university-educated young

---

[60] *To Vima*, 2010.   [61] I thank Neil Dooley for this point.   [62] Lynch 2015.
[63] Power and Nussbaum 2015.   [64] Kelpie 2014.

generations are often mentioned in *To Vima*, which concludes one of its editorials (without detectable irony!) with 'We need for Germany, France and UK to create a sort of economic directorship for Europe.' As Hertzfeld notes, quoting Mosse, '[E]ven the most articulate members of an oppressed population may strategically adopt the negative features attributed to it by those of higher status.'[65] This self-bashing by Greek opinion-makers amounts to more than adapting to the practical realities of discrimination; it actively contributes to the subordination.

Immature Pupil

A third and related figure in both Greek and German newspapers is that of Greece as the 'immature pupil' (with Germany cast as 'teacher'). This label is related to the tragedy image, but it differs because it offers the possibility of change and improvement of position.[66] As with the other labels, the 'underdog versus modernity' debate has a long history in Greek society. The self-labelling as 'immature' in Greece pre-dates the euro – and has an important relationship with a perception of not being 'modern', which is arguably synonymous with not being Western European enough. As one Greek editorial noted in 2010, '[I]t is no wonder that we will be thrown out of the Eurozone: we are backwards, our technological development is low, and we have a middle class with no interests besides consumption.'[67] In terms of understanding the production of hierarchy, it raises a number of questions. Is there a 'hegemonic' notion of European modernity acting as a yardstick against which PIIGS come up short in their own (and others') estimations? How did that emerge? How is it reproduced or changed in the Euro Crisis?

There are plenty of 'tailored' diagnoses of immaturity for Ireland, Portugal, Spain and Italy (the PIIGS). The specifics are different, but the dominant narratives of what went wrong in these countries come down to similar immaturity of political and economic governance for which Greece is castigated.[68] However, where Greece sees itself (and is seen) as the worst of the PIIGS and lowest in the ranking of Eurozone members, Italians perceive that their relegation to second-class status – compared to the first-class status enjoyed by Germany, France and the United Kingdom – is unjust. Associate evaluation matters for how states manage their relationship to other states.

<hr/>

[65] Hertzfeld 1987, 66.
[66] As illustrated in Antonis Samaras' charm offensive in Berlin in August for Germany's additional bail-out.
[67] Kathimerini 2010.   [68] Dooley 2014.

Germany's role as teacher is uncomfortable in an inter-state relation-ship in Europe, which is supposed to be based on equality and reciprocity. The perception of this role in Germany is far from homogeneous. Responding to the harsh criticism of Germany in Greek media, the German government organised an official six-hour state visit in 2012 where the German chancellor met with Greek Prime Minster Samaras. In preparation for the visit, Samaras explained: 'We will receive her as befits the leader of a great power and a friendly country . . . People know that this government means Greece's last chance. We will make it. If we fail, chaos awaits us.'[69] Samaras made an ambiguous statement: to be a 'great power' and a 'friend' are two different things, and the ambiguity is also reflected in Merkel's statements.

Keenly aware of the importance of symbolic gestures, Chancellor Merkel arrived in Athens in 2012 with the state plane flying the flags of Greece and Germany. The gesture set a tone of humility from the German camp. Merkel herself is very aware of the importance of renego-tiating (or concealing) the hierarchy between the two states: 'I have not come as a taskmaster . . . And nor have I come as a teacher to give grades, I have come as a friend to listen and be informed.'[70] However, her subsequent remarks confirmed the role of the teacher as Merkel began to evaluate the Greek reform efforts:

I come from East Germany and I know how long it takes to build reform . . . The road for the people of Greece is very tough, very difficult, but they have put a good bit of the path behind them. I want to say you are making progress!

Interestingly, Prime Minister Samaras contributed to the role-play. Greek officials underlined that Samaras was indeed a good pupil: 'Samaras showed a real will to change things,' as one Greek government official said to German newspapers. 'He stressed what Greece had to do, not what others had to do for Greece.' In addition, German officials responded by confirming this role: 'In our view Samaras is really trying to get things done', one German official said, requesting anonymity. 'Nobody should see this trip as a sign that all is perfect. But we recognise things are moving in the right direction.'[71]

Yet, the awkwardness of Greece's relationship with Germany was on display during the visit when Samaras stressed: 'Greeks are a proud people [and] our enemy is recession. But we are not asking for favours. In my discussion with the German chancellor I pointed out, however, that the Greek people are bleeding.'[72] This suggests that rather than being the

[69] McElroy 2012.   [70] Smith 2012.
[71] http://business.financialpost.com/news/economy/hostile-greeks-brace-for-merkels-visit.
[72] Smith 2012.

pupil 'making progress', Greece is a strong and full-grown nation suffering from the recession. Interestingly, the principle of equality of opportunity is stressed in the 'we are not asking for favours' remark. On the one hand, Samaras insists on taking on the responsibility for resolving the crisis, suggesting equality between Greece and Germany, and, on the other hand, suggesting that the crisis is more structural, putting Greece to its knees.

Conclusion

This chapter has argued that neither a narrow institutional nor a broad structural understanding of hierarchy alone can explain the position of Germany and Greece in the Eurozone. The two understandings of hierarchy need to be combined and complemented with an analysis of national identity. This is so because the Euro Crisis is not only about the skewed architecture of the Economic and Monetary Union or failed national policies. It is also a struggle over the sense of national self. Moreover, hierarchies (both when they appear as formal institutions and when they appear as broader societal discourses) are interpreted and reacted to. Examining Greek and German debates about each other's roles in the Euro Crisis, this chapter has demonstrated how the crisis strengthens self-reflexive and highly interactive debates on national identities, self-blame and self-stereotyping. This interactive dynamic means that both Greece and Germany can appear as innocent victims (the Greek oppressed and colonised victim, the naive German tax-payer) that suffer from the other's brutality (Nazism) or laziness (decadence). Tropes of Nazism in both German and Greek versions, criminality and colonialism are invoked as Eurozone members are forced to interact more closely as the Euro Crisis continues, both enforcing a sense of common destiny and creating ideological and political divides. This results in complex political struggles that often collide nations with their leaders or with particular groups.

There are important tensions between ideas of state sovereignty (equality) and principles and practices of ranking states (hierarchy). On the one hand, international organisations such as the European Union guarantee all member states the same status and obligations (formal equality of all Eurozone states and their equal obligations in economic and monetary politics under EU law). On the other hand, international law and multilateral governance pave the way for organised inequality through rankings of national performance. These institutional rankings have implications not just for economic policies, unemployment rates and domestic social unrest but also for structural and more encompassing classification of states and national identities. Within the EU system of formal equality, an institutional hierarchy is reinforced by mutual stereotyping and moral shaming. The German chancellor's delicate balancing acts during state visits to Athens indicate the difficulty of negotiating such hierarchical positions in a discourse of equality.

Mediatised labels and stereotypes suggest particular positions for states and make different kinds of political decisions possible. Depending on whether Greece is a bottomless pit or a spoiled pupil in need of more discipline, it will need to act differently. Likewise, it makes a difference for German strategy whether German economic dominance is labelled 'strict', 'oppressive' or downright 'hysteric' by Greek and German news-papers. The classifications of states in the Euro Crisis are volatile and ambiguous, making alternative political choices not only possible but also more likely. Hierarchies can involve a high degree of self-reproach, irony and – more generally – a heightened self-consciousness. States can seek to resist domination or to move up in the hierarchy, but in doing so they often end up expressing complicity with the very same order they seek to resist. In this sense, Greece is complicit in its own relegation to the bottom of the hierarchy. This complicity, however, also means that there are possibilities for change from within and below in the hierarchy. This raises all sorts of interesting questions: Are all states equally concerned about how they are viewed by others? Or are Germany and Greece more concerned about their international rankings than other states? If so, is this linked to their history and to their common fate and obligations in the Euro Crisis? More broadly, does the European project, rather than ensuring sovereign equality, strengthen hierarchy and thereby national shame? Answering these questions will require addressing how institu-tional and structural hierarchies interact – and how reflective practices contribute to the evolution, transformation and sometimes undermining of these hierarchies. Such practices are deeply political, and while their consequences are far from automatic, they show a pattern. This is, ultimately, the key added insight of focusing on the social production of international hierarchy and the interactions within it.

10   'Delinquent Gangs' in the International System Hierarchy

Shogo Suzuki

Russia's recent annexation of Crimea has brought the issue of international 'delinquency' into the spotlight once more. Russia's proclamation of the region as a part of its 'sphere of influence' and blatant use of power politics in ensuring that Crimea stays under its control have brought about considerable social opprobrium and sanctions from its critics. One of the sanctions included suspending Russia's membership of the G8, United States President Obama announced that Russia was being 'isolated' as punishment for its inappropriate behaviour. As reported by CNN:

> The annual summit of the world's industrial powers is scheduled for Russian Olympic venue Sochi in June, but the United States and other members have halted planning for the gathering amid calls for Russia to be kicked out. Once known as the G7, the group that also includes Germany, Britain, France, Italy, Japan and Canada agreed to add Russia in 1998 to reflect the changing geopolitical dynamic after the Cold War and breakup of the Soviet Union. Revoking Russia's membership would isolate Putin diplomatically to deny him the Western acceptance he has sought. 'He will be isolated more. He won't look good in front of his people,' CNN Chief International Correspondent Christiane Amanpour said Monday. Such isolation would bolster economic isolation and sanctions – a more effective strategy to pressure Putin. 'The G8 plus some others and all of them, every single one of them are prepared to go to the hilt in order to isolate Russia with respect to this invasion,' Kerry said Sunday on the CBS program 'Face the Nation'.[1]

A number of key assumptions undergird the G7's decision to exclude Russia. First, there is the assumption/hope that exclusion from a social grouping in the international community can eventually bring about some form of behavioural change from the Russians. This assumption, in turn, is supported by the belief that membership of the G8 and acceptance from the West somehow matter to Russia, possibly more than any other grouping in the international community. These policies are ultimately based on the premise that identities matter deeply to states. As Ringmar has noted,

---

[1] Cohen and Davidsen 2014.

social actors, including states, create 'narratives' – stories of what they 'are' and 'what they would like to be', and what they would like others to think they are – in the process of constructing their identities. Rejection of these narratives by one's peers effectively constitutes 'identity denial': it causing a mismatch between how the actor perceives himself or herself and how others see him or her and frequently culminates in identity crises.

Such identity crises are powerful drivers of behavioural change. In sociological theories of International Relations (IR), recognition, which can be defined as an act in which an actor's peers accept a social actor's 'narratives' of his or her identity, has always been a crucial concept that explains state behaviour. Constructivists have thus examined how the tactic of collective 'shaming', which effectively stigmatises a state and denies recognition of its preferred perception of its identity, has contributed to the diffusion of particular 'global norms'. Here shaming typically serves to deny a state's self-proclaimed claims to being a 'worthy and legitimate member of the international community', causing a crisis of identity within the 'shamed' state, and ultimately brings about conformist behaviour. States do this not only because they see particular norms as an inherent 'good' that is worth following: they also are typically assumed to desire membership of the international community (thus creating a 'new' identity for themselves) as a good in itself, and because of this, they ultimately seek recognition by their peers as 'worthy members' of this grouping.

There is a strong but perhaps under-acknowledged logic of social hierarchy behind this analysis. First, there is an assumption that social hierarchies – between 'good' and 'bad' states in this case – can and have emerged repeatedly in the international community despite the existence of sovereign equality.[2] Second, and following from this point, the existence of these hierarchies also means that there are certain groups of states who possess the social authority to impose particular negative labels on other states, which effectively moves the latter down the social rankings of states. Finally, it is presumed that states find it extremely difficult to escape these hierarchies because they ultimately care about their standing within this social hierarchy. Indeed, in most constructivist analyses, the story is often one of a 'happy ending',[3] where the 'rogue' eventually mends its wicked ways and adopts the norms propagated by the 'good' states, eventually re-joining the more respectable, morally superior grouping within the international community.

---

[2] Also see Chapter 9.
[3] Recent scholarship on norms has been complicating this narrative: see e.g. Towns 2012; Adler-Nissen 2014, 2015; Zarakol 2011, 2014.

But is this the only way in which states can negotiate hierarchy? If hierarchy does indeed exist and matter, is it a 'given' that the weak will eventually capitulate to the dominance of those at the apex? In this book, Sharman (Chapter 6) argues convincingly that many micro-states or dependencies are not in a subordinate relationship with great powers or metropoles but at times are able to subvert their relations with their more powerful counterparts. This leads Sharman to conclude that 'micro-states are institutional clones of other states, irrespective of the vast disparity in material capabilities', and there is therefore a 'relative rarity of hierarchy' in the international community today.[4] Accordingly, states – no matter how weak – can escape the logic of hierarchy thanks to the entrenchment of norms of sovereign equality, which have ensured that there is very little hierarchy left in the contemporary international order. This chapter concurs with the view that less powerful states can escape hierarchies (and have), but it also argues, contra Sharman, that this is done so despite the existence of deeper social hierarchies that continue to characterise the contemporary international order. Sharman's chapter defines hierarchy narrowly, in the sense of formal, institutionalised arrangements (such as a currency union, security alliances or the location of judicial control by the metropole state) that surrender part of a state's sovereign prerogatives to a more powerful state. This results in the former entering relations of domination, where the more powerful are able to exert control over the weak. Hierarchy is most likely to manifest in more direct exertions of power, where there exist 'relations between actors that allow one to shape directly the circumstances or actions of another'.[5]

Such overt forms of domination are indeed scarce today, thanks to decolonisation and the spread of the norm of sovereign equality. Yet, a narrow focus on formal institutions of control risks missing deeper structures of domination. There are other forms of hierarchy that allow certain actors to dominate the rules and procedures of the 'formal and informal institutions' between actors that 'guide, steer, and constrain the actions (or nonactions) and conditions of existence of others'.[6] They can also exert their influence over determining what is 'normal', 'natural', 'abnormal' or 'unthinkable' in social life as well.[7] In the context of international politics, Hedley Bull has provided a classic example of this in the case of decolonisation. Bull notes that although many former colonies attained formal 'equality' with the rest of the world through independence and the attainment of sovereign statehood, they could only do so by invoking Western norms of national self-determination and sovereignty. Put simply, in order to escape narrower forms of hierarchical control, they

---

[4] See Chapter 6.   [5] Barnett and Duvall 2005, 49.   [6] *Ibid.*, 51.   [7] *Ibid.*, 52–7.

had no choice but to accept a different form of hierarchy, where they had to accept an international order whose constitutive rules were originally written by the West and for the West.[8]

As has been pointed out elsewhere, this means that certain Western great powers have continued to enjoy greater moral authority than others, even in today's decolonised world. This means that this particular category of states is able to use their superior status to affect states' social standing within the international community. The labelling of non-democratic regimes as 'outlaw states' is intimately linked to the fact that the most powerful states in the post–cold war international community are liberal democracies. Critics have also noted the inconsistent manner by which certain states have been labelled as 'rogues' and argued that the category and its use are more a reflection of American foreign policy interests.[9] Furthermore, very few states can escape this hierarchy altogether: it is telling that even Lichtenstein, which Sharman uses as an example of a micro-state being able to successfully exercise (and even enhance) its autonomy vis-à-vis Switzerland, was unable to withstand the social shame (and subsequent moving down in the international social hierarchy) of being blacklisted by .the Financial Action Task Force for harbouring money laundering.[10] 'Stung by the criticism',[11] it has since reformed some of its financial regulatory laws.

This chapter thus takes as its theoretical starting point a broader view of hierarchy that encompasses economic and social hierarchies that exist beyond the formal institutional settings of equality. It forwards two main points. First, the chapter draws on sociological studies of delinquent subculture formation to highlight the existence of a more complex hierarchy of multiple social groups within the international community. In my use, the term 'deviant' can be defined simply as an actor defying 'commonly accepted societal norms'. In the context of international politics, this 'refers to a flouting of key norms of conduct espoused by the global community, or at least by those who have asserted a credible right to speak for it'.[12] This, of course, is not to suggest that the mainstream social grouping is 'good' and that subcultures are necessarily 'delinquent' or that the latter have readily observable characteristics that mark them out as such. While social groups whose behaviours deviate from the mainstream are often labelled as 'delinquent' or 'rogues', it is

---

[8] Bull 1984.

[9] See e.g. Simpson 2004; Hoyt 2000; Litwak 2001. For an attempt to forward a more analytically viable definition of a 'rogue state', see Caprioli and Trumbore 2003.

[10] To this day, Liechtenstein remains a country of 'primary concern' for serving as a money laundering base on the US Department of State's list.

[11] See (accessed October 24, 2015).   [12] Nincic 2005, 2 (emphasis added).

important to note that this act again reflects hierarchical power relations within a society, as those in dominant positions are more likely to be able to 'successfully' determine what constitutes deviancy or 'malicious' behaviour in the first place.

Second, this chapter argues that a state may be able to garner international status and prestige despite its refusal to conform to so-called global norms and subsequent failure to secure recognition by the 'mainstream' of the international community because it is able to secure social recognition from members of the alternative 'subculture'. As Adler-Nissen's contribution to this book (Chapter 9) highlights, most studies on status in international politics have tended to examine an actor's/state's interaction within one community (be it 'international' or 'regional') and have not fully explored the possibility of multiple sources of social recognition and their implications. This chapter, then, aims to add another layer of complexity to this picture and highlight the existence of multiple social groupings and hierarchies within an overarching 'international community'.

This is not simply for the sake of complexity. Conventional constructivist studies on socialisation have been hampered by in an implicit belief that it is impossible and unthinkable that any international recognition can be given to actors who reject (often progressive) values espoused by the mainstream of the international community. The West, which is implicitly assumed to be the 'liberal core' of the international community, is seen as 'the only game in town' and the only community that can bestow recognition on international actors. This has the effect of ignoring the potential existence of non-Western social groupings within the international community and reproducing Eurocentric narratives. Whether or not the Western-centric social group is really the only one that 'matters' should be an empirical question rather than something that is simply assumed. It is possible that some actors may be able to garner some form of international 'praise' or 'recognition' precisely because they refuse to conform to certain norms, and this may play a role in hindering the diffusion of 'international norms'.[13]

A brief case study of 'international subculture' formation is provided by examining China's attempts to break its international alienation by cultivating its relations with Africa in the 1960s. The Chinese case is interesting, as the People's Republic of China found itself alienated from both the communist camp and the capitalist camps during the cold war. Given the bipolar division that existed in the international community at that time,

---

[13] It must also be noted that negative recognition is a form of recognition (more on this later).

it may have been difficult for a state to survive this alienation for long. Yet, China managed to survive for more than ten years without necessarily becoming a 'hermit state'. While its normalisation of relations with the United States heralded the end of this period of imposed 'isolation', the period between has received less scrutiny and is worthy of our attention.

Socialisation, Alienation and Subculture Formation

The socialiser has a number of options that he or she can use to bring about behavioural change. First, there is persuasion, where the socialiser attempts to convince the socialisee that the norms being propagated are just and that it is in the best interests of the latter to accept them. Second, the socialiser can praise 'good' behaviour in an attempt to bring out further norms compliance. Third, there is the tactic of 'shaming', where the socialisee is stigmatised for his or her refusal to adopt certain norms. In this final case, constructivists have tended to look at the process by which states conform to 'international norms' in order to deal with their 'shaming' or 'alienation', and there appear to be three avenues by which an actor can respond to this situation.[14] While constructivists' normative commitment to demonstrating moral progress in international politics has often meant that there is a tendency to concentrate on successful cases of 'socialisation' into largely liberal norms emanating from the West, it is worth noting that there is no a priori guarantee that socialisation is going to be successful.

First, the actor can cut himself or herself off and 'withdraw' from the social environment. Second, the actor can attempt to change the very features that result in the withdrawal of his or her recognition by conforming as closely as possible to the norms that govern legitimate membership of the 'reference group'. This, of course, is the process that constructivist scholars have examined most in the context of international politics. Third, the actor can gather other actors with similar 'recognition' problems

and jointly ... establish new norms, new criteria of status which define as meritorious the characteristics they do possess, the kinds of conduct of which they are capable ... [s]uch new status criteria would represent new sub-cultural values different from and even antithetical to those of the larger social system.[15]

It is this third type of behaviour that can lead to the emergence of 'deviant subcultures'.[16] A subculture has been defined as 'a system of values,

---

[14] See Goffman 1963, 19–21, as well as Adler-Nissen 2014, 153–5; Zarakol 2011, Chapter 2.
[15] Cohen 1956, 66.   [16] See e.g. Cohen 1956; Willis 1977.

Table 10.1 *Status Frustration among Alienated States*

Group type/ conditions	Alienation from dominant group	Dissatisfaction with social standing in dominant group	Challenge to principles of membership in dominant group	Goals of group/ actor
Isolated actor	Yes	Yes/no	No	Withdrawal from dominant group and any other social groupings
Sub-cultural group member	Yes	Yes	Yes	Improving social status by attaining social recognition within sub-cultural group
Oppositional group member	No	No	No	Dispute and attain the group's goals in certain issue areas within dominant group; social recognition not a primary goal, although this may emerge

attitudes, modes of behaviour and life-styles of a social group which is distinct from, but related to the dominant culture of a society.'[17] Although there are various reasons why subcultures emerge, Albert K. Cohen argues in his study of gang culture that sub-cultural groups can emerge as a response to social alienation, which is of particular relevance here. Sub-cultural groupings in international politics share a number of traits that distinguish them from other groupings such as coalitions or oppositional groups which emerge specifically to win disputes over given issue areas, as summarised in the Table 10.1.

Sociological studies give us a number of examples of this type of behaviour. In his study of working-class subculture at school, Willis demonstrates that delinquent working-class 'lads' articulate a set of

[17] Abercrombie et al. 1994, 416. Dick Hebdige adopts a similar interpretation, describing subculture as 'a form of resistance in which experienced contradictions and objections to . . . ruling ideology are obliquely represented in style.' See Hebdige 2003, 133.

values that serve as an antithesis to 'obedient', 'good' behaviour at the school. The 'lads' receive recognition and status within this normative framework: for instance, under-aged drinking takes place 'because it is the most decisive signal to staff and "ear'oles" [conformist students] that the individual is separate from the school and has a presence in an alternative, superior and more mature mode of social being'.[18]

An ideal-type sub-cultural group will have three characteristics. First, as elaborated below, members of a sub-cultural grouping are alienated from the dominant group, and the emergence of the group is a reaction to the resulting lack of social recognition by the latter. Second, because of their isolation and expulsion from the mainstream social group, the sub-cultural group operates on different principles of membership. They should not be confused with oppositional groups which work within the framework of the dominant culture as the 'loyal opposition'. One example of the latter would be France and Germany's opposition to the American and British invasion of Iraq, which was over a procedural point. Both states did not challenge the arguably more fundamental normative goals of promoting democratic governance and the respect for human rights, which scholars have argued has become the benchmark for legitimate membership in the Western-dominated international community since the end of the cold war.[19]

Finally, one of the primary goals of a sub-cultural group is to engage in 'counter-stigmatization ("in-group alignment")', where representatives accept the stigma but turn it into an emblem of pride, identifying with the group of stigmatized'.[20] Insofar as 'recognition' requires an actor's peers to accept the narratives of the actor's identity, the sub-cultural group provides a ready audience to accept and positively affirm the actor's apparently 'deviant' identity. Members of the group challenge their alienation/stigmatisation by the international community by seeking social recognition and 'back-patting' through an alternative reference group. This, in turn, means that the actor in question may become 'relatively untouched by ... failure [to attain social recognition in "mainstream" society]' and may even believe himself or herself to be 'a full-fledged normal human being and that [the mainstream] are the ones who are not quite human'.[21]

---

[18] Willis 1977, 19 (emphasis added).
[19] See e.g. Clark 2005; Bowden 2004; Fidler 2001.   [20] Adler-Nissen 2014, 153.
[21] Goffman 1963, 17. Oppositional groups within the mainstream social group do not share this primary goal, as they do not suffer from a perceived lack of social recognition, although this is not to deny the possibility that 'back-patting' and other positive social influence are not exercised within the latter.

Sub-cultural Groupings in International Relations

When this concept is applied to international politics, we see similar characteristics to the aforementioned youth subcultures. First, as mentioned earlier, sub-cultural groupings are likely to emerge when there are a number of states that have been alienated from the dominant international social group and share dissatisfaction with their lack of social recognition. Yongjin Zhang has defined international alienation as a situation in which 'cordial relations between [states] have been broken and friendly feelings towards each other have been turned into bitterness and hostility'.[22] It is likely to take place when a 'state does not regard or is perceived not to regard as binding a set of common rules regulating relations between member states' of the international community, 'when that state withdraws or is prevented from sharing in the working of common institutions' and 'when that state does not hold that it has any stake, or interests, as others do, in maintaining the existing order within that society'.[23]

It is important to note, however, that alienation in itself does not necessary motivate an actor to form a sub-cultural group. As Figure 10.1 shows, a state, for instance, can choose a policy of isolation, by which it decides that it 'can best promote its national interests through minimum involvement in foreign affairs and alliances'.[24] Alternatively, a state might withdraw from some aspects of social life in the international community because it views its rules as unjust and sees very little stake in maintaining it. In both cases, the state is unlikely to be active in seeking the recognition of its peers and is not going to suffer from a mismatch between the social recognition it receives and desires.

This problem is more likely to occur if a state has been ostracised against its will and cannot attain the social recognition it desires. This form of alienation 'may be an act or the result of an act'.[25] It takes place when a state challenges or is perceived to pose a threat to the normative structures of the international community.[26] Whichever reason comes first, these two factors are mutually reinforcing and serve to deepen the state's isolation from the international community.[27]

Imposed isolation can cause several difficulties in the international realm. The withdrawal of diplomatic recognition, for example, may cause problems for an alienated state in communicating with other governments. Similarly, if a state is banned from international organisations,

---

[22] Zhang 1998, 44.   [23] *Ibid.*   [24] Geldenhuys 1990, 9.   [25] Zhang 1998, 45.
[26] Revolutionary states, for instance, have tended to be seen as inherently threatening to the international order and been subjected to hostile treatment. See Armstrong 1993; Walt 1996.
[27] Cohen 1956, 68; Zhang 1998, 45.

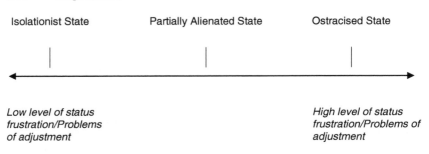

Figure 10.1 Status frustration among alienated states.

it may be unable to enjoy the benefits generated through its membership. Imposed isolation also has symbolic value. As can be seen from the recent case of suspending Russia from the G8, it can stigmatise a state as a 'pariah' and put its membership of the international community (and any other community, for that matter) into question. Taken to extremes, imposed isolation can also result in the denial of a state's identity. Isolation results in the loss of a community that can recognise and reconfirm an identity to which a social actor aspires, and the same applies to states. A case in point may be Taiwan, which continues to almost frantically construct the narrative of being a de jure state, the 'Republic of China'. Yet, most states recognise the People's Republic of China and by doing so cut off official diplomatic ties with Taiwan. Taiwan is thus diplomatically isolated and finds its aspired self-identity denied. As a state's self-identity can only emerge through interactions with others, a state is unable to construct a self-identity and maintain meaningful social relations within its community.[28] If the ostracised state aspires to a particular identity, one way to break out of this situation is to recover its identity through an alternative social arena. It is then when it begins its attempts to form a sub-cultural group.

Of course, as Geldenhuys points out, integration and alienation are not necessarily two concepts in a dichotomous relationship and are thus best thought of as a continuum.[29] A state can, for example, feel a profound sense of ambivalence towards certain institutions of the international community while simultaneously playing a part in maintaining others. Examples of this may include third world states' support of sovereignty and the sovereign state system while strongly opposing the human rights regime. This point also seems to indicate that there are also degrees of deviance. As shown in Figure 10.2, an actor's commitment to the norms of the sub-cultural group

[28] Gries 2005, 241.   [29] Geldenhuys 1990.

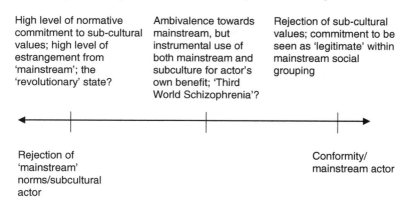

Figure 10.2 Degrees of 'delinquency' in the international community.

may vary depending on the degree of its alienation, how aggrieved it feels towards its social environment and the degree of its 'status frustration'. It may thus cooperate in maintaining some elements of the shared rules within the mainstream social grouping despite its ambivalence.

Second, there must be 'effective interaction' between these actors for a sub-cultural group to emerge.[30] Through these interactions, actors can discover similarities in identity (in the sense of being 'socially frustrated' and/or alienated from the mainstream social groups) and potentially articulate common interests that would lead to the emergence of the subculture. Typically, this takes the form of mutual signalling that certain behaviour that stands in opposition to the dominant culture will be supported and held in high esteem. Once the alienated state has decided that it stands to gain little from conforming to the existing norms of the international community, it can initiate the process of forming a subculture to resist its 'pariah' status and attain some form of international recognition. As a subculture requires members with similar 'status frustrations', the actor must first identify peers with similar problems and articulate a common 'frame of reference' that will serve as a rallying point. Typically, this will include hostile images of the dominant international social milieu,[31] as well as a set of alternative principles that will stand in opposition to those of the dominant community. Members of the sub-cultural group must then persuade each other of their commitment to the group and their intent to 'reward' or 'support' members,[32] and this can take either material or social forms, as described by constructivist scholarship.[33]

[30] Cohen 1956, 59.   [31] *Ibid.*, 68.   [32] Risse 2000.
[33] Johnston 2001, 501; Ringmar 2002, 119.

China's Relations with Africa in the 1950 and 1960s: A Case of Subculture Formation?

The rest of this chapter demonstrates this by examining China's attempts to break out of its international alienation in the 1960s by cultivating a sub-cultural group with African states. China's dealings with Africa in the late 1950s and 1960s makes an excellent case for examining the process of sub-cultural group formation as well as its limitations.

The People's Republic of China (PRC) satisfies a number of conditions necessary for the motivations to form a sub-cultural group. First, the PRC faced an unprecedented degree of international alienation in the 1950s and 1960s. Its initial pro-Soviet 'leaning to one side [*xiang sulian yibiandao*]' policy, the signing of the Sino-Soviet Friendship, Alliance and Mutual Assistance Treaty (1950), and decision to enter the Korean War had caused the United States to envision a monolithic communist bloc. Washington established a series of alliances to contain the threat of Chinese and Soviet communism in the Asia-Pacific, which was further complemented by trade embargos.[34] China was ostracised further by the Eastern bloc led by the Soviet Union when it clashed with Moscow over ideological lines. Both sides exchanged angry polemics, and relations deteriorated to a point where Beijing was accused of flouting the '"strict prohibition of factionalist activities within the Communist movement" and establishing "nothing but an anti-Leninist faction in the international Communist movement"'[35] and only narrowly escaped total excommunication.[36] Nevertheless, Beijing had few supporters, and it was expelled from the Eastern bloc in all but name.

Second, this 'international isolation' was imposed completely against Beijing's will, and China stood in 'angry isolation' at the time, as Richard Nixon aptly put it, despite Beijing's eagerness to establish diplomatic relations with members of the international community. The leaders of the Chinese Communist Party (CCP) had not only come to power on the basis of their revolutionary ideology, but their legitimacy also derived considerably from their credentials as a nationalist force. They were anxious that China be recognised as a legitimate member of the international community rather than a 'semi-civilised', semi-colony that it had been prior to the 1940s. With all these aspirations denied, China had been transformed from a weak state 'into a new giant, the most powerful

---

[34] The trade embargo, enforced by the China Committee of the Paris Coordinating Committee for Exports of Strategic Materials, was much more stringent than its counterpart imposed on the Soviet Union.

[35] Griffith 1964, 217. The quotations are from the Soviet theoretical journal *Kommunist*, published on October 18, 1963.

[36] Griffith 1964, 210–19.

ground military force in Asia, and the most frustrated and certainly most populous nation in the world'.[37] It is hardly surprising in this context that Beijing would see its international environment as fundamentally unjust and seek to realise its ambitions by forming a sub-cultural grouping: in fact, it had no other choice.

Searching for Soul Mates: Propagating the Sub-cultural Ideology

As discussed earlier, the formation of a sub-cultural group requires 'fellow members' who share similar frustrations, as well as a sufficient amount of interaction between them. In the Chinese case, the PRC was able to recruit a number of sympathetic members into the sub-cultural group because of a shared history of European domination. China propagated hostile images of both the United States and the Soviet Union as imperialists bent on neo-colonialism. 'In every conceivable way', Lin Biao's 1965 article roared, 'U.S. imperialism and its lackeys are trying to extinguish the revolutionary flames of people's war. The Khrushchov [sic] revisionists, fearing people's war like the plague, are heaping abuse on it. The two are colluding to prevent and sabotage people's war.'[38]

Why did these efforts pay dividends? There seems to be normative and material reasons for this. From the normative point of view, Beijing's signals for rewarding that 'anti-imperialist' behaviour (one of the first conditions needed for forming a sub-cultural group, as discussed earlier) were taken relatively seriously in the absence of costly material signalling because of its social identity,[39] and this compensated for its inability to send out 'costly' signals to an extent. Bourdieu has noted in his study of symbolic power that the 'power to impose upon other minds a vision, old or new, of social divisions depends on the social authority acquired in previous struggles'.[40] The Chinese did command a degree of authority within the third world because it was neither seen as white nor associated with imperialism[41] and had successfully thrown off the European and Japanese imperialist yoke. Moreover, China's militant anti-colonialism 'won [the Chinese] much respect, as her views reflected those of militantly nationalist African states and movements'.[42] This meant that the African states were more likely to be 'persuaded' or give a sympathetic hearing to Beijing's invitations to join the sub-cultural group. Second,

---

[37] *Ibid.*, 5 (emphasis added).   [38] Lin 1965, 10.

[39] As Johnston points out, an actor's 'credibility' depends on sending out 'costly' material signals to its peers. It also depends on its social identity, such as 'altruistic', 'reliable', 'selfish', 'opportunistic' and so on. Johnston 2001, 491.

[40] Bourdieu 1989, 23.   [41] Crabb 1968, 443; Ogunsanwo 1974, 166.

[42] Ogunsanwo 1974, 263.

many third world states were fearful of aligning themselves to both the Western and Eastern camps, fearing that such actions would be 'substituting one form or subordination for another'.[43] They saw the 'West . . . not simply as resisting progress in the shape of the drive against colonialism and racism, but as the dominant element in a political, social, and economic order that systematically exploited the Third World'.[44] This is consistent with Johnston's argument that actors are more open to persuasion when they have 'few prior, ingrained attitudes that are inconsistent with the counterattitudinal message'.[45]

The Soviet Union was similarly viewed with suspicion for several reasons, despite its professed opposition to colonialism. First, while many developing states were part of Soviet-led organisations by sheer dint of their anti-Western/anti-imperialist beliefs,[46] many Asian-African state leaders disliked Communist ideology. Second, the Soviet Union's sheer influence and size as one of the two superpowers made it susceptible to Asian-African suspicions.[47] Racial difference also played a part in hindering the Asian and African states' entry into the Eastern camp, as mentioned earlier. Finally, there was discomfort with the Soviet line of peaceful coexistence with the US-led Western bloc, which was seen as the leading force of colonialism.

The sub-cultural group was subsequently characterised by a number of alternative membership criteria. First, membership was limited to non-white states. This was signalled through a series of Chinese-organised international conferences such as the Afro-Asian Journalists Association (AAJA) or the Afro-Asian Writers' Association. The aim was 'to build international organizations that were both anti-US and anti-Soviet, and which would . . . help buttress China's own anti-imperialist and antirevisionist foreign policies'.[48] All organisations specifically excluded the Soviet Union, and in the 1963 AAJA conference in Jakarta, the USSR was reduced to observer status. It was, as Griffith noted,

the first time Moscow's representatives were specifically treated as 'second-class members' of Afro-Asian front organisations – a major tactical victory in China's drive towards the assumption of the leadership of communism and the national liberation movement in Asia, Africa and Latin America.[49]

---

[43] Mayall 1990, 127.   [44] Armstrong 1993, 166.   [45] Johnston 2001, 499.
[46] Crabb 1968, 434.
[47] In his speech at the 1963 AASC, Tanzanian President Julius Nyerere implicitly noted that the USSR was 'now beginning to use wealth for capitalist purposes, that is, for the acquisition of power and prestige'. Although his speech was made in the context of warning *both* Beijing and Moscow to refrain from polemics at the conference, it does indicate some discomfort with Soviet chauvinism and the inherent hierarchy behind it. See Hutchison 1975, 43. Also see Crabb 1968, 435.
[48] Van Ness 1970, 131.   [49] Griffith 1964, 126. Also see Hutchison 1975, 42.

The Chinese thus posited an aggressive, colonising Western world, thereby privileging the Asian and African states. By doing so, they attempted 'to set up a new and implicitly racist Communist international'.[50] In spite of Mao's call for 'all colours of the world, white, black, yellow, brown, etc., to unite to oppose the racial discrimination practised by U.S. imperialism', Beijing's 'othering' of white states pitted 'colonials against colonialists, "have nots" against "haves", colored against white, and East against West', and exploited the underlying sense of alienation felt by the Asian and African states. The racial card also served to marginalise the Soviet Union, which was seen by some Asian-African states as white, European and therefore fundamentally foreign.[51]

Second, the sub-cultural group was characterised by its commitment to continuous struggle towards imperialism, and this stood in direct opposition to US and Soviet camps' efforts towards détente.[52] The Chinese-led sub-cultural group's norms were characterised by an opposition to the 'revisionist' USSR line that socialist transformation was possible through democratic/political means and that peaceful coexistence with the capitalist camp was preferable to violent confrontation in a thermonuclear age.[53] This was seen as an abandonment of the revolutionary duty that socialist states owed to the peoples of the world, as it would mean abandoning the states and peoples under the yoke of imperialism for the sake of 'peace'. Thus, only states and their peoples who 'shared a common sense of deprivation and exploitation at the hands of the rich and powerful' and displayed true commitment to overthrowing imperialist oppression were qualified for membership,[54] and the Chinese leaders frequently noted the common identity that China and Africa shared in terms of their suffering under imperialism,[55] implicitly signalling that the Asian and African post-colonial states qualified for membership in the Chinese led sub-cultural group.

Empowering the Group and Its Members: Social Recognition of the Anti-mainstream

The sociological insights of sub-cultural groups suggest that strong signals of support and recognition/rewards need to be sent out for the group

---

[50] Griffith 1964, 22.   [51] Ibid., 191.

[52] It should also be noted that this was a reflection of Mao Zedong's own belief that military power was indispensable for revolutionary transformation. For a brief discussion on military power and its relations in Mao's thought, see Tsou and Halperin 1965, 84–5. Also see Halpern 1961.

[53] See 'The CCP's Proposal Concerning the General Line of the International Communist Movement, June 14, 1963', reproduced in Griffith 1964 and Piao 1965, 27.

[54] Van Ness 1993, 197.

[55] See e.g. Zhou Enlai's speeches given at Ghana, Mali, Guinea and Sudan, January 1964 in Foreign Languages Press 1964.

to maintain some form of cohesion and successfully empower itself in the face of social alienation. How, then, did the Chinese attempt to do this and consolidate its sub-cultural group? Signals for support and rewards primarily took the form of verbal and material support for the state's revolutionary/anti-colonial causes and economic aid. Material support from the PRC took the form of military and technical aid. The Chinese tended to promote labour-intensive projects that required a relatively low level of technical expertise. This meant that the receiving states were not left with a high level of dependence on the donor and reflected the 'self-reliance' development strategy. It also served to 'demonstrate the excellence of China's developmental model, as well as its relevance for African countries'.[56] Furthermore, the Chinese made a point of taking on projects neither the Soviet Union nor the West were prepared to support. The conditions attached to its aid were relatively generous compared to those of the Western states and the USSR. All of this no doubt served as a useful material reward for states adhering to Beijing's militant anti-imperialist line and joining the sub-cultural group.

Normative rewards – or 'back-patting' – for these states' revolutionary stance were given in the form of mutual praise of the each other's anti-colonial stance towards the US and Soviet camps. The Chinese-led sub-cultural group engaged in this by praising and bestowing international recognition on states that challenged the US and Soviet camps. This contested the superpowers' attempts to classify their opponents as pariahs. For instance, Chinese President Liu Shaoqi said to Guinean President Ahmed Sékou Touré in 1960 that the 'Chinese people have always regarded the victory of the Guinean people as their own victory, and the achievements of the Guinean people as their own achievements. We express profound admiration for the heroic Guinean people.'[57] Revolutionary movements that maintained frosty relations with the United States or opposed Soviet 'revisionism' were given positive endorsement, and some revolutionary movements were even invited to enter into 'diplomatic relations' with the PRC.[58] African leaders returned the gesture. President Sékou Touré of Guinea announced that the post-colonial world regarded the PRC as a model. China was 'a source of inspiration and an example of courage to all peoples subjected to the forces of oppression and exploitation in the world',[59] and its economic

[56] Hutchison 1975, 212.   [57] 'Chairman' 1960, 13.
[58] Such organisations included the Palestine Liberation Organisation, the South Vietnamese NFL, The Malayan National Liberation League, the Thailand Independence Movement and the Thailand Patriotic Front. See Van Ness 1970, 130.
[59] Foreign Languages Press 1964, 210; also see 'President' 1960, 19.

model of development was similarly of great applicability to developing countries.[60] As one Tanzanian diplomat put it:

I have had the opportunity to learn firsthand of the great commitment of the Chinese people not only for the development of their own country but also and above all to support all just causes ... I was most impressed by the modesty and humility demonstrated by such a powerful nation. The respect accorded to us, as to many other African colleagues with missions in Peking, was indeed overwhelming.[61]

Assessing Beijing's Success

The PRC's attempts to form a sub-cultural group were surprisingly successful in fulfilling its goals to overcome its lack of 'international legitimacy'. Beijing's activities were enough to worry Moscow and make the USSR attempt to remove China from the Communist International movement. China's anti-colonialist stand also helped it escape third world condemnation during the Sino-Indian dispute, when many African states refused to condemn Beijing, as they disagreed with Nehru's views on peaceful coexistence and his claim that colonialism had passed.[62]

Furthermore, an increasing number of African states began voting for the PRC's admission into the United Nations, which was a direct challenge to American-led attempts to deny China legitimate membership in the 'mainstream' international community – and ultimately, this was successful. Of course, not all UN members who voted for China did so because they were 'members' of the sub-cultural group. Rather, they simply recognised that the exclusion of the world's most populous and highly influential state was an anomaly that needed to be corrected. Beijing, however, needed every vote it could get to maximise its chances of beating its imposed alienation, and to this extent it would be somewhat foolish to claim that the formation of the sub-cultural group had little or no effect.

Membership in the Chinese sub-cultural group offered many African states (as well as China) a chance to demonstrate their own uncompromising stance towards imperialism. Crucially, a provocative stance towards mainstream group members was held in high esteem, and this again underscores the function of the sub-cultural group serving as

[60] See Kwame Nkrumah's speech on January 15, 1964 in Foreign Languages Press 1964, 156.
[61] Cited in Yu 1974, 95.
[62] Ogunsanwo 1974, 107–11. See Adie (1964) for a more sceptical view.

236   *Shogo Suzuki*

a means to enhance an actor's social standing. The PRC's alienated status meant that states with close relations would risk irritating both Washington and Moscow, and some African states found that this could also help them demonstrate that they were truly 'independent' of the superpowers and colonial powers, thus fulfilling their aspirations to change 'the status of their countries from that of mere "objects" of international relations to one in which they can be recognized as "subjects"'.[63] It was for this reason, Alaba Ogunsanwo argues, that 'Mauritania recognised Peking in 1965 ... mainly to prove that the President was not an imperialist stooge set up by the French to frustrate Morocco's "just" demands on Mauritania', to the point of even holding a written work of Mao Zedong when he visited Beijing.[64] Beijing's ardent anti-US (and, by extension, anti-imperialist) rhetoric 'unquestionably found a sympathetic response in certain neutralist nations'.[65]

Such normative attractions were buttressed by China's aid programmes, which effectively helped to 'reward' the sub-cultural group's 'members'. As noted earlier, Beijing's 'principled' aid programme was designed to show up both the USSR and the United States. The Chinese were prepared to undertake projects that both superpowers were unwilling to, and the conditions attached were comparatively generous. This was certainly appreciated by the African nations.[66] For China, however, aid provided a valuable means to attain international recognition. Assisting the developing countries in Africa could serve to 'demonstrate the excellence of her developmental model, thus strengthening her position as a champion of the Third World', while African praise (some of which was no doubt genuine) would 'demonstrate to her own population the esteem in which China is held',[67] as well as the rest of the world.

Limitations

These successes, however, must be put in context alongside the many limitations the Chinese faced. Most African states were half-hearted members of the Chinese sub-cultural group at the very best. Many African states were not alienated from the international community to the degree China was and maintained good relations with the United States or the Soviet Union. While they were dissatisfied with the continuing Western (and to some extent Soviet) domination of the international community and were sympathetic to Beijing's anti-imperialist stance, the Africans simultaneously relied on the superpowers to provide them with

---

[63] Ayoob 1989, 72. See also Snow 1994, 308.   [64] Ogunsanwo 1974, 266.
[65] Crabb 1968, 443.   [66] Prybyla 1964, 1136.   [67] Hutchison 1975, 206.

security and economic aid. In this sense, they displayed classic symptoms of what Mohammed Ayoob has called 'Third World schizophrenia'[68] and could never be full members of the PRC's sub-cultural group. Some were even more cynical and sought closer relations with Beijing simply to play the superpowers off one another and obtain more aid.

Furthermore, it could also be argued that even China was not fully committed to the membership rules of the sub-cultural group. Beijing simply did not have the resources to compete with Washington or Moscow,[69] and its ability to influence the African states to join the sub-cultural group was limited to only a handful of pro-China African nationalist leaders such as Nkrumah, the president of Ghana (who was deposed in 1966) and Mobido Keita of Mali (who was also deposed in 1968).[70] These facts notwithstanding, Beijing's half-hearted commitment to the sub-cultural group can be seen from the fact that Beijing conspicuously failed to support a number of communist-led anti-colonial movements because the governments in power maintained official relations with the PRC.[71] The Chinese also entered into diplomatic relations with capitalist states of the West around this time.

In this sense, then, Chinese attempts at forming a sub-cultural group are better thought of as a broader strategy to break its international alienation and regain what it considered its rightful position in the mainstream international community. Two factors contributed to this behaviour. First, it is important to keep in mind that the PRC was isolated against its will. Although its socialist system did mean that it adopted some foreign policies that were directly at odds with the West, its ultimate goal was a nationalist one, in that it sought to attain as much recognition from other states as possible. Second, China's socialisation into the Western-dominated international order in the late nineteenth century had arguably left a long-lasting legacy. Like Turkey and Japan, China had also 'joined European international society ... as stigmatized outsiders', and these 'insecurities created by that international environment have been built into the national [identity]' of the state.[72] This resulted in the emergence of 'occidentalism', which is a belief 'that a state's identity ... is deeply connected to Western recognition'.[73] This meant that the West constituted the most desirable social grouping to which the Chinese wished to belong and receive recognition from.[74] The 'third world' ultimately did not constitute the social group in which China

---

[68] Ayoob 1989.   [69] Adie 1964, 179; Taylor 2000, 96.   [70] Snow 1994, 297.
[71] Van Ness 1970, 94–101; Hutchison 1975, 160; Snow 1994, 296.
[72] Zarakol 2010, 4.   [73] Suzuki 2014, 634.
[74] This legacy arguably remains today despite the fact that China has become a much more powerful player in the international community.

wanted to belong, and its social recognition was inadequate for China's ontological security despite rhetorical statements that the PRC stood in solidarity with the post-colonial world. As Johnston has argued, an actor can maximise its 'social well-being' when there are more members in its social group.[75] The sub-cultural group was ultimately too small and did not provide Beijing with enough social recognition.

Such behaviour from Beijing ultimately only contributed to reinforcing the existing social hierarchy of the contemporary international order, in which the West continues to occupy the highest stratum. Drawing on Hegel's discussion of the master–slave relationship, Zarakol notes that social recognition from actors who are 'inferior' can be inherently dissatisfying.[76] Zarakol nevertheless points out that provided that such relations can be a 'very viable approximation' for the actor's ontological security needs, such relations of recognition can be highly sustainable.[77] Nevertheless, this scenario is in a relatively straightforward, two-way relationship between a social 'superior' and 'inferior'. When it becomes a three-way relationship between a 'superior', 'in between' and 'inferior', recognition from the 'inferior' becomes much more unstable for the actor who is placed 'in between'. The absence of social recognition from the 'top' and the fact that one is only accorded status by absolute 'inferiors' only serve to recreate the sense of inferiority for those in a limbo between the 'superior' and 'inferior'. Just as the 'slave becomes the natural slave', the 'in between' starts to reproduce its 'inferior' identity, thus contributing to the existing social pecking order.

Conclusion

In this chapter I have highlighted the social phenomenon of subculture formation in the international community that has been neglected by IR scholarship as an alternative source of international legitimacy. It now remains to discuss a number of implications.

From the point of IR theory, three points are worth noting. First, since the end of the cold war, there seems to be an increasing tendency to assume the existence of a single 'international community', albeit one that is placing increasing demands on legitimate membership.[78] Yet, the Chinese case here suggests that the international community should not be assumed to be 'homogeneous' as it is and that there could be multiple social groupings that are sources of different degrees of international recognition. Studies have shed much light on how the desire for social recognition can play a role in the global diffusion of norms, but we need

[75] Johnston 2001, 510.   [76] Zarakol 2011, 68.   [77] *Ibid.*, 69.   [78] Clark 2005.

a better conceptualisation of how the *social hierarchical structures* of the international community (rather than domestic societies) operate to better understand the dynamics by which norms spread (or may not spread) on an international scale.

Second, from the point of studying hierarchies in international politics, the Chinese case suggests the existence of a hierarchy of social groups that actors can look to in seeking social recognition. The case study here highlights that some actors/groups 'matter' more socially than others and that the most important social grouping is – at least for the PRC – the West. As noted earlier, the legacy of the West's expansion in the nineteenth century can still be felt in the form of what Barnett and Duvall have called 'productive power',[79] which has made it (perhaps almost) 'unthinkable' that a state can be regarded as a fully legitimate member of the international community without some form of social recognition from the West. It has produced a powerful social dynamic within the non-Western world that triggers ontological insecurities whenever alienation and stigmatisation from the West occur. It is perhaps not surprising that attempts to gain recognition on the back of sub-cultural groups – another example could include Japan's attempts to insert itself into a leading position in the Great East Asian Co-Prosperity Sphere – have not been successful since the nineteenth century. However, in the case of India, we see that its claim to legitimate great power status is partially based on its 'credibility' as a champion of the third world. It may be worth further examination to see how states can build up successful subcultures and whether these groupings are more successful in elevating the social status of the 'frustrated great powers'.

It is worth emphasising, however, that this should not mean that we can simply fall back on our Eurocentric 'default position' and not study alternative social groups in the international community. My third point relates to our study of 'revolutionary powers' in the international community and the threat they pose. Existing studies all agree that the emergence of revolutionary states is an inherent threat to the international order both because of their universalistic revolutionary ideology and because of misperceptions caused by their fundamentally different state goals, which tend to exacerbate fear among their neighbours.[80] These arguments are not wrong, but perhaps they are incomplete. Our discussions here show that the Chinese were surprisingly 'moderate' international revolutionaries. Beijing was not a particularly keen exporter of revolution, and neither did it seek outright confrontation with the Western camp, its ideological adversaries, shortly after the PRC was

---

[79] Barnett and Duvall 2005.   [80] Walt 1996, Chapter 2.

established. In fact, the Chinese leadership was willing to enter into diplomatic relations with capitalist and socialist states.[81] It was only after China had been deprived of international legitimacy that it adopted a 'revolutionary' stance, in the sense that it 'stands ... for fundamental change in the principles on the basis of which states conduct their relations with each other' and 'deliberately adopts a posture of confrontation with the society of states'.[82] It seems to me that one key causal factor for this policy is the 'revolutionary' state's (domestic) ideology. But the Chinese case seems to demonstrate that the PRC's 'revolutionary' stance was more a product of its acute status anxiety and its attempts to escape it rather than communist ideology. These findings may also have some implications for our thinking of how we deal with belligerent members of the international community.

[81] Zhang 1998, 32–6; Walt 1996, 318.   [82] Armstrong 1993, 3.

Part III

Conclusion

11   Beyond Hierarchy

Jack Donnelly

The preceding chapters have demonstrated, in a great variety of ways, the substantive importance and analytical value of focusing on hierarchy in International Relations (IR). This chapter steps back, situates IR's emerging "turn to hierarchy" within the historical evolution of the discipline, and takes a mildly critical approach to that turn. I fully endorse studying inequality, authority, and rule, which have been perversely marginalized in mainstream anarchy-centric IR. I question "hierarchy," though, as a frame for such work.

This chapter is divided into two parts. The first three sections critically examine the Waltzian anarchy-hierarchy binary and the associated idea of structural ordering principles, explicate the idea of hierarchy as a structure of stratification and differentiation, and argue against extending the concept to a broader range of authorities and inequalities. I conclude that the most promising path forward is to focus on the variety of forms of hierarchies (and other inequalities). The last three sections then offer brief excursions into that variety.

Beyond Anarchy and Ordering Principles

Hierarchy is usually understood in contemporary IR as opposed to anarchy, which itself is understood as the "fundamental"[1] feature of international relations. As Zarakol puts it, "even as IR's anarchy-centred view of world politics [has] receded from view, it nonetheless remain[s] largely undisturbed as a starting assumption."[2] I argue for not merely disturbing but displacing anarchy-centrism – but not with hierarchy-centrism.

Waltz's Anarchy-Hierarchy Binary

It is commonly held that IR has "from its earliest years, been structured by a discourse about anarchy."[3] I have shown elsewhere,[4] however, that

[1] Milner 1991, 67; Schmidt 1997, 1; Miller 2002, 10; Holmes 2011, 291. Cf. Lake 2009a, 2: "Virtually all scholars agree that relations between states are anarchic and that this is one of the most unique, important, and enduring features of world politics."
[2] See the Introduction.   [3] Schmidt 1997, 41.   [4] Donnelly 2015a.

prior to the publication of Waltz's *Theory of International Politics* (in 1979), anarchy was rarely employed as a central analytical concept or understood as the defining feature of international relations. For example, in a selection of 145 books published between 1895 and 1978, the median use of the terms "anarchy" and "anarchic" is two (and the mean is 6.9). In a similar set of sixty-two books published between 1979 and 2013, the median is twenty-four (and the mean is 35.5).[5] Before Waltz, even realists did not conceptualize the absence of an international government as "anarchy."[6] The absence of an international government was seen as a background condition rather than an ordering principle or a master explanatory variable.[7] The idea of substantive "effects of anarchy" was unknown.[8]

Even if we agree that absence of an international government is a "fact" that IR *must* comprehend, "anarchy" is only one of many ways to do that. And (Waltzian) "anarchy" is not only a recent discursive construction, but it also entered contemporary IR, especially in the United States, in a particular way: as the unique ordering principle of international systems opposed to hierarchy. If anarchy and hierarchy are mutually exclusive and inclusive ordering principles, and if all international systems are anarchic, then international systems cannot be structurally hierarchic – as Waltz argues at some length.[9]

The preceding chapters, building on two decades of growing discomfort with this conclusion,[10] have shown, in many ways and contexts, that hierarchy is a regular feature of international relations. As even Waltz acknowledges, "inequality is what much of politics is about," and "internationally, inequality is more nearly the whole of the political story."[11]

---

[5] Donnelly 2015a, 395, table 1.

[6] For example, the term is used only twice, in passing, in E. H. Carr's *The Twenty Years, Crisis* (1939 [2001], 28, 162), in George Kennan's *American Diplomacy* (1951, 33, 149), and in Henry Kissinger's *A World Restored* (1957, 17, 25). None of the seven editions of Morgenthau's *Politics among Nations* contains an index entry for anarchy. *Scientific Man versus Power Politics* (Morgenthau 1946, 117) uses "anarchy" only once – referring to "the international anarchy of our age" (not of international relations in general).

[7] As Waltz (1990, 36) puts it, for classical realists "anarchy is a general condition rather than a distinct structure. Anarchy sets the problem that states have to cope with."

[8] A Google Scholar search for "effects of anarchy" or "effects of international anarchy" and "international relations" yields only three insignificant results from 1900 to 1974. There is one result for 1975–9: Jervis' influential 1978 article "Cooperation Under the Security Dilemma" (Jervis 1978, 173). In the 1980s, "effects of (international) anarchy" appears in seven works, including major articles by John Ruggie (1983, 284), Harrison Wagner (1983, 385), Michael Doyle (1983, 232), and Joseph Grieco (1988, 502). In the 1990s, however, there are almost 100 results, almost 250 in the 2000s, and nearly 300 for 2010–16.

[9] Waltz 1975, 114–16.   [10] See Introduction, n. 3, for illustrative works.

[11] Waltz 1979, 142, 143.

"The inequality of nations is ... the dominant political fact of international life."[12]

David Lake in effect attempts to rescue the Waltzian account by arguing that *relational hierarchy* regularly coexists with *structural anarchy*.[13] Lake, however, continues to define hierarchy "as the antonym of anarchy,"[14] accepts Waltz's notion of ordering principles, and thus denies structural hierarchy.[15] In fact, however, nearly all international systems are *structurally* hierarchic; that is, ordered around systematic relations of super- and subordination and differentiation. Later I show this for the hard case of state systems.[16]

The pervasive presence of international hierarchy, however, does not mean that hierarchy is, as Hobson claims, "the core concept of IR."[17] "Hierarchy" is no less "the ordering principle" of national political systems and "the core concept" of comparative politics. It thus tells us nothing distinctive about international relations. Furthermore, much international authority and inequality, as I argue below, is not hierarchical. To understand the place of hierarchy – and of inequality and rule more broadly – we need to escape the Waltzian anarchy-hierarchy binary.

Abandoning Ordering Principles

Part of the problem is that neither anarchy nor hierarchy is a structural ordering principle. Absence of a government simply indicates one way in which a system is *not* ordered. It may demarcate international from domestic politics. It does not, however, even begin to tell us how an international system is structured/ordered. Similarly, hierarchy simply tells us *that* a system is stratified, not *how* (let alone how it is structured).

The fundamental problem, though, is not that international and national systems have some other ordering principles. Rather, it is Waltz's conception of structural ordering principles. In other fields, structure is not seen to involve "ordering principles."[18] Examining the works that Waltz identifies as having been especially useful in his

---

[12] Waltz 1979, 144. Distinguishing hierarchy and inequality (see the section "Centralization (Center-Periphery Differentiation)" below) makes these quotes somewhat less apposite than they first seem but does not undermine my basic point.

[13] Lake 2009a, 17; cf. x, 62, 133, 136, 174, 177, 179.   [14] *Ibid.*, 62.

[15] *Ibid.*, 61, 62. See also the section "Hierarchy" below.

[16] See the section "Stratification and Functional Differentiation in States Systems."

[17] Hobson 2014.

[18] In the first 300 results of a Google Scholar search in September 2013 for "ordering principle" and "structure," "ordering principle" is presented as a defining component of structure only in works by or citing Waltz. The same is true of the first 100 results of a search for "ordering principle" and "social structure."

thinking about systems theory and cybernetics,[19] from which he developed his conceptions of system and structure, I was unable to find the term "ordering principle" or anything close to the Waltzian concept. Structural ordering principles really do seem to be Waltz's original contribution.

That social and political systems have a singular ordering principle, however, is an aesthetic prejudice that flies in the face of the historical record. (For example, there was no ordering principle in early modern Europe, in the Mediterranean world of the third and second centuries BCE, or in China during the Spring and Autumn period [770–476 BCE].) Many international systems can be fruitfully understood in terms of multiple "ordering principles." (For example, the post-Napoleonic system was a system of sovereign states, a great power system, a concert system, and an antirevolutionary [pro-monarchical] system.) And claims that all international systems have the same basic structure (ordering principle) – "two, and only two, types of structures are needed to cover societies of all sorts"[20] – become obviously ludicrous once we stop pretending that anarchy orders (rather than demarcates[21]) international systems. International systems share little, if anything, else – let alone one thing that defines or determines the arrangement of their parts.

Hierarchy and IR

The fact of hierarchy, like the fact of the absence of a government, is of little positive analytical interest. The structures of most, if not all, international systems are both anarchic (lacking a government) and hierarchic (systematically stratified and differentiated). And which (if either) is more important in any particular system is an empirical, not a theoretical or conceptual, question. IR's Waltzian legacy may have given momentary remedial importance to insisting on the pervasive reality of hierarchies in international relations. Real analytical progress, however, requires getting past that moment as quickly as possible. Our attention should be focused

---

[19] Angyal 1939; Ashby 1964 [1956]; Bertalanffy 1968; Buckley 1968; Nadel 1957; Smith 1956, 1966; Watzlawick, Beavin, and Jackson 1967; Wiener 1961, cited in Waltz 1975, 78, n. 40; 1979, 40 n. *.

[20] Waltz 1979, 116.

[21] This basic analytical distinction is regularly ignored. That *A* differs structurally from *B* by *c* does not make *c* the structure of *A*. For example, mammals can be demarcated from other vertebrates as milk-producing animals with hair, three bones in their middle ear, a neocortex, and a lower jaw made of a single bone. These features, however, do not define the structure of mammals. In fact, demarcation criteria often have little analytical utility. For example, the two principal groups of dinosaurs, *Saurischia* and *Ornithischia*, are distinguished by their hipbones. This, however, provides little, if any, insight into their structure or functioning.

instead on the *multiple forms and sources* of hierarchy and on *how hierarchies matter* – on, as the title of this book puts it, *hierarchies* (not hierarchy) in world politics.

In the spirit of friendly constructive criticism, however, I want to suggest that hierarchy, although certainly deserving a place in the analytic arsenal of IR, is too narrow a frame (and thus [to change metaphors again] too blunt a tool) to comprehend adequately the phenomena addressed in this book, which I think are better described as authority, (in)equality, and rule.

The Language of Hierarchy in IR

Hierarchy, like anarchy, only became a central focus of IR after the publication of *Theory of International Politics*. Table 11.1 summarizes uses of "hierarchy" and "hierarchical" in a broadly representative selection of seventy-nine books published between 1895 and 1978 and sixty-two books published between 1980 and 2015.[22] Before 1979, the median is 1 and the mean is 3.5. After 1979, the median jumps to 13 and the mean to 18.0. Waltz's impact is underscored by the fact that post-1979 works that use "anarchy" or "anarchic" ten or more times employ "hierarchy" or "hierarchical" three times more often than those that refer to anarchy less frequently.

Substantively, the most common pre-1979 uses, in addition to "social hierarchy," refer to medieval, feudal, or ecclesiastical hierarchies,[23] a hierarchy of values or national interests,[24] hierarchies in bureaucracies or of offices or officeholders,[25] and the diplomatic hierarchy.[26] I could not find a single passage that contrasts hierarchy with anarchy, uses hierarchy to define domestic politics,[27] or treats hierarchy as a structural ordering principle. Even Waltz in *Man, the State and War* (1959) uses "hierarchy"

---

[22] The 1895–1978 sample includes a bit more than half the set used in Donnelly (2015a, appendices 1 and 2), which list all the books. The 1980–2015 selection includes the books listed in Donnelly (2015a, appendix 3) plus one more recent addition, Buzan and Lawson 2015.

[23] Hill 1911, 16; Potter 1922, 38, 47; Walsh 1922, 64; Barnes 1930, 15, 16; Mitrany 1933, 22; Sharp and Kirk 1940, 17, 100; Spykman 1942, 240; Wright 1964 [1942], 26; Herz 1959, 43; Wallerstein 2011 [1976], 58, 90, 156, 161, 214.

[24] Woolf 1916, 305; Hobson 1922, 54; Niebuhr 1932, 265; Lasswell 1935, 36; Sharp and Kirk 1940, 105; Wright 1964 [1942], 214, 245; Morgenthau 1951, 118; Aron 2003 [1966], 104, 236, 288, 323; Brodie 1973, 481; Gilpin 1975, 224; Bull 1977, 21, 74; Krasner 1978, 286, 341.

[25] Reinsch 1900, 53; Leacock 1906, 196, 197, 378; Wright 1964 [1942], 357; Organski 1958, 167; Haas 1964, 88, 105, 109, 110, 112, 534.

[26] Lawrence 1898 [1895], 263; Potter 1922, 73; Hodges 1931, 256, 533; Schuman 1933, 181, 182; Zimmern 1936, 481.

[27] Although Harold Laski does observe (1921, 80, 217, 240, 241) that contemporary governments are hierarchical, he does not see this as a defining feature of domestic

Table 11.1 *Uses of "Hierarchy" or "Hierarchical" in Selected Books*

	1895–1978 (n = 79)	1980–2015 (n = 62)	1895–1945 (n = 51)	1946–78 (n = 28)	Use of "anarchy" ≥ ten times (n = 48)	Use of "anarchy" < ten times (n = 14)
Median	1.0	13.0	1.0	2.0	16.0	5.0
Mean	3.5	18.0	1.5	7.2/3.7[a]	21.3	6.9

[a] The second figure (3.7) excludes one book (Kaplan 1957) that uses the terms more than 100 times (which amounts to almost half the total uses in the twenty-eight books).

only twice, in reference to the "hierarchy of human motivations" and the "hierarchy of the Chinese Communist Party."[28]

Furthermore, far from denying that hierarchy is characteristic of international relations, many prominent scholars note that international relations often is hierarchically stratified.[29] And they understand hierarchy as structural but not an ordering principle – an understanding to which, I suggest, IR ought to return.

Hierarchy: Structures of Stratification and Differentiation

The most relevant definition of "hierarchy" in the *Oxford English Dictionary* is "a body of persons or things ranked in grades, orders, or classes, one above another." Similarly, the *Merriam-Webster Dictionary* defines "hierarchy" as "a system in which people or things are placed in a series of levels with different importance or status." Zarakol, following this ordinary language sense, defines "hierarchies" as "structures of stratification and the differentiation of units."[30] Similarly, Waltz argues that in hierarchies "actors are formally differentiated according to the degrees of their authority, and their distinct functions are specified."[31]

politics in general. Quite the contrary, he argues (1921, 241) for the possibility and desirability of "coordinate" national politics.
[28] Waltz 1959, 22, 112.
[29] Organski 1958, 90, 213, 349; Aron 2003 [1966], 69, 441, 652; Osgood and Tucker 1967, 48; Gilpin 1975, 24; Bull 1977, 31, 36. In addition, Kaplan 1957, 55–7, develops an ideal-type model of "the hierarchical international system."
[30] See Introduction. This formulation, in addition to being precise and firmly rooted in ordinary language, requires only a modest modification of the familiar Waltzian framework. "Ordering principle" effectively means stratification; the presence or absence of relations of super- and subordination. We simply call stratification "stratification" (rather than "hierarchy") – and then address not its presence or absence but the forms it takes; hierarchies (not hierarchy).
[31] Waltz 1979, 81, cf. 97, 114.

Hierarchy thus understood includes an important but limited range of authorities, (in)equalities, and forms of rule. Hierarchies are *systems* of stratification and differentiation (not ad hoc, isolated, or purely interactional relations). They involve a rank or level *structure* that creates a *body* of ranked persons or things. Hierarchies involve differentiated social positions; difference in *roles and practices* (not just capabilities, control, or outcomes). Ranking people or groups in grades one above another is closely associated with the differential allocation of functions, benefits, burdens, and behaviors among those so ranked. Only when we have a structured system of ranks, levels, or grades that differentiate actors as parts of a complex whole – rather than simply array them along a scale of comparison – do we have a hierarchy.

Stratification and Functional Differentiation in States Systems

All international systems are structurally hierarchical. This is obvious – although in contemporary IR typically elided – in imperial and hegemonic international systems. And it is equally true of states systems.

Contemporary IR typically takes systems of separate autonomous polities ("sovereign states") as its working model of anarchic (and not hierarchic) international orders. States systems, however, are *defined* largely by the formal hierarchical superiority of states over nonstate actors. Great power states systems have a third level of stratification, with great powers placed above lesser states. In Georg Schwarzenberger's memorable formulation, states are the aristocrats of states systems and great powers the oligarchs among those aristocrats.[32]

This pattern of stratification is associated with a particular differentiation of functions. It simply is not true that "the states that are the units of international-political systems are not formally differentiated by the functions they perform."[33] States are formally differentiated from nonstate actors, with particular (contingent) legal rights and responsibilities. Great powers, as Waltz puts it, "take on special responsibilities," exercise "managerial functions," and perform "managerial tasks."[34] And the international political system, which Waltz explicitly addresses, is a functional subsystem of a broader international system.

There may be good reasons, for particular analytical purposes, to bracket or ignore these elements of hierarchy. But IR's dominant account of structure – and for all the criticism of structural realism, it must be stressed that Waltz's account of structure remains widely adopted across

[32] Schwarzenberger 1951, Chapters 6 and 7.   [33] Waltz 1979, 93.
[34] Waltz 1979, 198, 196; Chapter 9 is titled "The Management of International Affairs."

much of the discipline – instead denies the reality of hierarchy. It is therefore essential, for both analytic and normative reasons, that we emphasize that virtually all international systems, including systems of sovereign territorial states, are structurally hierarchical.

Extended Conceptions of Hierarchy

Despite the agreement of ordinary language, Waltz, and the explicit definition of this book, more expansive conceptions of hierarchy are regularly encountered both in the preceding chapters and in the broader IR literature on hierarchy.

Bilateral "Hierarchy"   For example, Alexander Cooley presents bilateral basing agreements as hierarchies (Chapter 7). Cooley does not, however, argue that these agreements either arise from or give rise to structures of stratification and differentiation – which are largely absent from his discussion. This understanding of hierarchy as a matter of asymmetric quasi-contractual bilateral relations draws on Lake's path-breaking and influential work over more than a decade that culminated in *Hierarchy in International Relations*.[35] Lake argues that "hierarchy is a dyadic relationship"[36] that is fruitfully conceptualized as a matter of quasi-voluntary (although rarely, if ever, entirely "free") choice and consent.

Vincent Pouliot's chapter (Chapter 5) effectively challenges the idea that hierarchies are intentional contractual constructs. Here I simply note that bilateral relations of super- and subordination are not, in themselves, necessarily hierarchical (except in Lake's stipulative sense of the term). (Hierarchies, as we have seen, are ranked *structures* that operate within a *body* of actors.) Furthermore, most structures of stratification and differentiation are not bilateral (and thus are perversely redefined by Lake's definition as *not* hierarchies). Given that Lake's stated aim is to "explicate"[37] hierarchy (not stipulate a new sense) and to provide a "general statement about the nature and implications of international hierarchy for international relations,"[38] this account is simply erroneous.

Lake's work also nicely illustrates the unfortunate tyranny of the Waltzian anarchy-hierarchy frame. The empirical chapters of *Hierarchy in International Relations* offer a rich account of practices of bilaterally divided sovereignty. But international hierarchy is not, as Lake would

---

[35] The bookends of this body of work are Lake (1996) and Lake (2009), which collectively have about a thousand Google Scholar citations.
[36] Lake 2009, 45, 61, cf. xi, xii, 96, 179.   [37] Lake 2009, x, 16.   [38] *Ibid.*, x, cf. xi, 67.

have it, "simply the counterpart to variable sovereignty."[39] Both international hierarchy and practices of divided sovereignty are obscured rather than clarified when they are equated.

What, though, about *extending* the notion of hierarchy to include bilateral relations of super- and subordination? I can see no analytical benefit to such an extension.

For example, the story that Rebecca Adler-Nissen (Chapter 9) tells of Greco-German relations over Greek debt is much more one of competing equalities and inequalities and conflicting authorities than of a ranked structure of status or power. The frame of hierarchy seems to me not only forced and uninformative but misleading. Greek claims to equality, sovereign authority, and self-rule are central parts of the story. They have nothing to do, though, with a Greco-German hierarchy (and would be elided from the story were the frame of hierarchy to be consistently applied).

Or consider Michael Barnett's discussion of paternalism (Chapter 3), a particular type of (often bilateral) authority relation. It seems to me forced (at best) to impose the idea of a ranked structure of social positions on the competing claims to authority and the competing equalities and inequalities involved. Paternalism involves very particular types of authority, (in)equality, and rule that, it seems to me, are obscured rather than illuminated by the frame of hierarchy. At best, "hierarchy" adds nothing to our understanding of paternalism.

Hierarchy and Inequality   Adler-Nissen's and Barnett's chapters (Chapters 3 and 9) also seem to suggest that hierarchy refers to pretty much any type of authority, inequality, or rule. Cooley's argument (Chapter 7) that "the term 'military base' has itself become associated as a marker of differential status between the host and center, even as a site of actual foreign influence and bilateral hegemony,"[40] seems to squeeze even influence into "hierarchy." Similarly, Pouliot (Chapter 5) writes, "When it comes to definition, I cannot improve on Towns ... 'Social hierarchy, which I use synonymously with social rank, concerns the ordering of actors as superior or inferior to one another in socially important respects.'"[41] Even more strikingly, Towns elsewhere notes that she uses "social hierarchy ... synonymously with social inequality, stratification, or rank."[42] As we saw earlier, though, this is inconsistent with both ordinary language and the sense adopted in this book.

---

[39] *Ibid.*, 51, cf. 7, 62.   [40] See Chapter 7.   [41] See Chapter 5, quoting Towns 2012, 188.
[42] Towns 2010, 44.

What, though, about stipulatively extending "hierarchy" to cover all inequalities? This, at best, abandons a perfectly good and useful term with a precise definition. At worst, it impedes our understanding. "Hierarchy" becomes a residual – whatever is not egalitarian – thus obscuring (and implicitly denigrating) the great variety of different types of authority, inequality, and rule in international relations (and social life more broadly).

What is analytically central is not *whether* practices or relations are egalitarian or inegalitarian, but *how* they are. Structures of stratification and differentiation are a distinctive and important type of authority that deserves to be studied separately from other types of inequality and authority – which are also obfuscated by lumping them under "hierarchy." For example, Sarah Stroup and Wendy Wong (Chapter 8) present an interesting and insightful account of the social position of "leading authority." This original formulation highlights the fact that the influence of international nongovernmental organizations (INGOs) rests heavily on moral authority, access to information, and their ability to mobilize capabilities and resources outside the control of states. But reframing "Leading Authority as Hierarchy," as the title of their chapter puts it, eliminates the precision of the notion and strips out all the interesting detail without enhancing our understanding of leading authorities.

To be fair, Adler-Nissen, Barnett, and Stroup and Wong, in order to further the collective enterprise of this book, have taken bodies of work conceived in different terms and "rethought" them in terms of hierarchy. This makes sense, though, only if we assume that all forms of authority and inequality are hierarchical – which is inconsistent with ordinary usage, the framing of this book, and analytical clarity and precision.

Types of Order

This section offers three largely separate mini-essays on hierarchy, authority, (in)equality, and rule in international relations, focusing on different ordering principles. Having established that hierarchies are pervasive in international relations, an obvious next step is to differentiate types of hierarchies. Zarakol in the Introduction focuses on the analytical distinction between agentic and structural approaches. Other typologies, though, are not only possible but necessary.

Hierarchy

In "simple" hierarchies, one axis of stratification operates over a single issue or domain. The formal hierarchy of offices in a bureaucracy is a good example.

Table 11.2 *A Typology of Hierarchical Stratification*

	Single axis	Multiple axes
Single issue	Simple	Contested
Multiple issues	Convergent	Tangled/Divergent

"Contested" hierarchies have multiple axes of stratification operating within a single issue or domain. Consider the often substantial divergence between an institution's formal hierarchy of authority and its informal hierarchy of influence.

In "convergent" hierarchies something like a single axis of stratification runs through a multifunctional group or organization. Separate hierarchies converge or coalesce to create *a* (singular) hierarchy that pervades the system. Modern states are a familiar political example.

"Tangled"[43] or "divergent" hierarchies have multiple patterns of stratification. For example, the American Congress, president, and federal courts comprise a structured body of authorities in which different branches are "on top" in different substantive domains.

Table 11.2 presents a simple typology of forms of hierarchical stratification, distinguishing first between hierarchies restricted to one issue, function, or domain and those that span multiple issues and then between hierarchies with one axis of stratification from those with multiple axes. The distinction between convergent and divergent hierarchies merits special note. There is nothing "natural" or even "normal" about multiple hierarchies converging, as in the case of nineteenth- and twentieth-century states operating in the modern states system. For example, medieval Europe was structured around crosscutting religious and secular hierarchies (as well as often tangled hierarchies within each domain). Early modern Europe moved only very slowly and irregularly toward a convergent hierarchy. And globalization is producing hierarchies that are increasingly tangled. *Divergent* hierarchy thus has been the norm in the Eurocentric world over most of the past millennium. It has, however, received almost no attention, under any name, in contemporary IR.

Centralization (Center-Periphery Differentiation)

"Hierarchy" typically draws attention to *higher* authority. Center-periphery differentiation, a fundamental structural dimension of both national and

[43] I take the term from Hofstadter 1979, Chapter 20.

international social systems, draws our attention instead to *central* authority and rule – not as an alternative but in addition to stratification, further illustrating the diversity of forms of authority, (in)equality, and rule in international relations.

Centers and Peripheries   Social systems have centers, specially valued "places" around which social life is integrated, and peripheries, which are in varying ways and degrees removed from the center. As Edward Shils put it in his seminal 1961 essay, "Centre and Periphery,"

> Society has a centre. There is a central zone in the structure of society ... Membership in the society, in more than the ecological sense of being located in a bounded territory and of adapting to an environment affected or made up by other persons located in the same territory, is constituted by relationship to this central zone.[44]

A society may have more than one center. Centrality may be rooted in normative, institutional, coercive, or productive resources.[45] Relations between centers and peripheries may take many forms, with very different balances between center and periphery. The creation of centers and peripheries, however, is a characteristic structural feature of social systems – and, I will argue, creates distinctive types of international systems.

A Typology of Center-Periphery Differentiation   A simple typology of center-periphery differentiation begins by distinguishing systems with one center from those with more than one. Single-center systems can be further divided into those that more or less uniformly integrate their peripheries and those that differentially integrate peripheries. Polycentric systems can be divided into those in which the centers are fundamentally territorial and those with fundamentally functional centers.

I call single-center polities that integrate their peripheries relatively uniformly "states." "Empires" are single centers that integrate their peripheries differentially. As Maurice Duverger puts it, empires "unite several ethnicities, several communities, several cultures, previously separate, still distinct."[46] This corresponds to the ordinary language definition of "an extensive territory under the control of a supreme

---

[44] Shils 1961, 117 = Shils 1975, 3. IR is much more familiar with the core-periphery frame of Immanuel Wallerstein (1974, 2011 [1976]), which I view as a particular perspective on center-periphery differentiation in the world economic system.

[45] Typically, though, there is a crucial normative element. Shils (1961, 117) goes so far as to argue that centrality is "a phenomenon of the realm of values and beliefs ... [that] partakes of the nature of the sacred."

[46] Duverger 1980, 10 (my translation).

ruler ... often consisting of an aggregate of many separate states or territories."[47]

"States systems" are composed of multiple multifunctional territorial centers. IR's standard depiction of states systems as anarchic takes the perspective of the unit (there is no higher authority) and defines structure negatively (absence of a government). This may not be inaccurate. It is not, however, particularly insightful. Viewed from the perspective of the system, in terms of centers and peripheries, and stated positively, a states system is structured around multiple peer polities.[48] States systems have several centers (not none). Authority *in the international system* is not absent, *pace* Waltz,[49] but disaggregated spatially and concentrated in privileged peer polities ("states"). The hierarchies in states systems converge on multiple territorial centers that provide nearly all the governance (authoritative rule) in the system, both nationally and internationally.

"Heterarchies" are composed of multiple functionally differentiated centers. "Heterarchy"[50] combines the root *arkhē* ("rule") or *arkhon* ("ruler") with the prefix "hetero-," indicating difference, variety, or the other. Heterarchy involves "differential rule" or "multiple rule" – in contrast to the "higher" rule of hierarchy and the "no rule(r)" of anarchy. Hegemony, understood as a system in which hegemons control the foreign policy of lesser powers that remain formally independent and substantially in control of their domestic policy,[51] is a relatively simple type of hybrid heterarchic states system. Medieval Europe is a classic historical example.

States, empires, and heterarchies may, in principle, be either polities in a larger "international" system or "international systems" (or regional subsystems). Because there has never been a world state, three types of international systems defined by centralization are of special interest: states systems, imperial international systems, and heterarchic international systems.

In imperial systems, authority is concentrated in a single imperial center. In states systems, authority is spatially dispersed (and concentrated) in

---

[47] *Oxford English Dictionary.*

[48] I take the notion of peer polities from Renfrew and Cherry 1986.

[49] "Nationally, relations of authority are established. Internationally, only relations of strength result." Waltz 1979, 112.

[50] The term was coined in neuroscience. See McCulloch 1945. It has been widely employed in cybernetics and computer science. "A program which has a structure in which there is no single, highest level, or monitor, is called a heterarchy." Hofstadter 1979, 134. In the social sciences, the concept has been employed fairly widely in Archaeology. Crumley (1987) and Ehrenreich, Crumley, and Levy (1995) are the seminal works – and in the study of business organization (e.g., Hedlund 1986, Stark 1999, Wall and van der Knaap 2012).

[51] E.g., Doyle 1986, 12, 40, 55–60; Watson 1992, 15–16, 27–8, 122–8.

separate centers. Authority in heterarchies – rather than being concentrated, relatively coherent, and monopolized by a single type of actor – is dispersed among functional centers that are often located in different places and operate at different scales, is often crosscutting, and usually is held by actors of different types. For example, in the early modern Holy Roman Empire, the emperor, electors, lesser princes (both secular and clerical), free cities, and imperial knights exercised different forms of authority at widely varying scales, resulting in most places being subject to multiple (often competing) authorities.[52]

Heterarchies underscore the fact that social functions and institutions are readily separable from one another and may operate at radically different scales. A multifunctional organization ruling more or less exclusively over a territory is only one possibility. Social or political units and territorial units can stand in very different kinds of relations – as globalization increasingly reminds us.

It is important to note that "centralization," as I understand it here, is *not* a matter of concentrating authority in a single place. That is indeed a standard ordinary language sense. By "centralization," however, I mean a social process that mutually co-constitutes centers and peripheries. Systems in which the center integrates peripheries uniformly are not "more centralized" than those in which the center integrates peripheries differentially. They are *differently* centralized. The same is true of systems with one center and with many. We are concerned here with the diverse ways in which centers and peripheries are constructed, defined, and related – because these differences generate different types of cooperation and conflict. Consider, for example, the differences between a rebellious province in an empire, a rival peer polity in a states system, and an encroaching or overreaching authority in a heterarchy or between self-help balancing in a states system, claims of authority in a heterarchy, and appeals to justice or privilege in an empire.

Stratification and Centralization Stratification differentiates social positions and actors as higher and lower. Centralization differentiates them as central and peripheral. Centrality and stratification do tend not only to overlap but to reinforce one another. Rarely, however, do they map perfectly onto one another. Although we can often translate center and periphery into top and bottom, something usually is lost in the translation. And the reverse translation regularly fails. (Many tops are not centers.)

---

[52] For an overview of the political structure of the early modern Empire, see Wilson 2011, Chapter 3.

Not all authority is best understood as higher authority. Not all rule is best understood as rule from above. The "central government" may be a higher authority, a central authority, or (most often) some combination of both. For example, complaints about "Washington" in the United States can be understood as expressing a belief that the federal government has become more a higher power than a central authority.

Centers center (and are central). They are cores, places, values, institutions, and practices around which societies are organized. Creating centers and peripheries in many ways constitutes a society or polity.

Centers attract (and are attractive), exerting a "gravitational" pull on their peripheries. Centers also radiate influence. This mix of attractive and radiating power exercised by central authorities differs fundamentally from the penetrating power of a higher authority reaching down into lower levels.

Networks provide a striking example. Nodes with a very high relative number of connections – centers – have special influence, sometimes even dominance. Central nodes, though, need not be, and often are not, "higher than" other nodes. They are central.

Or consider the standard representation of an empire as a rimless wheel (or a hub and spokes system).[53] The focus here is on centrality (rather than stratification).

Consider also Shmuel Eisenstadt's distinction between conquest empires (e.g., the empires of Alexander the Great, Charlemagne, and Genghis Khan) and bureaucratic empires (e.g., China, Rome, Sassanid Persia, Moghul South Asia, and the Ottoman Caliphate).[54] The peripheries of conquest empires remain more members of a collection than parts of a whole; more an aggregation of occupied territories and protectorates than parts of an integrated polity. We might thus say that in conquest empires the dominant polity or elite has not established itself as a true center. The conquerors sit, more or less heavily, on top of the conquered. The ruled remain conquered (by a higher power) rather than peripheralized (by a central power). Thus understood, the transformation of superiority to centrality marks the change from conquest to bureaucratic empire. (This framing, I think, could be usefully employed to extend Andrew Phillips's account (Chapter 2) of British and Mongol rule.)

Layering and Ranking

A similar set of distinctions arises from modeling international systems in terms of geographically more encompassing layers. In a very simple

---

[53] This representation goes back at least to Galtung 1971.   [54] Eisenstadt 1993 [1963].

representation, imagine three layers: the system, "regions," and localities. Relations among these layers may vary considerably.

States systems are focused on "regions" (in the form of states). In the modern international system, for example, states were the principal providers of both national governance (largely monopolizing jurisdiction and control over "their" localities) and international governance (through self-help and bilateral and multilateral agreements and institutions). But this pattern of strong intermediate-level "units" (states) dominating their localities and operating within a thin system is not universal or even normal.

Imperial international systems, for example, are focused on the system level. For example, "regions" in the Mediterranean world at the height of the *Pax Romana* were more subordinate provinces than autonomous polities ("states"). And most localities had little contact with the imperial center. The structure of Europe at the turn of the first millennium CE, after the collapse of the Carolingian Empire and the shocks of the Magyar and Viking invasions, was still different. Politics came to be focused on localities (small lordships or seigneuries dominated by castellans and small bands of armed men). "Regional" authorities (kings, dukes, and counts) had considerable status but little power. And there was only a thin culturally integrating religious overlay at the system level.

More complicated level structures are also possible. For example, globalization might be thought of has having created a five-level structure, with additional subnational and supranational levels, in which the levels stand in varying relations depending on place and issue area. And certain scenarios of globalization imagine a radically heterarchic system in which distinctions between levels are obscure and of little analytical interest.

The key point, again, is the variety of forms of structured (in)equality, authority, and rule in international relations. We should not assume that what is most important can always be found "on top" or can be adequately appreciated through the lens of higher authority.

Hierarchy (and Equality) as Ontology

My final excursus begins by returning to the original sense of "hierarchy." Although this will initially take us far beyond IR, it will lead us, I believe, to a deeper appreciation of the structures of status and power that order hierarchies.

Ontological Hierarchy in the West

Hierarchy was initially a religious notion, as its etymology suggests: *arkhē*, "rule or power," of a *hierarkhēs* (*hieros* ["sacred"] *arkhēs* ["ruler"]), a "hierarch"; "one who has rule or authority in holy things; an ecclesiastical ruler or potentate; a chief priest."[55] Consider the first two definitions in the *Oxford English Dictionary* (which, as the title of earlier editions put it, is organized "on historical principles"). "1. a. Each of the three divisions of angels, every one comprising three orders, in the system of Dionysius the Areopagite … Also, the collective body of angels, the angelic host. b. *transf.* of other beings … 2. a. Rule or dominion in holy things; priestly rule or government; a system of ecclesiastical rule."

The term was coined by (psuedo-)Dionysius (Denys the Areopagite),[56] a late fifth- or early sixth-century Syriac Greek neo-Platonist author who presented himself as the Athenian convert of St. Paul. For roughly a millennium, Dionysius provided the authoritative account of hierarchy in the Western Christian world.[57] Not coincidentally, two of Dionysius' major treatises, *On the Heavenly Hierarchy* and *On the Ecclesiastical Hierarchy*,[58] correspond to the two initial definitions of hierarchy.

According to Dionysius, God, "having fixed all the essences of things being, brought them into being."[59] And he arrayed them hierarchically, hierarchy being "a sacred order and science and operation, assimilated, as far as attainable, to the likeness of God."[60] "Each rank of the Hierarchical Order is led, in its own degree, to the Divine co-operation, by performing, through grace and God-given power, those things" appropriate to its nature.[61] Just as angels are above men, so on this Earth men, as rational beings, are placed at the top, closer to God than irrational sentient beings (who are in turn higher than "things which merely exist").[62]

The political implications of this ontology are clear. "The inferior Ranks cannot cross to the superior functions."[63] As St. Boniface (ca. 675–754) put it, there are "several dignities, each having its own function: there is an order of commanders and an order of subjects, an order of the wealthy and an order of the poor, an order of the old and an order of the

---

[55] *Oxford English Dictionary*.
[56] "By creating the abstract noun *hierarchy* from the cultic title *hierarch*, Dionysius invented a word for a structure or system for 'sourcing' or channeling the sacred, and linked it all inextricably to the single leader." Rorem 1993, 19, 21. The term then was directly transliterated into Latin by Johns Scotus Eriugena in his influential ninth-century translation and commentary (in contrast to Dionysius' first Latin translator, Abbot Hilduin of Saint Denis, who rendered it as *sacros principatus*, sacred rule, principle, or origin). Rorem 2005, 59.
[57] Rorem (1993) provides a commentary on Dionysius' texts and their influence – which was immense. For example, Giovanni Pico della Mirandola (1463–1494), one of the leading humanist philosophers of the Italian Renaissance, cites Dionysius more than thirty times in the three essays collected in Pico della Mirandola 1998.
[58] These works are available online at www.ccel.org/ccel/dionysius/works.html.
[59] *On the Heavenly Hierarchy* (cited here as HH), 4.1.   [60] HH 3.1.   [61] HH 3.3.
[62] HH 4.2.   [63] *On the Ecclesiastical Hierarchy*, 5.7, cf. HH 3.2.

young ... each with its own path to follow, as in the body each part has its own function."[64] This vision came to be expressed in the idea of a society composed of three orders – those who prayed, those who fought, and those who worked the land – ruled by the priests and princes. As Georges Duby puts it in his classic study, *The Three Orders*:

One part of society was worthy to rule over the remainder. Because they were morally of lesser value, "those behind" were subordinated to "those in front" (*prelati*) "who speak" (*predicators*), "who govern" (*rectores*), who are "powerful" (*potentes*) ... All hierarchy originated in the unequal distribution of good and evil, of flesh and spirit, of the heavenly and the terrestrial. As men were by nature differently inclined to sin, it was proper for the least culpable to assume responsibility, with care, affection, and firmness, for the leadership of the flock.[65]

All of reality is arranged in an elaborate level structure based on closeness to God. Proper social and political order is a matter of correspondence to the divinely ordained order of creation. In slightly broader terms, all of creation is ordered in a great chain of being – a hierarchical ontological vision that dominated Western philosophy into the eighteenth century.[66]

Ontological Hierarchy in India

Louis Dumont develops a strikingly similar account of the traditional Indian caste system – a system of ranked hereditary groups characterized by separation in marriage and contact and an interdependent division of labor[67] – which he presents as a model of hierarchical thinking. For Dumont, hierarchy is defined by a (typically religious) "principle by which the elements of a whole are ranked in relation to the whole."[68] In traditional India, this principle was "the opposition of the pure and the impure,"[69] which produced a linear order of castes based on distance from *Brahman* (reality/truth/godhead, the universal principle, and cause of all that is).

The resulting religious "status" hierarchy was classically sketched in the Vedic literature in the theory of the *varnas* (colors, classes, characters, or natures); orders or estates ranked according to function.[70] At the top were *Brahmins*, priests, who were most pure and who alone could perform sacrifices. *Kshatriyas*, kings and lesser rulers, provided public order. *Vaishyas* worked the land. *Shudras* performed servile tasks for the

---

[64] Quoted in Duby 1980 [1978], 74–5.   [65] *Ibid.*, 67.
[66] The classic account is Lovejoy 1936.
[67] Dumont 1980, 21, 30, 43, and, at much greater length, Chapters 3–6, building on the classic definition of Bouglé 1971 [1908].
[68] Dumont 1980, 66.   [69] *Ibid.*, 33, 43, 59 and, more generally, Chapter 2.
[70] *Ibid.*, Chapter 3.

three higher orders. And outside of (and below) this structure were "untouchables."

Traditional Indian society, however, also had a *power* "hierarchy."[71] As Dumont puts it, "Status ranking is not everything. It leaves out power and its distribution"[72]

Dumont insists, however, that in traditional India, at least in principle, "Status and power, and consequently spiritual authority and temporal authority, [we]re absolutely distinguished,"[73] and power was "absolutely inferior to status."[74] Unlike in the West (and most other places), "in India there has never been spiritual *power*, i.e., a supreme spiritual authority, which was at the same time a temporal power. The supremacy of the spiritual was never expressed politically."[75]

For our purposes here, the question of whether Dumont's account is overdrawn and overly intellectual is of largely academic interest. He does, however, explicitly raise three issues of broad relevance that are also implicitly raised by Dionysius and the theory of the three orders: the systemic totality of hierarchies, the place of status and power, and the contrast between hierarchical and egalitarian ontologies and social theories.

Hierarchies as Structured Systems

Dumont sees hierarchies as complex relational wholes that are characterized by both an encompassing unity and the differentiation of levels (distinguished by their relation to the organizing principle).[76] "The 'elements'" of the system are "the product of the network of relations" – so much so that the network of relations *is* the system; "a system of relations, in short, not a system of elements."[77]

To take an IR example, consider the modern system of sovereign states. Preexisting states did not confront each other in anything even vaguely resembling a state of nature and then, in order to overcome the incommodities of their situation, mutually recognize one another's sovereign authority. Rather, over several centuries, a great variety of material, institutional, and normative forces interacted to produce states, nonstate actors, diplomacy, international law, sovereign rights and prerogatives,

---

[71] Dumont reserves the term "hierarchy" for structures of religious/status ranking. "Hierarchy, in the sense that we are using the word here, and in accord with its etymology, never attaches itself to power as such, but always to religious functions." Dumont 1980, 260. I use "hierarchy" in the ordinary-language English sense to refer also to systems of political/power ranking.

[72] *Ibid.*, 77, cf. 66.   [73] *Ibid.*, 72, cf. 71.   [74] *Ibid.*, 74.   [75] *Ibid.*, 72.   [76] *Ibid.*, 239.

[77] *Ibid.*, 40.

a new kind of *respublica christiana*, the idea and practice of a European balance of power, and a variety of other institutions and practices that, taken together, at some point "made" (in the sense of resulted in) the modern states system. And these internal generative relations and logics continued to evolve in response to internal forces and external shocks, continuously reshaping states and the states system.

This appreciation of hierarchies as real relational structures adds a philosophical argument to the semantic and pragmatic arguments advanced above against extending "hierarchy" to encompass forms of authority, (in)equality, and rule not associated with structures of stratification and differentiation. It also suggests a certain skepticism toward using "hierarchy" to refer to "structures" that are largely constructs of external observers (rather than immanent in the practices of social actors).

For example, Lake claims that "by defining appropriate behavior, social norms create hierarchies of 'good' actors that substantially comply . . . and 'bad' actors that routinely violate or even deny the existence of the community standard."[78] In fact, though, there is nothing inevitable or even normal about using compliance to construct a ranked ordering of those subject to a norm. External analysts are, for their own purposes, free to make up or imagine such "hierarchies." Positive and negative sanctions, however, need not (and usually do not) create a structure of social positions ranked in grades one above another. Even when good compliance systematically generates high esteem or status and poor compliance produces low status or esteem, the resulting hierarchy is a contingent empirical result, not an inevitable consequence of the existence of a norm.

Consider Stroup and Wong's identification of leading authorities among INGOs (Chapter 8). They do this driven by a combination of substantive insights and data constraints. It seems to me, though, not only fair but necessary to ask whether the "hierarchy" of INGOs that they have identified is internal to the practice of these organizations or an external construct (a sort of rationalist "as if" model).

The ontology of hierarchies matters – even if we no longer see social hierarchies as instantiations of the hierarchical structure of reality. For example, Laura Sjoberg argues (Chapter 4) that gender hierarchies, gendered hierarchies, and gendered hierarchy *are* part of the structure of our social world. "The central contention of this chapter is that gender is implicated in and implicates all hierarchies in global politics"[79] – to which I would add "really," in the sense that all these types of hierarchies

---

[78] See Chapter 1. Towns similarly argues that "norms rank and set up relations of inequality" and has a subsection titled "Norms/Hierarchies." Towns 2010, 1, 44.

[79] See Chapter 4.

are part of the practices and meanings of real social actors. This also, it seems to me, underlies Pouliot's depiction of hierarchies as "heavy" (Chapter 5).

Status and Force

The distinctions between *Brahmins* and *Kshatriyas*, the first and second estates, and the lords spiritual and temporal – between spiritual and secular authority – raise the fundamental issue of the relation between "status" and "power" (or "authority" and "force") in the creation, maintenance, reproduction, and operation of hierarchies (and other forms of authority, (in) equality, and rule). Status (authority) is central to the effective operation of hierarchies. The initial cause of any particular hierarchy may (and often does) lie in force. But rule by force, which is extremely clumsy and expensive, is unlikely to persist unless it becomes institutionalized. (Conversely, the growing use of force by an autocratic ruler is the clearest sign that she is losing her grip on power; her status as a ruler.)

Hierarchies – as opposed to, for example, mere domination – arise from the transformation of superior strength (force, material capabilities) into superior status. Hierarchical authority or rule need not be legitimate in a substantive or even merely procedural sense of that term. It does, however, rest *in part* on a certain kind of legitimation, rooted in the "acknowledgment" by the subordinated of their inferior status.

Lake's language of consent and contract (Chapter 1) goes too far – or, rather, mistakes one source or type of hierarchy for the general form.[80] But so does Pouliot's suggestion (Chapter 5) that hierarchies are "heavy." It oddly suggests the individualist perspective of an abstract actor who is considered, or imagines herself, somehow outside the practice of hierarchy. And it ignores the fact that many hierarchies are experienced as "appropriate" or even "legitimate" rather than (or in addition to) "heavy." In fact, in many hierarchies of elected office, merit, or achievement, complaints of "heaviness" tend to be disparaged – "rightly" (when judged from within the practice).

Those enmeshed in hierarchal practices – especially those who have been made who they are *through* hierarchical practices – typically "play the game" from the positions they have. They practice their status. And these status-based practices make up – in an important sense *are* – hierarchies.

---

[80] Even within the social contract tradition, consent is understood primarily as tacit (Locke is the clearest example) or hypothetical (as in Kant's and Rawls' accounts of what a rational being properly situated would consent to). For a classic discussion of the problematic nature of the relationship between obligation and consent, see Pitkin 1965, 1966.

None of this is to deny that force is *also* part of the practice of hierarchies. Nor is it to deny that the relative mix of force and status is important to how particular hierarchies function. Hierarchies, however, are usually – I am inclined to say inescapably – matters of superior and inferior status. And status inequalities are an extremely important type of inequality, with a very particular character. We thus have one more reason to keep to the ordinary-language sense of hierarchy (rather than conflate hierarchy and inequality).

Hierarchy in an Egalitarian World

Nonetheless, to most modern readers there *is* something inherently suspect – "heavy" – about hierarchy. "We" live in an ontologically egalitarian world. Even if we are increasingly skeptical of "universal reason," we remain deeply committed to "universal human rights" and the equal and inherent worth and dignity of the human person. What jumps out at us about most social hierarchies is their inequality. And hierarchical inequalities, because they are systematic and structural, strike us as particularly problematic.

The moral core of modernity is egalitarianism. (In this reading, Burke is the last great political theorist of a hierarchical universe.) Since the French Revolution, hierarchy has been not merely on the defensive but on the retreat. Hierarchies based on religion, birth, wealth, and even race and gender have, at least in theory and in polite company, been banished. Others (e.g., disability, age, and gender identity or orientation) are under assault. I think that it is even fair to say that the fundamental justification for modernity – which, for its innumerable sins and shortcomings, is much in need of justification – is its success in suppressing ascriptive hierarchies. (Much of the implicit normative force of Sjoberg's chapter [Chapter 4] derives from her argument that these very basic ascriptive hierarchies have *not* in fact been eliminated.)

The contrast to hierarchical ontologies, in other words, helps us to see ourselves better; to appreciate as a distinctive historical achievement the egalitarianism that has become part of our nature. Even the idea of human nature as an attribute of all members of *Homo sapiens*, as opposed to an elite of "truly human" beings, is a modern idea.[81]

---

[81] See Donnelly (2015b), where I distinguish between taxonomic and normative humanity, which I argue have, at best, only been seen as largely overlapping sets since around 1960, when a widespread normative commitment to decolonization became solidified. As Dumont (1980, 16) puts it, summarizing Tocqueville, "where inequality reigns, there are as many distinct humanities as there are social categories" – as classical India illustrates in a particularly striking form.

It also, though, highlights the way our deep discomfort with inequality makes it difficult for us to understand or appreciate hierarchy. Dumont argues that "our contemporaries, who value equality, find scarcely anything to contrast it with except inequality."[82] The fact of inequality overwhelms an appreciation of its different forms. As Dumont puts it, "make distinction illegitimate, and you get discrimination."[83] Hierarchy thus becomes reduced to an imposition of force – or, conversely, we want to model "acceptable" (or at least tolerable) hierarchies as a matter of consent.

Traditional hierarchies, in sharp contrast, were rooted in differences of being. I certainly do not want to defend such hierarchies. They do, however, underline the vital point that in many (most?) hierarchies power is subordinated to status. And even today, the relative mix of power and status *and the grounds for the attribution of status* are vital considerations in both characterizing and evaluating hierarchies.

Beyond Hierarchies in World Politics

We thus return to the central theme of this chapter and, I think, of this book as a whole, namely, the need, for both analytic and evaluative purposes, to investigate, directly and systematically, the varied forms of authority, (in)equality, and rule that are central to international relations, anywhere and in any era. IR's Waltzian legacy makes hierarchy, for us today, an "obvious" entry point. I have argued, though, that authority, (in)equality, and rule cannot be adequately encompassed within the frame of hierarchy or even hierarchies. I thus read *Hierarchies in World Politics* as a call for IR to give central and sustained attention to practices and systems of international rule arising from complex interactions of differences in capabilities and authority that both are rooted in and give rise to a great variety of equalities and inequalities among international actors.

[82] Dumont 1980, 19. [83] *Ibid.*, 262.

12   Why Hierarchy?

Ayşe Zarakol

Previous chapters have illustrated the value of the hierarchy heuristic for the study of world politics. The chapters in Part I considered types and origins of hierarchies and whether they are purposefully designed by agents as institutions or experienced as structural settings of inequality. The chapters in Part II analysed how actors respond to, shape and act in the hierarchical settings in which they find themselves. Then, in Chapter 11, Donnelly provided a friendly dissent, arguing that while studying inequality, authority, and rule is a desirable goal for International Relations (IR), the concept of hierarchy may not be the best way of getting there. While Donnelly makes a compelling case for analytical precision, he over-estimates the notion of concepts as purely analytical tools. In this very brief conclusion, I will argue that hierarchy is a useful concept for IR not only because of its analytical value, which is considerable, as demonstrated in this book, but also because of the particular history of IR as a discipline and its relation to world politics at large. The assumption of anarchy upon which IR rests is a particular historically contingent conception that derives from and reproduces the political project of the nation-state. Rather than merely a neutral heuristic device, the lens through which mainstream IR analyses world politics is a particular ideology of anarchy, which is then naturalised as given. The concept of hierarchy unsettles these assumptions in ways that other concepts proposed by Donnelly do not.

Historicising Anarchy in IR

In the *Political Discourse of Anarchy*, Schmidt argues that from the inception of the discipline, the writings on the international took the existence of the state as their starting point.[1] When the American Political Science Association was formed in 1903, the study of political science 'was basically synonymous with the state', which was conceptualised

---

[1] Though he also shows that 'anarchy' was understood differently by successive approaches since the origins of the discipline. See also Donnelly 2015a.

juristically: '[t]his conception of sovereignty depicted the state as an expression of supreme authority over a territorially defined political community.'[2] From this perspective, 'states occupied a position similar to that of the individuals living in a state of nature', and therefore international law (which nineteenth-century jurists had recognised) did not embody the 'true characteristics of law'.[3] Tellingly, however, '[t]he agenda of the first annual APSA meeting in 1904, held in conjunction with the annual meeting of the American Economic Association, was overwhelmingly given over to problems posed by imperialism.'[4] In one sense, then, the juristic theory of the state forestalled 'an analytically distinct investigation of international relations'.[5] Yet, it did not preclude a preoccupation with imperial administration and racial conflict, which in fact characterised the early years of the discipline.

In other words, IR started with states first. As discussed by Donnelly in Chapter 11, the concept of anarchy came to dominate the field much later. Some may object here that it was always present in 'spirit' – after all, introductions to IR textbooks often attribute a long and distinguished intellectual lineage to this particular concept, going back several millennia: 'Waltz, for example, claimed that Thucydides' history represented 'an early recognition of the "anarchic character of international politics," which "accounts for the striking sameness of the quality of international life throughout the millennia".'[6] Other precursors believed to have written about the anarchic character of international politics include Machiavelli, Hobbes and Rousseau.[7] While it is undeniable that these thinkers discussed situations that resemble anarchy, a fact that is almost always overlooked is that none of these precursors talked about *anarchy*[8] per se. Though we recognise that there is a familial resemblance between the scenarios captured by Waltz's definition of anarchy versus the Hobbesian state of nature versus Thucydides' civil war, the differences in metaphor used to describe the absence of a supra-polity authority disclose the unspoken assumptions and the context the author is drawing upon, with significant consequences for our understanding of the international.

Consider, for instance, Thucydides. An APSR article comparing the views of Hobbes and Thucydides about anarchy takes the following passage as Thucydides' clearest statement about anarchy: 'Many harsh

---

[2] Schmidt 1997, 79.   [3] *Ibid.*   [4] Vitalis 2010, 927. See also Vitalis 2015.
[5] Schmidt 1997, 120.   [6] *Ibid.*, 40, quoting Waltz 1979.
[7] *Ibid.*, 27; see also Doyle 1996.
[8] Even Schmidt, whose primary goal was to write a critical history of the discourse of anarchy in IR, misses this point to some extent and fails to conceptually distinguish 'the state of nature' from 'anarchy'.

things befell cities on account of civil war, such as happen and will *always* happen so long as the nature of human beings is the same.'[9] However, if we were not so inclined to read this text anachronistically, we would notice that Thucydides is talking about (1) civil war (2) among cities (polis), not states. This is not a world that is governed by the structural dynamics of Waltzian anarchy but one where the 'enemy' is seen as part of the same community as literally declared in the conception of 'civil war'.

The word 'anarchy' is also barely mentioned in Hobbes' *Leviathan*, and when it is, it is in reference to something else altogether[10]; there is only one place – in Chapter XXI – where Hobbes characterises the state of nature as anarchy, but he does not use the terms interchangeably, and he is not referring to 'international relations'. Instead, Hobbes' views on international 'anarchy' are derived from the following passage: 'Like individuals in the state of nature, "kings" [stand] in the posture of gladiators; ... their weapons pointing, and their eyes fixed on one another.'[11] Notice, however, that Hobbes does not mention 'states', preferring to talk about 'kings' instead, and even though he likens them to individuals in the state of nature, he uses a metaphor he does not use to describe individuals in the state of nature: that of gladiators watching each other. Conduct among gladiators, though it may be fairly characterised as a fight to the death, is a metaphor invoking a much more formalised setting (with its codes of fighting, weaponry, salutes, etc.) to describe a survival situation than the nasty, brutish and short existence of individuals surviving in the state of nature as imagined by Hobbes, where violence is more random and unpredictable.

At issue is that both Thucydides' and Hobbes' descriptions of relations between polities imply certain communal and, in fact, normative features that are left out of modern-day conceptualisations of the international system as anarchy. In using the concepts and metaphors they did, these authors could not help but convey certain common understandings of their time, even as they rose above superficial observations with their incisive analyses that speak even to us across centuries. Similarly, it is no accident that modern IR has a particular understanding of world politics (or inter-polity relations). The particular way in which we conceptualise politics between polities has much to do with how we conceptualise the polity itself.

---

[9] PW 3.82.2, as cited by Ahrensdorf 2000, 537 (emphasis added by Ahrensdorf).

[10] 'For they that are discontented under monarchy call it tyranny; and they that are displeased with aristocracy call it oligarchy: so also, they which find themselves grieved under a democracy call it anarchy, which signifies want of government' (Chapter XIX).

[11] Hobbes 1946 [1651], 83, Chapter XIII.

Past intra-disciplinary debates within IR are a good example of this phenomenon. The neorealist tradition views the state as a unitary actor that exercises supreme authority over continuous territory. States then interact as billiard balls in the international stage. The neoliberal tradition sees the state as merely the sum of its parts and therefore has a more optimistic view of how those various parts may interact with their counterparts elsewhere to mitigate the problems arising from the systemic fact of anarchy. Both approaches agree on the fact of anarchy because, in thinking about world politics, they both start from the state, imagined in a particular, sovereign form that then renders the international as anarchy. And yet, the particular kind of sovereign state upon which both theorisations rest is a historically contingent institutionalisation of particular notions about how human life should be organised. The 'state' as a unit of 'international relations' is seemingly timeless only because we have anachronistically imposed our concepts back on the past – we often see in history what we want to see.

The notion of bounded community as represented by the nation-state is a modern invention (or at the very least its ubiquity is). It was not even until Renaissance that 'man and state for the first time came to be thought of as independent and self-directing entities'.[12] This could be traced to developments of the sixteenth and seventieth centuries, which 'had little to do with what happened or did not happen in Westphalia, but more to do with the shift in cosmological perspective that occurred at the beginning of [seventeenth] century when geographical and cartographical knowledge was being harnessed for state-building and imperial expansions'.[13]

At the time Hobbes was writing, these developments had not yet reached fruition: ideas about the universal community of the church had been undermined, and ideas about the bounded communities ruled by kings were in ascendance, but the match between territory, sovereign, and the people that nationalism eventually secured had not yet been made.[14] During Hobbes' time, it was much more 'natural' to assume a match between the ruler and the 'state'[15] he or she ruled. Around this

---

[12] Bruckhardt [1860] 1958, vol, II, 279–302, as cited by Ringmar 1996, 444.

[13] Bartelson 2009, 106.

[14] It was later that symbols of the past were recycled and new 'spatial symbols of identity that that could be deciphered in terms of those virtues that had been appropriated from the ancients', such as cathedrals and royal palaces of remarkable stylistic uniformity, were erected throughout Europe to link first the crown, and later the state, with a collective memory, a teleology and a certain destiny. See Bartelson 2009, 107. These symbols as well as the memory would become fully nationalized after the French Revolution when such monuments of the monarchy would be reclaimed by the nation as its own through the invention of the museum (101).

[15] If one could even call it that – territoriality would not develop until late eighteenth century. See e.g. Bartelson 2017; Benton 2010.

time, the prevailing belief had come to be that 'a state was not a state without a prince and a prince was not a prince without a state',[16] and the body metaphor was commonly used to describe this relationship. The world itself was compared to a 'stage',[17] and the state was a body or 'a person' acting on that stage, with the prince's reason guiding it on that stage.

The concept of 'a person', itself an early modern invention (due to changes in understanding of memory as constituting the identity of a person as continuous throughout time as well as the new belief in the mouldability of identity and fate due to personal choice), had come to describe the concept of the state. This was the context Hobbes was writing in: '[a]ccording to Hobbes, the state could be thought of as a "Feigned" or "Artificial" person, and as already the cover-page of his most famous work made clear, Leviathan was a superman who, with sword and sceptre in hand, brought peace to the individual men out of whom he was composed.'[18] In other words, although we can clearly see the beginnings of the modern equivalent of the state as a unitary actor trope in Hobbesian thought, he had a very different conception of 'state as a person' than modern-day realists. When Hobbes talked about kings standing in the posture of gladiators, he really did mean kings, and though he was using the metaphor of gladiators for kings, he was not using kings as a metaphor for states.

This is not a trivial point. Kings standing in the posture of gladiators with eyes affixed on each other invokes a very different kind of world than states as billiard balls bouncing off of each other. Hobbes means something else than we do when he talks about the state of nature, and it is problematic to stretch that concept to the international system without awareness of the historical context. It is problematic both because Hobbes did not understand inter-polity relations of his time to be a 'state of nature' in the sense that we understand today and also because the inter-polity relations of his time were not a 'state of nature' (let alone anarchy) in the sense we understand today. In fact, there are good reasons to believe that 'it took the French Revolution to fully bring the "state of nature" concept to fruition within the post-Reformation European states system'[19] in the sense that we understand the term. Prior to the French Revolution, the people were governed but not represented by the raison d'état. Eighteenth-century European politics was governed by the idea of monarchical rights.[20] Furthermore, '[n]either contiguity nor national

---

[16] Skinner 1989, 90–102, as paraphrased by Ringmar 1996, 445.

[17] Frye 1990, 196–211; Jacquot 1957; Magistretti 1971, all cited by Ringmar 1996, 445.

[18] Ringmar 1996, 446.   [19] Bukovansky 1999, 213; see also Bukovansky 2001.

[20] Bukovansky 1999, 205.

homogeneity were major priorities of 18th century monarchs, though territorial gains figured significantly. But there were other means of righting perceived imbalances, including money, titles, and prestige.'[21] Relations between eighteenth-century European states were governed by dynastic norms: '[t]he pre-revolutionary game was more constrained and rule-bound than it became in the nineteenth century, with nation-states throwing themselves at each other in zero-sum crusades.'[22]

Probing the Political Project of Anarchy

Within the European states system,[23] then, the transition from the Middle Ages to 'modernity' involved first the erosion and then the loss of conceptualisations of universal community (fifteenth and sixteenth centuries) and, next, the emergence of the particularising concept of the state as a person (sixteenth and seventeenth centuries). That was the world that Hobbes likened to the state of nature, but he conceded in a way that it was governed by dynastic norms.[24] Finally came the emergence of the nation-state after the French Revolution (nineteenth and twentieth centuries), until which point it was not even conceivable to think about the states in the terms used by neorealists. Indeed, it was not even until early nineteenth century that 'rule came to be denied exclusively in terms of territories with boundaries between homogeneous spatial authority claims'.[25] Before this development, it would have been inconceivable to think of 'states' in terms of territorial continuity, unitary rational agency or as existing in anarchy.

Anarchy, that is, what mainstream IR has taken to be a trans-historical fact about world politics, rests on a particular conception of the state that is so historically contingent and so far removed from practical reality that it has only ever been actualised for moments in history and that started coming apart the moment it was actualised. Even under the most hospitable of conditions, the nation-state never really obtained in the manner it is assumed by the literature. No state has ever been entirely convergent with its 'nation' or its bounded community. States have not had exclusive monopolies on continuous territories either (though many certainly have aspired to do so). Borders have always been porous to some extent, and competing claims to authority were never fully silenced. Furthermore,

---

[21] *Ibid.*   [22] *Ibid.*, 213. See also Reus-Smit (1999) on a variation of this argument.
[23] This is not to endorse the Eurocentrism of IR narratives; I am focusing on Europe because this is where these particular conceptualisations emerged.
[24] See also Bartelson's re-reading of Kant, which lends support to the idea that universal conceptions of humanity were on their last legs at this time.
[25] Branch 2011, 6. See also n. 15 above.

well into the middle of twentieth century many 'nation-states' were either imperial powers or colonies. Analysts started predicting the erosion and ultimate demise of the nation-state the moment it became the predominant model for organising human life around the world. In sum, anarchy neither captures the reality of international politics nor does it work as an analytical heuristic with explanatory powers: even 'understood as a general feature of international relations, [anarchy] is not an independent variable with universal and uniform effects (that may or may not be mitigated or overcome). It is an interactive and contextual variable associated with multiple equilibria.'[26] For all these reasons, the over-reliance first on the nation-state in IR as the main unit of analysis in world politics and then 'anarchy' is a supposedly timeless structural ordering principle should first be explained sociologically. The same goes, to some extent, for methods of challenging these assumptions: analytical purchase of a given concept, by itself, will not be enough.

Note that in the nineteenth century, while anarchism was in fact relatively ascendant as a left-wing political philosophy/ideology, the word 'anarchy' was not used to describe relations between the states. The favoured similar metaphors were 'state of nature' and later, borrowing from Darwin, 'survival of the fittest'. While similar conceptually, these terms have very different implications. It needs little demonstration that they were more fitting (and legitimising) metaphors for an age that included zero-sum wars among European powers and colonial conquest of non-European peoples.[27] More than a half century later, by the time neorealism adopted the concept of anarchy as the primary assumption of IR, anarchism as a political ideology had lost the influence it enjoyed in the nineteenth century and early twentieth century.[28] But in the way that the term was deployed by Waltz, there is an echo of the positive connotations the concept of anarchy had for anarchists.[29] After all, the state of nature that Hobbes depicts (and which realism invokes frequently for legitimation of certain aspects of its argument) is a condition from which one wants to escape. If the states are truly like the unitary rational actors in a Hobbesian state of nature, the logical conclusion should also be the Hobbesian one: the erection of a global Leviathan (this contradiction was not a problem for Hobbes because he was not confusing his own metaphor for reality). The substitution of the word 'anarchy' for what could also be called 'the state of nature' mediates this conclusion. Subtly

---

[26] Donnelly 2015a, 413.   [27] See e.g. Carr 2001 [1939].

[28] Though it is making a comeback now, with interesting implications for IR. See e.g. Prichard 2011.

[29] There is indeed a great deal of overlooked irony in the political journey of the concept of 'anarchy'.

implied here is the claim of anarchism-as-a-philosophy that anarchy is preferable to the alternative, that is, the centralised state or a world-sovereign.[30]

The second thing accomplished by describing the world as anarchy is to mask conditions of inequality in the system, making it difficult to talk about even political hierarchies that are not explicitly formalised, let alone economic or social inequalities that exist throughout the system. As Hobson notes, '[T]his conventional axiom constitutes an opaque veneer or an ideological veil that masks the dark hierarchical face of IR which promotes, defends and reifies, analytically and/or normatively, Western civilisation over non-Western states.'[31] In other words, the anarchy assumption has had the ironic consequence of making it much more difficult to talk about economic and social hierarchies in international relations than it is to talk about them in domestic societies, even though, arguably, citizens within the same society have much more formal equality than states, and the hierarchies that exist within domestic societies are not directly caused by the fact that domestic societies have formal sovereigns.

Why Hierarchy Then?

So what would it mean for IR if the historical contingency of the ideology underpinning the anarchy heuristic were exposed? Approaches that assume anarchy to be a trans-historical fact of inter-polity relations reduce (the past, the present and the future of) world politics to an international (i.e. inter-state) system. This is so because they take state sovereignty as a 'hard' given, that is, as an enduring fact of world politics, as clear in its boundaries, and as inextricable from state interests. In exposing the (historical and contemporary) softness of sovereignty – that is, its contingency and porosity – globalising processes have challenged scholars to more explicitly theorise world politics in a manner that does not analytically conflate states with their sovereignty and so, by extension, does not privilege sovereignty as the only defining feature of the primary units in world politics. By drawing our focus to structures of stratification and the differentiation of units, only the concept of hierarchy urges a perspective on world politics that accommodates but does not insist upon sovereignty and that is systemic in scope. That, in turn, may get us thinking further about the links between IR theory and modern political project.

---

[30] This is all the more true given the US dominance of the discipline.
[31] Hobson 2014, 559.

A turn towards hierarchy also forces us think about all the ways the concept anarchy does not explain world politics. The anarchy assumption obscures not only structural inequalities in world politics (broad hierarchies that modernity finds problematic, as Donnelly notes) but also makes it difficult to imagine institutional (narrow) hierarchies that may then be (part of the) solutions to those inequalities. To put it another way, the concept of anarchy has stunted our normative sense as a discipline both by robbing us of the language to speak about what is problematic and by constraining our imagination as to what types of solutions are possible. The concept of hierarchy (as articulated in this book in its broad and narrow variants) reopens both of these avenues. Finally, the excessive focus on anarchy is largely responsible for the ahistoricism of the discipline, cutting us off from large swaths of human history where our theories are self-evidently inadequate. Not being able to understand past and, by implication, the moments of systemic change has made us as a discipline entirely unequipped to deal with the current challenges that the modern international order is facing. The concept of hierarchy helps us to overcome such blind spots by offering a bridge into the near and distant past and therefore also the future. This kind of re-thinking is an absolute necessity if the discipline is to remain relevant into the new century.

Bibliography

Abbott, George C. 1971. "Political Disintegration: The Lessons of Anguilla." *Government and Opposition* 6(1): 58–74.

Abbott, Kenneth W., Robert O. Keohane, Andrew Moravcsik, Anne-Marie Slaughter, and Duncan Snidal. 2000. "The Concept of Legalization." *International Organization* 54(3): 401–19.

Abdul-Alim, Jamaal. 2015. "ISIS 'Manifesto' Spells Out Role for Women." *The Atlantic*, March 8; available at www.theatlantic.com/education/archive/2015/03/isis-manifesto-spells-out-role-for-women/387049/ (accessed May 25, 2015).

Abercrombie, Nicholas, Stephen Hill, and Bryan S. Turner. 1994. *The Penguin Dictionary of Sociology*. Harmondsworth: Penguin Books.

Abu-Lughod, Lila. 2014. *Do Muslim Women Need Saving?* Cambridge, MA: Harvard University Press.

Acharya, Amitav. 2004. "How Ideas Spread: Whose Norms Matter? Norm Localization and Institutional Change in Asian Regionalism." *International Organization* 58(2): 239–75.

Acker, Joan. 1990. "Hierarchies, Jobs, Bodies: A Theory of Gendered Organizations." *Gender & Society* 4(2): 139–58.

　2011. "Theorizing Gender, Race, and Class in Organizations," in Emma Jeanes, David Knights, and Patricia Yancey Martin (eds.), *Handbook of Gender, Work, and Organization*. London: Wiley.

Adler, Emanuel, and Michael Barnett. 1998. *Security Communities*. New York: Cambridge University Press.

Adler-Nissen, Rebecca. 2014. "Stigma Management in International Relations: Transgressive Identities, Norms and Order in International Society." *International Organization* 68(1): 143–76.

　2015. *Opting Out of the European Union: Diplomacy, Sovereignty and European Integration*. Cambridge: Cambridge University Press.

Adler-Nissen, Rebecca, and Ulrik Pram Gad, eds. 2013. *European Integration and Postcolonial Sovereignty Games*. London: Routledge.

Adie, W. A. C. 1964. "Chou En-lai on Safari." *China Quarterly* 18: 174–94.

African Development Bank. 2011. "Seychelles Country Strategy Paper 2011–2015."

Ahrensdorf, Peter. 2000. "The Fear of Death and the Longing for Immortality: Hobbes and Thucydides on Human Nature and the Problem of Anarchy." *American Political Science Review* 94(3): 579–93.

Akbar, Jay. 2015. "'I Rejoiced When We Had Our First Sex Slave, Forced Sex ISN'T Rape, and They Should Be Thankful': Chilling Rant of Twisted ISIS Jihadi Bride Who Justified Kidnapping and Abusing Yazidi Girls." *Daily Mail*, May 22, 2015; available at www.dailymail.co.uk/news/article-309294 6/I-rejoiced-sex-slave-forced-sex- ... g-rant-twisted-ISIS-jihadi-bride-justifies-kidnapping-abusing-Yazidi-girls.html (accessed May 25, 2015).

Alavi, Seema. 1998. *The Sepoys and the Company: Tradition and Transition in Northern India, 1770–1830*. Oxford: Oxford University Press.

Allen, Amy. 2000. *The Power of Feminist Theory*. Boulder, CO: Westview.

Aly, Ann. 2015. "'Jihadi Brides' Aren't Oppressed. They Join ISIS for the Same Reason Men Do." *The Guardian*, March 3; available at www.theguardian .com/commentisfree/2015/mar/04/jihadi-brides-arent-oppressed-they-join-isis-for-the-same-reasons-men-do (accessed May 25, 2015).

Ambrosetti, David. 2009. *Normes et rivalités diplomatiques à l'ONU. Le Conseil de Sécurité en audience*. Brussels: Peter Lang.

Monika Ambrus, Karin Arts, Ellen Hey, and Helena Raulus (eds.). 2014. *The Role of "Experts" in International and European Decision-Making Processes: Advisers, Decision Makers, or Irrelevant Actors?* New York: Cambridge University Press.

Andersen, Morten. 2011. "How Empires Emerge," Working Paper 786, Norwegian Institute of International Affairs, Oslo. Available at file:///H:/NU PI-WP-786-Skumsrud%20Andersen.pdf (accessed October 20, 2015).

Anderson, Benedict. 1991. *Imagined Communities: An Inquiry into the Origins and Spread of Nationalism*. New York: Verso.

Angyal, Andras. 1939. "The Structure of Wholes." *Philosophy of Science* 6(1): 25–37.

Anheier, Helmut, Mary Kaldor, and Marlies Glasius. 2012. "Lessons and Insights 2001–2011," in *Global Civil Society Yearbook*. London: Palgrave.

Anghie, Anthony. 2005. *Imperialism: Sovereignty and the Making of International Law*. Cambridge: Cambridge University Press.

Anievas, Alex, and Kerem Nişancıoğlu. 2015. *How the West Came to Rule*. London: Pluto.

Anievas, Alex, Nivi Manchanda, and Robbie Shilliam. 2015. *Race and Racism in International Relations: Confronting the Global Colour Line*. London: Routledge.

Antoniades, Andreas. 2013. "At the Eye of the Cyclone: The Greek Crisis in Global Media." *Greece's Horizons*, 11–25.

Appiah, Kwame. 2010. *The Ethics of Identity*. Princeton, NJ: Princeton University Press.

Applbaum, Arthur Isak. 2007. "Forcing People to be Free." *Philospohy and Public Affairs* 35: 359–400.

Archard, David. 1990. "Paternalism Defined." *Analysis* 50(1): 36–42.

Arendt, Hannah. 1965. *On Revolution*. New York: Penguin.

Armitage, David. 2007. *The Declaration of Independence: A Global History*. Cambridge, MA.: Harvard University Press.

Armstrong, David. 1993. *Revolution and World Order: The Revolutionary State in International Society*. Oxford: Clarendon Press.

Aron, Raymond. 2003 [1966]. *Peace and War: A Theory of International Relations.* New Brunswick, NJ: Transaction Publishers.

Arrighi, Giovanni. 1994. *The Long Twentieth Century: Money, Power, and the Origins of Our Times.* London: Verso.

Ashby, W. Ross. 1964 [1956]. *An Introduction to Cybernetics.* London: Chapman & Hall.

Ashley, Richard K. 1988. "Untying the Sovereign State: A Double Reading of the Anarchy Problematique." *Millennium* 17(2): 227–62.

Asian Development Bank. 2007. *Country Economic Report: Nauru.* Manila.

Axelrod, Robert. 1986. "An Evolutionary Approach to Norms." *American Political Science Review* 80(4): 1095–111.

Avant, Deborah. 2005. *The Market for Force: The Consequences of Privatizing Security.* New York: Cambridge University Press.

Avant, Deborah D., Martha Finnemore, and Susan K. Sell. 2010. "Conclusion: Authority, Legitimacy, and Accountability in Global Politics," in Deborah D. Avant, Martha Finnemore, and Susan K. Sell (eds.), *Who Governs the Globe?* Cambridge: Cambridge University Press.

Ayoob, Mohammed. 1989. "The Third World in the System of States: Acute Schizophrenia or Growing Pains?" *International Studies Quarterly* 33(1): 67–79.

2003. "Inequality and Theorizing in International Relations: The Case for Subaltern Realism." *International Studies Review* 4(3): 27–48.

Baldwin, David A. 1989. *Paradoxes of Power.* NY: Basil Blackwell.

Banerjee, Sikata. 2012. *Muscular Nationalism: Gender, Violence, and Empire in India and Ireland, 1914–2004.* NY: NY University Press.

Bar'al, Zvi. 2015. "ISIS' Sex Slave Market: How the Islamic State is Wiping Out Iraq's Yazidi Minority." *Haaretz* May 5, available at www.haaretz.com/news/middle-east/.premium-1.654925 (accessed May 25, 2015).

Barder, Alexander. 2015. *Empire Within: International Hierarchy and its Imperial Laboratories of Governance.* London: Routledge.

Barkawi, Tarak, and Mark Laffey. 2006. "The Postcolonial Moment in Security Studies." *Review of International Studies* 32(2): 329–52.

Barkey, Karen, and Frederic C Godart. 2013. "Empires, Federated Arrangements, and Kingdoms: Using Political Models of Governance to Understand Firms' Creative Performance." *Organization Studies* 34(1): 79–104.

Barnes, Harry Elmer. 1930. *World Politics and Modern Civilization: The Contributions of Nationalism, Capitalism, Imperialism and Militarism to Human Culture and International Anarchy.* NY: Knopf.

Barnes, Julian E. 2013. "Hagel Tours 'Secret' U.S. Air Base in Qatar." *Wall Street Journal*, December 10.

Barnett, Michael N. 2011. *Empire of Humanity: A History of Humanitarianism.* Ithaca, NY: Cornell University Press.

2012. "International Paternalism and Humanitarian Governance," *Global Constitutionalism* 1(3): 485–521.

Barnett, Michael N., and Raymond Duvall. 2005. "Power in International Politics." *International Organization* 59(1): 39–75.

Barnett, Michael N., and Martha Finnemore. 2004. *Rules for the World: International Organizations in Global Politics*. Ithaca, NY: Cornell University Press.

Bartelson, Jens. 2009. *Visions of World Community*. Cambridge: Cambridge University Press.

2017. "Dating Sovereignty." International Studies Association Convention, Baltimore, MD.

Bartman, Barry. 2002. "Meeting the Needs of Microstate Security." *The Round Table* 91: 361–74.

Bayly, Christopher. 2011. *Recovering Liberties: Indian Thought in the Age of Liberalism and Empire*. Cambridge: Cambridge University Press.

Beach, Derek. 2013. "The Fiscal Compact, Euro-reforms, and the Challenge for the Opt-Outs." In *Danish Foreign Policy Yearbook*, vol. 2013, pp. 113–33.

Beattie, David. 2004. *Liechtenstein: A Modern History*. London: IB Taurus.

Belich, James. 2011. *Replenishing the Earth: The Settler Revolution and the Rise of the Angloworld*. Oxford: Oxford University Press.

Ben-Porath, Sigal. 2010. *Tough Choices: Structured Paternalism and the Landscape of Choice*. Princeton, NJ: Princeton University Press.

Benton, Laura. 2010. *A Search for Sovereignty*. Cambridge: Cambridge University Press.

Berger, T. U. 1997. "The Past in the Present: Historical Memory and German National Security Policy." *German Politics* 6(1): 39–59.

Bernard, Chester I. 1962. *The Functions of the Executive*. Cambridge, MA: Harvard University Press.

Bertalanffy, Ludwig von. 1968. *General Systems Theory: Foundations, Development, Applications*. New York: George Braziller.

Best, Jacqueline. 2014. *Governing Failure: Provisional Expertise and the Transformation of Global Development Finance*. New York: Cambridge University Press.

Bially Mattern, Janice, and Ayşe Zarakol. 2016. "Hierarchies in World Politics." *International Organization* 7(3): 623–54.

Bicchieri, Cristina. 2006. *The Grammar of Society: The Nature and Dynamics of Social Norms*. New York: Cambridge University Press.

Biedermann, Zoltán. 2009. "The Matrioshka Principle and How It Was Overcome: Portuguese and Habsburg Imperial Attitudes in Sri Lanka and the Responses of the Rulers of Kotte (1506–1598)." *Journal of Early Modern History* 13(4): 265–310.

Biersteker, Thomas J., and Cynthia Weber (eds.). 1996. *State Sovereignty as Social Construct*. New York: Cambridge University Press.

Birnbaum, Maria. 2015. "Becoming Recognizable: Postcolonial Independence and the Reification of Religion." PhD thesis, European Union Institute.

Bisson, Thomas N. 2009. *The Crisis of the Twelfth Century: Power, Lordship, and the Origins of European Government*. Princeton, NJ: Princeton University Press.

Blaker, James R. 1990. *United States Overseas Basing: An Anatomy of the Dilemma*. New York: Praeger.

Blyth, Mark. 2013. *Austerity: The History of a Dangerous Idea*. Oxford: Oxford University Press.

Bob, Clifford. 2012. *The Global Right Wing and the Clash of World Politics*. New York: Cambridge University Press.

2005. *The Marketing of Rebellion: Insurgents, Media, and International Activism*. New York: Cambridge University Press.

Bolton, Doug. 2015. "Five Year Old Girls Are Dreaming of Becoming Jihadi Brides, Claims Police Chief." *The Independent*, May 23, 2015, available at www.independent.co.uk/news/uk/home-news/five-year-old-girls-are-dreaming-of-becoming-jihadi-brides-claims-police-chief-10271687.html (accessed May 15, 2017).

Bonham, James. 1999. "Practical Reason and Cultural Constraint: Agency in Bourdieu's Theory of Practice," in Richard Shusterman (ed.), *Bourdieu: A Critical Reader*. Oxford: Blackwell, pp. 129–52.

Boström, Magnus, and Christina Garsten (eds.). 2008. *Organizing Transnational Accountability*. Northampton, MA: Edward Elgar.

Boswell, C. 2009. *The Political Uses of Expert Knowledge: Immigration Policy and Social Research*. New York: Cambridge University Press.

Bouglé, Celestin. 1971[1908]. *Essays on the Caste System*. Cambridge: Cambridge University Press.

Bourdieu, Pierre. 1984. *Distinction: A Social Critique of the Judgement of Taste*. Cambridge, MA: Harvard University Press.

Bourdieu, Pierre. 1989. "Social Space and Symbolic Power." *Sociological Theory* 7(1):14–25.

1990. *The Logic of Practice*. Cambridge, UK: Polity Press.

1994. *Raisons pratiques. Sur la théorie de l'action*. Paris: Seuil.

2000a[1972]. *Esquisse d'une théorie de la pratique*. Paris: Seuil.

2000b[1997]. *Pascalian Meditations*. Stanford, CA: Stanford University Press.

2001. *Langage et pouvoir symbolique*. Paris: Seuil.

2003 [1997]. *Méditations pascaliennes*. Paris: Seuil.

Bourdieu, Pierre, and Loïc J. D. Wacquant. 1992. *An Invitation to Reflexive Sociology*. Chicago: University of Chicago Press.

Bowden, Brett. 2004. "In the Name of Progress and Peace: The 'Standard of Civilization' and the Universalizing Project." *Alternatives* 29(1): 43–68.

2009. *The Empire of Civilization*. Chicago: University of Chicago Press.

Branch, Adam. 2008. "Against Humanitarian Impunity: Rethinking Responsibility for Displacement and Disaster in Northern Uganda." *Journal of Intervention and Statebuilding* 2: 152–73.

Branch, Jordan. 2011. "Mapping the Sovereign State: Technology, Authority and Systemic Change." *International Organization* 65: 1–36.

2014. *The Cartographic State*. Cambridge: Cambridge University Press.

Brazys, Samuel, and Niamh Hardiman. 2015. "From 'Tiger' to 'PIIGS': Ireland and the Use of Heuristics in Comparative Political Economy." *European Journal of Political Research* 54(1): 23–42.

Brint, Stephen. 1996. *In an Age of Experts: The Changing Role of Professionals in Politics and Public Life*. Princeton, NJ: Princeton University Press.

Brodie, Bernard. 1973. *War and Politics*. New York: Macmillan.

Brooks, Stephen G., and William C. Wohlforth. 2008. *World Out of Balance: International Relations and the Challenge of American Primacy*. Princeton, NJ: Princeton University Press.

Brown, Chris, Terry Nardin, and Nicholas Rengger (eds.). 2002. *International Relations in Political Thought: Texts from the Ancient Greeks to the First World War*. New York: Cambridge University Press.

Bruckhardt, Jacob. [1860] 1958. *The Civilization of the Renaissance in Italy*, trans. S. G. C. Middlemore. New York: Harper Torchbooks.

Buckley, Walter Frederick. 1968. *Modern Systems Research for the Behavioral Scientist: A Sourcebook*. Chicago: Aldine Publishing Company.

Bukovansky, Mlada. 1999. "The Altered State and the State of Nature: The French Revolution and International Politics." *Review of International Studies* 25: 197–216.

2001. *Legitimacy and Power Politics: The American and French Revolutions in International Political Culture*. Princeton, NJ: Princeton University Press.

Bukovansky, Mlada, Ian Clark, Robyn Eckersley, Richard MacKay Price, Christian Reus-Smit, Nicholas J. Wheeler (eds.). 2012. *Special Responsibilities: Global Problems and American Power*. Cambridge: Cambridge University Press.

Bull, Hedley. 1977. *The Anarchical Society: A Study of Order in World Politics*. New York: Columbia University Press.

1984. "The Revolt against the West," in Hedley Bull and Adam Watson (eds.), *The Expansion of International Society*. Oxford: Oxford University Press.

Burbank, Jane, and Frederick Cooper. 2010. *Empires in World History: Power and the Politics of Difference*. Princeton, NJ: Princeton University Press.

Burnett, Christina Duffy. 2005. "The Edges of Empire and the Limits of Sovereignty: American Guano Islands." *American Quarterly* 57(3): 779–803.

Buruma, Ian. 1994. *The Wages of Guilt: Memories of War in Germany and Japan*. New York: Farrar Straus Giroux.

Butler, Judith. 1990. *Gender Trouble*. New York: Routledge.

1993. *Bodies that Matter*. New York: Routledge.

1997. *The Psychic Life of Power: Theories in Subjection*, Stanford, CA: Stanford University Press.

2003. "Violence, Mourning, Politics." *Studies in Gender and Sexuality* 4(1): 9–37.

Butt, Ahsan I. 2013. "Anarchy and Hierarchy in International Relations: Examining South America's War Prone Decade, 1932–41." *International Organization* 67(3): 575–607.

Buzan, Barry. 2004. *From International to World Society?: English School Theory and the Social Structure of Globalisation*. New York: Cambridge University Press.

Buzan, Barry, and George Lawson. 2015. *The Global Transformation: History, Modernity and the Making of International Relations*. Cambridge: Cambridge University Press.

Buzan, Barry, and Richard Little. 2000. *International Systems in World History*. Oxford: Oxford University Press.

Buzan, Barry, and Richard Little. 2011. "International Systems in World History: Remaking the Study of International Relations," in Stephen Hobden and

John M. Hobson (eds.), *Historical Sociology of International Relations.* Cambridge: Cambridge University Press, pp. 200–22.

Campbell, David. 1988. *Writing Security: United States Foreign Policy and the Politics of Identity.* Twin Cities: University of Minnesota Press.

Calder, Kent E. 2007. *Embattled Garrisons: Comparative Base Politics and American Globalism.* Princeton, NJ: Princeton University Press.

Caprioli, Mary, and Peter F. Trumbore. 2003. "Identifying 'Rogue' States and Testing their Interstate Conflict Behavior." *European Journal of International Relations* 9(3): 377–406.

Carpenter, R. Charli. 2007. "Studying Issue (Non)Adoption in Transnational Advocacy Networks." *International Organization* 61(3): 643–67.

2011. "Vetting the Advocacy Agenda: Network Centrality and the Paradox of Weapons Norms." *International Organization* 65(1): 69–102.

2014. "Lost Causes": Agenda Vetting in Global Issue Networks and the Shaping of Human Security. Ithaca, NY: Cornell University Press.

Carr, E. H. [1939] 2001. *The Twenty Years' Crisis, 1919–1939.* Reissued with a new introduction by Michael Cox. London: Palgrave Macmillan.

Cartledge, Paul. 1994. "The Greeks and Anthropology." *Anthropology Today* 10(3): 3–6.

Castells, Manuel. 2008. "The New Public Sphere: Global Civil Society, Communication Networks, and Global Governance." *Ann Am Acad Political Soc Sci* 616(1): 78–93.

Cederman, Lars-Erik, Kristian S. Gleditsch, and Halvard Buhaug. 2013. *Inequality, Grievances, and Civil War.* New York: Cambridge University Press.

Chandler, David G. 2006. *Empire in Denial: The Politics of State-Building.* New York: Pluto Press.

Chang, Michael G. 2007. *A Court on Horseback: Imperial Touring and the Construction of Qing Rule, 1680–1785.* Cambridge, MA: Harvard University Asia Center.

1960. "Chairman Liu Shao-chi's Speech at the State Banquet In Honour of President Toure." *Peking Review,* September 14.

Chatterjee, Partha. 1993. *The Nation and Its Fragments: Colonial and Postcolonial Histories.* Princeton, NJ: Princeton University Press.

Chesterman, Simon. 2008. "Globalization Rules: Accountability, Power, and the Prospects of Global Administrative Law." *Global Governance* 14(1): 39–52.

Chin, Christine B. N. 2009. "Claiming Race and Racelessness in International Studies." *International Studies Perspectives* 10:92–98.

Chipman, John. 1989. *French Power in Africa.* Oxford: Blackwell.

Chowdhry, Geeta, and Sheila Nair. 2004. *Power, Postcolonialism and International Relations: Reading Race, Gender and Class.* London: Taylor & Francis.

Chung, Seungwha Andy, Harbir Singh, and Kyungmook Lee. 2000. "Complementarity, Status Similarity and Social Capital as Drivers of Alliance Formation." *Strategic Management Journal* 21(1): 1–22.

Claassen, Rutger. 2014. "Capability Paternalism," *Economics and Philosophy* 30(1): 57–73.

Clark, Ian. 1989. *The Hierarchy of States: Reform and Resistance in the International Order*. Cambridge: Cambridge University Press.

2005. *Legitimacy in International Society*. Oxford: Oxford University Press.

2011. *Hegemony in International Society*. Oxford: Oxford University Press.

Clarke, Duncan, and Daniel O'Connor. 1993. "U.S. Base Rights Payments after the Cold War." *Orbis* 37(3): 441–457.

Coase, Ronald H. 1937. "The Nature of the Firm." *Economica* 16(4): 386–405.

Cohen, Albert. 1956. *Delinquent Boys: The Culture of the Gang*. London: Routledge & Kegan Paul.

Cohen, Shlomo. 2013. "Nudging and Informed Consent." *American Journal of Bioethics* 13(6): 3–11.

Cohen, Tom, and Dana Davidsen. 2014. "What can Obama do about Russia's invasion of Crimea?" CNN, March 4. Available at http://edition.cnn.com/2014/03/03/politics/us-ukraine-options/ (accessed April 15, 2014).

Collins, Harry, and Robert Evans. 2007. *Rethinking Expertise*. Chicago: University of Chicago Press.

Collins, Randall. 2004. "Civilizations as Zones of Prestige and Contact," in Said Amir Arjormand and Edward A. Tiryakian (eds.), *Rethinking Civilizational Analysis*. New York: Sage, pp. 132–47.

Conley, Sarah. 2013. *Against Autonomy: Justifying Coercive Paternalism*. Cambridge: Cambridge University Press.

Constantinou, Costas M., and Oliver P. Richmond. 2005. "The Long Mile of Empire: Power, Legitimacy and the UK Bases in Cyprus." *Mediterranean Politics* 10(1): 65–84.

Cooley, Alexander. 2001. "Imperial Wreckage: Property Rights, Sovereignty and Security in the Post-Soviet States," *International Security* 26(3): 55–67

2003. "Thinking Rationally about Hierarchy and Global Governance." *Review of International Political Economy* 10(4): 672–84.

2005. *The Logics of Hierarchy: The Organization of Empires, States and Military Occupations*. Ithaca, NY: Cornell University Press.

2008. *Base Politics: Democratic Change and the U.S. Military Oversea*. Ithaca, NY: Cornell University Press.

2012. *Great Games, Local Rules: the New Great Power Contest in Central Asia*. New York: Oxford University Press.

2014. "U.S. Bases and Democratic Politics in Central Asia," in Carnes Lord and Andrew Eirkson (eds.), *Rebalancing US Forces: basing and Forward Presence in the Asia-Pacific*. Annapolis, MD: US Naval Institute Press.

Cooley, Alexander, and James Ron. 2002. "The NGO Scramble: Organizational Insecurity and the Political Economy of Transnational Action." *International Security* 27(1):5–39.

Cooley, Alexander, and Daniel H. Nexon. 2013. "'The Empire Will Compensate You': The Structural Dynamics of the US Overseas Basing Network." *Perspectives on Politics* 11(4):1034–50.

Cooley, Alexander, and Hendrik Spruyt. 2009. *Contracting States: Sovereign Transfers in International Relations*. Princeton, NJ: Princeton University Press.

Council of Europe. Parliamentary Assembly and Dick Marty. 2006. *Alleged Secret Detentions and Unlawful Inter-State Transfers Involving Council of Europe*

Member States: Draft Report, Part II (explanatory memorandum). Brussels: Council of Europe Parliamentary Assembly.

Crabb, Jr., Cecil V. 1968. *Nations in a Multipolar World*. New York: Harper & Row.

Crossley, Pamela Kyle. 1999. *A Translucent Mirror: History and Identity in Qing Imperial Ideology*. Berkeley: University of California Press.

1990. *Orphan Warriors: Three Manchu Generations and the End of the Qing World*. Princeton, NJ: Princeton University Press.

Crawford, James. 2006. *The Creation of States in International Law*. New York: Cambridge University Press.

Crawford, Neta C. 2002. *Argument and Change in World Politics: Ethics, Decolonization, and Humanitarian Intervention*. New York: Cambridge University Press.

Crumley, Carole L. 1987. "Celtic Settlement before the Conquest: The Dialectics of Landscape and Power," in Carole L. Crumley and William H. Marquardt (eds.), *Regional Dynamics: Burgundian Landscapes in Historical Perspective*. San Diego: Academic Press.

Darby, Phillip, and A. J. Paolini. 1994. "Bridging International Relations and Postcolonialism." *Alternatives* 19(3):371–97.

Darwin, John. 2013. *Unfinished Empire: The Global Expansion of Britain*. New York: Bloomsbury.

2008. *After Tamerlane: The Global History of Empire since 1405*. New York: Bloomsbury.

De Certeau, Michel. 1980. *L'Invention du quotidien. 1. Arts de faire*. Paris: Gallimard.

De Grauwe, P. 2012. *Economics of Monetary Union*. Oxford: Oxford University Press.

Dearden, Lizzie. 2015. "Yazidi Sex Slaves Undergoing Surgery to 'Restore Virginity' after Being Raped by ISIS Militants," *The Independent*, April 27, 2015, available at www.independent.co.uk/news/world/middle-east/yazidi-sex-slaves-undergoi ... surgery-to-restore-virginity-after-being-raped-by-isis-militants-10207352.html (accessed May 25, 2015).

Delbrück, Jost. 1993. "International Law and Military Forces Abroad: U.S. Military Presence in Europe, 1945–1965," in Simon W. Duke and Wolfgang Krieger (eds.), *U.S. Military Forces in Europe: the Early Years, 1945–1970*. Boulder, CO: Westview, pp. 83–115.

Department of Defense. 2013. *Base Structure Report: FY 2013 Baseline*. Washington, DC: DOD.

Dickenson, Edwin DeWitt. 1972. *The Equality of States in International Law*. New York: Arno Press (original edition 1920; reprint).

Diefenbach, Thomas, and John A. A. Silince. 2011. "Formal and Informal Hierarchy in Different Types of Organization." *Organization Studies* 32(11): 1515–37.

Dirks, Nicholas B. 2001. *Castes of Mind: Colonialism and the Making of Modern India*. Princeton, NJ: Princeton University Press.

2006. *The Scandal of Empire: India and the Creation of Imperial Britain*. Cambridge, MA: Harvard University Press.

Donnelly, Jack. 2006. "Sovereign Inequalities and Hierarchy in Anarchy: American Power and International Society." *European Journal of International Relations* 12(2):139–70.

2009. "Rethinking Political Structures: From 'Ordering Principles' to 'Vertical Differentiation' – And Beyond." *International Theory* 1(1):49–86.

2012a. The Differentiation of International Societies: An Approach to Structural International Theory. *European Journal of International Relations* 18(1):151–76.

2012b. The Elements of the Structures of International Systems. *International Organization* 66(4):609–43.

2015a. "The Discourse of Anarchy in IR." *International Theory* 7(3):393–425.

2015b. "Normative versus Taxonomic Humanity: Varieties of Human Dignity in the Western Tradition." *Journal of Human Rights* 14(1):1–22.

Dooley, N. 2014. "Growing Pains? Rethinking the 'Immaturity' of the European Periphery." *Millennium* 42(3):936–46.

Doty, Roxanne L. 1996. *Imperial Encounters: The Politics of Representation in North-South Relations*. Minneapolis: University of Minnesota Press.

Dowdall, J. 1972. "Mintoff's Malta: Problems of Independence." *The World Today* 28(5):189–95.

Downs, George W., David M. Rocke, and Peter N. Barsoom. 1996. "Is the Good News about Compliance Good News about Cooperation?" *International Organization* 50(3):379–406.

Doyle, Michael W. 1983. "Kant, Liberal Legacies, and Foreign Affairs." *Philosophy and Public Affairs* 12 (3):205–35.

1986. *Empires*. Ithaca, NY: Cornell University Press.

DuBois, Thomas David. 2011. *Religion and the Making of Modern East Asia*. Cambridge: Cambridge University Press.

Duby, Georges. 1980 [1978]. *The Three Orders: Feudal Society Imagined*. Chicago: University of Chicago Press.

Duffield, Mark. 2001. *Global Governance and the New Wars*. New York: Zed Books.

Duflo, E. 2014. "Paternalism versus Freedom?" Tanner lectures, May.

Duke, Simon. 1989. *United States Military Forces and Installations in Europe*. Stockholm: SIPRI and Oxford University Press.

Duke, Simon, and Wolfgang Krieger (eds.). 1993. *U.S. Military Forces in Europe: The Early Years, 1945–1970*. Boulder, CO: Westview Press.

1966. *Homo hierarchicus. Le système des castes et ses implications*. Paris: Gallimard.

Dumont, Louis. 1980. *Homo Hierarchicus: The Caste System and Its Implications*, complete English edition, revised. Chicago: University of Chicago Press.

Dunne, Tim. 1998. *Inventing International Society*. London: Macmillan.

2003. "Society and Hierarchy in International Relations." *International Relations* 17(3):303–20.

Duursma, Jorri C. 1996. *Fragmentation and the International Relations of Micro-States: Self-Determination and Statehood*. Cambridge: Cambridge University Press.

Duverger, Maurice (ed.). 1980. *Le Concept d,empire*. Paris: Presses Universitaires de France.

Dworkin, Gerald. 1972. "Paternalism." *The Monist* 56:64–84.

2013. "Defining Paternalism," in Christian Coons and Michael Weber (eds.), *Paternalism: Theory and Practice*. New York: Cambridge University Press, pp. 25–38.

Ebrahim, Alnoor, and Edward Weisband (eds.). 2007. *Global Accountabilities: Participation, Pluralism, and Public Ethics*. New York: Cambridge University Press.

Eckstein, Harry. 1975. "Case Study and Theory in Political Science," in Fred I. Greenstein and Nelson W. Polsby (eds.), *Handbook of Political Science*. Reading, MA: Addison-Wesley.

Edkins, Jenny, Veronique Pin-Fat, and Michael J. Shapiro. 2004. *Sovereign Lives: Power in Global Politics*. New York: Psychology Press.

Egan, John W. 2006. "The Future of Criminal Jurisdiction over the Deployed American Soldier: Four Major Trends in Bilateral U.S. Status of Forces Agreements." *Emory International Law Review* 20:291–344.

Ehrenreich, Robert M., Carole L. Crumley, and Janet E. Levy(eds.). 1995. *Heterarchy and the Analysis of Complex Societies*. Arlington, VA: American Anthropological Association.

Eisenstadt, S. N. 1993 [1963]. *The Political System of Empires*. New Brunswick, NJ: Transaction Publishers.

Eldridge, Robert D. 2001. *The Origins of the Bilateral Okinawa Problem: Okinawa in Postwar U.S.-Japan Relations, 1945–1952*. New York: Garland Press.

Ellinas, A. A. 2013. "The Rise of Golden Dawn: The New Face of the Far Right in Greece." *South European Society and Politics* 2013:1–23.

Elliott, Mark C. 2006. "Ethnicity in the Qing Eight Banners," in Pamela Kyle Crossley, Helen F. Sui, and Donald S. Sutton (eds.), *Empire at the Margins: Culture, Ethnicity and Frontier in Early Modern China*. Berkeley: University of California Press, pp. 27–57.

2001. *The Manchu Way: The Eight Banners and Ethnic Identity in Late Imperial China*. Stanford, CA: Stanford University Press.

Elster, Jon. 2000. "Rational Choice History: A Case of Excessive Ambition." *American Political Science Review* 94(3):685–95.

Elverskog, Johan. 2006. *Our Great Qing: The Mongols, Buddhism, and the State in Late Imperial China*. Honolulu: University of Hawaii Press.

Enloe, Cynthia H. 1990. *The Morning After: Sexual Politics at the End of the Cold War*. Berkeley: University of California Press.

2000. *Bananas, Beaches and Bases: Making Feminist Sense of International Politics*. Berkeley: University of California Press.

Epstein, Charlotte. 2014. "The Postcolonial Perspective: An Introduction." *International Theory* 6(2):294–311.

Erickson, Andrew S., Ladwig C. Walter III, and Justin D. Mikolay. 2010. "'Diego Garcia and the United States' Emerging Indian Ocean Strategy." *Asian Security* 6(3):214–37.

Erickson, Richard J. 1994. "Status of Forces Agreements: A Sharing of Sovereign Prerogative." *Air Force Law Review* 37:137–53.

Farquhar, David M. 1978. "Emperor as Bodhisattva in the Governance of the Ch'ing Empire." *Harvard Journal of Asiatic Studies* 38(1):5–34.

Farrell, Henry, and Martha Finnemore. 2013. "The End of Hypocrisy: American Foreign Policy in the Age of Leaks." *Foreign Affairs* 2013:22–6.

Farrell, Theo. 2005. "World Culture and Military Power." *Security Studies* 14(3): 448–88.

Fassin, Didier. 2011. *Humanitarian Reason*. Berkeley: University of California Press.

Fassin, Didier, and R. Rechtman. 2009. *The Empire of Trauma: An Inquiry into the Condition of Victimhood*. Princeton, NJ: Princeton University Press.

Fazal, Tanisha M. 2007. *State Death: The Politics and Geography of Conquest, Occupation and Annexation*. Princeton, NJ: Princeton University Press.

Fearon, James D., and David D. Laitin. 2004. "Neotrusteeship and the Problem of Weak States." *International Security* 28:5–43.

Feldman, Ilana, and Miriam Ticktin. 2011. "Government and Humanity," in Ilana Feldman and Miriam Ticktin(eds.), *In the Name of Humanity: The Government of Threat and Care*. Durham, NC: Duke University Press, pp. 1–27.

Ferguson, Yale H., and Richard W. Mansbach. 2008. *A World of Polities: Essays on Global Politics*. London: Taylor & Francis.

Fidler, David P. 2001. "The Return of the Standard of Civilization." *Chicago Journal of International Law* 2(1):137–57.

Finnemore, Martha. 2009. "Legitimacy, Hypocrisy, and the Social Structure of Unipolarity: Why Being a Unipole Isn't All It's Cracked Up to Be." *World Politics* 61(1):58–85.

   2003. *The Purpose of Intervention: Changing Beliefs about the Use of Force*. Ithaca, NY: Cornell University Press.

Finnemore, Martha, and Kathryn Sikkink. 1998. "International Norm Dynamics and Political Change." *International Organization* 52(4):887–917.

Flathman, Richard E. 1980. *The Practice of Political Authority: Authority and the Authoritative*. Chicago: University of Chicago Press.

Foreign Languages Press. 1964. *Afro-Asian Solidarity against Imperialism: A Collection of Documents, Speeches and Press Interviews from the Visits of Chinese Leaders to Thirteen African and Asian Countries*. Beijing.

Foucault, Michel. 2007. *Security, Territory, and Population*. New York: Palgrave.

Fourcade, M. 2013. "The Material and Symbolic Construction of the BRICs: Reflections Inspired by the RIPE." *Review of International Political Economy* 20(2):256–67.

Frank, Andre Gudre. 1978. *Dependent Accumulation and Underdevelopment*. New York: Monthly Review Press.

Frieden, Jeffry A. 1994. "International Investment and Colonial Control: A New Interpretation." *International Organization* 48(4):559.

Friedman, Richard. 1958. "On the Concept of Authority in Political Philosophy," in Carl J. Friedrich (ed.), *Authority*. Cambridge, MA: Harvard University Press, pp. 56–91.

Frykenberg, Robert Eric. 1993. "Constructions of Hinduism at the Nexus of History and Religion." *Journal of interdisciplinary history* 23(3): 523–50.

Frye, Northrop. 1990. "The Stage Is All the World," in Robert D. Denham (ed.), *Myth and Metaphor: Selected Essays 1974–1988*. Charlottesville: University Press of Virginia.

Fukuyama, Francis. 1992. *The End of History and the Last Man.* New York: Free Press.

Gallagher, Julia. 2014. "Chopping the World into Bits: Africa, the World Bank, and the Good Governance Norm." *International Theory* 6(2):332–49.

Galtung, Johan. 1971. "A Structural Theory of Imperialism." *Journal of Peace Research* 8(2):81–117.

Garren, David. 2006. "Paternalism, Part I." *Philosophical Books* 47(4):334–41.

2007. "Paternalism, Part II." *Philosophical Books* 48(1):50–9.

Geldenhuys, Deon. 1990. *Isolated States: A Comparative Analysis.* Cambridge: Cambridge University Press.

Gereffi, Gary, John Humphrey, and Timothy Sturgeon. 2005. "The Governance of Global Value Chains." *Review of International Political Economy* 12(1):78–104.

Gerson, Joseph, and Bruce Birchard (eds.). 1991. *The Sun Never Sets: Confronting the Network of Foreign U.S. Military Bases.* Boston, South End Press.

Gert, Bernard, and Charles Culver. 1976. "Paternalistic Behavior," *Philosophy and Public Affairs* 6:45–58.

Gilpin, Robert. 1975. *U.S. Power and the Multinational Corporation: The Political Economy of Direct Foreign Investment.* New York: Basic Books.

1981. *War and Change in World Politics.* Cambridge: Cambridge University Press.

Giurlando, Philip. 2012. "Vicarious Evaluation: How European Integration Changes National Identities." *Review of European and Russian Affairs* 7(2):1–14.

Glanville, Luke. 2014. *Sovereignty and the Responsibility to Protect: A New History.* Chicago: University of Chicago Press.

Goddard, Stacie E. 2009. "Brokering Change: Networks and Entrepreneurs in International Politics." *International Theory* 1(2):249–81.

Goebel, Julius. 1923. *The Equality of States: A Study in the History of Law.* New York: Columbia University Press.

Goffman, Erving. 1963. *Stigma: Notes on the Management of Spoiled Identity.* London: Penguin.

1967. *Interaction Rituals: Essays on Face-to-face Behavior.* New York: Doubleday.

Goh, Evelyn. 2013. *The Struggle for Order: Hegemony, Hierarchy, and Transition in Post–Cold War East Asia.* Oxford: Oxford University Press.

Goldman, Michael. 2001. "The Birth of a Discipline: Producing Authoritative Green Knowledge, World Bank-Style." *Ethnography* 2(2):191–217.

Goldstein, Judith, Miles Kahler, Robert O. Keohane, and Anne-Marie Slaughter (eds.). 2001. *Legalization and World Politics.* Cambridge, MA: MIT Press.

Gourevitch, Peter A., David A. Lake, and Janice Gross Stein. 2012. *The Credibility of Transnational NGOs: When Virtue Is Not Enough.* Cambridge: Cambridge University Press.

Grahl, John, and Paul Teague. 2013. "Reconstructing the Eurozone: The Role of EU Social Policy." *Cambridge Journal of Economics* 37(3):677–92.

Grant, Ruth W., and Robert O. Keohane. 2005. "Accountability and Abuses of Power in World Politics." *American Political Science Review* 99(1):29–43.

Green, Donald P., and Ian Shapiro. 1995. *Pathologies of Rational Choice Theory: A Critique of Applications in Political Science.* New Haven, CT: Yale University Press.

Grey, Stephen. 2006. *Ghost Plane: The True Story of the CIA Torture Program.* New York: St Martins Press.

Grieco, Joseph M. 1988. "Anarchy and the Limits of Cooperation: A Realist Critique of the Newest Liberal Institutionalism." *International Organization* 42(3):485–507.

Gries, Peter Hays. 2005. "Social Psychology and the Identity-Conflict Debate: Is a 'China Threat' Inevitable?" *European Journal of International Relations* 11(2):235–65.

Griffith, William E. 1964. *The Sino-Soviet Rift.* Cambridge, MA: MIT Press.

Grill, Kalle. 2007. "The Normative Core of Paternalism." *Res Publica* 13:441–58.

Grint, K. 2010. "The Sacred in Leadership: Separation, Sacrifice and Silence." *Organization Studies* 31(1):89–107.

Gross, Leo. 1948. "The Peace of Westphalia, 1648–1948." *American Journal of International Law* 42(1):20–41.

Grovugui, Siba. 2006. *Beyond Eurocentrism and Anarchy: Memories of International Order and Institutions.* London: Palgrave Macmillan.

Grynaviski, Eric, and Amy Hsieh. 2015. "Hierarchy and Judicial Institutions: Arbitration and Ideology in the Hellenistic World." *International Organization* 69(3):697–729.

Guilhot, Nicolas (ed.). 2011. *The Invention of International Relations Theory.* New York: Columbia University Press.

Guzzini, Stefano 2006. "From (Alleged) Unipolarity to the Decline of Multilateralism? A Power-Theoretical Critique," in Edward Newman, Ramesh C. Thakur, and John Tirman (eds.), *Multilateralism under Challenge? Power, International Order, and Structural Change.* Tokyo: United Nations University Press, pp. 119–38.

Haas, Ernst B. 1964. *Beyond the Nation State: Functionalism and International Organization.* Stanford, CA: Stanford University Press.

Hafner-Burton, Emilie M., and Alexander H. Montgomery. 2006. "Power Positions: International Organizations, Social Networks, and Conflict." *Journal of Conflict Resolution* 50(1):3–27.

Hafner-Burton, Emillie M., Miles Kahler, and Alexander Montgomery. 2009. "Network Analysis for International Relations." *International Organization* 63(3):559–92.

Halpern, Abraham M. 1961. "The Foreign Policy Uses of the Chinese Revolutionary Model." *China Quarterly* 7:1–16.

Hannerz, Ulf. 1989. "Culture between Center and Periphery: Toward a Macroanthropology." *Ethnos* 54(3–4):200–16.

Hansen, Jonathan M. 2011. *Guantánamo Bay: An American History.* New York: Hill & Wang.

Hansen, Lene. 2000. "Gender, Nation, Rape: Bosnia and the Construction of Security." *International Feminist Journal of Politics* 3(1):55–75.

Hardt, Micheal, and Antonio Negri. 2001. *Empire.* Cambridge, MA: Harvard University Press.

Harkavy, Robert E. 1989. *Bases Abroad*. Oxford: Oxford University Press and SIPRI.
  2005. "Thinking about Basing." *Naval War College Review* 58(3):12–42.
Harrell-Bond, Barbara. 1986. *Imposing Aid: Emergency Assistance to Refugees*. New York: Oxford University Press.
Hartogh, Den. 2011. "Can Consent be Presumed?" *Journal of Applied Philosophy* 28(3):294–307.
Haskell, T. L. (ed.). 1984. *The Authority of Experts: Studies in History and Theory*. Bloomington: Indiana University Press.
Havercroft, Jonathan. 2011. *Captives of Sovereignty*. New York: Cambridge University Press.
  2012. "Was Westphalia 'All That'? Hobbes, Bellarmine, and the Norm of Non-Intervention." *Global Constitutionalism* 1(1):120–40.
Hebdige, Dick. 2003. *Subculture: The Meaning of Style*. London: Routledge.
Hechter, Michael. 2013. *Alien Rule*. Cambridge: Cambridge University Press.
Hedlund, Gunnar. 1986. "The Hypermodern MNC: A Heterarchy?" *Human Resource Management* 25(1):9–35.
Henderson, Errol A. 2013. "Hidden in Plain Sight: Racism in International Relations Theory." *Cambridge Review of International Affairs* 26(1):71–92.
Henrich, J., R. McElreath, A. Barr, J. Ensminger, C. Barrett, et al. 2006. "Costly Punishment across Human Societies." *Science* 312(5781):1767–70.
Herz, John H. 1959. *International Politics in the Atomic Age*. New York: Columbia University Press.
Herzfeld, Michael. 1987. *Anthropology through the Looking-Glass: Critical Ethnography in the Margins of Europe*. Cambridge: Cambridge University Press.
  2013. "The European Crisis and Cultural Intimacy." *Studies in Ethnicity and Nationalism* 13(3):491–7.
Hill, David Jayne. 1911. *World Organization as Affected by the Nature of the Modern State*. New York: Columbia University Press.
Hinsley, F. H. 1986. *Sovereignty*, 2nd edn. New York: Cambridge University Press.
Hoare, Michael. 1986. *The Seychelles Affair*. London: Paladin.
Hobson, John A. 1922. *Problems of a New World Order*. New York: Macmillan.
Hobson, John M. 2012. "The Twin Self-Delusions of IR: Why, Hierarchy, and Not, Anarchy, Is the Core Concept of IR." *Millennium* 42(3):557–75.
  2013. *The Eurocentric Conception of World Politics*. Cambridge: Cambridge University Press.
  2014. "The Twin Self-Delusions of IR: Why 'Hierarchy' and Not 'Anarchy' Is the Core Concept of IR." *Millennium* 42(3):557–75.
Hobson, John M., and J. C. Sharman. 2005. "The Enduring Place of Hierarchy in World Politics: Tracing the Social Logics of Hierarchy and Political Change." *European Journal of International Relations* 11(1):63–98.
Hochshild, Adam. 2006. *Bury the Chains Prophets and Rebels in the Fight to Free an Empire's Slaves*. San Francisco: Mariner Books.
Hodges, Charles. 1931. *The Background of International Relations: Our World Horizons, National and International*. New York: Wiley.

Hofstadter, Douglas R. 1979. *Gödel, Escher, Bach: An Eternal Golden Braid.* New York: Basic Books.

Holmes, Marcus. 2011. "Something Old, Something New, Something Borrowed: Representations of Anarchy in International Relations Theory." *International Relations of the Asia-Pacific* 11(2):279–308.

Hopgood, Stephen. 2009. "Moral Authority, Modernity and the Politics of the Sacred." *European Journal of International Relations* 15(2):229–55.

   2014. *The Endtimes of Human Rights.* Ithaca, NY: Cornell University Press.

Howland, Douglas, and Luise White. 2009. "Introduction: Sovereignty and the Study of States," in Douglas Howland and Luise White (eds.), *The State of Sovereignty: Territories, Laws, Populations.* Bloomington: Indiana University Press, pp. 1–18.

Hoyt, Paul D. 2000. "The 'Rogue State' Image in American Foreign Policy." *Global Society* 14(2):297–310.

Hudson, Alan. 2002. "Advocacy by UK-based development NGOs." *Nonprofit and Voluntary Sector Quarterly* 31(3):402–18.

Hudson, Valerie, Bonnie Ballif-Spanvill, Mary Caprioli, and Chad F. Emmett. 2012. *Sex and World Peace.* New York: Columbia University Press.

Hughes, Helen. 1964. "The Political Economy of Nauru." *Economic Records* 40(92):508–34.

   2004. "From Riches to Rags: What Are Nauru's Options and How Can Australia Help?" Centre for Independent Studies Issue Analysis 50, Sydney, Australia.

Hurd, Ian. 2007. *After Anarchy: Legitimacy and Power in the United Nations Security Council.* Princeton, NJ: Princeton University Press.

Hurrell, Andrew. 2007. *On Global Order: Power, Values, and the Constitution of International Society.* Oxford: Oxford University Press.

Hunt, Lynn. 2007. *Inventing Human Rights: A History.* New York: W.W. Norton.

Husak, Douglas N. 2003. "Legal Paternalism," in Hugh LaFollette (ed.), *The Oxford Handbook of Practical Ethics.* New York: Oxford University Press, pp. 387–412.

Hutchison, Alan. 1975. *China's African Revolution.* London: Hutchinson.

Hyde, Susan D. 2011. *The Pseudo-Democrat's Dilemma: Why Election Monitoring Became an International Norm.* Ithaca, NY: Cornell University Press.

   2012. "Why Believe International Election Monitors," In Peter Gourevitch, David Lake and Janice Gross Stein(eds.), *The Credibility of Transnational NGOs: When Virtue Is Not Enough.* New York: Cambridge University Press.

Ikenberry, G. John. 2000. *After Victory: Institutions, Strategic Restraint, and the Rebuilding of Order after Major Wars.* Princeton, NJ: Princeton University Press.

   2012. *Liberal Leviathan: The Origins, Crisis, and Transformation of the American World Order.* Princeton, NJ: Princeton University Press.

Inayatullah, Naeem, and David Blaney. 2004. *International Relations and The Problem of Difference.* London: Routledge.

International Monetary Fund. 2013. "St Kitts and Nevis: Fourth Review under the Stand-By Arrangement." Country Report 13/42. Washington, DC.

Ishay, Micheline R. 2008. *The History of Human Rights: From Ancient Times to the Globalization Era.* Berkeley: University of California Press.

Jabri, Vivienne. 2012. *The Postcolonial Subject: Claiming Politics/Governing Others in Late Modernity.* London: Routledge.

Jabri, Vivienne. 2014. "Disarming Norms: Postcolonial Agency and the Constitution of the International." *International Theory* 6(2):372–90.

Jacquot, Jean. 1957. "Le Theatre du Monde." *Revue de Litterature Comparee* 31.

Jackson, Patrick Thaddeus. 2002. "Jeremy Bentham, Foreign Secretary, or the Opportunity-Costs of Neo-Utilitarian Analyses of Foreign Policy." *Review of International Political Economy* 9(4):735–53.

Jackson, Patrick Thaddeus, and Daniel H. Nexon. 1999. "Relations before States: Substance, Process and the Study of World Politics." *European Journal of International Relations* 5(3):291–332.

Jackson, Robert H. 1990. *Quasi-States: Sovereignty, International Relations and the Third World.* New York: Cambridge University Press.

Jackson, Robert H., and Carl G. Rosberg. 1982. "Why Africa's Weak States Persist: The Empirical and Juridical in Statehood." *World Politics* 35(1):1–24.

Jayawickrama, Sherine, and Neil McCullagh. 2009. "What Makes International NGOs Distinctive? Contributions, Characteristics and Challenges." The Hauser Center for Nonprofit Organizations at Harvard University. Available at https://cpl.hks.harvard.edu/files/cpl/files/distinctive_contributions_of_ngos.pdf

Jeffery, Keith. 1982. "The Eastern Arc of Empire: A Strategic View 1850–1950." *The Journal of Strategic Studies* 5(4):531–45.

Jervis, Robert. 1978. "Cooperation under the Security Dilemma." *World Politics* 30(2):167–214.

Johnson, Chalmers (ed.). 1999. *Okinawa: Cold War Island.* Cardiff, CA: Japan Policy Institute.

   2000. *Blowback: The Costs and Consequences of American Empire.* New York: Owl Books.

Johnson, Chalmers. 2004. *The Sorrows of Empire: Militarism, Secrecy and the End of the Republic.* New York: Metropolitan Books.

Johnston, Alastair Iain. 2001. "Treating International Institutions as Social Environments." *International Studies Quarterly* 45(4):487–515.

   2008. *Social States: China in International Institutions, 1980–2000.* Princeton, NJ: Princeton University Press.

   2012. "What (If Anything) Does East Asia Tell Us about International Relations Theory?" *Annual Review of Political Science* 15(1):53–78.

Jones, Branwen Gruffydd. 2008. "Race in the Ontology of International Order." *Political Studies* 56:907–27.

Kang, David C. 2004. "The Theoretical Roots of Hierarchy in International Relations." *Australian Journal of International Affairs* 58(3):337–52.

   2010a. "Hierarchy and Legitimacy in International Systems: The Tribute System in Early Modern East Asia." *Security Studies* 19(4):591–622.

   2010b. *East Asia before the West: Five Centuries of Trade and Tribute.* New York: Columbia University Press.

Kaplan, Morton A. 1957. *System and Process in International Politics*. New York: Wiley.

Kaplan, Robert D. 2005. *Imperial Grunts: The American Military on the Ground*. New York: Random House.

Kapyla, Juha, and Denis Kennedy. 2014. "Cruel to Care? Investigating the Governance of Compassion in the Humanitarian Imaginary." *International Theory* 6(2):255–92.

Kaufman, Chaim D., and Robert A. Pape. 1999. "Explaining Costly International Moral Action: Britain's Sixty-Year Campaign against the Atlantic Slave Trade." *International Organization* 53(4):631–68.

Kaufman, S. J., Richard Little, and William C. Wohlforth (eds.). 2007. *The Balance of Power in World History*. London: Palgrave.

Kayaoğlu, Turan. 2010. *Legal Imperialism: Sovereignty and Extraterritoriality in Japan, the Ottoman Empire, and China*. Cambridge: Cambridge University Press.

2010. "Westphalian Eurocentrism in International Relations Theory." *International Studies Review* 12(2):196–215.

Keck, Margaret E., and Kathryn Sikkink. 1998. *Activists beyond Borders: Advocacy Networks in International Politics*. Ithaca, NY: Cornell University Press.

Keck, Zachary. 2014. "Russia Says it's Building Naval Bases in Russia, Latin America." *The Diplomat*, February 28.

Keene, Edward. 2002. *Beyond the Anarchical Society*. Cambridge: Cambridge University Press.

2007. "A Case Study of the Construction of International Hierarchy: British Treaty-Making against the Slave Trade in the Early Nineteenth Century." *International Organization* 61(2):311.

2013. "Social Status, Social Closure and the Idea of Europe as a 'Normative Power.'" *European Journal of International Relations* 19(4):939–56.

Kelman, Steven. 1981. "Regulation and Paternalism." *Public Policy* 29(2):219–54.

Kelpie, G. 2014. "The Irish Took Austerity Lying Down: German Poll." *The Independent*, November 20.

Kennan, George F. 1951. *American Diplomacy, 1900–1950*. New York: New American Library.

Kennedy, D. 2004. "Challenging Expert Rule: The Politics of Global Governance." *Sydney Law Review* 27:1–24.

Keohane, Robert O. 2005. *After Hegemony: Cooperation and Discord in the World Political Economy*. Princeton, NJ: Princeton University Press.

2003. "Political Authority after Intervention: Gradations in Sovereignty," in J. L. Holzgrefe and Robert O. Keohane (eds.), *Humanitarian Intervention: Ethical, Legal, and Political Dilemmas*. New York: Cambridge University Press, pp. 275–98.

Kim, Taeykoon. 2011. "Contradictions of Global Accountability: The World Bank, Development NGOs, and Global Social Governance." *Journal of International and Area Studies* 18(2):23–47.

Kingston, Lindsey N., and Kathryn R. Stam. 2013. "Online Advocacy: Analysis of Human Rights NGO Websites." *Journal of Human Rights Practice* 5(1):75–95.

Kinsella, Helen. 2011. *The Image before the Weapon*. Ithaca, NY: Cornell University Press.

Kirby, Paul. 2013. "How Is Rape a Weapon of War? Feminist International Relations, Modes of Critical Explanation, and the Study of Wartime Sexual Violence." *European Journal of International Relations* 19(4):797–821.

Kissinger, Henry A. 1957. *A World Restored: Metternich, Castlereagh and the Problems of Peace, 1812–22*. Boston: Houghton Mifflin.

Klabbers, Jan. 2014. "The Virtues of Expertise," in Monika Ambrus, Karin Arts, Ellen Hey, and Helena Raulus (eds.), *The Role of "Experts" in International and European Decision-Making Processes*. New York: Cambridge University Press, pp. 82–101.

Klotz, Audie. 1995. *Norms in International Relations: The Struggle Against Apartheid*. Ithaca, NY: Cornell University Press.

Kösebalaban, Hasan. 2008. "Torn Identities and Foreign Policy: The Case of Turkey and Japan." *Insight Turkey* 10(1):5–30.

Koskenniemi, Martti. 2002. *The Gentle Civilizer of Nations: The Rise and Fall of International Law 1870–1960*. New York: Cambridge University Press.

Kothari, Uma, and Rorden Wilkinson. 2013. "Global Change, Small Island State Response: Restructuring and the Perpetuation of Uncertainty in Mauritius and the Seychelles." *Journal of International Development* 25(1):92–107.

Kouvelakis, Stathis. 2012. "The End of Europeanism," in Costas Lapavitsas (ed.), *Crisis in the Eurozone*. London: Verso, pp. xiv–xxi.

Kramer, Paul A. 2006. *The Blood of Government: Race, Empire, the United States and the Philippines*. Chapel Hill: University of North Carolina Press.

2011. "Power and Connection: Imperial Histories of the United States in the World." *American Historical Review* 116(5):1348–91.

Krasner, Stephen D. 1978. *Defending the National Interest: Raw Materials Investments and U.S. Policy*. Princeton, NJ: Princeton University Press.

1999. *Sovereignty: Organized Hypocrisy*. Princeton, NJ: Princeton University Press.

2004. "Sharing Sovereignty: New Institutions for Collapsed and Failing States." *International Security* 29:85–120.

2005. "The Case for Shared Sovereignty." *Journal of Democracy* 16:69–83.

Kreps, Sarah. 2013. "Ground the Drones? The Real Problem with Unmanned Aircraft." *Foreign Affairs Snapshot*, December 4.

Kreps, Sarah, and Michael Zenko. 2014. "The Next Drone Wars: Preparing for Proliferation." *Foreign Affairs* 93(2).

Kylander, Nathalie, and Christopher Stone. 2012. "The Role of Brand in the Nonprofit Sector," *Stanford Social Innovation Review* 37.

Lafeber, Walter. 1998. *The New American Empire*, 35th Anniversary edition [1963]. Ithaca, NY: Cornell University Press.

Lake, David A. 1996. "Anarchy, Hierarchy and the Variety of International Relations." *International Organization* 50(1):1–33.

2007. "Escape from the State of Nature: Authority and Hierarchy in World Politics." *International Security* 32(1):47–79.

2009a. *Hierarchy in International Relations*. Ithaca, NY: Cornell University Press.

2009b. "Regional Hierarchy: Authority and Local International Order." *Review of International Studies* 35(S1): 35–58.

2010. "Rightful Rules: Authority, Order, and the Foundations of Global Governance." *International Studies Quarterly* 54(3): 587–613.

2013. "Legitimating Power: The Domestic Politics of U.S. International Hierarchy." *International Security* 38(2): 74–111.

Lake, David A. and Wendy H. Wong. 2009. "The Politics of Networks: Interests, Power, and Human Rights" in Miles Kahler, ed. *Networked Politics: Agency, Power, and Governance*. Ithaca, NY: Cornell University Press, pp. 127–150.

Lancaster, T. and G. Montinola. 1997. "Toward a Methodology for the Comparative Study of Political Corruption." *Crime, Law and Social Change* 3(27): 185–206.

Larmour, Peter. 2002. "Conditionality, Coercion and other Forms of 'Power': International Financial Institutions in the Pacific." *Public Administration and Development* 22(2): 249–260.

Larson, Deborah Welch, T.V. Paul, and William C. Wohlforth. 2014. "Status and World Order," in T. V. Paul, Deborah Welch Larson, and William C. Wohlforth (eds.), *Status in World Politics*. New York: Cambridge University Press.

Larson, Deborah Welch, and Alexei Shevchenko. 2010. "Status Seekers: Chinese and Russian Responses to U.S. Primacy." *International Security* 34(4):63–95.

Larson, M. S. 1984. "The Production of Expertise and Constitution of Expert Power," in T. L. Haskell (ed.), *The Authority of Experts: Studies in History and Theory*. Bloomington: Indiana University Press.

Laski, Harold J. 1921. *The Foundations of Sovereignty and Other Essays*. NY: Harcourt, Brace and Company.

Lasswell, Harold D. 1935. *World Politics and Personal Insecurity*. NY: The Free Press.

Lasswell, Harold D. and Abraham Kaplan. 1950. *Power and Society: A Framework for Analysis*. New Haven, CT: Yale University Press.

Lawrence, T. J. 1898 [1895]. *The Principles of International Law*. 2nd ed. Boston: D. C. Heath & Co.

Leacock, Stephen. 1906. *Elements of Political Science*. Boston: Houghton Mifflin Company.

Le Grand, Julian and Bill New. 2015. *Government Paternalism: Nanny State of Helpful Friend?* Princeton: Princeton University Press.

Lebow, Richard Ned. 2008. *A Cultural Theory of International Relations*. Cambridge: Cambridge University Press.

Leibold, James. 2007. *Reconfiguring Chinese Nationalism: How the Qing Frontier and Its Indigenes Became Chinese*. London: Palgrave Macmillan.

Levine, Daniel. 2012. *Recovering International Relations: The Promise of Sustainable Critique*. Oxford: Oxford University Press.

Levy, Neil. 2014. "Forced to be Free? Increasing Patient Autonomy by Constraining It." *Journal of Medical Ethics* 40(5):1–8.

Lewis, Jeffrey. 2005. "The Janus Face of Brussels: Socialization and Everyday Decision Making in the European Union." *International Organization* 59(4): 937–71.

Liberatore, Angela and Silvio Funtowicz. 2003. "'Democratising' Expertise, 'Expertising' Democracy: What does this mean, and why Bother?" *Science and Public Policy* 30(3): 146–50.

Lippmann, Walter. 1922. "The world outside and the pictures in our heads." *Public opinion* 4: 1–22.

Lipson, Charles. 2003. *Reliable Partners: How Democracies Have Made a Separate Peace*. Princeton, NJ: Princeton University Press.

Litwak, Robert S. 2001. "What's in a Name? The Changing Foreign Policy Lexicon." *Journal of International Affairs* 54(2):375–92.

Lloyd, Robert. 2008. "Promoting Global Accountability: The Experiences of the Global Accountability Project." *Global Governance* 14(3):273–81.

Long, David. 2005. "Paternalism and the Internationalization of Imperialism: J. A. Hobson on the International Government of the 'Lower Races,'" in David Long and Brian C. Schmidt (eds.), *Imperialism and Internationalism in the Discipline of International Relations*. Albany, NY: SUNY Press.

Lovejoy, Arthur O. 1936. *The Great Chain of Being: A Study of the History of an Idea*. Cambridge, MA: Harvard University Press.

Loveman, Brian. 2010. *No Higher Law: American Foreign Policy and the Western Hemisphere since 1776*. Chapel Hill: University of North Carolina Press.

Lowell, Stephanie, Brian Trelstad, and Bill Meehan. 2005. "The Ratings Game." *Stanford Social Innovation Review*, Summer.

Lu, Catherine. 2006. *Just and Unjust Interventions in World Politics*. New York: Palgrave Macmillan.

Lundestad, Geir. 2003. *The United States and Western Europe Since 1945: From "Empire" by Invitation to Transatlantic Drift*. Oxford: Oxford University Press.

Lutz, Catherine (ed.). 2009. *The Bases of Empire: The Struggle Against U.S. Military Posts*. New York: New York University Press.

Lynch, S. 2015. "Merkel Urges Greece to Follow Irish Example." *Irish Times*, March 21, available at www.irishtimes.com/news/world/europe/merkel-urges-greece-to-follow-irish-example-1.2147628 (accessed May 31, 2015).

Lynn, Matthew. 2010. *Bust: Greece, the Euro and the Sovereign Debt Crisis*. Hoboken, NJ: Wiley.

MacKinnon, Catharine. 2011. *Sex Equality*. New York: Thomson-West.

Magee, Joe C., and Adam D. Galinsky. 2008. "Social Hierarchy: The Self-Reinforcing Nature of Power and Status." *Academy of Management Annals* 2(1):351–98.

Magistretti, Paul A. 1971. "All the World a Stage: LEsthetics and Space in Medieval Drama." PhD dissertation, 2 vols, Yale School of Drama, New Haven, CT.

Mamdani, Mahmood. 2012. *Define and Rule: Native as Political Identity*. Cambridge, MA: Harvard University Press.

Mancham, James R. 2009. *Seychelles Global Citizen: The Autobiography of the Founding President of the Republic of Seychelles*. St Paul: Paragon House.

Mann, Michael. 1986. *The Sources of Social Power*, Vol. 1: *A History of Power from the Beginnings to AD 1760*. Cambridge: Cambridge University Press.

March, James C., and Johan P. Olsen. 1998. "The Institutional Dynamics of International Political Orders." *International Organizaiton* 52(4):943–69.

Marcus, Jeffrey. 2014. "U.N. Report Details ISIS Abuse of Women and Children." *New York Times*, October 3, available at www.nytimes.com/2014/10/04/world/middleeast/un-report-isis-abuse-women-children.html?_r=0.

Martin, Lisa L. 2000. *Democratic Commitments: Legislatures and International Cooperation*. Princeton, NJ: Princeton University Press.

Matthijs, Matthias, and Mark Blyth (eds.). 2015. *The Future of the Euro*. Oxford: Oxford University Press.

Matthijs, Matthias, and Kate McNamara. 2015. "'The Euro Crisis' Theory Effect: Northern Saints, Southern Sinners, and the Demise of the Eurobond." *Journal of European Integration* 37(2):229–45.

Mawby, Spencer. 2012. "Overwhelmed in a Very Small Place: The Wilson Government and the Crisis Over Anguilla." *Twentieth Century British History* 23(2):246–74.

Mayall, James. 1990. *Nationalism and International Society*. Cambridge: Cambridge University Press.

McCarthy, Thomas. 2009. *Race, Empire and the Idea of Human Development*. Cambridge: Cambridge University Press.

McCulloch, Warren S. 1945. "A Heterarchy of Values Determined by the Topology of Nervous Nets." *Bulletin of Mathematical Biophysics* 7(2):89–93.

McElroy, D. 2012. "Snipers on the Rooftops as Angela Merkel Visits Crisis-Torn Greece," October 8, available at www.telegraph.co.uk/news/worldnews/europe/greece/9594714/Snipers-on-the-rooftops-as-Angela-Merkel-visits-crisis-torn-Greece.html (accessed May 31, 2015).

McNeill, William H. 1982. *The Pursuit of Power: Technology, Armed Force, and Society since AD 1000*. Chicago: University of Chicago Press.

Mead, Lawrence. 1997. "The Rise of Paternalism," in Lawrence Mead (ed.), *The New Paternalism: Supervisory Approaches to Poverty*. Washington, DC: Brookings Institution, pp. 1–38.

Mearsheimer, John J., and Stephen M. Walt. 2013. "Leaving Theory Behind: Why Simplistic Hypothesis Testing Is Bad for International Relations." *European Journal of International Relations* 19:427–58.

Mehta, Uday Singh. 1999. *Liberalism and Empire*. Chicago: University of Chicago Press.

Metcalf, Thomas R. 1997. *Ideologies of the Raj*. Cambridge: Cambridge University Press.

Meyer, John W., John Boli, George M. Thomas, and Francisco O. Ramirez. 1997. "World-Society and the Nation-State." *American Journal of Sociology* 103(1):144–66.

Meyer, John W., and Ronald L. Jepperson. 2000. "The 'Actors' of Modern Society: The Cultural Construction of Social Agency." *Sociological Theory* 18(1):100–20.

Miller, Benjamin. 2002. *When Opponents Cooperate: Great Power Conflict and Collaboration in World Politics*. Ann Arbor: University of Michigan Press.

Milner, Helen. 1991. "The Assumption of Anarchy in International Relations Theory: A Critique." *Review of International Studies* 17(1):67–85.

Milliken, Jennifer. 1999. "The Study of Discourse in International Relations." *European Journal of International Relations* 5(2):225–54.

Mitchell, George E., and Sarah Stroup. N.d. "The Power of Reputation for INGOs." Working paper, available on request.

2016. "The Reputations of NGOs: Peer Evaluations of effectiveness." *The Review of International Organizations*: 1–23.

Mitrany, David. 1933. *The Progress of International Government*. New Haven: Yale University Press.

Moon, Katharine Hyung-Sun. 2012. *Protesting America: Democracy and the US-Korea Alliance*. Berkeley: University of California Press, 2012.

Morgenthau, Hans J. 1946. *Scientific Man versus Power Politics*. Chicago: University of Chicago Press.

1951. *In Defense of the National Interest: A Critical Examination of American Foreign Policy*. New York: Alfred A. Knopf.

Morozov, Viacheslav. 2013. "Subaltern Empire? Toward a Postcolonial Approach to Russian Foreign Policy." *Problems of Post-Communism* 60(6):16–28.

Morrow, James D. 2014. *Order within Anarchy: The Laws of War as an International Institution*. New York: Cambridge University Press.

Mosse, D. 2011. *Adventures in Aidland: The Anthropology of Professionals in International Development*. New York: Berghahn Books.

Mosser, Michael W. 2001. "Engineering Influence: The Subtle Power of Small States in the CSCE/OSCE," in Erich Reiter and Heinz Gärtner (eds.), *Small States and Alliances*. New York: Physica-Verlag, pp. 456–466.

Motyl, Alexander J. 2006. "Is Everything Empire? Is Empire Everything?" *Comparative Politics* 38(2):229–49.

2013. *Imperial Ends: The Decay, Collapse, and Revival of Empires*. New York: Columbia University Press.

Moyes, Richard, and Thomas Nash. 2011. "Global Coalitions: An Introduction to Working in International Civil Society Partnerships." *Action on Armed Violence*.

Mill, John Stuart. 1975. *On Liberty*. New York: W.W. Norton.

Milner, Helen. 1991. "The Assumption of Anarchy in International Relations Theory: A Critique." *Review of International Studies* 17:67–85.

Murdie, Amanda, and David R. Davis. 2012. "Shaming and Blaming: Using Events Data to Assess the Impact of Human Rights INGOs." *International Studies Quarterly* 56(1):1–16.

Nadel, S. F. 1957. *The Theory of Social Structure*. Glencoe: Free Press.

Narangoa, Li, and Robert Cribb. 2014. *Historical Atlas of Northeast Asia, 1590–2010: Korea, Manchuria, Mongolia, Eastern Siberia*. New York: Columbia University Press.

Nash, Frank. 1957. "United States Overseas Military Bases." White House Report. Washington, DC (declassified February 1990).

Nexon, Daniel H. 2007. "Discussion: American Empire and Civilizational Practice," in Martin Hall and Patrick Thaddeus Jackson (eds.), *Civilizational Identitynu: The Production and Reproduction of "Civilizations" in International Relations*. New York: Palgrave Macmillan, pp. 109–18.

2009. *The Struggle for Power in Early Modern Europe: Religious Conflict, Dynastic Empires, and International Change*. Princeton, NJ: Princeton University Press.

Nexon, Daniel H., and Thomas Wright. 2007. "What's at Stake in the American Empire Debate." *American Political Science Review* 101(2):253–71.

Neumann, Iver B. 2014. "Status Is Cultural: Durkheimian Poles and Weberian Russians Seek Great Power Status," in T. V. Paul, Deborah Welch Larson, and William C. Wohlforth (eds.), *Status in World Politics*. New York: Cambridge University Press.

Neumann, Iver B., and Sieglinde Gstohl. 2006. "Introduction: Lilliputians in Gulliver's World," in Christine Ingebritsen, Iver B. Neumann, Sieglinde Gstohl, and Jessica Beyer (eds.), *Small States in International Relations*. Seattle: University of Washington Seattle/University of Iceland, pp. 3–38.

Neumann, Iver B., and Ole Jacob Sending. 2010. *Governing the Global Polity: Practice, Mentality, Rationality*. Ann Arbor: University of Michigan Press.

Newbury, Colin Walter. 2003. *Patrons, Clients, and Empire: Chieftaincy and Over-Rule in Asia, Africa, and the Pacific*. Oxford: Oxford University Press.

Niebuhr, Reinhold. 1932. *Moral Man and Immoral Society: A Study in Ethics and Politics*. New York: Charles Scribner's Sons.

Nincic, Miroslave. 2005. *Renegade Regimes: Confronting Deviant Behavior in World Politics*. New York: Columbia University Press.

Niva, Steve. 1998. "Tough and Tender: New World Order Masculinity and the Gulf War," in Marysia Zalewski and Jean Parpart (eds.), *The "Man" Question in International Relations* Boulder, CO: Westview Press.

North, Douglass C., and Barry R. Weingast. 1989. "Constitutions and Commitment: The Evolution of the Institutions of Public Choice in 17th Century England." *Journal of Economic History* 49(4):803–32.

Nowotny, H. 2003. "Democratising Expertise and Socially Robust Knowledge." *Science and Public Policy* 30(3):151–56.

Omissi, David. 1991. "'Martial Races': Ethnicity and Security in Colonial India 1858–1939." *War & Society* 9(1):1–27.

O'Neil, Patrick H. 2014. *Post-Communism and the Media in Eastern Europe*. London: Routledge.

Onuf, Nicholas. 1998. *The Republican Legacy in International Thought*. New York: Cambridge University Press.

Oostindie, Gert, and Inge Klinkers. 2003. *Decolonising the Caribbean: Dutch Policies in Comparative Perspective*. Amsterdam: University of Amsterdam Press.

Organski, A. F. K. 1958. *World Politics*. New York: Alfred A. Knopf.

Organski, A. F. K., and Jacek Kugler. 1980. *The War Ledger*. Chicago: University of Chicago Press.

Ogunsanwo, Alaba. 1974. *China's Policy in Africa 1958–1971*. Cambridge: Cambridge University Press.

Osgood, Robert E., and Robert W. Tucker. 1967. *Force, Order, and Justice*. Baltimore: Johns Hopkins University Press.

Osiander, Andreas. 2001. "Sovereignty, International Relations, and the Westphalian Myth." *International Organization* 55(2):251–87.

Otero, Eva. 2010. "Evaluation of Oxfam GB's Climate Change Campaign." Oxfam GB, Oxford.

Pain, Rachel. 2014. "Everyday Terrorism: Connecting Domestic Violence and Global Terrorism." *Progress in Human Geography* 38:531–50.

Pain, Rachel. 2015. "Intimate War." *Political Geography* 44:64–73.

Pain, Rachel, and S. J. Smith (eds.). 2008. *Fear, Critical Geopolitics, and Everyday Life*. Aldershot: Ashate.

Panchanathan, K., and R. Boyd. 2004. "Indirect Reciprocity Can Stabilize Cooperation without the Second-Order Free Rider Problem." *Nature* 432(7016):499–502.

Papadimitriou, Dimitris, and Sotirios Zartaloudis. 2015. "European Discourses on Managing the Greek Crisis: Denial, Distancing and the Politics of Blame," in Georgios Karyotis and Roman Gerodimos (eds.), *The Politics of Extreme Austerity: Greece in the Eurozone Crisis*. London: Palgrave Macmillan, pp. 34–45.

Paris, Roland. 2004. *At War's End: Building Peace after Civil Conflict*. Cambridge: Cambridge University Press.

Parker, Geoffrey. 1996. *The Military Revolution: Military Innovation and the Rise of the West, 1500–1800*. Cambridge: Cambridge University Press.

Paul, T.V., Deborah Welch Larson, and William C. Wohlforth. 2014. *Status in World Politics*. Cambridge: Cambridge University Press.

Pennington, Brian K. 2005. *Was Hinduism Invented? Britons, Indians, and the Colonial Construction of Religion*. Oxford: Oxford University Press.

Peterson, Susan Rae. 1977. "Coercion and Rape: The State as a Male Protection Bracket," in Mary Vetterling-Braggin, Frederick A. Elliston, and Jane English (eds.), *Feminism and Philosophy*. Totowa, NJ: Littlefield, Adams, pp. 360–71.

Pérez, Louis A. 1991. *Cuba under the Platt Amendment, 1902–1934*. Pittsburgh: University of Pittsburgh Press.

Peterson, V. Spike. 2010. "Gendered Identities, Ideologies, and Practices in the Context] of War and Militarism," in Laura Sjoberg and Sandra Via (eds.), *Gender, War, and Militarism: Feminist Perspectives*. Santa Barbara, CA: Praeger Security International, pp.17–29.

1992. "Transgressing Boundaries: Theories of Knowledge, Gender, and International Studies." *Millennium* 21(2):183–201.

Pettyjohn, Stacie L., and Alan J. Vick. 2013. *The Posture Triangle: A New Framework for U.S. Air Force Global Presence*. Washington, DC: RAND Corporation.

Pettyjohn, Stacie L., and Anne Sisson Runyan. 2013. *Global Gender Issues in a New Millennium*. Boulder, CO: Westview Press.

Pettman, Jan Jindy. 1996. *Worlding Women: Toward a Feminist International Politics*. London: Routledge.

Phillips, Andrew. 2014. "Civilising Missions and the Rise of International Hierarchies in Early Modern Asia." *Millennium* 42(3):697–717.

2011. *War, Religion and Empire*. Cambridge: Cambridge University Press.

Phillips, Andrew, and Jason C. Sharman. 2015. *International Order in Diversity: War, Trade and Rule in the Indian Ocean*. Cambridge: Cambridge University Press.

Philpott, Daniel. 2001. *Revolutions in Sovereignty: How Ideas Shaped Modern International Relations*. Princeton, NJ: Princeton University Press.

Piao, Lin. 1965. "Long Live the Victory of People's War!" *Peking Review* 35: 10.

Pickles, Kate. 2015. "ISIS Slaughters 400 Mostly Women and Children in Ancient Syria City of Palmyra Where Hundreds of Bodies Line the Street," *Daily Mail*, May 24, available at www.dailymail.co.uk/news/article-3094956/ISIS-slaughters-400-women-children-ancient-Syria-city-Palmyra-hundreds-bodies-line-street.html (accessed May 25, 2015).

Pico della Mirandola, Giovanni. 1998. *On the Dignity of Man*. Indianapolis, IN: Hackett.

Pisani-Ferry, J. 2012. *The Euro Crisis and the New Impossible Trinity* (No. 2012/01). Bruegel Policy Contribution.

Pitkin, Hanna. 1965. "Obligation and Consent, part I." *American Political Science Review* 59(4):990–999.

1966. "Obligation and Consent, part II." *American Political Science Review* 60(1):39–52.

Podolny, Joel M. 2001. "Networks as the Pipes and Prisms of the Market." *American Journal of Sociology* 107(1):33–60.

Ponzio, Richard. 2007. "Transforming Political Authority: UN Democratic Peacebuilding in Afghanistan." *Global Governance* 13(2):255–75.

Potter, Pitman B. 1922. *An Introduction to the Study of International Organization*. New York: Century Company.

Pouliot, Vincent. 2008. The Logic of Practicality: A Theory of Practice of Security Communities. *International Organization* 62(2):257–88.

2010. *International Security in Practice. The Politics of NATO-Russia Diplomacy*. Cambridge: Cambridge University Press.

2011. "Diplomats as Permanent Representatives: The Practical Logics of the Multilateral Pecking Order." *International Journal: Canada's Journal of Global Policy Analysis* 66(3):543–61.

2014. "Setting Status in Stone: The Negotiation of International Institutional Privileges," in T. V. Paul, Deborah Welch Larson, and William C. Wohlforth (eds.), *Status in World Politics*. Cambridge: Cambridge University Press.

2016a. *International Pecking Orders: The Politics and Practice of Multilateral Diplomacy*. Cambridge: Cambridge University Press.

2016b. "Hierarchy in Practice: Multilateral Diplomacy and the Governance of International Security." *European Journal of International Security* 1(1):5–26.

Power, S. A., and D. Nussbaum. 2015. "'The Fightin' Irish? Not When It Comes to Recession and Austerity," *The Guardian*, available at www.theguardian.com/science/head-quarters/2014/jul/24/the-fightin-irish-not-when-it-comes-to-recession-and-austerity (accessed May 31, 2015).

"President Toure's Speech at the Peking Rally." 1960. *Peking Review*, September 14.

Price, Richard. 1998. "Reversing the Gun Sights: Transnational Civil Society Targets Land Mines." *International Organization* 52(3):613–44.

2008. *Moral Limits and Possibility in World Politics*. New York: Cambridge University Press.

Prichard, Alex. 2011. "What Can the Absence of Anarchism Tell Us about the History and Purpose of International Relations?" *Review of International Studies* 37:1647–69.

Prybyla, Jan S. 1964. "Communist China's Economic Relations with Africa 1960–1964." *Asian Survey* 4(11):1135–43.

Pumain, Denise. 2006. *Hierarchy in Natural and Social Sciences*. New York: Springer.

Putnam, Robert D. 2000. *Bowling Alone: The Collapse and Revival of American Community*. New York: Simon & Schuster.

Qizilbash, Mozaffar. 2011. "Sudgen's Critique of Sen's Capability Approach and the Dangers of Libertarian Paternalism." *International Review of Economics* 58(1):21–42.

Ramos, Jennifer M. 2013. *Changing Norms Through Actions: The Evolution of Sovereignty*. New York: Oxford University Press.

Rand, Gavin, and Kim A Wagner. 2012. "Recruiting the 'Martial Races': Identities and Military Service in Colonial India." *Patterns of Prejudice* 46(3–4):232–54.

Rawls, John. 2001. *The Law of the Peoples*. Cambridge, MA: Harvard University Press.

Rawski, Evelyn S. 1996. "Presidential Address: Re-envisioning the Qing: The Significance of the Qing Period in Chinese History." *Journal of Asian Studies* 55(4):829–50.

Rayner, S. 2003. "Democracy in the Age of Assessment: Reflections on the Roles of Expertise and Democracy in Public Sector Decision-Making." *Science and Public Policy* 30(3):161–70.

Recchia, Stefano. 2009. "Just and Unjust War Reconstruction: Just How Much Interference Can Be Justified?" *Ethics and International Affairs* 23:165–87.

Redfield, Peter. 2005. "Doctors, Borders, and Life in Crisis." *Cultural Anthropology* 20(3):328–61.

Reid, Elizabeth J., and Janelle A. Kerlin. 2006. *The International Charitable Nonprofit Subsector in the United States*. Washington, DC: Urban Institute.

Reid, Helen Dwight. 1932. *International Servitudes in Law and Practice*. Chicago: University of Chicago Press.

Reinsch, Paul S. 1900. *World Politics at the End of the Nineteenth Century, As Influenced by the Oriental Situation*. New York: Macmillan.

Renfrew, Colin, and John F. Cherry (eds.). 1986. *Peer Polity Interaction and Socio-Political Change*. Cambridge: Cambridge University Press.

Reus-Smit, Christian. 1999. *The Moral Purpose of the State: Culture, Social Identity, and Institutional Rationality in International Relations*. Princeton, NJ: Princeton University Press.

    2005. "Liberal Hierarchy and the License to Use Force." *Review of International Studies* 31(S1):71–92.

    2013. *Individual Rights and the Making of the International System*. Cambridge: Cambridge University Press.

Richardson, Hayley. 2015. "ISIS 'Using Paedophile Grooming Tactics' to Lure Young Jihadi Brides." *Newsweek*, March 16, 2015, available at www.newsweek.com/isis-using-paedophile-grooming-tactics-lure-young-jihadi-brides-314140 (accessed May 15, 2017).

Ringmar, Erik. 1996. "On the Ontological Status of the State." *European Journal of International Relations* 2(4):429–66.

2002. "The Recognition Game: Soviet Russia Against the West." *Cooperation and Conflict* 37(2):115–36.

Risse, Thomas. 2000. "Let's Argue!: Communicative Action in World Politics." *International Organization* 54(1):1–40.

Roberts, Susan M. 1995. "Small Place, Big Money: The Cayman Islands and the International Financial System." *Economic Geography* 71(3):237–56.

Ron, James, Howard Ramos, and Kathleen Rodgers. 2005. "Transnational Information Politics: NGO Human Rights Reporting, 1986–2000." *International Studies Quarterly* 49(3):557–88.

Rorem, Paul. 1993. *Pseudo-Dionysius: A Commentary on the Texts and an Introduction to Their Influence.* Oxford: Oxford University Press.

2005. *Eriugena's Commentary on the Dionysian Celestial Hierarchy.* Toronto: Pontifical Institute of Medieval Studies.

Rosenau, James. 1997. *Along the Domestic-Foreign Frontier: Exploring Governance in a Turbulent World.* Cambridge: Cambridge University Press.

Rosenberg, Justin. 2013. "The 'Philosophical Premises' of Uneven and Combined Development." *Review of International Studies* 39(3):569–97.

Roy, Kaushik. 2011. "The Hybrid Military Establishment of the East India Company in South Asia: 1750–1849." *Journal of Global History* 6(2):195–218.

2001. "The Construction of Regiments in the Indian Army: 1859–1913." *War in History* 8(2):127–48.

Roy, Tirthankar. 2013. "Rethinking the Origins of British India: State Formation and Military-Fiscal Undertakings in an Eighteenth Century World Region." *Modern Asian Studies* 47(4):1125–56.

Ruggie, John G. 1983. "Continuity and Transformation in the World Polity: Toward a Neorealist Synthesis." *World Politics* 35(2):261–85.

1993. "Territoriality and Beyond: Problematizing Modernity in International Relations." *International Organization* 47(1):139–74.

(ed.). 1993. *Multilateralism Matters: The Theory and Praxis of an Institutional Form.* New York: Columbia University Press.

Rumelili, Bahar. 2003. "Liminality and Perpetuation of Conflicts: Turkish-Greek Relations in the Context of Community-Building by the EU." *European Journal of International Relations* 9(2):213–48.

Runyan, Anne Sisson, and V. Spike Peterson. 2013. *Global Gender Issues in the New Millennium.* Boulder, CO: Westview Press.

Ryner, M. 2012. "Financial Crisis, Orthodoxy and Heterodoxy in the Production of Knowledge about the EU." *Millennium* 40(3):647–73.

Sagoff, Mark. 2013. "Trust versus Paternalism." *American Journal of Bioethics* 13(6):20–1.

Sandars, Christopher T. 2000. *America's Overseas Garrisons: The Leasehold Empire.* New York: Oxford University Press.

Scarr, Deryck. 1999. *Seychelles Since 1770: History of a Slave and Post-Slavery Society.* Trenton, NJ: Africa World Press.

Schatzki, Theodore R., Karin Knorr-Cetina, and Eike von Savigny. 2001. *The Practice Turn in Contemporary Theory.* New York: Psychology Press.

Schimmelfennig, Frank. 2015. "Liberal Intergovernmentalism and the Euro Area Crisis." *Journal of European Public Policy* 22(2):77–195.

Schmidt, Brian. 1997. *The Political Discourse of Anarchy: A Disciplinary History of International Relations*. Albany, NY: SUNY Press.

Schrefler, L. 2014. "Reflections on the Different Roles of Expertise in Regulatory Policy Making," in Monika Ambrus, Karin Arts, Ellen Hey, and Helena Raulus (eds.), *The Role of "Experts" in International and European Decision-Making Processes*. New York: Cambridge University Press.

Schuman, Frederick Lewis. 1933. *International Politics: An Introduction to the Western State System*. New York: McGraw-Hill.

Schwarzenberger, Georg. 1951. *Power Politics: A Study of International Society*. 2nd edn. London: Stevens/F. A. Praeger.

Scott, James C. 1985. *Weapons of the Weak. Everyday Forms of Peasant Resistance*. New Haven, CT: Yale University Press.

  1990. *Domination and the Arts of Resistance: Hidden Transcripts*. New Haven, CT: Yale University Press.

Seth, Sanjay. 2011. "Postcolonial Theory and the Critique of International Relations." *Millennium* 40(1):167–83.

Sharman, J.C. Interviews: Basseterre, St Kitts, January 2004 and April 2013; Vaduz, Liechtenstein, January 2004 and June 2013; Avarua, Cook Islands, June 2004 and December 2009; Oranjestad, Aruba, January 2005; Nauru, August 2008; Willemstad, Curaçao, February 2009; Victoria, the Seychelles, February 2013; Charleston, Nevis, April 2013.

  2011. *The Money Laundry: Regulating Criminal Finance in the Global Economy*. Ithaca, NY: Cornell University Press.

  2013. "International Hierarchies and Contemporary Imperial Governance: A Tale of Three Kingdoms." *European Journal of International Relations* 19:189–207.

Sharp, Walter R., and Grayson L. Kirk. 1940. *Contemporary International Politics*. New York: Farrar & Rinehart.

Sheffer, Gabriel. 1997. "The Security of Small Ethnic States: A Counter Neo-Realist Argument," in Efraim Inbar and Gabriel Sheffer (eds.), *The National Security of Small States in a Changing World*. London: Frank Cass. pp. 9–40.

Shepherd, Laura. 2008. *Gender, Violence, and Security*. London: Zed Books.

Shiffrin, Seana. 2000. "Paternalism, Unconscionability Doctrine, and Accommodation." *Philosophy and Public Affairs* 29(3):205–50.

Shilliam, Robbie (ed.). 2010. *International Relations and Non-Western Thought: Imperialism, Colonialism and Investigations of Global Modernity*. London: Routledge.

  2014. "'Open the Gates Mek We Repatriate': Caribbean Slavery, Constructivism, and Hermeneutic Tensions." *International Theory* 6(2):349–72.

  2015. *The Black Pacific: Anticolonial Struggles and Oceanic Connections*. London: Bloomsbury Academic Press.

Shillington, Kevin. 2009. *History of the Modern Seychelles*. Houndsmill: Macmillan.

Shils, Edward. 1961. "Centre and Periphery," in *The Logic of Personal Knowledge: Essays Presented to Michael Polanyi*. Glencoe: Free Press, pp. 117–30.

1975. *Center and Periphery: Essays in Macrosociology.* Chicago: University of Chicago Press.

Shubert, Atika, and Bharait Naik. 2014. "From Food Recipes to AK-47s: Inside Online World of the Women of ISIS." CNN, September 10, 2014, available at www.cnn.com/2014/09/10/world/meast/iraq-syria-isis-women/ (accessed May 25, 2015).

Shumate, Michelle, Janet Fulk, and Peter Monge. 2005. "Predictors of the International HIV–AIDS INGO Network over time." *Human Communication Research* 31(2):482–510.

Siméant, Johanna. 2013. "Committing to Internationalisation: Careers of African Participants at the World Social Forum." *Social Movement Studies* 12(3): 245–63.

Simmons, Beth A. 2009. *Mobilizing for Human Rights: International Law in Domestic Politics.* Cambridge: Cambridge University Press.

Simon, Herbert A. 1976. *Administrative Behavior: A Study of Decision-Making Processes in Administrative Organization,* 3rd edn. New York: Free Press.

Simpson, Gerry. 2004. *Great Powers and Outlaw States: Unequal Sovereigns in the International Legal Order.* Cambridge: Cambridge University Press.

Singer, Peter. 2003. *Corporate Warriors: The Rise of the Privatized Military Industry.* Ithaca, NY: Cornell University Press.

Singh, Amrit, and David Berry. 2013. *Globalizing Torture: CIA Secret Detention and Extraordinary Rendition.* New York: Open Society Foundations.

Sjoberg, Laura. 2012. "Gender Hierarchy, International Structure, and the Causes of War." *International Theory* 4(1):1–38.

2013. *Gendering Global Conflict: Toward a Feminist Theory of War.* New York: Columbia University Press.

Sjoberg, Laura, and Jessica Peet. 2011. "A(nother) Dark Side of the Protection Racket: Targeting Women in Wars." *International Feminist Journal of Politics* 13(2):163–82.

Skaale, Sjurur (ed.). 2004. *The Right to National Self-Determination: The Faroe Islands and Greenland.* Leiden: Martinus Nijhoff.

Skjaelsbaek, Inger. 2001. "Sexual Violence and War: Mapping Out a Complex Relationship," *European Journal of International Relations* 7(2):211–37.

Skendaj, Elton. 2014. "International Insulation from Politics and the Challenge of State Building: Learning from Kosovo." *Global Governance* 20(3):459–81.

Skinner, Quentin. 1989. "The State," in Terence Ball, James Farr, and Russell L. Hanson (eds.), *Political Innovation and Conceptual Change.* Cambridge: Cambridge University Press.

Smith, A. 2012. "Angela Merkel Is Unshakeable as Athens Resounds with Angry Chants." *The Guardian,* October 9, available at www.theguardian.com/world/2012/oct/09/angela-merkel-unshakeable-athens-resounds (accessed May 31, 2015).

Smith, Amelia. 2014. "ISIS Publish Pamphlet on How to Treat Female Salves." *Newsweek,* December 9, 2014, available at http://europe.newsweek.com/isis-release-questions-and-answers-pamphlet-how-treat-female-slaves-290511 (accessed May 25, 2015).

Smith, M. G. 1956. "On Segmentary Lineage Systems." *Journal of the Royal Anthropological Institute of Great Britain and Ireland* 86 (2):39–80.

    1966. "A Structural Approach to Comparative Politics," in David Easton (ed.), *Varieties of Political Theories*. Englewood Cliffs, NJ: Prentice-Hall.

Snow, Philip. 1994. "China and Africa: Consensus and Camouflage," in Thomas W. Robinson and David Shambaugh (eds.), *Chinese Foreign Policy: Theory and Practice*. Oxford: Clarendon Press.

Solzhenitsyn, Aleksandr. 1963. *One Day in the Life of Ivan Denisovich*. London: Penguin.

Soros, George. 2012. "How to Save the Euro." *NY Review of Books*.

Soss, Joe, Richard Fording, and Sanford Schram. 2011. *Disciplining the Poor: Neoliberal Paternalism and the Persistent Power of Race*. Chicago: University of Chicago Press.

Spykman, Nicholas J. 1942. *America,s Strategy in World Politics: The United States and the Balance of Power*. New York: Harcourt, Brace and Company.

Stachowitsch, Saskia. 2012. "Military Gender Integration and Foreign Policy in the United States: A Feminist International Relations Perspective." *Security Dialogue* 43(4):305–21.

Stanley, Brian. 2001. "Christianity and Civilization in English Evangelical Mission Thought, 1792–1857," in Brian Stanley (ed.), *Christian Missions and the Enlightenment*. Grand Rapids, MI: Curzon Press.

Stark, David. 1999. "Heterarchy: Distributing Authority and Organizing Diversity," in John Heny Clippinger III (ed.), *The Biology of Business: Decoding the Natural Laws of Enterprise*. San Francisco: Jossey-Bass.

Steele, Brent. 2008. *Ontological Security in International Relations: Self-Identity and the IR State*. London: Routledge.

Steffek, Jens. 2010. "Public Accountability and the Public Sphere of International Governance." *Ethics and International Affairs* 24(1):45–64.

Stone, Randall W. 2011. *Controlling Institutions: International Organizations and the Global Economy*. Cambridge: Cambridge University Press.

Strang, David. 1996. "Contested Sovereignty: The Social Construction of Colonial Imperrialism," in Thomas J. Biersteker and Cynthia Weber (eds.), *State Sovereignty as Social Construct*. New York: Cambridge University Press, pp. 22–49.

Streets, Heather. 2004. *Martial Races: The Military, Race and Masculinity in British Imperial Culture, 1857–1914*. Manchester: Manchester University Press.

Stroup, Sarah S. 2012. *Borders among Activists*. Ithaca, NY: Cornell University Press.

Stroup, Sarah S., and Amanda Murdie. 2012. "There's No Place like Home: Explaining International NGO Advocacy." *Review of International Organizations* 7(4):425–48.

Stroup, Sarah S., and Wendy Wong. 2013. "Come Together? Different Pathways to International NGO Centralization." *International Studies Review* 15(2): 163–84.

Stroup, Sarah S., and Wendy Wong. 2017. *The Authority Trap: Strategic Choices of International NGOs*. Ithaca, NY: Cornell University Press.

Stuvøy, K. 2010. "Symbolic Power and (In)Security: The Marginalization of Women's Security in Northwest Russia." *International Political Sociology* 4(4):401–18.

Subotic, Jelena, and Ayşe Zarakol. 2013. "Cultural Intimacy in International Relations." *European Journal of International Relations* 19(4):915–38.

Sunstein, Cass. 1997. *Free Markets and Social Justice*. New York: Oxford University Press.

2006. "Preferences, Paternalism, and Liberty." *Royal Institute of Philosophy Supplement* 59:233–64.

2013. "Behavioral Economics and Paternalism." *Yale Law Journal* 122(7): 1826–99.

Sunstein, Cass, and Robert H. Thaler. 2003. "Libertarian Paternalism Is Not an Oxymoron." *University of Chicago Law Review* 70(4):1159–202.

Suzuki, Shogo. 2005. "Japan's Socialization into Janus-Faced European International Society." *European Journal of International Relations* 11(1): 137–64.

2009. *Civilisation and Empire: China and Japan's Encounter with the European International Society*. London: Routledge.

2014. "Journey to the West: China Debates Its 'Great Power' Identity." *Millennium* 42(3):632–50.

Swidler, Ann 2001. "What Anchors Cultural Practices," in Theodore Schatzki, K. Knorr-Cetina, and Eike von Savigny (eds.), *The Practice Turn in Contemporary Theory*. London: Routledge, pp. 83–101.

Talbott, William J. 2010. *Human Rights and Human Well-Being*. Oxford: Oxford University Press.

Tarrow, Sidney. 2005. *The New Transnational Activism*. Cambridge: Cambridge University Press.

Taylor, Ian. 2000. "The Ambiguous Commitment: The People's Republic of China and the Anti-Apartheid Struggle in South Africa." *Journal of Contemporary African Studies* 18(1):91–106.

Thaler, Robert H., and Cass R. Sunstein. 2008. *Nudge: Improving Decisions About Health, Wealth, and Happiness*. New Haven, CT: Yale University Press.

2003. "Libertarian Paternalism." *American Economic Review* 93(2):175–9.

Tharoor, Ishaan. 2015. "ISIS Burns Woman Alive for Refusing to Engage in 'Extreme' Sex Act, UN Says." *The Independent*, May 24, 2015, available at www.independent.co.uk/news/world/middle-east/isis-burns-woman-alive-for-refusing-to-engage-in-extreme-sex-act-un-says-10272832.html (accessed May 25, 2014).

Thompson, Alexander. 2009. *Channels of Power: The UN Security Council and U.S. Statecraft in Iraq*. Ithaca, NY: Cornell University Press.

Thompson, Dennis. 1990. *Political Ethics and Public Office*. Cambridge, MA: Harvard University Press.

Thomson, Janice. 1994. *Mercenaries, Pirates, and Sovereigns: State-Building and Extraterritorial Violence in Early Modern Europe*. Princeton, NJ: Princeton University Press.

Thongchai, Winichakul. 1997. *Siam Mapped: A History of the Geo-body of a Nation*. Honolulu: University of Hawaii Press.

Thrall, A. Trevor, Dominik Stecula, and Diana Sweet. 2014. "May We Have Your Attention Please? Human-Rights NGOs and the Problem of Global Communication." *International Journal of Press/Politics*.

Tickner, Arlene. 2003. "Seeing IR Differently: Notes from the Third World." *Millenium* 32(2): 295–324.

Tickner, J. Ann. 1992. *Gender in International Relations*. New York: Columbia University Press.

Tilly, Charles. 1990. *Coercion, Capital, and European States, AD 990–1990*. Cambridge, MA: Blackwell.

Tönnies, Ferdinand. 2011. *Community and Society*. Mineola, NY: Dover Publications.

Tóth, Judit. 2008. "EU Member States' Complicity in Extraordinary Renditions," in Elspeth Guild (ed.), *Security versus Justice? Police and Judicial Cooperation in the European Union*. Aldershot: Ashgate.

Towns, Ann E. 2010. *Women and States: Norms and Hierarchies in International Society*. Cambridge: Cambridge University Press.
    2012. "Norms and Social Hierarchies: Understanding International Policy Diffusion 'from Below.'" *International Organization* 66(2):179–209.

True, Jacqui, and Michael Mintrom. 2001. "Transnational Networks and Policy Diffusion: The Case of Gender Mainstreaming." *International Studies Quarterly* 45(1):27–57.

Tsai, George. 2014. "Rational Persuasion as Paternalism." *Philosophy & Public Affairs* 42(1):78–112.

Tsou, Tang, and Morton H. Halperin. 1965. "Mao Tse-tung's Revolutionary Strategy and Peking's International Behavior." *American Political Science Review* 59(1):80–99.

Tsui, Josephine. 2013. "The Effectiveness of Measuring Influence," *GSDRC Helpdesk Research Report 911*. GSDRC, University of Birmingham, UK.

Tsygankov, Andrei P. 2016. *Russia's Foreign Policy: Change and Continuity in National Identity*. London: Rowman & Littlefield.

Tversky, Amos, and Daniel Kahneman. 1981. "The Framing of Decisions and the Psychology of Choice." *Science* 211(448):453–8.
    1974. "Judgment under Uncertainty: Heuristics and Biases." *Science* 185(4157):1124–31.

Tzogopoulos, George. 2013. *The Greek Crisis in the Media: Stereotyping in the International Press*. London: Ashgate.

Van Ness, Peter. 1970. *Revolution and Chinese Foreign Policy: Peking's Support for Wars of National Liberation*. Berkeley: University of California Press.
    1993. "China as a Third World State: Foreign Policy and Official National Identity," in Lowell Dittmer and Samuel S. Kim (eds.), *China's Quest for National Identity*. Ithaca, NY: Cornell University Press.

VanDeVeer, Donald. 1986. *Paternalistic Intervention: The Moral Bounds of Benevolence*. Princeton, NJ: Princeton University Press.

Verdier, Nicholas. 2006. "A Short History of Hierarchy," in Denise Pumain (ed.), *Hierarchy in Natural and Social Sciences*, pp. 13–39.

Verovšek, P. J. 2014. "Memory and the Euro-Crisis of Leadership: The Effects of Generational Change in Germany and the EU." *Constellations* 21(2):239–48.

Vine, David. 2009. *Island of Shame: A Secret History of the U.S. Military Base on Diego Garcia.* Princeton, NJ: Princeton University Press.

Vinograd, Cassandra. 2014. "Jihadi Brides Swap Lives in the West for Front Line with Syria Militants." NBC News, July 8, 2014, available at www.nbcnews.com/storyline/iraq-turmoil/jihadi-brides-swap-lives-west-front-line-syria-militants-n150491 (accessed May 25, 2015).

Vitalis, Robert. 2000. "The Graceful and Generous Liberal Gesture: Making Racism Invisible in American International Relations." *Millennium: Journal of International Studies* 29(2):331–56.

　2006. "Birth of a Discipline," in David Long and Brian C. Schmidt (eds.), *Imperialism and Internationalism in the Discipline of International Relations.* Albany, NY: SUNY Press, pp. 159–82.

　2010. "The Noble American Science of Imperial Relations and its Laws of Race Development." *Comparative Studies in Society and History* 52(4):909–38.

　2015. *White World Order, Black Power Politics.* Ithaca, NY: Cornell University Press.

Viviani, Nancy. 1970. *Nauru: Phosphate and Political Progress.* Canberra: Australian National University Press.

Wagner, R. Harrison. 1983. "The Theory of Games and the Problem of International Cooperation." *American Political Science Review* 77(2): 330–46.

Walker, Rob B. J. 1993. *Inside/Outside: International Relations as Political Theory.* Cambridge: Cambridge University Press.

Wall, Ronald, and Bert van der Knaap. 2012. "Centrality, Hierarchy, and Heterarchy of Worldwide Corporate Networks," in Ben Derudder, Michael Hoyler, Peter J. Taylore, and Frank Witlox (eds.), *International Handbook of Globalization and Cities.* Cheltenham: Edward Elgar.

Wallerstein, Immanuel. 1974. "The Rise and Future Demise of the World Capitalist System." *Comparative Studies in Society and History* 16(4):387–415.

　1984. *The Politics of World Economy: The States, the Movements and the Civilizations.* Cambridge: Cambridge University Press.

　2011[1976]. *The Modern World-System I: Capitalist Agriculture and the Origins of the European World Economy in the Sixteenth Century, with a New Prologue.* Berkeley: University of California Press.

Walsh, Edmund A. (ed.). 1922. *The History and Nature of International Relations.* New York: Macmillan.

Walt, Stephen M. 1996. *Revolution and War.* Ithaca, NY: Cornell University Press.

Waltz, Kenneth N. 1959. *Man, the State and War: A Theoretical Analysis.* New York: Columbia University Press.

　1975. "Theory of International Relations," in Nelson W. Polsby and Fred I. Greenstein (eds.), *Handbook of Political Science, Volume 8: International Politics.* Reading, MA: Addison-Wesley.

　1979[2010]. *Theory of International Politics.* Long Grove, IL: Waveland Press.

1985. "Political Structures," in Robert O. Keohane (ed.), *Neorealism and Its Critics*. New York: Columbia University Press.

1990. "Realist Thought and Neo-Realist Theory." *Journal of International Affairs* 44(1):21–37.

Watson, Adam. 1992. *The Evolution of International Society: A Comparative Historical Analysis*. London: Routledge.

Watzlawick, Paul, Janet Helmick Beavin, and Don D. Jackson. 1967. *Pragmatics of Human Communication: A Study of Inter-Actional Patterns, Pathologies, and Paradoxes*. New York: W.W. Norton.

Weber, Cynthia. 1995. *Simulating Sovereignty: Intervention, the State and Symbolic Exchange*. Cambridge: Cambridge University Press.

1999. *Faking It: U.S. Hegemony in a Post-Phallic Era*. Minneapolis: University of Minnesota Press.

Weingast, Barry R. 1997. "The Political Foundations of Democracy and the Rule of Law." *American Political Science Review* 91(2):245–63.

Weldes, Jutta, Mark Laffey, Hugh Gusterson, and Raymond Duvall. 1999. *Cultures of Insecurity: States, Communities, and the Production of Danger*. Twin Cities: University of Minnesota Press.

Wendt, Alexander. 1999. *Social Theory of International Politics*. Cambridge: Cambridge University Press.

Wendt, Alexander, and Michael Barnett. 1993. "Dependent State Formation and Third World Militarization." *Review of International Studies*. 19:321–347.

Wendt, Alexander, and Daniel Friedheim. 1995. "Hierarchy under Anarchy: Informal Empire and the East German State." *International Organization* 49(4):689–721.

Westerbrook, Robert. 2000. "An Uncommon Faith: Pragmatism and Religious Experience," in Stuart Rosenbaum (ed.), *Pragmatism and Religion*. Urbana: University of Illinois Press.

White, Julie. 2000. *Democracy, Justice, and the Welfare State: Reconstructing Public Care*. University Park, PA: Penn State University Press.

Wiener, Norbert. 1961. *Cybernetics, or Control and Communication in the Animal and Machine*, 2nd edn. Cambridge, MA: MIT Press.

Wilcox, Lauren. 2009. "Gendering the 'Cult of the Offensive.'" *Security Studies* 18(2):214–40.

Wilkinson, Ian. 2015. "Social Suffering and Critical Humanitarianism." *World Suffering and Quality of Life* 56:45–54.

Williams, Michael C. 2006. "The Hobbesian Theory of International Relations: Three Traditions," in Beate Jahn (ed.), *Classical Theory in International Relations*. New York: Cambridge University Press, pp. 253–76.

Williamson, Oliver E. 1975. *Markets and Hierarchies: Analysis and Anti-Trust Implications*. New York: Free Press.

1985. *The Economic Institutions of Capitalism*. New York: Free Press.

2002. "The Theory of the Firm as Governance Structure: From Choice to Contract." *Journal of Economic Perspectives* 16(3):171–95.

Willis, Paul. 1977. *Learning to Labor: How Working Class Kids Get Working Class Jobs*. New York: Columbia University Press.

Willoughby, W. W., and Charles G. Fenwick. 1974. *The Inquiry Handbooks*, vol. 16, reprint edn. Wilmington, DE. Original edition, *Types of Restricted Sovereignty and of Colonial Autonomy*.

Wilson, Peter H. 2011. *The Holy Roman Empire 1495–1806*. Houndmills, Basingstoke: Palgrave Macmillan.

Wivel, Anders, and Kajsa Noe Oest. 2010. "Security, Profit or Shadow of the Past? Explaining the Security Strategies of Micro-states." *Cambridge Review of International Affairs* 23(3):429–52.

Wohlforth, William C. 2009. Unipolarity, Status Competition, and Great Power War. *World Politics* 61(1):28–57.

Wong, Wendy. 2012. *Internal Affairs: How the Structure of NGOs Transforms Human Rights*. Ithaca, NY: Cornell University Press.

Woodliffe, John. 1992. *The Peacetime Use of Foreign Military Installations under Modern International Law*. Dordrecht, Netherlands: Martinuus Nijoff.

Woolf, Leonard. 1916. *International Government: Two Reports*. London: Allen & Unwin.

World Bank. 2015. *World Development Report: Mind, Society, and Behavior*. Washington, DC: World Bank Press.

Wright, Quincy. 1964 [1942]. *A Study of War*. Chicago: University of Chicago Press.

Xiang, Gao. 2013. "Expounding Neo-Confucianism: Choice of Tradition at a Time of Dynastic Change: Cultural Conflict and the Social Reconstruction of Early Qing." *Social Sciences in China* 34(2):105–33.

Yang, Guobin. 2005. "Environmental NGOs and institutional dynamics in China." *China Quarterly* 18(1):44–66.

Yeo, Andrew. 2011. *Activists, Alliances, and Anti-US Base Protests*. New York: Cambridge University Press.

Yoshida, Kensei. 2001. *Democracy Betrayed: Okinawa under U.S. Occupation*. Bellingham: Center for East Asian Studies, Western Washington University.

Young, Iris Marion. 2003. "The Logic of Masculinist Protection: Reflections on the Current Security State." *Signs* 29(1):1–25.

Yu, George T. 1974. "The Maoist Model: Appeal, Relevance, and Applicability," in James Chieh Hsiung (ed.), *The Logic of "Maoism": Critiques and Explication*. New York: Praeger.

Zarakol, Ayşe. 2010. "Ontological Insecurity and State Denial of Historical Crimes: Turkey and Japan," *International Relations* 24(1):3–23.

2011. *After Defeat: How the East Learned to Live with the West*. Cambridge: Cambridge University Press.

2014. "What Made the Modern World Hang Together: Socialisation or Stigmatisation?" *International Theory* 6(2):311–32.

Zhang, Yongjin. 1998. *China in International Society since 1949: Alienation and Beyond*. Basingstoke: Macmillan.

Zimmern, Alfred E. 1936. *The League of Nations and the Rule of Law, 1918–1935*, 2nd edn. London: Macmillan.

Index

a la carte hierarchies, 152
AAJA. *See* Afro-Asian Journalists Association
Abkhazia, 168–70
Acharya, Amitav, 44
actor behavior
  credibility and, 231
  hierarchies and, 10–13
  overview about, 12–13
Adler-Nissen, Rebecca, 11–12, 132, 223, 251–2
Afghanistan, 168–70
Africa
  empowerment of group related to, 233–5
  limitations faced by PRC related to, 236–8
  PRC relations with, 230–8
  subcultural ideology propagation and, 231–3
  success of PRC related to, 235–6
Afro-Asian Journalists Association (AAJA), 232–3
After Defeat (Zarakol), 11–12, 120, 238
anarchy
  anarchy-hierarchy binary of Waltz, 243–5
  historicising, 266–71
  IR and, 2–3, 266–71
  neorealism and, 2–3
  order versus demarcation and, 246
  Political Discourse of Anarchy, 266–7
  probing political project of, 271–3
  rationale for study of hierarchy related to, 273–4
  scholarship influenced by, 3
  state of nature and, 272–3
  structural realism and, 2–3
  Theory of International Politics and, 2–3
Arendt, Hannah, 80–1
Atambayev, Almazbek, 168–70
authority. *See also* consent-based authority
  acceptance of, 19

compacts and contracts and, 113–14
decisionist view of, 114–15
defined, 76–7
equity and, 20–1
factors related to, 76–7
in or of, 77
INGOs and, 176–7, 196
kinds of, 77
laws and, 18–19, 25–6
legitimacy and, 18–19, 20–1, 25–6
limiting abuse of, 20
norms legitimating, 25–6
ontological hierarchy and, 263–4
overview, 113–14
paternalism and, 76–7
political struggle and, 19–20
responsibility and, 79–83
as right granted, 19
Avgi, 206–7

backpatting, 226, 234–5
Bakiyev, Kurmanbek, 168–70
banner system, 55–6
Barder, Alexander, 7–8
bargaining-based arguments, 47
Barnett, Michael, 110, 119, 239, 251
beyond hierarchy
  anarchy-hierarchy binary of Waltz, 243–5
  bilateral hierarchy, 250–1
  extended conceptions of hierarchy, 250–2
  hierarchy and inequality, 251–2
  language of hierarchy in IR and, 246–8
  ontology and, 258–65
  order types
    centralisation, 253–7
    hierarchical stratification typology, 252–8
    layering and ranking, 257–8
  ordering principles and, 243–6
  overview, 243
  stratification and differentiation in states systems, 249–50

beyond hierarchy (cont.)
structures of stratification and
differentiation, 248–9
in world politics, 265
bilateral hierarchy, 250–1
BILD, 206, 210–11, 213
Bodies That Matter (Butler), 107–9
Bourdieu, Pierre, 117–18, 121–4
Brahmins, 260–1
Britain
Charity Commission of England and
Wales, 184
foreign military bases, 161–2
INGOs headquartered in, 183–4
British India. *See also* empire
conclusions about, 60–5
ethnic military mobilization in, 58–60
ideal type of empire and, 44
Indian Mutiny in, 58–9
martial races and, 59–60
organising imperial identities in, 56–60
religious patronage and, 56–8
temporality and, 62–3
broad hierarchies
concept of, 138–41
delinquent gangs and, 222–3
empires and, 60–5
gender and, 96, 107, 112
INGOs and, 176
laws and norms and, 17–18
micro-states, dependencies and, 137–8
narrow approach compared with, 9
overview of topics related to, 9–10, 12–13
paternalism and, 66–7
Buddhism. *See* Tibetan Buddhism
Bukovansky, Mlada, 5, 117–18
Bull, Hedley, 221–2
Butler, Judith, 107–9

Calvo Doctrine, 34–6
Campbell, David, 7–8
Cartledge, Paul, 211–13
Cayman Islands
diplomacy and constitutional affairs,
148–51
overview about, 142, 152
centralisation
centers and peripheries and, 254
beyond hierarchy and, 253–7
stratification and, 256–7
typology of center-periphery
differentiation, 254–6
"Centre and Periphery" (Shils), 254
Charity Commission of England and
Wales, 184

Charity Navigator (CN), 181–2, 184
Charter of the Organization of American
States, 34–5
China. *See* People's Republic of China;
Qing China
Civilization and Empire (Suzuki), 11–12
Clark, Ian, 117–18
CN. *See* Charity Navigator
coercion-based arguments, 47
Cohen, Albert K., 224–5
colonialism, liberalism and, 87–9
compacts, 113–14
compassion, 80–1
complicity, 124
Concordat of Worms, 30–1
consent, 71–2, 263
consent-based authority
beyond authority I, 118–21
beyond authority II, 129–31
born within hierarchy and, 121–9
complicity and, 124
conclusions about, 131–3
constitutive effects of hierarchy and,
121–4
contract view and, 115–17
embodiment and, 121–9
hierarchies within ourselves and, 124–9
overview, 114–15
pecking order and, 126–8
problems with, 114–18
public conformity without private
acceptance and, 118–21
sense of place and, 124–9
social compact view and, 117–18
social stratification and, 129–31
contract theory
of hierarchies, 4–7
Hierarchy in International Relations
and, 4–5
contract view
consent-based authority and, 115–17
informal governance and, 116
rational interest and, 115–16
voluntarism and, 116–17
contracts, 113–14
Convention on Rights and Duties of
States, 34–5
Cook Islands
diplomacy and constitutional affairs,
148–51
economies of scale and, 145–8
overview about, 142, 152
Cooley, Alex, 138–9, 250–2
Corruption Perception Index, 202
counter-stigmatization, 226

covert sites, 172
Crash, 209–11
Crimea, 219–20
Crossley, Pamela, 52–3
Cuba, 164–5
cuius regio, eius religio (whose realm, his religion), 31
Curaçao
    defence and security and, 142–5
    economies of scale and, 145–8
    overview about, 142, 152
customisation, 44–5, 50

Daesh. *See* Islamic State of Iraq and the Levant
delegated authority, 77
delinquent gangs
    alienation and, 224–6
    broad hierarchies and, 222–3
    conclusions, 238–40
    counter-stigmatization and, 226
    empowerment of, 233–5
    introductory analysis related to, 219–24
    isolation and, 227–8
    limitations faced by PRC related to, 236–8
    narrow hierarchies and, 221–2
    PRC relations with Africa and, 230–8
    social recognition of, 233–5
    socialisation and, 224–6
    status frustration and, 225
    subcultural grouping in IR and, 227–9
    subcultural ideology propagation and, 231–3
    subculture formation and, 224–6
    success of PRC related to, 235–6
Department of Defense, US (DOD), 167
dependencies
    a la carte hierarchy in, 152
    broad hierarchies and, 137–8
    conclusions about, 152–3
    defence and security and, 142–5
    diplomacy and constitutional affairs, 148–51
    economies of scale and, 145–8
    narrow hierarchies and, 137–8
    overview related to, 137–8, 142
    scarcity of hierarchy and, 141–2
devalorisation, 102–3
Dionysius, 258–65
diplomacy and constitutional affairs, 148–51
discursive practices, 7–8
divide and rule, 49

DOD. *See* Department of Defense, US
Donnelly, Jack, 2–3, 13–14, 130–1, 193–4, 266
Drago Doctrine, 34–6
Drakopoulos, Giorgos, 210
drones. *See* unmanned aerial vehicles
Duby, Georges, 258–65
Dumont, Louis, 130–1, 260–1
Duverger, Maurice, 254–5
Dworkin, Gerald, 70–1

each king is an emperor in his own realm.
    See rex est imperator in regno suo
East India Company (EIC). *See* British India
Economic and Monetary Union (EMU)
    Italy and, 203–4
    sovereign equality and, 200–1
economies of scale, 145–8
EIC. *See* East India Company
Elphinstone, Lord, 49
embodiment, 121–9
empire
    agency centered account of, 61–2
    bargaining-based arguments for rise of, 47
    broad hierarchies and, 60–5
    Civilization and Empire, 11–12
    coercion-based arguments for rise of, 47
    conclusions about, 60–5
    customisation and, 44–5, 50
    defined, 43, 45–8
    difference curatorship and, 48–51
    divide and rule and, 49
    ethnic military mobilization and, 51
    explanations for, 45–8
    foreign military bases and, 154–5
    Holy Roman Empire, 30–1
    ideal type of, 44
    imperial statecraft and, 48–51
    narrow hierarchies and, 44–5, 60–5
    religious patronage and, 50
    revolution and secession and, 45
    rule of difference and, 45
    status-based arguments for rise of, 47–8
    temporality and, 62–3
EMU. *See* Economic and Monetary Union
equality
    hierarchy and inequality, 251–2
    non-intervention and, 32–4
    as ontology, 258–65
    racial inequality and, 33–4
ethnic military mobilization, 51, 58–60
Eurasia, 168–70
euro crisis

euro crisis (cont.)
  austerity narrative, 204
  civilising narrative, 204
  conclusions, 217–18
  German oppressor and, 209–11
  Golden Dawn movement and, 211–13
  Greece as immature pupil and, 215–17
  Greek tragedy and, 214–15
  hierarchy as interactive and, 198–9
  labeling and, 200–3
  narratives behind, 204–5
  negotiating victimhood and, 213–17
  overview, 198–200
  searching for labels of Greece and
    Germany in, 206–7
  sinners-saints narrative, 204–5
  teacher role of Germany in, 216–17
  trope of Nazism in, 208–13
Europe. *See also specific countries*
  conditional decolonisation bargains and,
    161–2
  negotiating hierarchies in, 203–5
Eurozone, sovereign equality and, 200–1
expert authority, 77
expertise, paternalism and, 82–3

Faroe Islands
  economies of scale and, 145–8
  overview about, 142, 152
feminist approach, to hierarchies, 112.
    See also gender; gender hierarchies;
    gendered hierarchies; hierarchies
    in global politics, as gendered;
    women
Flathman, Richard, 19
Focus, 213–14
foreign military bases
  Britain and, 161–2
  case example, 168–70
  conclusions, 174
  contracts and rights, 163–6
  covert sites, 172
  empire and, 154–5
  in Eurasia, US and Russian views of,
    168–70
  European conditional decolonisation
    bargains, 161–2
  France and, 161
  as global multinational company, 157
  hidden hierarchy and, 171–4
  as hierarchical legacies, 163
  as imperial legacies, 159–63
  Japan and, 160–1
  overview related to, 155–6
  political consequences related to, 158–9

  political dynamics and, 155–6
  PSCs and, 171–2
  relational contracting and, 156–9
  Russia and, 162, 168–70
  SOFAs as use rights and, 165–6
  sovereignty and, 166–7
  as status symbols, 167–8
  as symbols of subordination and
    influence, 166–70
  taboo and, 167–8
  UAVs and, 172–3
  unofficial basing, 171–4
  US imperial and wartime basing
    acquisitions of, 160–1
  use rights in basing contracts, 163–5
Fourcade, M., 202–3
France, 161
Franco, Francisco, 163–4
Frankfurter Allgemeine, 206

G8, 219–20
gender. *See also* women
  broad hierarchies and, 96, 107, 112
  as hierarchical structure in global politics,
    98–100
  overview of topics related to, 96
  relative position among states and, 100
gender hierarchies
  capability distribution and, 100
  femininity devalued and, 97–8
  Google search for, 95
  ISIS recruitment and, 101–2
  sex inequality as global, 97
  violence against women and, 96–7
  workplace and, 97
gendered hierarchies. *See also* hierarchies in
    global politics, as gendered
  defined, 102
  devalorisation and, 102–3
  enemy subordination and, 104
  labeling and, 103–4
  power and, 103
  sexual abuse and, 104–7
Germany
  conclusions, 217–18
  German oppressor and, 209–11
  Golden Dawn movement and, 211–13
  Greece as immature pupil and, 215–17
  Greek tragedy and, 214–15
  negotiating victimhood and, 213–17
  overview related to, 199–200
  search results related to, 207–8
  searching for labels of, 206–7
  teacher role of, 216–17
  trope of Nazism in, 208–13

globalisation, IR and, 1. *See also* hierarchies in global politics, as gendered
Goffman, Erving, 124–9
Goh, Evelyn, 117–18
Golden Dawn movement, 211–13
Good Neighbor policy, 34–5, 36–7
Google, 95, 206
Greece
  conclusions, 217–18
  German oppressor and, 209–11
  Golden Dawn movement and, 211–13
  as immature pupil, 215–17
  negotiating victimhood and, 213–17
  overview related to, 199–200
  search results related to, 207–8
  searching for labels of, 206–7
  teacher role of Germany for, 216–17
  tragedy, 214–15
  trope of Nazism related to, 208–13
Gregory VII, 30–1

harm principle, 91
Hawkesworth, Mary, 103–4
Henry IV, 30–1
Herzfeld, Michael, 210, 211–13, 214–15
heterarchies, 255
hidden hierarchy, 171–4
hierarchies. *See also* beyond hierarchy; broad hierarchies; gender hierarchies; gendered hierarchies; narrow hierarchies; ontological hierarchy
  a la carte, 152
  actors experience of, 10–13
  agentic-contractual accounts of, 4–7
  bargained, 4–7
  concept of, 138–41
  conclusions about research areas related to, 13–14
  constitutive effects of, 121–4
  contract theory of, 4–7
  as deep structures of organised inequality, 7–8
  defined, 1–2
  discursive practices and, 7–8
  dynamics generated by, 1–2
  feminist approach to, 112
  hidden, 171–4
  incentives and, 6–7
  as interactive, 198–9
  IR research and, 3–4
  nature of, 4–10
  negotiating, 203–5
  origins of, 4–10
  within ourselves, 124–9

paternalism and, 66–94
questions addressed regarding, 3–4
rationale for study of, 273–4
rules and, 17
social status and, 11
socialising effects of, 10–13
trade-off explanation of, 4–7
as ubiquitous, 1–2
hierarchies in global politics, as gendered
  bodies and, 107–9
  gendered logics and, 107–9
  ISIS and, 110–12
  masculinity valorised and, 109–10
  materiality and, 107–9
  overview, 107
  parity and, 109
  paternalism and, 110
Hierarchy in International Relations (Lake), 4–5
Hinduism, 56–8
Hobbes, Thomas, 268–71
Hobson, John M., 117–18, 273
Holy Roman Empire, 30–1
Homo Hierarchicus (Dumont), 130–1
humanitarians, 81
Hurd, Ian, 117–18
Hurrell, Andrew, 117–18

Ikenberry, G. John, 5, 115–17
illusio, 123
imperial hierarchies
  agency centered account of, 61–2
  conclusions about, 60–5
  constitution of, 48–51
  overview about, 43–5
  temporality and, 62–3
imperial simultaneity, 52–3
in authority, 77
incapacity, 77–9
incentives, 6–7
incompetence, paternalism and, 77–9
India, 260–1. *See also* British India
Indian Mutiny, 58–9
inequality
  deep structures of organised, 7–8
  hierarchy and, 251–2
  racial, 29, 33–4
  sex, 97
inferiority, paternalism and, 77–9
international non-governmental organizations (INGOs)
  audience reception and, 177
  audiences, 177–91
    media, 178–9, 182–8
    overview, 177–9
    peers, 178, 179–81

(INGOs) (cont.)
    public, 178, 181–2
    authority and, 176–7, 196
    broad or narrow hierarchies and, 176
    conclusions, 196–7
    counting, 184–5
    defined, 175–6
    different authorities and, 189–91
    headquartered in US and Britain, 183–4
    hierarchy as lens for, 192–6
    identifying leading, 188–9, 190
    literature on, 175
    numbers of, 175
    overview, 175
    positionality and, 192–3
    public good and, 175–6
    sampling and, 187
    stratification variation within, 193–4
    ties to, 185
    trade-offs and, 194–5
    wealthiest, 187
    world news publications mentions of,
        186–7
international principle, non-intervention
    and, 29–40
international relations (IR)
    anarchy and, 2–3, 266–71
    anarchy-hierarchy binary of Waltz and,
        243–5
    fragmented field of, 1
    globalisation and, 1
    hierarchies research and, 3–4
    historicising anarchy in, 266–71
    language of hierarchy in, 246–8
    neorealism and, 2–3
    pluralist research program in, 113
    subcultural groupings in, 227–9
investiture controversy, 30–1
IR. See international relations
Ireland, 214
Islamic State of Iraq and the Levant (ISIS)
    denaturalisation and, 111
    hierarchies in global politics, as gendered,
        and, 110–12
    jihadi brides and, 95
    media reports of, 100–1
    rearticulation and, 111–12
    recruitment and, 101–2
    sexual abuse and, 104–7
    women, oppression of, within, 100–1
Italy, 203–4

Jackson, Patrick Thaddeus, 139–40
Japan, 160–1
jihadi brides, 95

Kasidiaris, Ilias, 211–13
Kathimerini, 206–7, 210–11
Krasner, Stephen D., 118–21
Kreps, Sarah, 172–3
Kshatriyas, 260–1
Kugler, Jacek, 10–11
Kyrgyzstan, 168–70

labeling
    euro crisis and, 200–3
    gendered hierarchies and, 103–4
    morality and, 202–3
    other and self, 207–8
    positive or negative, 202
    searching for, 206–7
    sense of self and, 203
    social, as markers of hierarchy, 202–3
    sovereign equality and, 200–1
    stigmatization and, 202
Lake, David, 4–5, 115–17, 122–3, 126–8,
        154–5, 244–5, 250–1
Laski, Harold, 247–8
Latin America, non-intervention and, 35–6
laws
    authority, legitimate, and, 18–19, 25–6
    broad hierarchies and, 17–18
    intentional quality of, 17–18
    interaction of norms and, 18–29
    narrow hierarchies and, 17–18
    norms legitimating, 25–6
    overview about, 18
    principles and, 24–5
    principles strategically translated
        into, 26–7
    promote principles and norms, 27–9
    rules and, 18–19
    self-interest and, 21
    as socially constituted hierarchy, 18–21
layering, 257–8
legal paternalism, 74
legitimacy
    authority and, 18–19, 20–1, 25–6
    dimensions of, 92–3
    paternalism and, 68–9
Leviathan (Hobbes), 268–71
Liberal Leviathan (Ikenberry), 5, 116
liberalism
    colonialism and, 87–9
    paternalism and, 87–90
libertarian paternalism, 74–5
Liechtenstein
    defence and security and, 142–5
    economies of scale and, 145–8
    money laundering and, 222
    overview about, 142, 152

MacKinnon, Catherine, 102–3
Madrid Pacts, 163–4
Man, the State and War (Waltz), 247–8
Manas Transit Center, 168–70
Manchu Raj. *See* Qing China
Mao Zedong, 233, 235–6
Markets and Hierarchies (Williamson),
    139–40
martial races, 59–60
masculinity, valorised, 109–10
maternalism, 70
media
    INGOs and, 178–9, 182–8
    ISIS and, 100–1
Merkel, Angela, 208–13, 216–17
Metaxas, Ioannis, 211–13
micro-states
    a la carte hierarchy in, 152
    broad or narrow hierarchies and, 137–8
    conclusions about, 152–3
    defence and security and, 142–5
    diplomacy and constitutional affairs,
        148–51
    economies of scale and, 145–8
    overview related to, 137–8, 142
military bases. *See* foreign military bases
Mill, John Stuart, 78–9, 87–9
    harm principle and, 91
money laundering, 222
Mongolia, 53–5
moral authority, 77
multinational company concept, 157

narrow hierarchies
    broad approach compared with, 9
    concept of, 138–41
    defined, 6
    delinquent gangs and, 221–2
    empire and, 44–5, 60–5
    INGOs and, 176
    laws and norms and, 17–18
    micro-states, dependencies and, 137–8
    overview of topics related to, 9–10, 12–13
    paternalism and, 66–7
Nauru
    defence and security and, 142–5
    economies of scale and, 145–8
    overview about, 142, 152
Nazism
    German oppressor and, 209–11
    Golden Dawn movement and, 211–13
    trope of, 208–13
negotiating hierarchies, 203–5
negotiating victimhood, 213–17
neorealism, 2–3, 272–3

New Zealand, 165
non-intervention
    conclusions about, 40–2
    current debate surrounding, 37–40
    development of principle of, 29
    equality and, 32–4
    failed states and, 40
    forcible actions and, 37
    history surrounding, 30–2
    international principle and, 29–40
    investiture controversy and, 30–1
    Latin America and, 35–6
    legalisation and, 34–7
    newly independent states and, 37
    overview about, 29
    Peace of Augsburg and, 31
    racial inequality and, 33–4
    social norms, role of, in, 32–4
    Thirty Year's War and, 31
    US and, 36–7
norms, social
    as ambiguous, 23
    authority legitimated by, 25–6
    broad hierarchies and, 17–18
    conclusions about, 40–2
    as decentralised, 21–2
    defined, 21–2
    equality, 32–4
    interaction of laws and, 18–29
    as judgmental, 22
    law promotes, 27–9
    laws legitimated by, 25–6
    legalisation of, 23–4
    narrow hierarchies and, 17–18
    non-intervention and, 29–40
    origin of, 17–18, 23
    overview about, 18
    principles and, 24–5
    principles conditioned by, 26
    racial inequality, 29, 33–4
    role of, 32–4
    as socially constituted hierarchy, 21–4
Nussbaum, D., 214
Nyerere, Julius, 232

Obama, Barack, 167, 219–20
of authority, 77
Ogunsanwo, Alaba, 235–6
ontological hierarchy
    egalitarian world and, 264–5
    equality and, 258–65
    in India, 260–1
    status and force, 263–4
    structured systems and, 261–3
    in West, 258–65

Opting out of the European Union (Adler-
  Nissen), 11–12
ordering principles
  abandoning, 245–6
  beyond hierarchy and, 243–6
Organski, A. F. K., 10–11
Overseas Base Structure report
  (DOD), 167

Panama, 164–5
Papantoniou, Yiannos, 213–14
Papoulias, Carolas, 214–15
paternalism
  authority and, 76–7
  broad and narrow hierarchies and, 66–7
  conclusions about, 91–4
  consent and, 66–7, 71–2
  defined, 66, 70–2
  as domination, 66–7
  expertise and, 82–3
  as form of rule, 69
  harm principle and, 91
  hierarchies and, 66–94
  hierarchies in global politics, as gendered,
    and, 110
  humanitarians and, 81
  inferiority, incompetence, incapacity
    and, 77–9
  is not same thing as . . ., 72–6
  judgment and, 77–8
  legal, 74
  liberalism and, 87–90
  maternalism and, 70
  overview, 69–70
  persuasion and, 73–4
  post-colonialism and, 89–90
  power and, 71
  propriety and legitimacy and, 68–9
  purpose of, 85
  scope and, 84–5
  self-interest and, 75–6
  sphere of autonomy and, 71
  structural sources of, 67–8
  substitution of judgment and, 71
  superiority, competence, responsibility
    and, 79–83
  variations of, 83–90
patronage. *See* religious patronage
Paul, T. V., 11
Peace of Augsburg, 31
Peace of Westphalia, 31
pecking order, 126–8
People's Republic of China (PRC)
  empowerment of group related to, 233–5
  limitations faced by, 236–8

relations with Africa, 230–8
  subcultural ideology propagation and,
    231–3
  subculture formation and, 224–6
  success of, assessing, 235–6
  trade embargo and, 230
  UN and, 235
persuasion, 73–4
Peterson, V. Spike, 102–3
Philippines, 167
Phillips, Andrew, 117–18, 129
PIIGS. *See* Portugal, Ireland, Italy, Greece
  and Spain
Political Discourse of Anarchy (Schmidt),
  266–7
Portugal, Ireland, Italy, Greece and Spain
  (PIIGS), 198–9, 215. *See also specific
  countries*
post-colonialism, paternalism and, 89–90
Pouliot, Vincent, 251–2, 263
power
  consent and, 71–2
  as formative force, 109
  gendered hierarchies and, 103
  materiality and, 107–9
  ontological hierarchy and, 263–4
  paternalism and, 71
  sense of place and, 124–9
  *Special Responsibilities: Global Problems
    and American Power*, 5
  transition theory, 10–11
  Waltz on countries with great, 249
Power, S. A., 214
PRC. *See* People's Republic of China
principles
  cuius regio, eius religio, 31
  law promotes, 27–9
  laws and norms and, 24–5
  non-intervention, 29–40
  norms conditioning, 26
  rex est imperator in regno suo, 31
  strategically translated into law, 26–7
private security contractors (PSCs), 171–2
Proto Thema, 206–7
PSCs. *See* private security contractors
public conformity without private
  acceptance, 118–21
Putin, Vladimir, 219–20

Qing China. *See also* empire
  banner system and, 55–6
  as barbarian dynasty, 52
  conclusions about, 60–5
  ethnic sovereignty and, 52
  ideal type of empire and, 44

imperial simultaneity and, 52–3
Mongolia and, 53–5
organising imperial identities in, 51–6
rise of, 51–2
temporality and, 62–3
Tibetan Buddhism and, 54–5

R2P. *See* Responsibility to Protect; Right to
     Protect
racial inequality, 29, 33–4
ranking, 257–8
rational-legal authority, 77
Rawls, John, 87–9
relational contracting
   foreign military bases and, 156–9
   multinational company concept and, 157
   political consequences related to, 158–9
religious patronage, 50, 56–8
responsibility
   authority and, 79–83
   paternalism and, 79–83
Responsibility to Protect (R2P), 89–90
Reus-Smit, Christian, 118–21
revolution and secession, 45
rex est imperator in regno suo (each king is an
     emperor in his own realm), 31
Right to Protect (R2P), 40
Roosevelt, Theodore, 36–7
rule
   of difference, 45
   hierarchies and, 17
   laws and, 18–19
Russia, 164–5, 167–8
   foreign military bases and, 162, 168–70
   G8 and, 219–20

Samaras, Antonis, 216–17
saviours, 81
Schäuble, Wolfgang, 214–15
Schlarmann, Josef, 210–11
Schmalkaldic War, 31
Schmidt, Brian, 266–7
Schwarzenberger, Georg, 249
secession, 45
self-interest, 75–6
selfish altruists, 75–6
sense of place, 124–9
sex inequality, 97
sexual abuse, 104–7
Seychelles
   defence and security and, 142–5
   diplomacy and constitutional affairs,
       148–51
   economies of scale and, 145–8
   overview about, 142, 152

Sharman, J. C., 11–12, 115–18
Shils, Edward, 254
Shogo Suzuki, 11–12
Shudras, 260–1
Sjoberg, Laura, 61–2, 262–3
social compact view, 117–18
social norms. *See* norms, social
social relations
   overview of approach to, 76
   of paternalism, 76–7
   two elements of, 76
SOFAs. *See* Status of Forces Agreements
solidarity, 72–3
sovereign equality
   contingent promise of, 201
   EMU and, 200–1
   as guiding principle, 201
   hierarchy in world of, 200–1
   legal recognition of, 200–1
sovereignty
   ethnic, 52
   foreign military bases and, 166–7
   history surrounding, 30–2
Spain, 163–4
*Special Responsibilities: Global Problems and
     American Power* (Bukovansky), 5
sphere of autonomy, 71
St Kitts and Nevis
   defence and security and, 142–5
   economies of scale and, 145–8
   overview about, 142, 152
state of nature, 272–3
status
   arguments based on, 47–8
   empire and, 47–8
   force and, 263–4
   frustration, 225
   social, 11
   symbols, 167–8
Status in World Politics (Paul et al), 11
Status of Forces Agreements (SOFAs),
     165–6
stratification, 248
   centralisation and, 256–7
   consent-based authority and, 129–31
   differentiation in states systems and,
       249–50
   structures of, 248–9
   typology, 252–3
   variation within INGOs, 193–4
Stroup, Sarah, 251–2, 262
structural realism, 2–3, 249–50
subculture
   formation, 224–6
   groupings in IR, 227–9

subculture (cont.)
  isolation and, 227–8
  PRC relations with Africa and, 230–8
  propagation of ideology of, 231–3
substitution of judgment, 71
Sunstein, Cass, 74–5
superiority, paternalism and, 79–83
Swidler, Ann, 118–21

Tageszeitung (*TaZ*), 206
Talbott, William, 74
TaZ. See Tageszeitung
Thaler, Robert, 74–5
Theory of International Politics (Waltz), 2–3,
  243–5
Thirty Year's War, 31
The Three Orders (Duby), 258–65
Thucydides, 267–8
Tibetan Buddhism, 54–5
TNGO. *See* Transnational NGO Initiative
To Vima, 206–7, 210, 214–15
Towns, Ann E., 11–12
transaction cost economics, 139–40
Transnational NGO Initiative (TNGO),
  179–81

UAVs. *See* unmanned aerial vehicles
Al Udeid Air Base, 170
United Nations (UN)
  Article 2 (7) of Charter of, 34–5
  PRC and, 235
United States (US). *See also* foreign military
    bases
  CN and, 184
  DOD, 167
  Eurasian military bases, Russian and
    US views of, 168–70
  imperial and wartime basing acquisitions
    of, 160–1
  INGOs headquartered in, 183–4
  military bases as global multinational
    company, 157

non-intervention and, 36–7
unmanned aerial vehicles (UAVs), 172–3
US. *See* United States

Vaishyas, 260–1
Vattel, Emmerich de, 32–4
victims, 81
voluntary self-binding, 74–5

Waltz, Kenneth N., 100, 118–21
  anarchy-hierarchy binary of, 243–5
  on countries with great powers, 249
  Man, the State and War by, 247–8
  ordering principles abandoned and,
    245–6
  Theory of International Politics by, 2–3,
    243–5
The War Ledger (Organski & Kugler),
    10–11
Westphalian sovereignty. *See* non-
    intervention
whose realm, his religion. *See cuius regio, eius
    religio*
Wilberforce, William, 87–9
Williamson, Oliver E., 139–40
  relational contracting and, 156–9
Wolff, Christian von, 32
women
  femininity devalued and, 97–8
  oppression of, within ISIS, 100–1
  sex inequality as global for, 97
  violence against, 96–7
  workplace and, 97
Women and States (Towns), 11–12
Wong, Wendy, 251–2, 262
Writing Security (Campbell), 7–8

Yongjin Zhang, 227
Yoshida Shigeru, 160–1

Zarakol, Ayşe, 11–12, 120, 132, 198–9,
    203, 238, 243

Cambridge Studies in International Relations

136 Ole Jacob Sending, Vincent Pouliot and Iver B. Neumann (eds.)
Diplomacy and the Making of World Politics

135 Barry Buzan and George Lawson
The Global Transformation
History, Modernity and the Making of International Relations

134 Heather Elko McKibben
State Strategies in International Bargaining
Play by the Rules or Change Them?

133 Janina Dill
Legitimate Targets?
Social Construction, International Law, and US Bombing

132 Nuno P. Monteiro
Theory of Unipolar Politics

131 Jonathan D. Caverley
Democratic militarism
Voting, wealth, and war

130 David Jason Karp
Responsibility for human rights
Transnational corporations in imperfect states

129 Friedrich Kratochwil
The status of law in world society
Meditations on the role and rule of law

128 Michael G. Findley, Daniel L. Nielson and J. C. Sharman
Global shell games
Experiments in transnational relations, crime, and terrorism

127 Jordan Branch
The cartographic state
Maps, territory, and the origins of sovereignty

126 Thomas Risse, Stephen C. Ropp and Kathryn Sikkink (eds.)
The persistent power of human rights
From commitment to compliance

125 K. M. Fierke
Political self-sacrifice
Agency, body and emotion in international relations

124 Stefano Guzzini
The return of geopolitics in Europe?
Social mechanisms and foreign policy identity crises

123 Bear F. Braumoeller
The great powers and the international system
Systemic theory in empirical perspective

122 Jonathan Joseph
The social in the global
Social theory, governmentality and global politics

121 Brian C. Rathbun
Trust in international cooperation
International security institutions, domestic politics and American multilateralism

120 A. Maurits van der Veen
Ideas, interests and foreign aid

119 Emanuel Adler and Vincent Pouliot (eds.)
International practices

118 Ayşe Zarakol
After defeat
How the East learned to live with the West

117 Andrew Phillips
War, religion and empire
The transformation of international orders

116 Joshua Busby
Moral movements and foreign policy

115 Séverine Autesserre
The trouble with the Congo
Local violence and the failure of international peacebuilding

114 Deborah D. Avant, Martha Finnemore and Susan K. Sell (eds.)
Who governs the globe?

113 Vincent Pouliot
International security in practice
The politics of NATO-Russia diplomacy

112 Columba Peoples
Justifying ballistic missile defence
Technology, security and culture

111 Paul Sharp
Diplomatic theory of international relations

110 John A. Vasquez
The war puzzle revisited

109 Rodney Bruce Hall
Central banking as global governance
Constructing financial credibility

108 Milja Kurki
Causation in international relations
Reclaiming causal analysis

107 Richard M. Price
Moral limit and possibility in world politics

106 Emma Haddad
The refugee in international society
Between sovereigns

105 Ken Booth
Theory of world security

104 Benjamin Miller
States, nations and the great powers
The sources of regional war and peace

103 Beate Jahn (ed.)
Classical theory in international relations

102 Andrew Linklater and Hidemi Suganami
The English School of international relations A contemporary
reassessment

101 Colin Wight
Agents, structures and international relations
Politics as ontology

100 Michael C. Williams
The realist tradition and the limits of international relations

99 Ivan Arreguín-Toft
How the weak win wars
A theory of asymmetric conflict

98 Michael Barnett and Raymond Duvall (eds.)
Power in global governance

97 Yale H. Ferguson and Richard W. Mansbach
Remapping global politics
History's revenge and future shock

96 Christian Reus-Smit (ed.)
The politics of international law

95 Barry Buzan
From international to world society?
English School theory and the social structure of globalisation

94 K. J. Holsti
Taming the sovereigns
Institutional change in international politics

93 Bruce Cronin
Institutions for the common good
International protection regimes in international security

92 Paul Keal
European conquest and the rights of indigenous peoples
The moral backwardness of international society

91 Barry Buzan and Ole Wæver
Regions and powers
The structure of international security

90 A. Claire Cutler
Private power and global authority
Transnational merchant law in the global political economy

89 Patrick M. Morgan
Deterrence now

88 Susan Sell
Private power, public law
The globalization of intellectual property rights

87 Nina Tannenwald
The nuclear taboo
The United States and the non-use of nuclear weapons since 1945

86 Linda Weiss
States in the global economy
Bringing domestic institutions back in

85 Rodney Bruce Hall and Thomas J. Biersteker (eds.)
The emergence of private authority in global governance

84 Heather Rae
State identities and the homogenisation of peoples

83 Maja Zehfuss
Constructivism in international relations
The politics of reality

82 Paul K. Ruth and Todd Allee
The democratic peace and territorial conflict in the twentieth century

81 Neta C. Crawford
Argument and change in world politics
Ethics, decolonization and humanitarian intervention

80 Douglas Lemke
Regions of war and peace

79 Richard Shapcott
Justice, community and dialogue in international relations

78 Phil Steinberg
The social construction of the ocean

77 Christine Sylvester
Feminist international relations An unfinished journey

76 Kenneth A. Schultz
Democracy and coercive diplomacy

75 David Houghton
US foreign policy and the Iran hostage crisis

74 Cecilia Albin
Justice and fairness in international negotiation

73 Martin Shaw
Theory of the global state
Globality as an unfinished revolution

72 Frank C. Zagare and D. Marc Kilgour
Perfect deterrence

71 Robert O'Brien, Anne Marie Goetz, Jan Aart Scholte and Marc Williams
    Contesting global governance
    Multilateral economic institutions and global social movements

70 Roland Bleiker
    Popular dissent, human agency and global politics

69 Bill McSweeney
    Security, identity and interests
    A sociology of international relations

68 Molly Cochran
    Normative theory in international relations
    A pragmatic approach

67 Alexander Wendt
    Social theory of international politics

66 Thomas Risse, Stephen C. Ropp and Kathryn Sikkink (eds.)
    The power of human rights
    International norms and domestic change

65 Daniel W. Drezner
    The sanctions paradox
    Economic statecraft and international relations

64 Viva Ona Bartkus
    The dynamic of secession

63 John A. Vasquez
    The power of power politics
    From classical realism to neotraditionalism

62 Emanuel Adler and Michael Barnett (eds.)
    Security communities

61 Charles Jones
    E. H. Carr and international relations
    A duty to lie

60 Jeffrey W. Knopf
    Domestic society and international cooperation
    The impact of protest on US arms control policy

59 Nicholas Greenwood Onuf
    The republican legacy in international thought

58 Daniel S. Geller and J. David Singer
   Nations at war
   A scientific study of international conflict

57 Randall D. Germain
   The international organization of credit
   States and global finance in the world economy

56 N. Piers Ludlow
   Dealing with Britain
   The Six and the first UK application to the EEC

55 Andreas Hasenclever, Peter Mayer and Volker Rittberger
   Theories of international regimes

54 Miranda A. Schreurs and Elizabeth C. Economy (eds.)
   The internationalization of environmental protection

53 James N. Rosenau
   Along the domestic-foreign frontier
   Exploring governance in a turbulent world

52 John M. Hobson
   The wealth of states
   A comparative sociology of international economic and political change

51 Kalevi J. Holsti
   The state, war, and the state of war

50 Christopher Clapham
   Africa and the international system
   The politics of state survival

49 Susan Strange
   The retreat of the state
   The diffusion of power in the world economy

48 William I. Robinson
   Promoting polyarchy
   Globalization, US intervention, and hegemony

47 Roger Spegele
   Political realism in international theory

46 Thomas J. Biersteker and Cynthia Weber (eds.)
   State sovereignty as social construct

45 Mervyn Frost
Ethics in international relations
A constitutive theory

44 Mark W. Zacher with Brent A. Sutton
Governing global networks
International regimes for transportation and communications

43 Mark Neufeld
The restructuring of international relations theory

42 Thomas Risse-Kappen (ed.)
Bringing transnational relations back in
Non-state actors, domestic structures and international institutions

41 Hayward R. Alker
Rediscoveries and reformulations
Humanistic methodologies for international studies

40 Robert W. Cox with Timothy J. Sinclair
Approaches to world order

39 Jens Bartelson
A genealogy of sovereignty

38 Mark Rupert
Producing hegemony
The politics of mass production and American global power

37 Cynthia Weber
Simulating sovereignty
Intervention, the state and symbolic exchange

36 Gary Goertz
Contexts of international politics

35 James L. Richardson
Crisis diplomacy
The Great Powers since the mid-nineteenth century

34 Bradley S. Klein
Strategic studies and world order
The global politics of deterrence

33 T. V. Paul
Asymmetric conflicts
War initiation by weaker powers

32 Christine Sylvester
    Feminist theory and international relations in a postmodern era

31 Peter J. Schraeder
    US foreign policy toward Africa
    Incrementalism, crisis and change

30 Graham Spinardi
    From Polaris to Trident
    The development of US Fleet Ballistic Missile technology

29 David A. Welch
    Justice and the genesis of war

28 Russell J. Leng
    Interstate crisis behavior, 1816–1980
    Realism versus reciprocity

27 John A. Vasquez
    The war puzzle

26 Stephen Gill (ed.)
    Gramsci, historical materialism and international relations

25 Mike Bowker and Robin Brown (eds.)
    From cold war to collapse
    Theory and world politics in the 1980s

24 R. B. J. Walker
    Inside/outside
    International relations as political theory

23 Edward Reiss
    The strategic defense initiative

22 Keith Krause
    Arms and the state
    Patterns of military production and trade

21 Roger Buckley
    US-Japan alliance diplomacy 1945–1990

20 James N. Rosenau and Ernst-Otto Czempiel (eds.)
    Governance without government
    Order and change in world politics

19 Michael Nicholson
    Rationality and the analysis of international conflict

18 John Stopford and Susan Strange
Rival states, rival firms
Competition for world market shares

17 Terry Nardin and David R. Mapel (eds.)
Traditions of international ethics

16 Charles F. Doran
Systems in crisis
New imperatives of high politics at century's end

15 Deon Geldenhuys
Isolated states
A comparative analysis

14 Kalevi J. Holsti
Peace and war
Armed conflicts and international order 1648–1989

13 Saki Dockrill
Britain's policy for West German rearmament 1950–1955

12 Robert H. Jackson
Quasi-states
Sovereignty, international relations and the third world

11 James Barber and John Barratt
South Africa's foreign policy
The search for status and security 1945–1988

10 James Mayall
Nationalism and international society

9 William Bloom
Personal identity, national identity and international relations

8 Zeev Maoz
National choices and international processes

7 Ian Clark
The hierarchy of states
Reform and resistance in the international order

6 Hidemi Suganami
The domestic analogy and world order proposals

5 Stephen Gill
American hegemony and the Trilateral Commission

4 Michael C. Pugh
   The ANZUS crisis, nuclear visiting and deterrence

3 Michael Nicholson
   Formal theories in international relations

2 Friedrich V. Kratochwil
   Rules, norms, and decisions
   On the conditions of practical and legal reasoning in international
   relations and domestic affairs

1 Myles L. C. Robertson
   Soviet policy towards Japan
   An analysis of trends in the 1970s and 1980s

For EU product safety concerns, contact us at Calle de José Abascal, 56–1°,
28003 Madrid, Spain or eugpsr@cambridge.org.

www.ingramcontent.com/pod-product-compliance
Ingram Content Group UK Ltd.
Pitfield, Milton Keynes, MK11 3LW, UK
UKHW020341140625